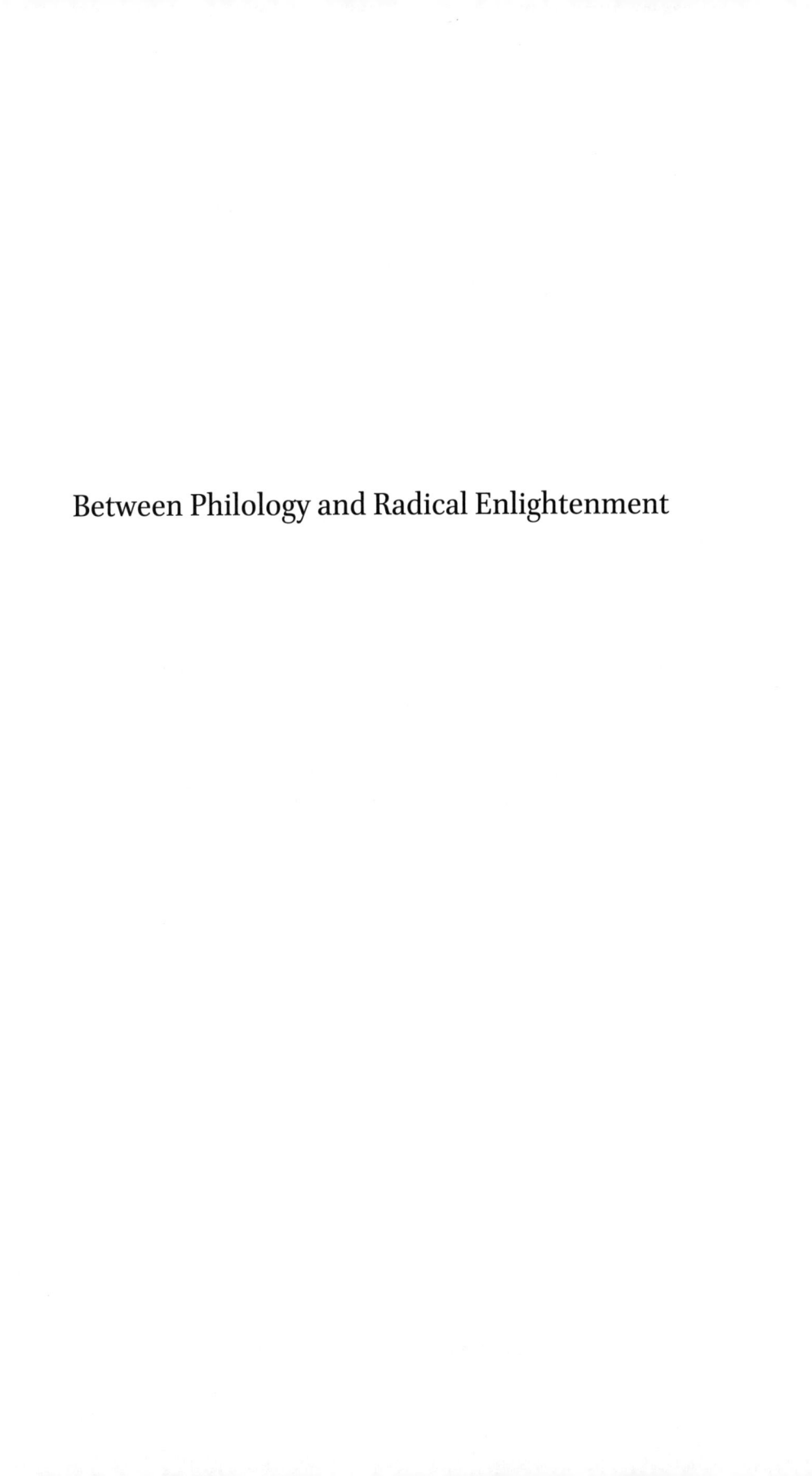

Between Philology and Radical Enlightenment

Brill's Studies in Intellectual History

Between Philology and Radical Enlightenment

Hermann Samuel Reimarus (1694–1768)

Edited by

Martin Mulsow

BRILL

LEIDEN · BOSTON
2011

Cover illustration: Frontispiece of *Cassii Dionis Historiae Romanae* Volumen II, ed. Johann Albert Fabricius / Hermann Samuel Reimarus (Hamburg: Herold, 1752). (copy of the editor).

This book is printed on acid-free paper.

Library of Congress Cataloging-in-Publication Data

Between philology and radical Enlightenment : Hermann Samuel Reimarus (1694–1768) / edited by Martin Mulsow.
    p. cm. — (Brill's studies in intellectual history, ISSN 0920-8607 ; v. 203)
    Chiefly proceedings of a conference held Mar. 4, 2006 at Rutgers University.
    Includes index.
    ISBN 978-90-04-20946-6 (hardback : alk. paper)
1. Reimarus, Hermann Samuel, 1694–1768. I. Mulsow, Martin. II. Title. III. Series.

B2699.R44B48 2011
211'.5092—dc23

2011028629

This publication has been typeset in the multilingual "Brill" typeface. With over 5,100 characters covering Latin, IPA, Greek, and Cyrillic, this typeface is especially suitable for use in the humanities. For more information, please see www.brill.nl/brill-typeface.

ISSN 0920-8607
ISBN 978 90 04 20946 6

MIX
Paper from responsible sources
FSC® C004472

PRINTED BY DRUKKERIJ WILCO B.V. - AMERSFOORT, THE NETHERLANDS

CONTENTS

PREFACE

Hermann Samuel Reimarus (1694–1768) was the most significant biblical critic in eighteenth-century Germany and an eminent Enlightenment philosopher. He was teaching as a professor at the Gymnasium illustre in Hamburg, and during the 1740s his house became an important meeting place for the enlightened citizens of Hamburg. Reimarus, however, never published his own *Apologie oder Schutzschrift für die vernünftigen Verehrer Gottes*, his main biblical critical work, during his lifetime. He needed to protect his career and his family. If the public had known that this respected man, who had allegedly been a loyal supporter of church and faith, was the author of such a subversive attack on revelation, both his fame and renown would have come to an abrupt end. But after Reimarus' death the famous German dramatist Gotthold Ephraim Lessing published, between 1774 and 1778, a series of fragments from this work under the title "Fragments from an Undisclosed Author," thus triggering the famous "fragment controversy", one of the most important disputes of the German Enlightenment. The entire work, to be sure, did not see the light of the day until 1972, when Gerhard Alexander published it, and a critical edition is still wanted today.

But Reimarus was not only a biblical critic. He was a much-valued classicist – editor of an edition of Cassius Dio –, one of the most significant popular philosophers of late-Enlightenment Germany (author of the *Vernunftlehre* and the *Vornehmsten Wahrheiten der christlichen Religion*), and a pioneer of ethology (*Allgemeine Betrachtungen über die Triebe der Thiere*).

His significance notwithstanding, research on Reimarus has so far not been particularly prolific, and many aspects remain untouched. The present volume has two aims. Firstly, it tries to uncover previously neglected areas of scholarship. Among the contributions are those about Reimarus as classicist, antiquary, and expert on Judaism. Other articles provide a new evaluation of Reimarus' relationship to Johann Lorenz Schmidt, another important figure of the German Enlightenment, as well as some observations about Reimarus' philosophical and theological development in regard to his commentary on the Book of Job. Secondly, we seek to expand the available primary source material on Reimarus. So far, hardly

any of the numerous letters, diary entries, notes, and lecture drafts – basically the manuscript material – have been used. But this corpus should no
longer be ignored. These printed contributions draw extensively for the
first time on such sources as household books, diary fragments, learned
correspondence, and early drafts of the *Apologie*.

But this volume may also serve as an introduction for the English-
speaking public to the multi-layered work of Reimarus. So far, works in
English about Reimarus have been completely missing. The scholarship of
Jonathan Israel and others about the Radical Enlightenment, however, has
shown that it has become essential to situate Reimarus in this context and
not to allow this international debate to ignore him any longer.

Most of these contributions have sprung from a conference organized
on March 4th, 2006 at Rutgers University. Almut and Paul Spalding have
kindly agreed to submit a contribution specifically for this volume, and
Wilhelm Schmidt-Biggemann's entry is a translation of an article that was
published in German in 1998 [Wolfgang Walter, ed., *Hermann Samuel
Reimarus, 1694–1768: Beiträge zur Reimarus-Renaissance in der Gegenwart*
(Göttingen: Vandenhoeck & Ruprecht, 1998), pp. 23–52].

Special credit goes to Ulrich Groetsch, who has not only been actively
involved in the organization of the conference, but has also translated
two contributions into English. The Rutgers Department of History has
supported this conference financially. To them I am also grateful. Finally,
my thanks go to Martin Wilson, who has read the whole manuscript with
great care and suggested numerous corrections and improvements.

Martin Mulsow
Erfurt, Summer 2010

FROM ANTIQUARIANISM TO BIBLE CRITICISM?
YOUNG REIMARUS VISITS THE NETHERLANDS
With an edition of the travel diary fragment of 1720/1

Martin Mulsow

I. Visiting Le Clerc

"Le Clerc has the face of an ox."[1] This is the first sentence of the diary, which we still possess, of Reimarus' academic travels to Holland and England. At the age of twenty-five, Reimarus embarked on his *peregrinatio academica* from Hamburg in the spring of 1720, after he had received plenty of advice and manuscript copy requests from his mentors Johann Albert Fabricius and Johann Christoph Wolf.[2] Laid low by sickness in Leiden during the first four months, Reimarus thereafter started his most productive time in libraries, interrupted only by visits to scholars and excursions. Sometime between late summer 1720 and his departure to England in June 1721 he must have visited Jean Le Clerc, the famous remonstrant theologian and philologist in Amsterdam.[3]

It is certainly possible to verify Reimarus' impression of his physiognomy. Many young Germans visited Le Clerc, who was so busy that his visitors often had to come back five or six times until they were let in. Among them was Gottlieb Stolle, who wrote similarly in 1703, but phrased it more tactfully: "He has a very broad face [...], his colour no different

---

[1] See the text in the appendix. In the following footnotes I indicate only the page numbers of the citations. Here: p. 1. – I am grateful to Ulrich Groetsch for his translation of this contribution. For important suggestions I would like to thank Anthony Grafton, Jonathan Israel, Dietrich Klein and Ulrich Groetsch.

[2] See Carl Mönckeberg, *Hermann Samuel Reimarus und Johann Christian Edelmann* (Hamburg, 1867), p. 19; Wilhelm Schmidt-Biggemann, "Einleitung," in Reimarus, *Kleine gelehrte Schriften. Vorstufen zur Apologie oder Schutzschrift für die vernünftigen Verehrer Gottes* (Göttingen, 1994), pp. IX–XI. Reimarus himself remembers his journey in a 1723 oration with the title "Omnes homines aeque felices esse" (p. 25f.), printed in *Kleine gelehrte Schriften*, p. 64f. On contemporary travels by scholars see Winfried Siebers, "Beobachtung und Räsonnement. Typen, Beschreibungen und Öffentlichkeitsbezug der frühaufklärerischen Gelehrtenreise," in: Hans-Wolf Jäger (ed.), *Europäisches Reisen im Zeitalter der Aufklärung* (Heidelberg, 1992), pp. 16–34.

[3] On Le Clerc see Annie Barnes, *Jean Le Clerc (1657–1736) et la République des lettres* (Paris, 1938).

from Budde's, cheerful and serious as he appears."[4] At a time when cam-
eras did not exist, comparisons with other well-known people were often
the only way to record another person's appearance, even if that meant
comparing him to Professor Budde from Halle.

At the time of his *peregrinatio*, Reimarus was still entirely orthodox by
conviction, an offspring of Wittenberg University of the purest kind. Not
surprisingly then, after his astonishment about Le Clerc's appearance had
died down, he wrote: "He is very frank in his judgment and criticism of
everybody," and, somewhat scornfully, he adds, "he seemed to me a little
profane, when he claimed that he criticised the Bible no differently than
if he had Aristophanes before him."[5] Not just the sacrilege of comparing
the Bible with profane texts, but even with the comic poet Aristophanes!
Le Clerc certainly intended this remark to sound provocative, just as Reimarus perceived it. Reimarus' mentor Johann Christoph Wolf's visit to Le
Clerc was then already twelve years in the past. Wolf had stood at Le
Clerc's front door on 14 August 1708. Just a few days before that, he had
had a conversation with other scholars in Hamburg about Le Clerc, and
the Latin term *Ars nihil credendi* was repeatedly used in reference to Le
Clerc's *Ars critica*.[6] After the conversation with Le Clerc in Holland, Wolf
had had to admit that he expressed his thoughts in speech as pointedly
as he did in his books. Elements of the conversation had included John
Mill's variant edition of the New Testament, as well as Grotius' theological
anthropology. Reimarus, too, talked with Le Clerc about editions and manuscripts, especially about his collection of letters by Libanios, about which
Wolf had probably requested some information.[7] But all scholarly conver-

---

[4] Gottlieb Stolle, Travel diary 1703/4, Ms. Cod. IV oct. 49, Biblioteka Uniwersytecka, Wro-
claw. See the edition that I am planning: Stolle, *Eine Reise durch die Gelehrtenrepublik*, ed.
Martin Mulsow and Olaf Simons. See as well Johann Burkhard Mencke, *Das Holländische
Journal 1698–1699*, ed. Hubert Laeven, (Hildesheim, 2005), p. 86. Mencke visited Le Clerc
on August 22, 1698 and describes his impression as follows: "Sonst hat er eine leichtsinnige
Physiognomie und scheinen die Augen an ihm ganz dunkel und gläsern, vielleicht weil er
sie bey seinem unermüdetem Fleiße zu wenig geschonet."

[5] Reimarus, Diary fragment; see edition in appendix. Here: p. 1; Le Clerc amends Aristophanes in his *Ars critica*, part III, p. I, Chap. XVII, 30f. I use the edition Amsterdam
1730, vol. 2, pp. 287–290; soon afterwards follows a passage on the Codex Beza of the New
Testament.

[6] SUB Hamburg, Cod. geogr. 84, fol. 2rf. On Wolf see Martin Mulsow, "Johann Chris-
toph Wolf (1683–1739) und die Geschichte der verbotenen Bücher in Hamburg," in Johann
Anselm Steiger (ed.), *500 Jahre Theologie in Hamburg. Hamburg als Zentrum christlicher
Theologie und Kultur zwischen Tradition und Zukunft* (Berlin, 2005), pp. 81–112.

[7] On Wolf's research on Libanios see Mulsow, "Wolf" (footnote 6), p. 93, 96f. Note also
Reimarus' efforts to provide information about the Karaites – a culture in which Wolf was

sation notwithstanding, in the back of his mind Reimarus still maintained his reservation about Le Clerc as a dangerous muddler of *philologia sacra* and *philologia profana*. Who would have guessed that Reimarus himself would eventually become a much more rigorous biblical philologist than Le Clerc, one who would relentlessly read the Bible as a "profane" piece of writing, which had been composed by human hands for human purposes and was full of craftiness, cunning, and deception?

The development of Reimarus from an offspring of Hamburgian and Wittenbergian orthodoxy to the author of the *Apology* remains a process that has not yet been fully understood. Since at least the work of Peter Stemmer in 1983, it has become clear that this process was not initiated by Reimarus' travels to Holland and England.[8] Older scholarship had assumed that it was this journey that brought Reimarus into contact with deism, and that he then almost automatically became a biblical-critical sceptic. Subscribing to this assumption underestimates the tremendous firmness of the orthodox Lutheran worldview around 1720 and maintains a too simplified concept of what constitutes influence in the history of ideas. Indeed, the diary fragment presented and transcribed here for the first time in its entirety supports Stemmer's conclusion that in the course of his academic travels, neither deism nor Le Clerc would have been able to shake Reimarus' belief. The attempt to locate apparently early shoots of unbelief cannot lie at the heart of the significance of an analysis of the diary fragment. However, it leads to a better acquaintance with Reimarus' intellectual horizons and his interests. Only then, after taking a carefully considered step, would we be able to ask further if his early profile contains elements that may have supported Reimarus after 1735, when he embarked on his own theological journey. These would have to be elements that developed a critical potential of their own that they did not originally possess. At around that time, as is generally known, Reimarus rejected on the one hand the concept of purely sacred hermeneutics, and

---

interested as well. In 1721, Wolf was preparing the second edition of his *Notitia Karaeorum* (1st ed. Hamburg, 1714). On June 20, 1721, Reimarus writes to him from Leiden (SUB Hamburg, Sup. ep. 438r, cit. after Schmidt-Biggemann, "Einleitung" [footnote 2], p. IX): "Sed ut verum fatear non sine magnis impensis id fieri potest, quoniam custos Bibliothecae, qui perpetuo assidat evolventibus Msta., erit pro navata opera solvendus. Ipsa vero haec Warneriana de Karraeis excerpta ita comparata sunt, ut lucem non mereantur, nisi simul autores, ex quibus petita sunt, et qui maximam partem in hac ipsa bibliotheca latent sedulo et accurate consultantur. Cras, Deo volente, Anglicam iter aggrediar, ubi spero majorem mihi fore copiam Tibi satisfaciendi, si qua forte in re Tibi mea prosit servare industria."

[8] Peter Stemmer, *Weissagung und Kritik. Eine Studie zur Hermeneutik bei Hermann Samuel Reimarus* (Göttingen, 1983), pp. 88ff. But see below footnote 54.

on the other hand developed a reasonable theology of a loving God, which became the norm of his criticism of the biblical narrative. The divine qualities that could be derived from reason alone were not supposed to contradict the revealed text. If that was the case, then the revealed character of the Bible needed to be given up.[9] What in fact supported this abandonment of the text's revealed character and what is already apparent from his journey to Holland, I suggest, is Reimarus' interest in antiquarianism.

II. An Appreciation for Realia

Reading the ten closely written pages of the diary, it becomes quickly obvious that, unlike Wolf or Stolle on their journeys, they do not discuss only books or manuscripts. Reimarus reveals his broad interests. He is interested in being introduced to the workings of a silk mill[10] just as much as how peat is processed: "Dutch peat is made from rich, muddy, and marshy soil, which is deposited on hard soil, dried, and then cut; I have tried it, and such peat burns for over twenty-four hours."[11]

In Utrecht Reimarus visited the famous physicist Nicolaas Hartsoeker.[12] First Hartsoeker showed Reimarus his magnet – as he did with Uffenbach over ten years earlier. Uffenbach, who just like Reimarus was generally instantly interested in texts and techniques, records a magnet that was tiny but could pull a hundred times more than its own weight.[13] Something similar happened before Reimarus' eyes: "He showed us a magnet that was round and was about 2/3 of a shoe in diameter, but was capable of pulling 200 pounds, and once he held a needle with his hand over it,

---

[9] Schmidt-Biggemann, "Einleitung" (footnote 2), pp. XVIIff. See also Wilhelm Schmidt-Biggemann's contribution to this volume. The argument becomes especially clear in the preliminary stages of the *Apologie*.

[10] Diary fragment, p. 7.

[11] Diary fragment, p. 2.

[12] On Hartsoeker (1656–1725) see Alice Stroup, "Science, politique et conscience aux débuts de l'Académie Royale de Sciences," *Revue de synthèse*, 4th series, Nos. 3–4 (July–Dec. 1993), pp. 423–53; Christiane Berkvens-Stevelinck, "Nicolas Hoartsoeker contre Isaac Newton ou pouquoi les planètes se meuvent-elles?," *Lias* 2 (1975), pp. 313–28. For his experiments see his *Principes de physice* (Paris, 1696), *Conjectures physiques* (Amsterdam, 1706), *Essai de dioptrique* (Paris, 1694), and *Eclairecissements sur les conjectures physiques* (Amsterdam, 1710).

[13] Zacharias Conrad von Uffenbach, *Merkwürdige Reise durch Niedersachsen, Holland und England*, 3 vols. (Frankfurt, 1753–54), vol. 3, p. 730. On early 18th-century-research on magnetism see Albert Kloss, *Geschichte des Magnetismus* (Berlin, 1994).

and it rose up perpendicularly."[14] Apparently, Hartsoeker barely stopped performing one demonstration after another one: dozens of keys were pulled by the magnet, poles were changed, and burning glasses melted metals. Hartsoeker was fussy about Tschirnhaus' theories and eventually went on to talk about dangerous theories concerning conception from semen.[15]

In Rijnsburg Reimarus attended a service of the Collegians.[16] He heard that they reduced their faith to only a few articles, which did not include the Trinity. He realised that the service was remarkably similar to the Quakers', because everybody could speak freely and according to his intuition. But Reimarus was dismayed by it: "Among those whom I heard perorate, I found only one who was saying something interesting; the others produced a babble, especially since they remained fairly general at all times and since they were not very learned."[17] This impression would remain fixed in his mind. A section in the *Apology* that treats the apostles' speaking in tongues during Pentecost reads: "The Apostles must have behaved like a group of drunkards, who yell at each other and gesture around as if they were insane and crazy." And to this Reimarus adds: "This insanity has been transmitted to our time. We have now fanatics, inspirationists, convulsionaries, just as the Ancients had their sibyls and pythians."[18]

Above all, Reimarus' diary reveals that the culture of the Netherlands of the early eighteenth century was entirely antiquarian in nature. It was a culture of art galleries, coin collections, stacks of paintings, instruments, statues, manuscripts, mounted animals, and dried plants. Although Reimarus was unable to see the famous cabinet of Nicolas Chevalier in Amsterdam[19] because it was just being sold at that time, he visited the collection of Jacob de Wilde, a bureaucrat suffering from gout, who enjoyed studying and collecting antiques in his spare time and who would

---

[14] Diary fragment, p. 5.

[15] See Clara Pinto-Correia, *The Ovary of Eve: Egg and Sperm and Preformation* (Chicago, 1997).

[16] Diary fragment, p. 4. On the Collegiants see Andrew Fix, *Prophecy and Reason. The Dutch Collegiants in the Early Enlightenment* (Princeton, 1991).

[17] Ibid.

[18] *Apologie oder Schutzschrift für die vernünftigen Verehrer Gottes*, ed. Werner Alexander, 2 vols. (Frankfurt, 1972), vol. 2, pp. 350f.

[19] See Anne Goldgar, *Impolite Learning. Conduct and Community in the Republic of Letters, 1680–1750* (New Haven, 1995), pp. 188–194. For the connection between the collections and the development of medicine see most recently Harold J. Cook, *Matters of Exchange: Commerce, Medicine, and Science in the Dutch Golden Age* (New Haven, 2007).

occasionally even publish specimens from his coin studies.[20] When Uffenbach visited de Wilde he tried to decipher coins, just like the famous con-
noisseur Philipp von Stosch before him. Magnifying glasses in their hands,
they would all hunch over these small objects of desire.[21] De Wilde showed
Reimarus his poetic attempts at distiches and requested him to sign his
guestbook, which he maintained just like Chevalier and in which numerous famous names were recorded.

The painter Willem van Mieris showed him his collection of animals
preserved in alcohol.[22] Uffenbach described it in his travel journal as well.[23]
Mieris was at that time only beginning to collect antiques. The problem of
forgeries, especially those of ancient coins and gems seems to have been a
matter of concern at the time. Johan Heyman for example, told Reimarus
about an oriental traveller by the name of Paul Lucas who "took false,
imitated ancient medallions with him and exchanged them for genuine
ones."[24] Elsewhere, Reimarus even heard about how such forgeries were
produced: "Ancient gems and sigilla can be reproduced by putting them
into a well-polished metal ring and hardening them by means of a tripod
(?) in the oven. The shaped tripod is placed in another clay instrument
in the metal oven through which evenly distributed flames harden it on
a plate."[25]

This demonstrates Reimarus' extraordinary interest in realia and material knowledge. It shows a critic in preparation who knows how to apply
acquired practical norms to the history he reads. Recent literature on
intellectual history is full of connections to material culture. Examples
include Neil Kamil's work on Huguenot ceramics, Anne Goldgar's work on

---

[20] On de Wilde's (1645–1721) biography see Thieme-Becker, *Lexikon der bildenen Kün-stler* (Leipzig, 1907–1950), vol. 30, p. 256; Peter Berghaus, "Si vis amari, ama. Johann Georg Graevius (1632–1703) und Jacob de Wilde (1645–1721)," in *Ars et amicitia. Beiträge zum Thema Freundschaft*, Festschrift für Martin Bircher (*Chloe* 28) (Amsterdam, 1998), pp. 409–426.

[21] Uffenbach (footnote 13), vol. 3, pp. 630ff.; on Uffenbach's visit to Stosch in The Hague see ibid. p. 490ff. On Stosch see Peter und Hilde Zazoff, *Gemmensammler und Gemmen-forscher. Von einer noblen Passion zur Wissenschaft* (München, 1983).

[22] Diary fragment, p. 1. On van Mieris (1662–1747) see Jonathan Israel, *The Dutch Repub-lic. Its Rise, Greatness, and Fall 1477–1806* (Oxford, 1995), pp. 1051–1053. On his paintings see Pamela H. Smith, *The Body of the Artisan. Art and Experience in the Scientific Revolution* (Chicago, 2004), esp. pp. 203–215.

[23] Uffenbach (footnote 13), vol. 3, pp. 422ff.

[24] Diary fragment, p. 8. On Lucas see footnote 144 below. On the problem of gem forgery see Peter und Helde Zazoff, *Gemmensammler* (footnote 21), esp. pp. 186ff.

[25] Diary fragment, p. 1.

tulips, and Pamela Smith's study of craftsmanship.[26] Reimarus fits neatly into it. His case offers a connection between material culture and biblical philology, to which Antiquarianism is the key.

Antiquarianism – the attempt to restore the cultural connections of past cultures by means of material objects – had been a companion to humanism since the sixteenth-century, and from the seventeenth-century at least became a companion to biblical scholarship.[27] In order to avoid any misunderstandings, however, it is important to point out that it was not only antiquarianism in its narrow sense that furnished biblical commentaries with background knowledge about realia. For quite some time, the field of rhetorical hermeneutics and the rationalistic tradition of biblical hermeneutics had instructed readers to pay attention to the factual and material contexts of a text, and the burgeoning travel literature of the early modern period provided cultural background information about the Near East. If the title of this contribution addresses the development "from antiquarianism to biblical criticism," then it is a reference to a broader concept of antiquarianism that includes this tradition. Still, it remains hard to ignore the fact that the collecting mania of the seventeenth and early eighteenth centuries, the cabinets of curiosities, the natural sciences and travel accounts, added to the existing traditions of hermeneutics that relied heavily on realia.

However, the antiquarianism that accompanied biblical philology was not in itself critical. Well into the eighteenth-century, the works of Campegius Vitringa, Adriaan Relant, Samuel Bochart, and many others, were faithful companions of students of theology. Wherever it was permissible, however, namely in the reconstruction of pagan religions, the critical potential of antiquarianism became evident in the course of the seventeenth-century. In the Netherlands, for example, Antonius van Dale used his antiquarian learning for his reconstruction – or one might even say exposure – of Greek oracles as a form of brainwashing.[28]

---

[26] Neil Kamil, *Fortress of the Soul. Violence, Metaphysics, and Material Life in the Huguenots' New World, 1517–1751* (Baltimore 2005); Anne Goldgar, *Tulipmania: Money, Honor and Knowledge in the Dutch Golden Age* (Chicago 2007); Pamela H. Smith, *The Body of the Artisan* (footnote 22).

[27] On antiquarianism see the classic study by Arnaldo Momigliano, "Ancient History and the Antiquarian", *Journal of the Warburg and Courtauld Institutes* 13 (1950) pp. 285–315, as well as Alain Schnapp, *The Discovery of the Past. The Origins of Archaeology* (London: British Museum Press, 1996) and Ingo Herklotz, *Cassiano dal Pozzo und die Archäologie des 17. Jahrhunderts* (München, 1999).

[28] Antonius van Dale, *De oraculis ethnicorum* (Amsterdam, 1683); see Martin Mulsow, "Antiquarianism, Libertinism, Religion: Antonius van Dale," (forthcoming) in Peter N.

The Mennonite Van Dale had apparently been animated by the presence of fortune-telling and divine inspiration in Dutch religious culture of his time and he became an antiquarian working to expose them. The statement by Reimarus on the convulsions of the sibyls and pythians quoted earlier may in fact have been influenced by van Dale, who even believed in the possible use of drugs during ancient ceremonies. Another contemporary of van Dale, Johann Peter Späth alias Moses Germanus, was equally moved – in his case by the experience of apparent immaculate conceptions among enthusiasts he befriended – to doubt the Virgin conception of Mary.[29] False prophets like Sabbatai Zwi caused a heightened sensibility to the religious critical theories of their time, such as the one of the "three impostors" Moses, Jesus, and Mohammed.[30] One can only speculate whether knowedge about practices of forgery, with all their technical details, as was the case with the gems, may have helped sharpen Reimarus' critical spirit as well.

Indeed, Reimarus remained throughout his life suspicious about potential trickery, credulity, and false conclusions. When he read Sir Thomas Browne's notorious *Religio Medici*, he was moved to start a sheet of notes entitled "False Conclusions." The passage in Browne cautions about those statements that are "familiarly concluded from the text, wherein (under favour) I see no consequence."[31] This note is among a disorderly array of sheets that are – under the record number A7 – part of the Reimarus papers in Hamburg dating from 1729 to 1764. Under the heading "False Conclusions" Reimarus made at different times three entries which

---

Miller (ed.), *The Age of Antiquaries in Europe and China*. On comparative history of religion at that time see the contributions in *Archiv für Religionsgeschichte* 3 (2001), as well as Mulsow, "Antiquarianism and Idolatry. The 'Historia' of Religions in the Seventeenth Century," in Gianna Pomata and Nancy G. Siraisi (eds.), *Historia. Empiricism and Erudition in Early Modern Europe* (Cambridge, Mass., 2005), pp. 181–210.

[29] Letter from Johann Peter Späth to Eleonora Petersen, in: [Johann Peter Spaeth,] *Send-Schreiben Eines gewesenen Pietisten / Der sich selbst Mosen Germanum nennet und vor wenig Jahren Ein Jude worden / mit nöthigen Anmerckungen publiciret Von Friedrich Christian Büchern* (Danzig, 1699), p. 9; see Mulsow, "Den 'Heydnischen Saurteig' mit den "Israelitischen Süßteig" vermengt: Kabbala, Hellenisierungsthese und Pietismusstreit bei Abraham Hinckelmann und Johann Peter Späth", *Scientia Poetica* 11 (2007), pp. 1–50.

[30] Richard H. Popkin, "Scepticism and Irreligion in the Seventeenth and Eighteenth Centuries", in idem and Arjo Vanderjagt (eds.), *Scepticism and Irreligion in the Seventeenth and Eighteenth Centuries* (Leiden, 1993), pp. 1–12.

[31] Sir Thomas Browne, *Religio Medici* (London, 1642), I,22; German translation: *Religio Medici. Ein Versuch über die Vereinbarkeit von Vernunft und Glauben*, tr. Werner von Koppenfels (Berlin, 1978), p. 47.

seemed important to him.[32] The first one refers to the then still popular allegorical interpretation of the Mosaic account of creation. Scholars from Burnet to Middleton and from Dickinson to Beverland had argued according to the theory of accommodation, which held that the apparently most learned Moses converted his scientific knowledge into a simple story for the common people.[33] "Moses was most likely instructed in the wisdom of the Egyptians and in hieroglyphics. Ergo, his *Historia creationis* needs to be read as an allegory." That is for Reimarus a *non sequitur*. It cannot really be deduced from the Bible.

The second example refers to an interpretation, which Johan Franz Budde, Reimarus' teacher in Jena, mentions in his *Historia ecclesiastica*, of the treatise *De paradiso* by the tenth-century Syrian Christian writer Moses Bar Cepha.[34] According to it, the first parents Adam and Eve lived for about thirty years in a state of paradise. From that it has been deduced that the Saviour spent thirty years on earth. Although Budde explicitly endorsed this argument, Reimarus rejected it.

The most exciting example, however, is the third. Reimarus revealed himself as a profound expert on the mysterious history of the Khazars, who collectively adopted the Mosaic faith in the eighth century. He makes a reference to Johann Buxtorf's preface to his edition of Jehuda Halevi's *Kuzari*,[35] which states: "The Argument of the Kings of the Khazars for Judaism was: The Christian claims that the Jewish religion is better than the Turkish, and the Turk says that the Jewish religion is better than the Christian; therefore, the Jewish religion must be the best, which follows from *a dicto secundum quid ad dictum simpliciter*." When Reimarus rejects this conclusion as sophistry, he may belong to a line of people who think that the dispute between Judaism, Christianity, and Islam could not be

---

[32] Nachlaß A7, fol. 73. See text in appendix. Reimarus refers to *Religio Medici* I,23, but the passage refers back to I,22, because it begins: "These are but the conclusions, and fallible discourses of man upon the word of God."

[33] See for example Paolo Rossi, *The Dark Abyss of Time. The History of the Earth and the History of Nations from Hooke to Vico* (Chicago, 1984), esp. pp. 123ff.

[34] Johann Franz Budde, *Historia ecclesiastica veteris testamenti*, 4 vols. (Halle, 1709). Moses Bar Cepha, *De paradiso commentarius* (Antverp, 1569). On the author see *Hebrew Bible / Old Testament. The History of ist Interpretation*, ed. Magnus Sæbø, vol. I/2: *The Middle Ages* (Göttingen, 2000), pp. 562f.

[35] *Liber Cosri* (Basel, 1660). The editor was Johann Buxtorf the younger. On the Buxtorf family and especially his father see Stephen G. Burnett, *From Christian Hebraism to Jewish Studies: Johannes Buxtorf (1564–1629) and Hebrew Learning in the Seventeenth Century* (Leiden, 1996). On Jehuda Halevi see Y. Silman, *Philosopher and Prophet: Judah Halevi, the Kuzari, and the Evolution of his Thought* (Albany, 1995). On the Khazars see Michael Borgolte, *Christen, Juden, Muselmanen* (Siedler Geschichte Europas vol. 2) (Berlin, 2006).

resolved easily, but that all three stand in a mutual relationship with each
other. That is also the approach of the *Kuzari* in regard to the *De tribus
impostoribus*, which sees all three of them grounded in deception.[36]

But let us turn from this note to antiquarianism. Reimarus was very
well acquainted with all those antiquarian authors whom Fabricius had
meticulously listed in his *Bibliographia antiquaria*.[37] The footnotes in his
Cassius Dio illustrate how he was a master in employing them to clarify
obscure passages. Ezechiel Spanheim, whose numismatic scholarship Reimarus in his commentary calls admiringly "immortalis," receives the highest praise of all of them.[38] Spanheim's monumental *De praestantia et usu
numismatum antiquorum*, which is based upon the study of coins,[39] had
already served as a model for Van Dale's reconstruction of ancient religions from realia.[40] Where he praises Spanheim's book, Reimarus uses it to
comment on Nero's participation in athletic competitions. One debatable
question required clarification: was the winner crowned after the time of
Nero with the *pinus* (spruce) or with the *apium* (marshwort)? Spanheim
was able to resolve the issue by means of images on coins: it was the
apium (marshwort).[41] But antiquarianism does not deal only with banal
and apparently inconsequential issues. In his *Apology*, Reimarus adduces

---

[36] This passage in Reimarus is, however, still also comprehensible in an Christian
apologetic context. See on the complex tradition of the comparison between the three
monotheistic religions, to which the Kuzari belongs as well as the treatise on the three
impostors, Friedrich Niewöhner, *Veritas sive Varietas. Lessings Toleranzparabel und das
Buch von den drei Betrügern* (Heidelberg, 1988).

[37] Johann Albert Fabricius, *Bibliographia antiquaria, sive Introductio in notitiam scriptorum qui Antiquitates Hebraicas, Graecas, Romanas et Christianas Scriptis Illustrarunt*
(Hamburg, 1713).

[38] Cassius Dio, *Historia romana*, ed. Reimarus, vol. 2 (Hamburg, 1752), p. 1033, n. 49. On
this work see Ulrich Groetsch's contribution to this volume.

[39] Ezechiel Spanheim, *Dissertationes de praestantia et usu numismatum antiquorum*
(Rome, 1664; expanded, Amsterdam, 1671; again expanded, London, 1706 and Amsterdam,
1717).

[40] Van Dale, *Dissertationes novem antiquitatibus quin et marmoribus, cum Romanis, tum
potissimum Graecis, illustrandis inservientes cum figuris aeneis* (Amsterdam, 1702I; see Mulsow (footnote 28).

[41] Dio Cassius (footnote 38), p. 1032f. (= Lib. 63, cap. 9); Reimarus comments, p. 1033
footnote 49: "Post Neronis tamen aetatem demum revocatam esse pinum, probant adhuc
Neronis numi, quos produxit Spanhemius in immortali opere, de U. N. Diss. VI. p. 314.
in quibus corona Isthmica non e pinu sed ex apio contexta cernitur. Unde Spanhemius
judicat, Dionem ex suis temporibus Neronia aestimasse, et primum jam sub Nerone in usu
rursus fuisse, putasse. Vide de Isthmis quoque eundem Spanh. epist. ad Morellum I. § 5.
p. 469." Thus Spanheim corrects Dio from his evidence; according to Spanheim, Dio had
judged Nero anachronisticly from his own time. See *De usu et praestantia* (footnote 39)
(London, 1706), p. 314: "Adeo ut dicto Dionis loco, ubi Nero traditur inter relatas e quatuor
Graecorum agonibus coronas, postremo loco e pinu adeptus, respexerit ibi omnino Auctor

Spanheim when he quotes Julian the Apostate's "cheap" absolution of Christians from sin.[42] In the plentiful notes to *Césars de l'empereur Julien*, which take up about nine-tenths of each page, Spanheim also refers to parallel passages to Julian's criticism of Christianity, such as Celsus' from Origen's *Contra Celsum*. These passages repeatedly drew Reimarus' interest, as his notes reveal.[43] To support his argument Reimarus uses a number of other antiquarian authors besides Spanheim. How then shall we evaluate this use of antiquarianism?

III. A GLANCE ON REIMARUS' SCHOLARLY PRACTICES

In 1737 Reimarus ceased lecturing on sacred hermeneutics at the *Gymnasium illustre*. Evidently he wanted to avoid presenting to his students prophetic proofs that he himself no longer believed.[44] He continued, however, to lecture on biblical antiquities.[45] This certainly means that antiquarian learning was innocent enough to be practised without causing a conflict of conscience. On the other hand, it also means that this type of literature

---

ad morem suorum temporum, quibus non ex Apio amplius, sed e Pinu constabant Isthmionicarum coronae, quodque ille iam sub Nerone obtinuisse censuerit."

[42] *Apologie* (footnote 18), vol. 1, pp. 156f.: "Denn das Christentum hat schon von Alters her darin einen Vorzug vor allen andern Religionen gesucht, daß es auch den ruchlosesten Sündern Vergebung, und Trost für ihre Gewissens-Bisse verkündigte; welche seine Feinde nicht gantz unrecht zu einem bittern Vorwurf gebraucht haben." On this passage Reimarus comments in a footnote: "Der Kayser Julianus zielt auf diese so gar leichte Entsündigung im Christenthum, wenn er am Ende seiner Satyre auf die Kayser, den Constantinum M. mit seinem Sohn, als Christen, und doch höchst lasterhafte, so redend eingeführt: 'Wer Weibsleute geschändet, wer sich mit Mordthaten befleckt hat, der komme getrost hieher; ich will ihn alsobald rein machen, wenn er mit diesem Wasser wird gewaschen seyn. Und wofern er sich von Neuem mit eben diesen Verbrechen verschuldet hat: so will ich ihn dennoch wieder reinschaffen, wenn er sich nur vor den Kopf und vor die Brust schlägt.' Spanheim wird in seinen Anmerkungen, und Beweisen der Anmerkungen, bey dieser Stelle, mehr ähnliche von anderen Heyden an die Hand geben. Des Celsus Worte bey dem Origine lib. III. p. 147 sind vorzüglich merkwürdig, da er sagt: bey ihren Geheimnissen rieffe der Herold vorher aus: Heran! wer unschuldige Hände hat, sich nichts arges bewust ist, und gerecht gelebt hat; dem verspreche man die Entsündigung; bey den Christen aber würden alle Sünder, Ungerechte, Diebe, Mörder, zu der Reinigung und zu den Geheimnissen eingeladen." See Spanheim, *Les Césars de l'empereur Julien* (Amsterdam, 1728), pp. 278f.

[43] See e.g. Nachlaß A7, fol. 43, where the exorcism of demons in Judaism is the topic.

[44] See Stemmer (footnote 8), p. 90.

[45] See Stemmer (footnote 8), pp. 6off. as well as the list of lectures in Wilhelm Schmidt-Biggemann, *Hermann Samuel Reimarus. Handschriftenverzeichnis und Bibliographie* (Göttingen, 1979).

was a daily resort of Reimarus and – while he wrote his *Apology* – that he was also influenced by it.

We need to be aware that during the 1730s and 1740s many things occur in parallel patterns in Reimarus' life: his work on his Cassius Dio as well as his large religious-critical project, which slowly evolves into the *Vernunftlehre*, the *Vornehmsten Wahrheiten*, and his biblical-critical *Apology*.[46] Results – with the exception of the *Apology* – appear only during the fifties. The period to the early fifties remains then a latent period in Reimarus' life, similar to the "silent Kant" of the 1760s and 70s.[47]

The implication of these parallel works becomes clear if we incorporate the observations from our reading of the diary fragment: we need to see what role antiquarianism played within this ensemble of skills and motives, which turned Reimarus into a biblical critic. Once Reimarus rejected revelation and started to believe in a rational religion, antiquarianism was also able to develop a critical potential, which it previously did not have. This potential became reality in the process of the labour that Reimarus devoted to biblical criticism.[48] But how did he proceed? What means did he use in regard to antiquarian sources?

Some preserved notes for the *Apology* reveal that Reimarus originally wrote some segments in Latin. The Goethe Museum in Frankfurt owns a sheet of early notes, which, upon closer inspection, can be identified as an early draft for chapter V.2 in the *Apology* about the doctrine of the messiah.[49] Drawing on the *Sanhedrin* treatise in the Talmud, he suggests in the *Apology* that the "famous Rabbi Hillel had already claimed that the Jews need no longer expect the coming of a messiah, because he had already arrived with Hiskias," and the text then continues with Joseph Albo's medieval abandonment of the doctrine of a messiah;[50] the same

---

[46] See Gerhard Alexander, "Einleitung," in Reimarus, *Apologie* (footnote 18); Schmidt-Biggemann, "Einleitung" (footnote 2).

[47] See Wolfgang Carl, *Der schweigende Kant. Die Entwürfe zu einer Deduktion der Kategorien* (Göttingen, 1989).

[48] See also Wilhelm Schmidt-Biggemann, "Die destruktive Potenz philosophischer Apologetik: Der Verlust des biblischen Kredits bei Hermann Samuel Reimarus," in idem, *Theodizee und Tatsachen. Das philosophische Profil der deutschen Aufklärung* (Frankfurt, 1988), pp. 73–87, here p. 80 on Reimarus's position at the time of the commentary on Hoffmann 1734: "Nicht die Suffizienz der Bibel war sein Ausgangspunkt, sondern Realienkunde."

[49] Freies Deutsches Hochstift Frankfurter Goethe Museum, document 60983–84.

[50] *Apologie*, vol. 1, p. 725; on Albo see Sina Rauschenbach, *Joseph Albo (um 1380–1444): jüdische Philosophie und christliche Kontroverstheologie in der frühen Neuzeit* (Leiden, 2002). On the topic of the messiah see also Dietrich Klein's contribution to this volume.

text in Latin appears in these notes.[51] One significant difference, however, becomes evident: the Latin notes provide plenty of references to sources and literature. Apart from the reference to Albo's *Sefer iqqarim*, it lists a dissertation from Rostock and Georg Eliser Edzardi's works on the Talmud, as well as the works of Lightfoot, Buxtorf, Schudt, and others.[52]

---

[51] Goethe-Museum (footnote 49). I cite only the beginning of the document. The heading is "Messias iam venit". Then follows: "Ita nonnulli Iudaeorum. In Tract: Sanhedr. cap <...> fol. 98 col. 2. fol. 99. col. 1 R. Hillel dixit: Non habituri Ysraelitae Messiam, quia dudum <...> tempore Hiskiae." These notes can be situated between Reimarus' lectures on biblical antiquarianism on the one hand and the *Apologie* on the other hand. This case shows in fact how both fit neatly together and that there is a continuity between the two. I add some more extracts from the document. Under the heading "Messias venturus tempore <...>" we read: "Iudaei quidem, <...> cum diffiteri non <...> tempus Messiae jam praeterisse, fingunt peccata sua adulatum Messiae <....> Rabbinorum testimoniis respondet. Seb: Edzardt Disp. ex Philologia Hebraica et Iudaeorum Magistri Witteb: 1695. §.7.8. conf. et Schudt. Comp.9.9. p. 533. sqq ubi testimonia Iudaeorum de vitiis tempore Messiae respectantibus Schia: Bach: Happ. I.139. Locum pasalt: cum. Matth: X.35 sqq. ex Talm: Bab: v. Praef. *Opp.* Lightfoot **a. vide et Talm: Bab. Sanhedr. fol. 97.1. Lightf: Hor. Matth. X.27.p. 317. XII. 39. p. 325. Reland: Antiqu. P.II.C.II. v. ult. p. 154.f. Multa hanc in rem loca congessit Edz: A.S.C.I. p. 24 ff. conf. ed. Wagens. ad Misn. Solr. IX.15. qui et extat Sanhedr. Conaj. p. 344.f." And under the heading "Messias nullum templum reale sed spirituale exstructurus" there are, among others, the following lines: "Communis est sententia Iudaeorum, Messiam templum rursus exaedificaturum. v. Maimon: tract: de Regib. c. XI. §.1. Paraphrasin Chald: in Cant. I.17. Probare hoc solent ex Ezechiele potissimum et eo derivant loca de templo secundo sub Cyro aedificando. Sed R. Moses Aljshech in Hag. XI. 12. Templum <...> non erit materiale, ubi eaedem peragendae sint caerimoniae quae olim usu obtinuere, sed templum <...> spirituale exspectandum et <...> parietes spirituales: quia homines pii praecipuum templum. Hoc observavit etiam l'Empereur praef: in Meddoth et Peringerus in notis ad Maimonid: c. XI. Tract: de regibus. p. 10." The cited authors: Constantin l'Empereur, *Talmudis Babylonici codex Middoth sive de mensuris Templi, una cum versione Latina* [...] *Additis commentariis* (Leiden, 1630). On l'Empereur's Middoth-commentary see Peter T. van Rooden, *Theology, Biblical Scholarship and Rabbinical Studies in the eventeenth Century* (Leiden, 1989), pp. 102ff. Gustav Peringer, *R. Mosis Maimonidae Tractatus De Primitiis Cap. Sextum* [*et*] *Septum, quae ex Hebraeo in sermonem Latinum converta* (Uppsala, 1695).

[52] See also the notes in Nachlaß A7, fol. 44f. on the belief in a messiah. In these notes a considerable number of authors is mentioned: "Bochart, Seldenus, Scaliger, Salmasius, Th. Hyde, La Croze, Jablonski, Gagnier, Herbelot, Kämpfer, Wagenseil, Ludolf." See also Reimarus' lecture on biblical antiquarianism on the basis of Conrad Iken, *Antiquitates hebraicae, secundum triplicem Judaeorum statum, ecclesiasticum, politicum et oeconomicum breviter delineatae* (Bremen, 1732). In § 11, Iken had mentioned the "errores de Messia". In the handwritten record of Reimarus' lecture (Ms. orient. 71 of the Universitätsbibliothek Rostock (I am grateful to Ulrich Groetsch for letting me use his photocopy of the manuscript) it says on p. 36 about this passage: "Errores de Messia praecipui sunt: quod plerumque negent, illum venisse et venturum esse ad redimendos homines, sed potius ad exsules et afflictos Judaeos in palaestinam reducendos et templum tertium, cum regno terreno, omni felicitate affluendum erigendum. Cum vero dicta scripturae de duplici Messiae statu atque adeo adventu conciliare nequeant, fingunt duplicem Messiam, alterum ben Joseph, vilis conditionis et prosterendum ab Armillo, sive Antichristo; alterum ben David, gloriosum et omnes populos subacturum. Vide iterum Lentium de moderna theol.

The following conclusion may thus be possible: Reimarus created from an amalgam of extremely learned and philological Latin references, filled with antiquarian sources, an extremely readable German text with only very few references. He uses Gottsched's and Mosheim's *German Society* as his model and distinguishes himself by his exemplarily clear and beautiful language.[53] Reimarus thus produced a reduction. Many references, which were worked into the *Apology*, became invisible. According to Dietrich Klein, numerous English deist works, clandestine, religious-critical texts, as well as works of the radical Enlightenment, are part of this invisible pool too.[54] Since Reimarus had still hoped – at least until 1760 – to publish the *Apology* himself, it was useful not to mention them. The mass of these works would become evident only if we attempted to restore his original working text again (possibly by means of a critical edition). The reader would then quickly realize that in regard to scholarly practice, the Cassius Dio edition and the *Apology* are not as different from each other as they appear to be. Indeed, already in his early scholarly works such as his *De Machiavellismo ante Machiavellum* it appears very clear that Reimarus was adept at using footnotes when he wanted to.[55]

---

jud. Cap. XII. p. 370 seqq. qui et peculiari Schediasma de pseudomesiis Judaeorum commentatus est." The reference is to Johannes van Lent, *De moderna theologia judaica* (Herborn, 1694), and idem, *Schediasma historico-philologicum de Judaeorum Pseudo-Messiis* (Herborn, 1697).

[53] On this language society (Sprachgesellschaft) see Thomas Charles Rauter, *The Eighteenth-Century "Deutsche Gesellschaft": A Literary Society of the German Middle Class* (Ph.D. diss., University of Illinois at Urbana-Champaign, 1970).

[54] An example of a clandestine text would be the treatise *De tribus impostoribus*: See the manuscript copies with the provenace Reimarus ULB Halle Ms. Stolb.-Wern. Zd 56, fol. 1–12, and UB Kiel, Ms. K.B. 89. Reimarus' extensive knowledge of English deist writings is apparent from his excerpts in Nachlaß A7, esp. fol. 14–18 and 59–63. The texts from which Reimarus took excerpts (Anthony Collins, *Grounds and Reasons of the Christian Religion* [London, 1724]; idem, *The Scheme of Literal Prophecy considered* [London, 1727], as well as works by Thomas Woolsten and Samuel Clarke) were all published before 1730. Thus, I assume that the notes belong to the preparatory work for Reimarus' *Vindicatio dictorum Veteris Testamenti in Novo allegatorum* (Ms. Kall 311, 4°, St. 7, of the Royal Library Copenhagen) of 1731. In this book, as Peter Stemmer (footnote 8) has shown, Reimarus still rejects deism and its critique of Christian proofs from prophecy. On the other hand, the intensity of Reimarus' concern with this English debate is amazing, so that we might ask whether the deist argument did not have an impact on Reimarus already in these early years, which became effective once Reimarus gave up his orthodox position in the course of the controversy about the Wertheim Bible. On this controversy see the contribution by Ursula Goldenbaum in this volume.

[55] Reimarus, *Dissertatio schediasmate de Machiavellismo ante Machiavellum* (Wittenberg, 1719); reprinted in *Kleine gelehrte Schriften* (footnote 2), pp. 1–48.

IV. Criteria for Divine Revelation

How then did Reimarus apply his sense of realia in his *Apology*? In those passages where he examines the biblical text, two things are usually important: the demonstration that apparently miraculous events are either a source of deception or could be explained naturally, and a moral criticism of the biblical protagonists. They are closely connected to each other. Reimarus uses as his starting point Christian Wolff's observation on miracles, which looks for "characteristics of divine revelation."[56] Wolf suggests the following criterion: "If it had pleased God to provide human beings through certain mediators or divine messengers with supernatural and joyful revelation, then he would have selected those who had the ultimate goal themselves to present what had been revealed to them to as many human beings as possible."[57] Since those mediators represent God, they would not be allowed to misbehave themselves because that would then ultimately refer back to God himself. Those determined to follow their calling need to be morally pure. From this premise Reimarus deduces his programme of research: the biblical text needs to be examined based upon whether the protagonists Moses, David, Isaiah, or Peter acted in accordance with this moral norm. In this procedure Reimarus proposes an unprejudiced attitude, which means that the sacred nature of these men should not be assumed.[58]

In our search for a general characterization of how Reimarus proceeds in his examination of the Bible it is almost appropriate to use the term "aggressive coolness." This coolness towards texts is already apparent in his Cassius Dio edition, especially when Reimarus attacks Nicolaus Carminius Falco.[59] But this coolness emanated also from philologists such as Jean Le Clerc and Jean Hardouin, at least when they examined and emended profane authors. How could this coolness be justified? Reimarus appears to have possibly followed the ideal of a "tempered reason"[60] in the

---

[56] Christian Wolff, *Vernünftige Gedancken von Gott, der Welt und der Seele des Menschen, auch allen Dingen überhaupt, den Liebhabern der Wahrheit mitgetheilet. Neue Auflage hin und wieder vermehret* (Halle, 1751), §§ 1011ff.; §§ 1040ff.: "Wenn es Gott gefallen hätte eine übernatürliche und seligmachende Offenbarung durch gewisse Mittelspersonen oder göttliche Boten an das menschliche Geschlecht zu bringen: so würde er solche dazu ausersehen, welche selbst den Endzweck hätten die ihnen offenbarte Religion allen Menschen so viel wie möglich kund zu machen und unter ihnen zu befördern."

[57] *Apologie* (footnote 18), vol. 1, p. 184.

[58] Ibid., p. 186.

[59] See the contribution by Ulrich Groetsch to this volume.

[60] See, for example, *Apologie* (footnote 18), vol. 2, p. 348.

sense of dispassion and impartiality, which Johann Lorenz Mosheim in particular defined in the preface to his history of heresy.[61] Jean Mabillon pleaded for this kind of impartiality in the preface to his *Traité des études monastiques*.[62] However, daring to subject the Bible to this philological coolness was unusual.

If, as a result, Reimarus points out, the deeds of the biblical protagonists "coincide with fleshly intentions" instead of being suitable for the spread of true religion, then it would be impossible to recognize them as divine messengers, and it would also prove that the Bible was not a book of divine revelation.[63] Reimarus does not directly deny the possibility of miracles and revelation; rather, he suggests an empirical-hermeneutical investigation, which leans on the recognition of revelation. It is a textual verification of an epistemological condition.

Wolff did not take this avenue himself. He puts forth the criteria that either "wherever nature is sufficient, the expected intention suffices" or wherever an old miracle, which is already well-known, is sufficient, no miracle has occurred. For God, who thinks in economic terms, would in such cases not put in extra effort. Wolff then draws a connection to the morality of the biblical figures. Not even the radical Wolffian Carl August Gebhardi, who wrote in 1743 an anonymous criticism of a belief in miracles and revelation, does that. He also expresses epistemological ideas in regard to the criteria: a prophet would accordingly not be capable of distinguishing between supernaturally conceived and naturally conceived ideas.[64] But Gebhardi does not continue these thoughts towards the moral criteria for the prophet.

Reimarus, however, moves in this direction, and he may in fact have been influenced by Pierre Bayle's criticism of apparent heroes such as King David. Although Bayle does not go as far as to explicitly deny the prophetic character of David, he claims that "the deep respect, which we

---

[61] Johann Lorenz Mosheim, *Versuch einer unpartheiischen und gründlichen Ketzergeschichte* (Helmstedt, 1746), introduction. See Martin Mulsow, "Eine 'Rettung' des Michael Servet und der Ophiten? Der junge Mosheim und die heterodoxe Tradition," in idem et al. (eds.), *Johann Lorenz Mosheim (1693–1755). Theologie im Spannungsfeld von Philosophie, Philologie und Geschichte* (Wiesbaden, 1997), pp. 45–92.

[62] See Jean Mabillon, *Traité des études monastiques* (Paris, 1691). On Mabillon see Blandine Kriegel, *Les historiens et la monarchie*, vol. 1: *Jean Mabillon* (Paris, 1988).

[63] *Apologie* (footnote 18), vol. 2, p. 348.

[64] *Vernünftige Gedanken von dem Gebrauch der strengen Lehrart in der Theologie welche in der Gesellschaft der Wahrheitsfreunde entworfen hat A–X, Amsterdam auf Kosten des Autors* [1743], § 7; see Martin Mulsow, *Freigeister im Gottsched-Kreis. Wolffianismus, studentische Aktivitäten und Religionskritik* (Göttingen, 2007) (with an edition of the text).

have towards this great King and the great prophets should not prevent us from pointing out the faults and blemishes in their lives and castigating them."[65]

Reimarus takes up this thought and combines it with Wolff's search for prophetic criteria. By this means, natural theology becomes the moral measuring stick for the characters in the Bible.

V. Antiquarianism and Enlightened Biblical Criticism

This is where antiquarianism comes again into play. In order to reconstruct the behaviour and potential deception of these characters, a profound knowledge of ancient geography as well as customs and rituals is necessary. For his study of the passage where Moses performed a miracle by striking a rock on Mount Sinai with his rod and water sprang from it, Reimarus uses travel accounts from Egypt. Already on his travels through Holland he had been fascinated by the accounts of Johan Heyman about Egypt. In his *Apology* he relied on the reports by Balthasar de Monconys and Pietro della Valle, which reveal that in the rock under Mount Horeb numerous springs of water can be found, as water had trickled into the crevices in the mountain.[66] And where Moses narrates the passage of the Israelites through the Red Sea after God's parting of the waves in order to lead the Israelites through it, Reimarus calculates, with one eye towards the then prevailing conditions, that this report could simply not have been true. In just the same way as he himself tried to find out during his journey in Holland how many hours peat stays alight, and using Le Clerc's calculations as his starting point,[67] he examines how many Israelites were

---

[65] Pierre Bayle, *Dictionnaire historique et critique*, 2nd edition (Rotterdam, 1702), Art. "David", Rem. D. German translation: *Historisches und kritisches Wörterbuch. Eine Auswahl*, translated and ed. by Günter Gawlick and Lothar Kreimendahl (Hamburg, 2003), p. 52.

[66] *Apologie* (footnote 18), vol. 1, p. 355; Balthasar de Monconys, *Iornal des voyages des Monsieur des Monconys, publié par le Sieur de Liergues son fils, vol. I: Voyage de Portugal, Provence, Italie, Égypte, Syrie, Constantinople, & Natonie* (Lyon, 1665); new edition of the part on Egypt by Henry Amer (Cairo, 1973); Pietro della Valle, *Eines vornehmen römischen Patritii Reiß-Beschreibung in unterschiedliche Theile der Welt, nemlich in Türckey, Egypten, Palestina, Persien, Ost-Indien und andere weit entlegene Landschafften; erstlich von dem Authore selbst in italienischer Sprach beschrieben und in 54 Send-Schreiben in 4 Theile verfasset; anjetzo aber auß dem Original in die Hoch-Teutsche Sprach übersetzet* (Geneva, 1674).

[67] *Apologie* (footnote 18), vol. 1, p. 296: Le Clerc on Exodus 12,37: *Genesis sive Mosis prophetae liber primus. Ex translatione Joannis Clerici, cum ejusdem paraphrasi perpetua, commentatio philologico, dissertationibus criticis quinque, et tabulis chronologici. Editio secunda auctior et emendatior* (Amsterdam, 1710), p. 60 (of the separate pagination for the

part of the exodus, how long it took to load the carriages, and how long the passage through the Red Sea must have taken. The result: the trail of ten thousand carriages including those with goods and cattle must have measured about four hundred thousand yards, and with its speed of at most one and a half mile per hour, it could never have crossed the Red Sea in a single night.[68] But that is what is recorded in the Bible.

Reimarus, who exhibits an interest in all types of technical details and conditions, thrives on such calculations. The manuscript notes to the *Apology* still show them.[69] Let us listen to Reimarus's description of the vibration of the bars of chimes on his journey to Holland: "The dead spots of the bars of the chimes cannot completely be calculated mathematically, because the quality of the ore changes the tone and therefore one should take dry sand and place the chime horizontally so that the sand remains sitting on both dead spots when it is played."[70] Let us also listen to him speak in the *Apology* about the miracle in Exodus 16, when bread and quails fall from the sky in order to feed the Israelites who have been wandering in the desert for forty years. Reimarus bases his analysis here on Bochart's *Hierozoicon*, which maintains that migrating birds such as quails pass through Egypt on their journey and exhausted birds often fall from the sky.[71] He adds to this antiquarian work the account of Frederik

commentary on Exodus), footnote: "Ut essent 600000 aetate militari, minimum 3000000 esse oportuit: nam vix sexta pars, ut hodierna constat experientia, est virorum eorumque adultorum." Reimarus quotes this passage up to this point. Le Clerc's text continues: "Mulieres puellae et pueri una cum servis, minimum quinque partes populorum conficiunt. Hoc cum ita sit, duo hic solvendi proponuntur Interpretibus nodi, 1. qui potuerint tot homines ex septuaginta capitibus ducentorum quindecim annorum spatio nasci? 2. qui tanta multitudo, praeter veteres Aegyptios, aliosque qui in inferiorem Aegyptum confluxerant potuerit sedes illic habere et vivere?" In order to estimate the population of the Israelites, Reimarus seems to have used the book by Robert Wallace, *A Dissertation on the Numbers of Mankind in Antient and Modern Times: In which the Superior Populousness of Antiquity is Maintained* (Edinburgh, 1753), from which he takes long extracts in his notes in Nachlaß A7, fol. 21–24.

[68] *Apologie* (footnote 18), pp. 299–326.

[69] Staatsarchiv Hamburg, 622–1 Nachlaß Familie Reimarus, A 14d, p. 35. The calculation refers to the length of the entire trail of the Israelites in the final version of the *Apologie* vol. 1, pp. 308f. In his earlier drafts, Reimarus still counts with different numbers, for example with a longer distance between the marching lines, so that he arrives at a total length of 2992900 (rather than of 490000) steps.

[70] Diary fragment, p. 9.

[71] *Apologie* (footnote 18), pp. 337ff. See Samuel Bochart, *Hierozoicon sive biparti operis de animalibus scripturae Pars posterior, in qui agitur Libris sex de avibus, serpentibus, insectis aquaticis, et de fabulosis animalibus* (London, 1663: this was appartently the edition that Reimarus used), lib. I, Cap. 15, col. 100, 104, 106ff. I shall quote only Bochart's summary of the chapter, col. 96: "Hae ceturnices unde venerint? Resp. Num. xi. 31. e mari. Non, quod in

Hasselquist's travels, which confirms that quails do in fact inhabit the area around the Red Sea.[72] Then, however, he starts with his own calculations. How much manna and how many quails did the Israelites then receive, given their number in the Bible? Most likely in accordance with his lectures at the *Gymnasium illustre*, Reimarus explains here: "Did the author of the passage also take into consideration what a chomer constitutes? I shall calculate it for him; but please let us not confuse omer and chomer. Ten omer are the equivalent of an ephta and ten ephta make a chomer, which is often also referred to as 'cr'. That means that one chomer contains one hundred omer and ten chomer accordingly one thousand omer. The daily ration of food in regard to the manna was only one single omer. Ten chomer would then contain enough food for one thousand people. Even if every collecting head of a family had to provide for ten people in his hut and family, he would still have needed over thirty days only about three hundred omer. That is not even one third of ten chomer."[73] These types of calculations often run over pages until Reimarus arrives at the result that six hundred thousand grown men could collect twenty-five thousand nine hundred and twenty million quails. Each of the three million Israelites could then eat two hundred and eighty-eight quails per day. "So, have it then until you are sick of the meat!" he exclaims mockingly about the absurd result and triumphantly adds, "How could they even have killed all of the gathered quails one month in advance, plucked their feathers, and got rid of their entrails; and how could they have preserved the meat for a month from vermin, maggots, and decay?"[74]

---

mari natae sint, ut volunt Arabes: sed quod, eo trajecto, volarunt in castra Israelitarum. Cur ad eas advehendas Eurum excitaverit Deus Psal. lxxviii. 26. cum Aegyptus, unde venerunt, sit ad occasum Arabiae, ubi tum erant Judai. Ex Graeca et Vulgata versione hic nodus non solvitur. Sed Eurus hoc loco idem, qui Auster, quod prolixe probatur. Refellitur, quod objiciunt Austro flante non volare coturnices. Venti Ornithyae qui sunt, et unde spirent. Coturnices aves migratoriae. Ex Aegypto venerunt, quo tempore migrare solent."

[72] Frederik Hasselquist, *Reise nach Palaestina in den Jahren 1749 bis 1752* (Rostock, 1762).

[73] *Apologie* (footnote 18), vol. 1, pp. 338f.: "Hat [der Schreiber] auch bedacht, was ein Chomer enthalte? Ich will es ihm vorrechnen; nur bitte ich, daß man die beiden Wörter, Omer und Chomer nicht mit einander verwechsele. Zehn Omer machen einen Ephta, und zehn Ephta machen einen Chomer, sonst auch cor genannt. Folglich hielte ein Chomer 100 Omer, und also zehn Chomer 1000 Omer. Nun wird das tägliche Maaß Speise, bey dem Manna, nur auf einen Omer gerechnet. Mithin würden zehn Chomer für 1000 Personen Speise enthalten. Wenn dann ein jeder sammelnde Hausvater auch 10 Personen in seiner Hütte und Familie gehabt hätte: so würde er doch auf 30 Tage nur 300 Omer gebraucht haben. Das macht noch nicht den dritten Theil von zehn Chomer aus."

[74] Ibid. p. 340: "Nun so friß denn, daß Du des Fleisches satt werdest [...] wie sie die auf einen gantzen Monat voraus gesammlete Wachteln eintzeln tödten, rupffen und

It would certainly be worthwhile to check Reimarus' Hamburg lectures on these calculations to find out how he conducted them without drawing these religious-critical conclusions. In his lectures there must have been certain breaks that enabled him to continue his antiquarian explanations without adding any explosive character to them. Reimarus must either have stopped his factual explanations just at the point where they would have reached a destructive consequence for the biblical text, or have repeated affirmatively the traditional approaches to these factual issues, without believing them himself. This demonstrates that once the intellectual framework to render factual explanations into vehicles that expose flaws or inconsistencies exists, it is no longer so easy to practice antiquarianism uncritically and not subversively. This conclusion still holds today. Now that Israel Finkelstein and Neil Silberman are able to produce archaeological evidence against the biblical story of King David, they cannot view him as much more than an insignificant tribal leader of a small urban unit.[75] They work with calculations similar to those that Reimarus had introduced, and as they appear – still on entirely peripheral subjects – in Reimarus' diary fragment from Holland.

---

ausnehmen können; oder womit sie dennoch das Fleisch einen Monat lang vor Ungeziefer, Maden und Verwesung bewahret haben."

[75] Israel Finkelstein and Neil A. Silberman, *The Bible Unearthed: Archaeology's New Vision of Ancient Israel and the Origin of Its Sacred Texts* (New York, 2002).

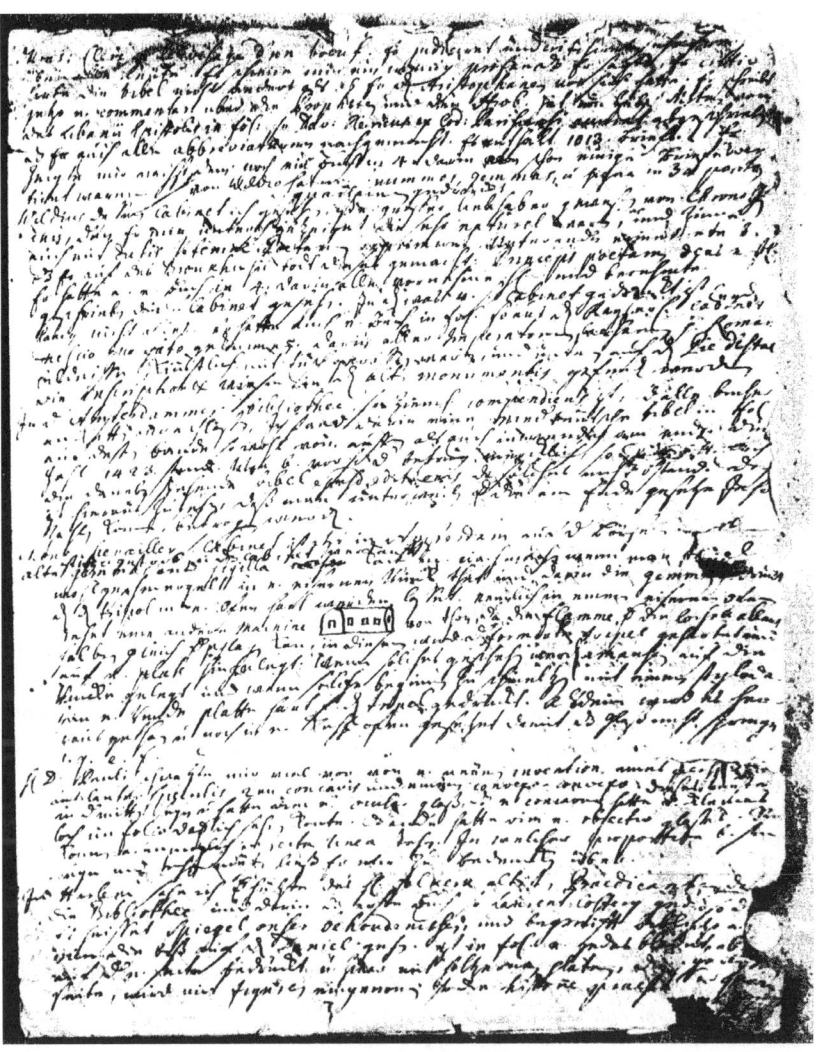

Figure 1. Reimarus, Travel Diary Fragment, 1720/21. Staatsarchiv Hamburg, Nachlaß Familie Reimarus IIIb 4a.

APPENDIX I

REIMARUS, TRAVEL DIARY FRAGMENT, 1720/21
STAATSARCHIV HAMBURG, NACHLASS FAMILIE REIMARUS IIIB 4A[76]

About the edition: For certain words, Reimarus uses his own abbreviations such as b for "aber", f for "auf", a break with a tilde above it for "nicht", d with a twirl for "durch", etc. Such abbreviations have tacitly been spelled out. Square brackets, however, are used to indicate where those abbreviations have been spelled out that Reimarus had marked by a simple break (e.g. "e[in]" for "e."). Abbreviations and squiggles at the end of words have mostly been spelled out as well without further indicating them. Punctuation marks have been added to facilitate the reading of passages. Modern umlauts have been added where Reimarus does not use them or where they appear barely legible on the manuscript copy. Words that have remained illegible have been marked by <...>. At times, a commentary in square brackets has been added in cursive about the general condition of the text such as: insertion, ink stain on paper. Numbers in square brackets "[1]" mark the page of the manuscript.

[1] [...] Clerc a le visage d'un boeuf.[77] Er judiciert und critisiert sehr frei [? fein?] über alle leute. Es schiene mir ein wenig profan, das er sagte, er critisirte die bibel nicht anders, als ob er den Aristophanes vor sich hatte. Er schreibt jetzo e[inen] commentar über die Propheten und den Hiob.[78] Hat ein hübsch manuscriptum von des Libanii epistolis in fol., so <Hr.?> Clericus ex Cod[ice] Parisiensi accurat abgeschrieben, als er auch alle abbreviaturen nachgemacht. Es enthält 1013 briefe.[79] Er zeigte mir nächst dem noch ein buch in 4, darin aber schon einige briefe convertiret waren. Von Wildio hat er nummos, gemmas u[nd] signa in 3a partes quartainen

---

[76] I am greatful to Julian Holzapfl for his excellent raw transcript of this text, which was often very difficult to decipher.

[77] The fact that Le Clerc had bestial facial features is testified also through the reports by Stolle and Mencke. See above footnote 4.

[78] *Veteris testamentae prophetae ab Esaia ad Malachiam usque ex translatione Joannis Clerci, cum ejusdem commentario philologico et paraphrasi* [...] (Amsterdam, 1731); *Veteris testamenti libri hagiographi, Jobus, Davidis Psalmi, Salomonis Proverbia, Concionatrix et Canticum Canticorum ex translatione Joannis Clerci, cum ejusdem commentario philologico in omnes memoratos libros et paraphrasi in Jobum ac Psalmos* (Amsterdam, 1731).

[79] Reimarus was expecially attentive to Libanius, because he knew that his teacher Wolf was going to undertake an edition of the Libanius letters, which claimed to be as comprehensive as possible. See the eventual outcome: *Libanii Sophistae Epistolae. Quas nunc primum maximam partem e variis codd. manu exaratis, edidit* [...] *Wolfius* (Amsterdam, 1738).

gedruckt.[80] Wildius, dessen cabinet ich gesehen, ist e[in] grosser liebhaber gewesen von Chronodistichis,[81] den er mir auch noch gezeiget, die sehr naturel waren, und zum e[xempel] auch mit dictis veterum poetarum exprimiret, unter andern erinn(er)t er <...>, das er auf des Broukhusii[82] todt dieses gemacht: Princeps poetarum deus noster.[83] Er hatte a[uch] e[in] buch in 4, darin alle vornehmen h[erren] und berühmte geschrieben, die s[ein] cabinet gesehen.[84] Zu dem, was v[on] s[einem] cabinet gedrukt, ist lang nicht alles. Er hatte auch e[in] buch in fol[io] so aus dem kayserl. cabinet nesquio quo fato gekommen, darin aller imperatoren, caesaren f. rome bildnisse künstlich mit tusch gerissen waren, und unten auf dem piedestal die inscriptiones, wie sie an den alten monumentis gefunden werden.[85]

In der amsterdammer bibliothec, so zieml[ich] compendieus ist, s[in]d alle bücher an ketten angeschlossen, ich fand darin eine niederteutsche bibel in fol[io] an dessen bande so wohl von aussen als auch inwendich am ende die Zahl 1423 stand. war aber vor s[ich] der betrug merklich, so <...> auch die daneben stehende bibel <...> editionis, da solches nicht stand. Des[..?] ist hieraus zu sehen, daß man unterweilen durch am ende gesetze jahr zahlen konnte betrogen werden.

---

[80] *Selecta numismatica antiqua musaeo Jacobi de Wilde, Amsterdam 1692; Signa antiqua e museo Jacobi de Wilde veterum poetarum carminibus illustrata et per Mariam filiam aeri inscripta, Amsterdam 1700; Gemmae selectae antiquae ex museo Jacobi de Wilde, sive L. tabulae diis deabusque gentilium ornatae per possessorem conjecturis, veterumque poetarum carminibus illustratae* (Amsterdam, 1703). On De Wilde's collections see M. Maaskant-Kleibrink, *Catalogue of the engraved Gems in the Royal Coin Cabinett the Hague. The Greek, Etruscan and Roman Collections* (The Hague, 1987), pp. 15ff. (with footnotes 1ff. on literature).

[81] Jacob de Wilde; see footnote 20. See also the travel report by Uffenbach (footnote 13), vol. 3, pp. 634f. Chronodistichon: an elegant encryption of the Roman ciphers of the date of a year in a distich, i.e. in a verse consisting of two lines (one hexameter and one pentameter).

[82] Johan van Broekhuizen (1649–1707), military career, neo-Latin poet. See also Stolle's visit (footnote 4): pp. 879ff.

[83] More precisely one should read: prInCeps poetaruM Deus noster. This amounts to MDCI, i.e. the year 1601; Broekhuizen, however, had died in 1707 – consequently Reimarus here notes only the beginning of the Chronodistich – the rest had to entail the numerical value that is still missing.

[84] Compare the similar case of a visitor's book in Nicolas Chevalier's cabinet, about which we learn from Anne Goldgar. See footnote 19.

[85] See Uffenbach (footnote 13), vol. 3, p. 636. Reimarus seems to refer to Jacobo Strada's book. On Strada's illustrations of the portraits on coins see Francis Haskell, *History and its Images: Art and the Interpretation of the Past* (New Haven, 1993), chapter I,2.

Mons. Chevaillers[86] cabinet ist jetzt in amsterdam auf der börse <...>
[*Insertion:* ist ietzt gestorben u[und] s[ein] cabinet verkaufft] Alte gemmas
und sigilla kan m[an] nachmachen, wenn man <...> wohl geschmergeltt
in e[inen] eisernen rink [?][87] thut und darin die gemmas <...> d[urch?]
d[en] tripod [?] in e[einem] ofen hart werden lasset, nemlich in einem
eisernen ofen, stehet eine andere machine [*here a drawing is inserted into
the text*] von thon, da die flamme durch die locher allenthalben gleich
durch schlagen kan, in diesem wird der formirte tripod [?] gehertet und
auf e[ine] plate hingelegt: Wenn solichs geschehen, werden <...> auf die
rincke gelegt, und wenn soliche beginnen zu schmeltzen, mit einem stylo
daran e[ine] runde platte hart auf d[en] tripod [?] gedrückt. Alsdann wird
es herraus gethan u[nd] noch in e[inen] kühl ofen gesetzet, damit das
glass nicht springe. I[n] q[uod] e[st] f[inis].

H[err] D[oktor] Pauli[88] schwatzte mir viel vor von e[iner] neuen invention
eines persp<...> mit lauter speculis, 2en concavis und einem convexo.
Convexo: der hat müssen in der mitten seyn, u[nd] hatte vorn e[in] ocult
glass, der e[inen] concavus hatte e[in] klaines loch im folio, das ich sehen
konte, der andere hatte vorn e[in] objectio gl<...>. <...> a[ber] unmoglich
in recta linea sehe, in welchem proportion aber sie sayn und müsten, liess
er mir zu bedenkcen über.

In Harlem sahe ich durch hülfe des H. Gelkern[89] [c]alv[in]ist[ischem] [?]
Praedicanten die Bibliothec, und darin das erste buch, so Laurent Coftern[90]
gedr<druckt> es heisset ‚Spiegel onser behoudenichen',[91] und begreifft
bibli[sche] [Histo]rien, die biß auf den Daniel gehen, ist in fol[io] a[uch]
jedes blad <...> auf der e[inen] seite bedruckt, u[nd] jenes mit höltzer-

---

[86] On Chevailler see footnote 6.
[87] Reimarus seems to mean a ringshaped edging. On techniques of counterfeiting coins
see Wayne G. Sayles, *Classical Deception: Counterfeits, Forgeries and Reproductions of
Ancient Coins* (Iola, 2001).
[88] Pauli, a physician and inventor from Dresden (see footnote 136), is not further
identifiable.
[89] Not identified.
[90] Laurent Kofter, publisher in Haarlem.
[91] *De Spieghel der menscheliker behoudenesse.* On this *Speculum humanae salvationis*
(1324) see the facsimile edition edited by Margit Krenn, *Heilsspiegel* (Darmstadt, 2006). See
also Bert Cardon, *Manuscripts of the Speculum humanae salvationis in the Southern Netherlands* (Leuven, 1996); Adrian Wilson, *A Medieval Mirror* (Berkeley, 1984); M. Fr. Daniels, *De
Spieghel der menscheliker behoudenesse: De middelnederlandse vertaling van het Speculuma
humanae salvationis* (Lannoo, 1949), and many other writings.

nen platen, die <andere?> seite wird mit figuren eingenommen, so die historien praesent<ieren> [2] beschrieben wird, keine Jahrzahl stehet dabey. Es ist a[uch] ohne titul, sondern nur das harlemmer wapen darauf geklebt, u[nd] ein ander zettel, darauf stehet ‚gedrukt tot harlem', diesem war beygebunden e[in] anderes buch, ebenvals ohne titul, fing sich so an: ‚Incipit liber Alex[andri] M[agni] Regis macedon[ens]is de proeliis', was lateinisch, und <...> s., u. anderes b. tit. ‚Petri Scriverrii Laure-Crans, voor Laurens Corfter van Harlem, erste vender van de boekdrukerey tot Harlem, by Adriaan Rooman, ordinary stadt boek druker, 1628', wahr mit papier beklebt, damit es das folio ausfullete. Voran war auf e[inem] Kupfer Cofterus vorgebildet, in der linken hand den buchstaben A haltend, in der rechten e[ine] taffel, darauf stand: N. S. consulari Laurentio Cofterio harlemensi, alteri cadmo artisty [*blot*] circa an. dni. 1430, inventori primo, bene de literis ac toto [ur]be merenti, hanc <...> statuam, quia aeream non habuit pro monumento posuit civis gratis[?] Adrian[us] Romanus Typogr[aphus] 1630. Unten standen in 2 columnen die verse:

Vana quid archetypos et praela moguntia iactas
harlemi archetypos praelaque nata sitas
Extulit hic non stante deo laurentii artem
dissimulare eium hunc dissimulare Deum est
Ments meint vant eerste boek vyl hak pie ghefonden,
tot harlem is noch thans de Drukery ghefonden
deer Laurens heft de konst med godt deer voort gebracht
verswigt man desen man, so word ook godt veracht

P. Scriverius[92]

[*blot*] ist die Bibliothec eben [?] klein, sie haben aber noch einige manuscripta, die ich, soviel das mädchen [?] so auch Luseke [?] kheinen schlüssel dazu hatten, nur per transeundem gesehen, e[xempli] g[ratia] Suetonium, Terentium, Plutarchium, Donatum in Vergilium etc.

Auf dem Westhause verwahrt m[an] noch andere exemplaria, u[nd] eben diesem speculo hum[anae] sapientiae,[93] welche an den H. Gelkern offerirt, in die bibliothecen zu geben, der sie aber wegen der sorge zu bewahren, <nicht?> annehmen wollen. Es sollen a[uch] da noch platten seyn, damit

---

[92] Petrus Scriverius (Peter Schryver) (1576–1660) was a late humanist poet.
[93] Correctly it should read: Speculum humanae salvationis (see footnote 91).

solches buch gedruckt, a. die einwohner des cofterischen Hauses haben e. nachm[als?] geb<...>es buch in e[inem] kästchen verwahret.

D[er] hollandische torft wird aus kostigter, schlammigter, u[nd] morastigter erde gemacht, welche auf das feste land aufgeschüttet, getrocknet, und alsdann abgestochen wird, ich habe probiret, das e. solche torft über 24 stunden feuer halten kann.[94]

Thysii[95] Bibliotheca ist klein, sie stehet auf e. saale in dem eidhause an der queerhaften gracht. Es sind nicht mehr den[n] 2 manuscipta darin: Terentii und Ovidii, [*loss of paper at the edge*] davon das erste nicht über 300, das andere kaum 200 jahre alt seyn mag. Das [*loss of paper at the edge*] soll wieder aufs neue gedruckt werden. Es hat an jetzo Ms: [*loss of paper at the edge*] [g]eneral staaten da weren darüber. Es ist ein legatten dabey, davon vor 100 jahr [*loss of paper at the edge*] alle jahr solten dazu gekauft werden, welches aber nicht geschehen, da [*loss of paper at the edge*] solche art innerhalb einigen 60 jahren, so lange die Bibliothec [be]standen was falsches hette können dazu kommen. Ich sahe auch [3] auf dieser bibiothec e[in] curieuses pulpet,[96] so auf e[iner] waltze was <...> hatte, die auf der waltze konten herum gedrehet werden, so das, wenn alle gl[eich] auf ihnen beleget waren, dennoch kaines herunter fiele.

Der weg von Leyden nach Leydendorp ist eine klaine stunde, plaisant, und eine continuirliche allée, fast gantz hin mit feldsteinen u[und] klunkern gepflastert.[97] Gleich dabei lieget ein prechtig hauss, einem schlosse ähnlich, so dem H[errn] [*lacuna*] aus Amsterdam gehörig, und schon 300 000 g[ulden] soll gekostet haben, ob es gl[eich] noch nicht fertig. Es s[ind] a[uch] schöne plantagen dabei.

---

[94] On the contemporary techniques of cutting the peat, see *Zedlers Universal-Lexicon*, vol. 44, col. 1308–1310.

[95] Antonius Thysius (1603–1665), classicist, professor in Leiden, editor of Aulus Gellius, Velleius Paterculus etc.

[96] pulpitum (lat.): wooden scaffold. Reimarus seems to refer to a roller for books, which enables one to read several books simultaneously. Similar machines were used by Duke August in his library in Wolfenbüttel, and by Gabriel Harvey. See Anthony Grafton and Lisa Jardine, "Studied for Action: How Gabriel Harvey Read his Livy", *Past and Present* 129 (1990), pp. 3–51.

[97] Leydendorp is located a few miles east of Leiden.

Das Pesthaus bestehet aus 8 zimmern, die e[inen] 4eckten platz einschlie-
ßen, worin e[in] garthen und durchfliessendes wasser. Es s[in]d vor 200
personen betten darinn. Es komt e[inem] e[in] kleiner schauer an, wenn
m[an] hinnein komt in die zimmer, ich glaube aber, das es einbildung
sey, weil in diesem hause noch niemand gestorben, das erst zur zeit der
vorigen pest, oder vieleicht nachher gebauet worden.

Von der Werfte,[98] mahler in Rotterdam, excelieret in mignaturen. Moor[99]
in Leyden, der vom kayser geadelt, in grossen contrefaiten, und sauberen
zeichnungen.

Zu Schevelingen[100] ist e[ine] curieuse maschine zu kauffen, damit man
sonder feuer diverse metalla zu filamenten separiren kann, so das, wenn
das verdeckte <...> einige mahl herumgedrehet worden, ein jedes metall
unten in einem aparte schachtelchen liegend gefunden wird. M[onsieur]
L. hatte si dahin machen lassen, da in e[inem] porcellainen deckel die
schensten farben in figuren gebrannt waren.

V. der Marck[101] in Harlem ist e. grosser bucher narre, so das er allerwerts
die besten editiones der bücher mit schwerem gelde aufgekaufft, soll selber nichts verstehen, und s[ein] capital minimiret [?] haben, das er e[s]
der bibliothec verkauffen musste, andere sagen jedoch, das er mit den
buchern schachere u[nd] profit damit gemacht habe.[102] Er hat e[ine] bibel
mit schönen kupfern auf s[eine] kosten drucken lassen.

Crenius ist im hanoverischen prediger gewesen, sol aber im <...> gemachet [?] und ist daher removiret worden.[103]

Sal[omon] van Till.[104] hat e[ine] gemaine hure geheurathet, so das m[an]
ihm die e[ntziehung?] des Erbs gedrohet, daran er s[ich] aber nicht

---

[98] Adriaan vander Werft (1659–1721), painter.

[99] Carel de Moor (1656–1738), portrait paiter.

[100] Apparently: Scheveningen.

[101] Hendrik Adriaan (Henricus Hadrianus) vander Marck.

[102] Indeed, there is a sales catalogue *Bibliotheca Marckiana*, which was published in The
Hague in 1712, but then was republished in 1727. One can infer that in 1712 probably the
sale of the library did not occur.

[103] Thomas Theodor Crenius (originally: Crusius) (1648–1728) had been a minister in
Celle, which he left because of accusations concerning his conduct (homosexuality?). In
Holland, he adopted the name Crenius and taught classics in Leiden.

[104] Salomon van Til (1643–1713), reformed theologian and professor in Leiden.

gekehret, ainige sagen, er sey <...> letzte wahnwitzig worden, u[nd] sey auf soliche art noch bey dem dienste geblieben.[105]

Von der Aa[106] druckt supplementa zu den tomis antiquit[a]t[um]:[107] hat schöne manuscripta, ist aber sehr theuer damit. Sonsten hat er a[uch] e[ine] selecta [*written in the line above*: bibliotheca] anzahl von raren büchern, davon er aber keine verkauffen will.

Oryphaeus,[108] commercien raht in Cassel, hat e[in] perpetuum mobile erfunden, so 4 ½ cent[ner?] bewegt, welches er curieusen zeiget, er machet sonst a[uch] e[inen] besonders schonen u[nd] starken phosphorn vom urin.

In Wien ist die Windhagensche Bibliothec,[109] bey den dominicanern, welche täglich morgens u[nd] nachmittags e[inem] jeden offen stehet, und da <...> die dinte u[nd] papier gemachet wird. Sie soll schöne bücher und manuscripta haben. Uffenbach o[der] Oppenbach[110] in F[rank]furt am Mayn hat a[auch] e[ine] schöne bibliothec, sonders an raren büchern, die er seinen freunden zeiget, u[nd] dazu e[in] stambuch offerirert, darinn m[an] s[einen] nahmen schreiben muss.

Albers in Nieuenhoft[111] in dem Haag, zu eußerm end der stad von Uetwerff [?] hat schöne alte bücher und rare a[lte?] manuscripta.

Die Rhedereiken oder Rhetoriken ist e[ine] compagnie poeten in Holland, so der alten meister sangern unsers teutschlandes glaichet, die ist jetzo a[us] lauter bauren <...>, welche a[ll?] hier e[ine] comoedie gespielet, aber elend zeug vorbrachten, der oberste davon schreibet alle jahr ain jed[er?] zeit u[nd] thema, aus welchen si gearbeitet werden in gewisser

---

[105] Compare the similar problems that the philologist Burmann had to face: Blanche T. Ebeling-Koning, "The *Catalecta Petrulliana* and the Burmann Affair: Sex, Religion, and Feuding in Eighteenth-Century Netherlands", *Harvard Library Bulletin* 11 (2000), pp. 3–27.
[106] Pieter van der Aa (1654–1733), publisher in Leiden.
[107] Jacob Gronovius, *Thesaurus graecarum antiquitatum* (Leiden, 1697–1702).
[108] Not identified.
[109] Library, bequeathed to the Dominicans of Vienna by the Count of Windhagen.
[110] Zacharias Konrad von Uffenbach (1683–1734), Frankfurt patrician and book collector. See footnote 13.
[111] Not identified.

qualitaet u[nd] art v[on] reimen. Vor dem sind vornehme leute darin [gewesen?]. [4]

Sonsten ist a[uch] noch e[ine] societaet poeten, die pro symbolo hat: nil volentibus arduum.[112] Macht die comoedien in Amsterdam, sind viele honete leute darin.

[Un?]weit leyden ist e[in] bauer, der die schönsten verse machet, dabey doch s[inen] pflug noch abtraghet.

Zu Leyden ist e[ine] zusammenkunfft bey e[iner] gewissen frauen, die nichts thut <in?> ihrem gottesdienst, als bibelerklaren, d[ie] s[ich] sogar auf den grund text berufft. Es gehen auch vornehme leute hinein.

Auf dem rahthause in leyden u[und] in den Haag liegen die codices autentici von der staatenbibel in Kasten verwahret, welche wo nur recht alle 3 Jahr visitirt, u[nd] conferiret werden, auf den gedruckten, es geschiht mit grossen solennitaeten.

Alle Jahr wird i[n] den vereinigten provinzen e[ine] synody gehalten, <...> aus 40 capitibus bestehend. Die Stadt wechselt alle jahr um.

In leyden ist a[uch] e[in] teutsches collegium, als e[in] convictorium, die studenten werden jährl[ich] von den professoribus 4 mahl examiniert u[nd] zway mahl sind a[uch] die curatores dabey.

Henr[ici] canisii lectiones antiquae tom. VI fol. curante Iac[obi] Basnagi werde bey den Wetsteini in Amsterdam wider aufgeleget.[113] Havercamp hat zu s[einem] Josepho auch Relandi hinterlassene observationes bekomen, erwartet a[uch] aus Copenhagen e[ine] Collation v[on] e[inem] m[anu]s[crip]to.[114]

---

[112] Nothing is impossible for those who have the will. On the "Kunstgenootenschap," which chose this motto for itself, see Albert Jacob Kronenberg, *Het kunstgenootenschap Nil volentibus arduum* (Deventer, 1875); Antonius J. Harmsen, *Onderwys in de tooneel-poëzy* (Rotterdam, 1989).

[113] *Thesaurus monumentorum ecclesiasticorum et historicorum, sive Henrici Canisii lectiones antiquae*, ed. Jacques Basnage, 10 vols. (Amsterdam: Wetstein, 1725).

[114] *Flavii Josephi opera omnia*, ed. Sigbert Haverkamp (Amsterdam-Leiden-Utrecht, 1726). See also Haverkamp's correspondence, which is preserved in the university library in Leiden. On Adriaan Reland (Hadrian Reland) see below footnote 139.

In Reinburg[115] ist in pfingsten u[nd] zur zeit der Rotterdamischen kirmeß versamlung von indifferentisten, sie sind durch alle provinzen <...> und kommen hier 2 mahl im jahr zusammen, das abendmahl zu geniessen. Sie sind von differenten religionen, doch meist socinianer, restringiren aber orthodoxiam fidei salvificae nur auf gantz wenige capita, worunter ich nicht die trinitaten habe nennen horen, daß übrige sprechen sie, gehöre nicht ad essentiam fidei, und sey nur ein modus loquendi, den e[iner] vor dem andern bedürfte, oder wäre nicht in der bibel enthalten oder bestünde in zweiffelhafften erklerungen der schrift.[116] Die art ihres gottesdienstes ist fast quäkerisch, weil predigen sagen, abendmahl austheilen e[inem] jeden frey stehet, dem es der geist eingiebt. Ich habe unter d[enen] die ich peroriren hörte, nur e[inen] gefunden, der was gescheites vorbrachte, die übrigen machten e[in] gewasche m[it] worten, um so ein mehr, weil sie allezeit in generalibus blieben, und ungelehrt waren.

[Eine?] Pagoden der Elephanten oder e[ine] Müntze v[on] e[inem] Elephanten, den der <Herr?> von Campen, ein gewesner prediger in Ostindien hat in leyden <...> rare sachen o[der] g[ar?] idola. Der Schefer, die zodiacus pfennige[117] complet in gold und in silber, unter jenen fehlt ihm <aber?> der aquarius <...> rechte ist e[in] alt monum[entum] Malabar[ium] auf 21 eisenern platen gravirt, die in e[inem] grossen einigefangen. Die buchstaben <...> niemand wist, e[in] dito mit 3 blettern, e[in] derselben celeber [?] <...> pfennig, da auf der e[inen] seite viele stengel mit figuren u[nd] nahmen, <...> fortuna amore <...> etc. [*one line loss of text*][118] [5]

Zu Utrecht ist M[on]s[ieur] Martin Minister françois, der die ganze bibel mit noten edirt, auch das dictum ‚3 sind, die da zeugen' defendirt und vindiciert hat, welches er jetzt zum 2ten mahl wieder u[und] gewisser <...>land defendiren will, ein alter aber dabey vigoureuser und lustiger mann, der e[ine] schöne suadam[119] hat.[120] Da selbst ist a[uch] de la Foy, ein

---

[115] Rhijnsburg near Leiden.
[116] Reimarus refers to the Collegiants. See footnote 16.
[117] See also Uffenbach (footnote 13), vol. 3, pp. 635f.; and p. 514–21 in general on von Campen's collection.
[118] See, in general, Paula J. Turner, *Roman Coins from India* (London, 1989); Edward J. Rapson, *The Coinage of Ancient and Medieval India* (San Diego, 1969).
[119] Literally: (goddess of) cajolery.
[120] David Martin (ed.), *La Sainte-Bible* [...] *revue sur les originaux et retouchée dans la langage*, 3 vols. (Amsterdam, 1707). On Martin see Erich Haase, *Einführung in die Literatur des Refuge* (Berlin, 1959), passim.

jung[er] Pred[iger], der wieder den Tolland[121] geschrieben, it[em] Dr. Engel Medius[122] [?] d[er] e[in] schön[es] antiquitäten. u[nd] münczen cabinet gehabt, so er jetzt an den könig von spanien verkaufft hat. Der <...> van der Waater[123] hat a[uch] e[inen] sohn, der secretarius beym dohmcapittel ist, e[in] gelehrter jurist, der schon einige schöne sachen geschr[ieben]. Hartsoeker[124] e[in] <...> privatus, und guter Mathemat[icus], Physicus u[nd] Mechanicus, Membr[um] Soc[ietatis] Gallicae.[125] Er hat v[on] dem vorigen churfursten v[on] der pfaltz e[ine] pension gehabt. Er zeigte uns e[inen] Magneten, der kugel rund gemacht war ohngefehr 2/3 schuh im diametro, konte 200 lb. ziehen, wenn er e[ine] nadel in der hand über dessen polen hielte, richtete s[ich] dieselbe in der hand perpendiculariter in die höhe. Wenn er e[inen] Schlüssel über dessen Polum hielte, so konte derselbe e[inen] anderen schlüssel tragen, ließ ihn a[uch] nicht fallen, biß er zieml[ich] hoch über den selben gehoben wurde. Er hatte 2 laminas[126] von eysen, davon beyde enden nach den beyden polis dieses magneti bestrichen waren. Wenn er dessen gleiche polos zusammen über ein ander hielte, war ihre krafft verdoppelt, und konten sie e[inen] ziemlichen schlüssel halten. Legte er die contrairen polos uber e[in] ander, so wolten sie nichts ziehen, dabey er observirte, daß wenn m[an] e[in] eisen mit einem Magneten mit einem polo von a – b striche, und hernachen wieder <...> der mit demselben polo von b – a oder mit dem contrairen polo von a – b, so würde die vorige mitgetheilte krafft wieder weg genommen, worauß mir zu folgen scheinet, das wenn es mit dem contrairen polo von b – a streichen den an krafft nicht weggenommen, sondern vieleicht verdoppelt werden. Er konte a[uch] die e[ine] laminem mobilem machen auf e[ine] art, so das er da auch das bekante experiment machen konte, ut contrarii poli se sequant non [?] fugiant. Er meinte, wenn nur e[in] magnet (N[ota] B[ene] immer [?]) in dem <...> wäre, so konte m[an] durch denselben so viele magneten machen, als man begehrte, wie er d[enn] mit d[en] erwehnten lamellen soliches probirte, die also bald s. bestrichenen diese die krafft haben, schlüssel zu halten, sonder er habe a 12 a 10 solicher lamellanien mit messing an e[in] ander fügen lassen, welche 25 lb. halten konten, wunderwürdig war es, das e[in]

---

[121] John Toland. To whom Reimarus refers with "de la Foy" I could not determine.
[122] Not identified.
[123] Not identified.
[124] Nicolaas Hartsoeker (Hartsoecker). See footnote 12. See as well *Zedlers Universal-Lexicon* vol. 12, col. 653f.
[125] Member of the Académie royale des sciences, Paris.
[126] Sheet metal plates.

kleiner magnet, als e[ine] mittelmaßige haselnuß groß, wohl 20 schlüssel halten konte. Nachst diesem zeigte er uns e[inen] bren spiegel, der convex war, und auf 9 schuh brante. Er war in e[iner] machina mobili in s[einem] garten aufgerichtet, so das man ihn nicht nur rechts u[nd] links nach der sonne drehen, sondern a[uch] nach deren hohe tief herunter lassen konte, er hatte a[uch] e[inen] andern concavum, dessen focus [6] auf 7 fuß s[ich] erstreckte, u[nd] aus e[inem] 28 füßigen sphaere war, jedoch nicht aus einem stücke, sondern wohl aus 12en zusammen gesetzet. Er observirte dabey, daß Tschernhausen tort hatte, wenn er mainte, das a[uch] die metalle durch dergleichen prennspiegel könten in glaß verwandelt werden,[127] denn er hette das metall allemahl in e[ine] Kohle oder erde gehalten, die si dann schmeltzen, die asche mit melliert, und so e[in] gläsernes corpus daraus gemacht. Er hat a[uch] gleser zu e[inem] tube von 600 fuß et von 70, welchen er vor dem zar probiret, weil dazumahl die leute auf dem ostindischen hause zu s[einen] diensten gestanden, da er s[ie] dem e[in] gehäuse von holcz machen lassen, u[nd] praecarium, das es nicht krumb würde, hat er es mit fleiß krum beugen lassen, da es sich im aufrichten von selbsten wieder gleich gegeben. Er discursirte auch von der hypothesi, die H[err]n Franzosen [?] verlese, der H. Boerhave[128] auch defendiert, das nemlich alle pflantzen und Blumen ex semine masculino et foeminino generiret würden, indem er es mit hampf probiert, und mit fleiß alle mänchen aus gerottet, da es dessen ohngeachtet saamen gegeben. Er hat a[uch] wieder die hypothesen geschrieben, weil sie aber von der societate gallica[129] approbieret war, worin er gewesen, u[nd] e[ine] pension genossen, so haben sie ihm die pension entzogen. Er zeigte uns auch wohl 1000 nachgemachte gemmas, aus emaillen, d[as] i[st] glaßen, u[nd] aller hand couleuren, die in venedig gemacht werden, auch referirte Hartsoeker in Neuburg.

Unweit Utrecht lieg e[in] lusthauß, Hemste[130] genannt, so jetzo e[in] bildhauer in Amsterdam, Dirck [*above the line is inserted*: auf der <…> gracht], vor 30 000 gulden gekaufft. Es muß wohl 400.000 g. gekostet haben, es

---

[127] See Ehrenfried Walter von Tschirnhaus, *Experimente mit dem Sonnenfeuer* (exhibition in the Dresden Zwinger), ed. Wolfram Dotz (Dresden, 2001).

[128] Herman Boerhaave (1668–1738), professor of botany and medicine in Leiden. See in general on the question of male or female fertilization: Thomas Laqueur, *Making Sex. Body and Gender from the Greeks to Freud* (Cambridge, Mass., 1990); on Hartsoeker see p. 171.

[129] See footnote 125.

[130] Heemstede palace near Houten close to Utrecht. For an illustration of the garden, see Cook (footnote 19), p. 319.

hat es der H[err] v[on] Felthysen,[131] presid[ent] der staat v[on] Utrecht
bauen lassen, es sind unvergleichlich lange, hohe und dicke alleen darin,
welche zu gleich so artig rengiret sind, das m[an] von e[iner] <stelle?>
in der mitten durch 12 alleen sehen kan, und allemahl wenn <man?>
weiter gehet, diverse ordnung der alleen gemacht wird. M[an] sagt, der
jetzige eigenthümer habe daraus schon 30 000 stamme <ver?>kaufft (welches aber nicht e[in] mahl zu sehen war), u[nd] habe er es nur zu dem
mitzwecke erhandelt, um auf soliche art geld darauß zu machen. Es giebt
a[uch] schöne fontainen, und unzählige marmorne statuen darinn, welche mich zwar beyde divertiert, aber jene ziemlich betrogen. Hinten ist
a[uch] e[in] schöner garten, worin wild, auch <schwedische?> <...>.

So waren wir a[uch] zu Ausdegte,[132] so e[in] leibgedinge der prinzessin
von Ostfriesland ist, welche wir zugleich nebst ihren jungen printzen und
dem landgrafen von Hessen Cassel mit s[einem] 3ten printzen, [7] dem
baron Dalwick u[nd] andere cavaliers taffel halten sehen, sonsten ist der
garten schlecht, wird u[nd] übel gewartet, u[nd] liegt auf m[eist?] san-
digsten erdreich, distinguiert s[ich] aber doch mit schönen alleen. Diver-
tiherter u[nd] properer ist Seist,[133] welches dem so genannten herrn von
Seist,[134] e[inem] filio nat[ivo] des Königs Williams zugehoret, der aber
jetzo unter die staaten v[on] Utrecht e[in] membrum ist. Solches ist recht
fürstlich, ja königlich. Das hauß presentiert s[ich] auswerts mit beyden
flugeln, und den großen vorpletzen admirabel, inwendig ist es auch sehr
proper, und wegen fontainen so a[uch] im hause und vor den fenstern
springen, angenehm. Oben ist sonderl[ich] e[in] saal, der vorn und hinten balcons gegen e[in] ander über hat, darauß m[an] a[uch] e[ine] in
dem garten und hinter dem selben gelegene allee siehet, ferne über feld
in e[ine] andere nemliche, beyde a parte de vue, gehen. Es sind im garten
schone fontainen, grotten, orangerie, statuen, u[nd] was man nur ange-
nehmes in e[inem] garten erdenken kan, weliches uns so viel angenehmer
war, je hoflicher der H[err] selbst, als welicher so bald er uns erblickte, so
gleich e[inen] Diener [?] schickte, der uns herumfuhren solte, a[aber?]

---

[131] Probably Huybert van Velthuysen.
[132] Reimarus refers to the Stadskasteel Oudaen in Utrecht, which was built in the thir-
teenth century.
[133] Seyst (Zeist) palace. The palace was built between 1670 and 1680 and is located
amidst today's small town of Zeist, east of Utrecht.
[134] Lodewijk Adriaan van Nassau (1670–1742), son of the builder of the palace, Count
Willem Adriaan van Nassau, who was an illegitimate descendant of Prince Maurits of
Orange.

d[er] s[eine] compagnie, aus der stuben, darin er saß, s[ich] retirierte, damit wir das zimmer besehen konten.

It[em] zu Utrecht in der vorstadt ist a[uch] die seiden mühle[135] remarquabel, welche mit e[inem] großen wasser rade getrieben wird, welche aber in unzehligen andere kamräder und trillinge greifft, unten sind wohl 500 spuhlen, von welichen die seide auf lange spindel gewunden wird, an der einer ende e[in] hammer u[nd] e[ine] glocke ist, welche, wenn sie schlaget, an d[en] tag giebt, das genueg zu e[inem] strange abgewunden sey, a[uch] unten <auf?> dem unteren rade gehet e[in] strick nach oben, der e[in] anderes rad ergreiffet, doch nur alsd<ann>, wenn das rad so beweglich mit e[iner] lade von etwa 40 lb. angezogen wi[rd], welches, wenn es auf gehalten wird, die gantze obere mach[ine] stehen machet. Auf der selben wird die rohe seide von großen strengen auf kleine spulen gewunden, um das grobe davon abzumachen, welche hernacher in das unterste zimmer komen. In beyden sind e[in] hauffen leute, die acht geben müssen, das der faden nicht reiße, oder s[ich] was grobes dar unter menge. Das negste rad bringet zugleich in die oberste etage, mit kleinen daran gemachten kuegeln [?], daraus rechen gehen, wasser in e[inen] trog, welches den fall <...> [here apparently a passage is missing].

[8] [...] giebt zu sehn, und fontainen, die perpetuirlich im garten springen, sonders war darin curieus e[ine] grotte, die erst halb fertig war, worin aus den schönsten muscheln blumen töpfe mit blumen, gantze gesichter mit naturlichen farben, rahmen s[o] g[ar?] gantz natürlich zusammen gesetzet waren, deren columnen man zugeschwungen [?], die uberaus kunstlich nach der architectur auch mit muscheln bekleidet waren.

Dr. Pauli,[136] e[in] mediciner aus Dresden, hat e[ine] invention, microscopia zu machen ohne glaß, it[em] ein kupfer ins kleine zu bringen mit der accuratesten proportion aller distantzen in kleinsten peritoren [?], ohne das man darauf ziehen konnte, und zugleich so, das es so zu end in e[inem] augenblicke zu machen.

---

[135] On contemporary silk mills see *Zedlers Universal-Lexicon* vol. 36, col. 1428–30.
[136] See above footnote 88.

M[onsieur] le Pleng,[137] in London wohnhafft, hat e[ine] invention, mit farbe zu drucken, so schön, als wenn es gemahlet wäre, wie ich d[enn] aus der anatomie e[in] specimen gesehen, nemlich die serie auf e[inem] folio blade, so aber 4 gulden kostete. Er wird a[uch] die gantze anatomie so verfertigen.

M[onsieur] Bizot historia Belgii numismatica ist frantzosisch und hollandisch herauß, doch sol die hollandische edit[ion] 1690 4. besser seyn, in dem die supplementa mit e[in] gerucket sind.[138] M[an] sagt aber, d[aß] es wieder [?] in Den Haag sol aufgeleget w[er]d[en].

Der H[err] Millig in Utrecht lest Relands analecta rabbinica wieder auflegen, auch zu dem andern tomo etwas von s[einer] arbeit mit zufügen.[139]

Basnage und Wequeforten, von dem hollendischen staat.[140]

Die auditoria in Utrecht sind schlecht, doch ist die stube remarquabel, welche die Schurmann[141] gehabt hat, u[und] zwischen iren auditoriis gelegen ist, da sie den lectiones zugehoret und nachgeschrieben.

Bei v[on] de[r] Aa habe e[inen] atlas gesehen in lenglicht 8, sehr commode bey s[ich?] zu sehen, u[nd] s[eine] special karten vorgehen [?] in 9 a 10 bänden.[142]

H[err] Heyman ist in der türckey, palaestina und aegypten e[ine] lange zeit gereyset. In Smyrna hatte er M. Tournefort[143] gesehen, in pal[aestina]

---

[137] Reimarus probably refers to a man by the name of Leblanc or Le Planque. See in general K. B. Roberts and J. D. W. Tomlinson, *The Fabric of the Body: European Traditions of Anatomical Illustrations* (Oxford, 1992).

[138] Pierre Bizot, *Medalische historie der Republyk van Holland* (Amsterdam, 1690); *Histoire metallique de la République de Hollande* (Amsterdam, 1690).

[139] Adriaan Relant (see footnote 114), *Analecta rabbinica, editio secunda* (Utrecht, 1723).

[140] Probably Jacques Basnage, *Annales des Provinces-Unies* (The Hague: Le Vier, 1719); Abraham de Wicquefort, *Histoire des Provinces-Unies des Pays-Bas* (The Hague, Johnson 1719).

[141] Anna Maria van Schürmann (Schuurman) (1607–1678), a universally learned Dutch woman; she lived in Utrecht from 1623 on.

[142] Pieter van der Aaa (see footnote 106) had specialized mainly in maps.

[143] Joseph Pitton de Tournefort, *Relation d'une voyage du Levant*, 2 vols. (Amsterdam: Compagnie, 1718). Johan Heyman's travels have been published in: *Travels trough Part of Europe [...]* (London, 1759).

und ägypten M[onsieur] Lucas, von dem wir die ‚voyage en egypte' haben.[144]
Er referirte, das derselbe nichts als s[ein] französisch verstanden, zum
wenigsten e[ine] orientalische sprache nichts gewußt und daher immer
[9] e[inen] maroniten[145] bey s[ich] gehabt, der s[ein] interpres[146] gewesen. Er glaubte auch, das er nicht so wohl auf anlaß des königs, als vielmehr s[eine] eigene gereyset, und das er nur zu mehren eclat den titul
davon gefuhret. Im übrigen habe er viel medaillen merkandiret, sey aber
darin so malae fidei gewesen, das er aus frankreich falsche nach gemachte
medaillen der alten mit s[ich] genommen, und die selben da gegen gute
vertauscht. In sonderheit habe er den den venetianischen ambasadeur in
C[onstantino]pel, der e[inem] nobili di venetia e[in] münz cabinet verehr-
ren wollen, und, weil er selbst nichts davon verstanden, dessen Lucas die
commission gegeben, so lesterlich mit s[inen] nummis adulterinis betrogen, das er darüber aus C[onstantino]pel habe müssen weichhaft werden,
so das der H[err] Heyman meinte, wer in den einen e[in] falsarius[147] wäre,
dem sey a[uch] in andern stücken nicht viel zu trauen. Der H[err] Heyman
selbst hatte s[ich] auch e[ine] schöne collection von müntzen mit heraus
gebracht, hat aber das unglück gehabt, das im dieselben in holland auf
e[inem] schiffe verbrandt sind. Er selbst ist in aegypten nicht weiter als
alexandria kommen. M[onsieur] Lucas aber ist a[ber] in ober aegypten
gewesen, quod non cuivis contingit,[148] weil es sehr gefährlich ist. Von der
hieroglyphischen Logie[149] [?] verstünde m[an] heute zu tage in aegypten
nichts mehr, denn die türken, die da wären, bekümmerten s[ich] nicht
darum, ja suchten vielmehr, alle monumenta antiquitatis aus dem wege zu
räumen, weil sie argumenta contra ipsorum doctrinam[150] waren, die christen wären dumm, u[nd] wüsten nichts als messe lesen, die juden wären
wenig und hatten a[uch] weder verstand noch curiositaet genuug dazu.

Die Schweden haben, um ihr eysen vor den russen zu salviren, alles auf einen
hauffen getragen, und holcz darauf geschüttet, und solches angezündet,

---

[144] Paul Lucas, *Voyage du Sieur Paul Lucas au Levant* (The Hague, 1705); *Voyage* […] *fait
in MDCCXIV* (Amsterdam, 1720).
[145] Maronites are Christians of Syriac origin, living mainly in Lebanon, but also in Syria,
Palestine, Egypt and Cyprus.
[146] Translator.
[147] Forger, Falsifier.
[148] What does not happen to everybody.
[149] Writing, Script.
[150] Arguments against their doctrine.

da es dann, weil es glühend geblieben, an einigen tagen nicht hat können angefasset werden.

Ein glockenspiel von stäben, die composition dazu ist die beste von kupfer und zinn, denn stahl rostet bald, und beirrt also die helligkeit und reinigkeit des klangs. Die dote pletze[151] auf jedem stabe können nicht allemahl mathemathice aus gerechnet werden, weil die unsauberkeit des ertztes den thon variiert, man nehme daher trockenen sand u[nd] lege den stab wage recht, so wird der sand wenn man schlaget auf den beyden todten pletzen liegen bleiben, unter den staben, da es hol ist, kan m[an] eine laminam mobilem[152] von holtz machen, die als ein pedal kann getreten und beweget werden, weliches mit dem schale admirabel spielet und ihn magis sonorum machet, e[rgo?] tremulum potium.[153]

[10] Miris[154] in leyden hat einen schönen anfang zu e[inem] cabinet v. ausländischen thieren in spiritu, dit. v[on] insecten u[nd] vögeln, u[nd] muscheln, u[nd] müntzen, die zur holl[ändischen] historie gehörn. Fengt a[uch] an, antiques zu samlen.

Die christen in asien, davon einige e[inen] patriarchen zu antiochien haben, welche mit der griechischen kirche übereinkommen, andere zu babylon, welche nestorianer sind, haben die syrische sprache als e[ine] linguam sanctam et eruditam noch unter sich behalten. Sie erkennen unter den libris N[ovi] T[estamen]ti die II Petri, III Johannis ep[istolae], judae et Apocalypsin nicht vor genuin. Lud[ovicus] de Dieu hat die Apocalypsis zu erst im syrischen aus der leydenschen bibliothec edirt, andere die andern bucher, da sie hernach in die polyglottis beygefüget sind.[155] Widmanstadii seine edition hat er auch noch nicht.[156]

---

[151] "dead spots" – Reimarus seems to refer to those areas in which because of interference with oscillation there is no resonance.

[152] See above footnote 126.

[153] more tuneful, thus more vibrating.

[154] Willem van Mieris (see footnote 22).

[155] Ludovicus (Lodevijk) de Dieu (Hg.), *Gelyana d-Yuhannan qaddisa id est, Apocalypsis, Ex Manuscripto exemplari è Bibliotheca* [...] *Iosephi Scaligeri deprompto, Edita Charactere Syro,* [*et*] *Ebrao, cum versione Latina,* [*et*] *Notis* [...] (Leiden: Elzevier, 1627).

[156] Johann Albrecht von Widmanstadt (Widmanstetter) (ed.), *Ketaba d-ewangelyon qaddisa de-maran w-alahan Yesu mesi.ha:* [...] *Liber Sacrosancti Evangelii* [...] *lingua Syra* [...] (Vienna, 1562).

Creech hat a[uch] d[en] lucretium[157] in englische verse übersetzet, und nicht weniger den Manilium[158] (ni fallor),[159] wobei er große reputation erworben. Mr. Dryden[160] b[ei?] s[einer] jalousie brachte ihn darauf, das er sollte d[en] Horatium übersetzen, weil er wuste, das es e[in] schwerer auctor wäre, und er demselben nicht würde gewachsen seyn. Creech übersetzt ihn, verliert aber s[eine] reputation dabey.[161] Dieses, sagen einige, habe ihn so chagriniert, das er s[ich] deshalb erhenckt, andere aber, weil er s[ich] <mit> e[inem] maedchen eingelassen in s[einer] jugend, das nunmehr, da er e[ine] reputation bekommen, weit unter s[einem] stand gewesen; hat s[ich] in e[ines] apothequers hause auf dem boden erhenckt, da sie es den 5ten tag erst gewahr worden, er hat a[ber] vor gehabt, den Justinem martyrem zu ediren, s[einer] annotationum hat s[ich] grabius[162] bedient. Ist nicht über 37 jahr alt worden.

Der erste engl[ische] Poet ist nunmehro M[onsieur] Prior[163] und M[onsieu]r Poël hat Homerum übersetzet.[164]

Chaquespare[165] ist schon alt h[at] a[ber] ein grosses renomée.

---

[157] Titus Lucretius Carus, *De rerum natura, libros sex, Interpretatione et Notis illustravit Thomas Creech*, 2nd edition (London, 1717) (first edition in 1682).

[158] *The Five Boocks of M[arcus] Manilius, Containing a System of the Ancient Astronomy and Astrology Together with the Philosophy of the Stoicks: Done into English Verse with Notes* (London, 1697).

[159] If I am not wrong.

[160] John Dryden (1631–1700), English poet.

[161] *The Odes, Satyrs, and Epistles of Horace* (London, 1684).

[162] Johann Ernst Grabe (1666–1711), German philologist and expert on the Church fathers, who emigrated to England. See Justin Martyr, *Apologia* (Oxford, 1700).

[163] Matthew Prior (1664–1721), English poet. See Charles K. Eves, *Matthew Prior, Poet and Diplomatist* (New York, 1939). – It seems as if Reimarus' interest in these last passages is directed more and more towards England. Thus it may be that they were written immediately before his departure for England on June 21, 1721. In Leiden there were many people (e.g. the illustrator "Le Pleng," footnote 137), who were familiar with English culture and circumstances.

[164] Reimarus seems to refer to Alexander Pope, *The Iliad of Homer* (London, 1715-20).

[165] Shakespeare. – The misleading spelling of the names of Pope and Shakespeare leads to the conclusion that these notes were written before the journey to England and not after it.

APPENDIX II

REIMARUS, NOTES
STAATSARCHIV HAMBURG, NACHLAß FAMILIE REIMARUS A7, FOL. 73

Falsche Schlüsse[166]

Th: Brownes Relig: Medici P. I. Sect: XXIII. p. 203. schließt so: Moses ist in aller Weisheit d[er] Egyptier auch der Hieroglyphischen unterrichtet nach Act: VII.22. ergo ist s[eine] Historia creationis allegorice zu verstehen.

Ex Mose Bar Cepha de paradiso P. I. circa fin[em] (utante Buddeo Hist. Eccl. P. I. p. 112.) constat iam tum nunnullos existimasse, triginta annos in statu integritatis primos parentes perstitisse / iuxta numerum annorum quibus inter mortales fuerit servator. (postrema haec forte adjecta a Buddeo).

Arg[umen]tum Regis Cosaraeorum p[ro] Relig[ione] Jud[aica]: d[er] Christe sagt die Israelistische Relig[ion] ist besser als die Türkische, der Türcke sagt, die Israelistische Religion ist besser als die Christliche, ergo ist die Israelitische Religion die beste, concludit a dicto secundum quid ad dictum simpliciter vid Buxt[orf] praef[atio] ad libr[um] Cosri D. 3.16.sqq

---

[166] On the texts cited see footnotes 31–35.

EDIFYING VERSUS RATIONAL HERMENEUTICS:
HERMANN SAMUEL REIMARUS' REVISION OF
JOHANN ADOLF HOFFMANN'S 'NEUE ERKLÄRUNG
DES BUCHS HIOB'

Wilhelm Schmidt-Biggemann

In 1734, a substantial volume in quarto was published in Hamburg by "the publisher of the widow of the late Theodor Christoph" under the title

Johan Adolf Hoffmann's
Neue Erklärung
des Buchs Hiob,
darin
das Buch selbst aus der Grund-Sprache
mit dem darin liegenden Nachdruck
ins Teutsche übersetzet;
Hienächst aus denen Alterthümer und der Morg-
genländischen Philosophie erläutert; überhaupt aber die
darin verborgene tieffe Weisheit gezeiget wird.
Jetßo nach des Verfassers seel. Abschiede mit Fleiß übersehen,
und mit einer Paraphrasi, wie auch Vorbericht
von Hiobs Person, Buche und dessen Auslegern
vermehret.

It was an odd work. The dedication to the mayor of Hamburg, Rutger Ruland, was signed by Hermann Samuel Reimarus; the typeface was intricate: fonts such as Schwabacher, Antiqua, and Fraktur were used. The nature of the book was imposing, yet discordant.

Like all books, this one also has its own history. It is the story of how a hermeneutical rationalist handled the work of an edifying writer. Not unexpectedly, it is a tense relationship. What makes this affair, however, most interesting is the fact that the encounter with edifying literature should befall the arch critic of all biblical miracles.

I

However Reimarus may have come to work on Johann Adolf Hoffmann's "Neue Erklärung des Buchs Hiob," it does not appear to have occurred entirely on a voluntary basis. The slightly morose tone of his introduction, in which he "openly" admits that he was drawn into the project "completely" against his "intention and expectation" conveys this sense as much as it provides clues to a potential group of people who may have harboured an interest in the publication of this half-exegetical and half-edifying work.[1] It is possible that Reimarus' own father-in-law Johann Albert Fabricius, the great Greek scholar and secretary of the Patriotic Society of Hamburg, persuaded Reimarus to take on the manuscript that his former and in many ways strange compatriot Johann Adolf Hoffmann had left behind; perhaps Reimarus' eminent Hebrew teacher Johann Christoph Wolf was to blame. He was minister at St. Catherine's in Hamburg and also a member of the Patriotic Society, which published the "Patriot" as its moral weekly. Together with the major of Hamburg, Rutger Ruland (1665–1742),[2] both men had been instrumental in recruiting Reimarus back from the City School of Wismar to the Academic College in Hamburg.[3]

Whichever way one views it, Reimarus inherited someone else's pet project. It was less because of the extreme philological demands that the study of the Book of Job generally poses[4] than because Reimarus, as an antiquarian philologist, encountered here a biblical text and its exegesis that generally fell between arcane scholarship and an edificatory genre. A matter-of fact type of philologist, Reimarus had little patience for that kind of work. This uneasiness about a text that neither met his expectations in regard to the philological dignity of its translation nor corresponded to Hoffmann's theological-edificatory approach, becomes evident in Reimarus' choice of words in his preface. Hoffmann's "opinion," Reimarus frowns, "goes entirely towards the belief that the philosophy of the Ancients was far more thorough and profound than today's; for this reason he explains from time to time the hieroglyphs and symbolic images of Egyptians and other oriental peoples and links them to the meaning of the Book of Job. His commitment to religion becomes evident whenever

---

[1] See p. 13* in Johann Adolf Hoffmann, *Neue Erklärung des Buchs Hiob, darin das Buch selbst aus der Grund-Sprache mit dem darin liegenden Nachdruck ins Teutsche übersetzet* [...] (Hamburg, 1734); *title page, preface* (= Vorrede), and *prologue* (= Vorbericht) are unpaginated: "Ich gestehe aber gleich Anfangs offenherzig, daß ich ganz wieder meine Absicht und Vermuthen hinein gezogen bin."

[2] Reimarus delivered the eulogy at Rutger Ruland's funeral service. See Hermann Samuel Reimarus, *Handschriftenverzeichnis und Bibliographie*, ed. and intr. by Wilhelm Schmidt-Biggemann (Göttingen, 1979), p. 56, num. 34.

[3] See minutes of the meeting of City Council of Wismar from 10 November 1727.

[4] See Reimarus' lecture "Animadveriones criticae ad versionem vernaculam Vet. Test. a Luthero concinnatam," in *Commentationes Theologicae* ed. Ernest Friedrich Karl Rosenmüller, vol. 2 (Leipzig, 1827), pp. 143– 186, especially p. 163.

a particular passage allows for it, so that he diligently explains salvation through a redeemer, the trinity of the divine figures, divine providence, the immortality of souls, and resurrection; (not to mention the occasionally interspersed fine expression of morality). Apart from many other beautiful passages, which I cannot possibly all mention here, one only has to take a look at what he wrote about chapters XIV and XIX. However, I cannot forbear to admit that at times he induced me to reflect further and to arrive at explanations that others perhaps may never have helped me find."[5]

Of course, when Reimarus wrote this preface in 1733, there were no indications that he had already become the radical biblical critic into which he would turn at the end of the decade that still lay ahead. He was never driven towards spiritual interests, which explains why he did not want to adopt Hoffmann's interpretation, which had a flavour partly of Neoplatonism and partly of Baroque gnosis. An interpretation of "Behemoth" as demolisher of both man's brutish strengths or "Naphesch" and his vitality or "Neschamah", seemed just as implausible to Reimarus as viewing "Leviathan" as the agent of worldly doom. Likewise, the not very delicate reduction of this speculation that "this ought to mean nothing else than that in human beings both mind and body are corrupt"[6] equally illustrates the considerable distance between the pious translator and exegete Hoffmann and Reimarus, the reviser and editor of the work.

This distance reached such an extent that, in addition to the commentary, Reimarus eventually decided to write an alternative translation. The scholarly necessity of this contribution occurred to him only in the course of preparing the work for print, to which he was adding consecutively his own philological annotations. "Moreover", Reimarus writes, "I realized

---

[5] *Preface*, p. 8*f.: "Seine Meynung gehet durchgehends dahin, daß der Alten ihre Philosophie weit gründlicher und tieffer gewesen sey als die heutige; wesfals Er hin und wieder der Egyptier und andrer Morgenländischen Völcker ihre Hieroglyphische und Symbolische Bilder erläutert und mit dem Sinn des Buches Hiob zusammen hält. Ins besondere sieht man seinen guten Zweck für die Religion bey allen Stellen wo davon zu reden Gelegenheit ist, so daß er die Ordnung des Heils durch den Erlöser, die Dreyfaltigkeit der göttlichen Personen, die göttliche Providenz, die Unsterblichkeit der Seelen, und die Auferstehung der Todten fleissig darthut; (daß ich der hin und wieder eingestreuten artigen Moral nicht einmahl erwehne.) Man sehe zum Exempel an, was er über das XIV und XIX Capittel geschrieben; ausser viele andere schöne Stellen die mir unmöglich sind alle umständlich zu erzehlen. Unterdessen kan ich nicht umhin zu bekennen, daß er mir selbst hin und wieder Gelegenheit gegeben weiter nachzudencken, und auf Erklärungen zu gerathen, dazu ich vieleicht durch andere nimmer würde gekommen seyn."

[6] Ibid., p. 10*f.: "So ferne nun dieses nichts weiter heissen sollte, als daß bey dem Menschen beides Leib und Geist verdorben sind [...]."

that, although the literal translation by Hoffmann might be useful for those who would want to learn how the original reads, it does not properly reveal the full context to its German reader. Therefore, once I had progressed to the fifth chapter, I decided to add a short paraphrase, beginning with the third chapter where the difficult style sets in, and to append those chapters which I had already left out to the end. I have prepared this paraphrase in such a way that it would not appear dissolute and arbitrary; instead, I have used *Schwabacher* typeface to express the proper meaning of the Hebrew text. To be sure, I did not simply replace the Hebrew words by their respective German equivalents (for I believe that it would not be a translation if the words in it are deprived of any meaning). Rather, I have tried to render the Hebrew into sensible German; for those places where the German coincides with the Hebrew, I have provided a literal translation, but where the Hebrew either did not make sense at all in German or would distort the true meaning, I have provided an equivalent that is common in German and still close to the meaning of the original. However, since the curtailed and lofty Oriental style of the book may still not be sufficiently clear, I have decided to insert explanations in fraktur typeface wherever it is necessary."[7]

It only *seems* as if an old exegetical genre was used hereto present the biblical text with both commentary and paraphrase. But in our case, one textual component does not serve to explain the other. On the contrary, with the paraphrase correcting the other text continuously, a tension between them arises. The focus lies on philology and not on the compre-

---

[7] Ibid., p. 13*f.: "Zu dem so sahe ich wohl daß die Hoffmannische buchstäbliche Uebersetzung denen angenehm seyn könnte, die gerne wissen mögten wie es eigenlich nach dem Grund-Texte lautete, aber daß sie doch den deutlichen Zusammenhang teutschen Lesern nicht völlig auf ein mahl vor Augen legte. Kurz, ich entschloß mich da ich bey dem fünften Capittel war, eine kurze jedoch bewiesene Paraphrasin von dem dritten Capittel an, da der schwere Stylus anfängt, dabey zu fügen, und die Capittel die ich versäumet hatte in dem Anhange nachzuholen. Diese Paraphrasin habe ich so angestellet, daß sie nicht wild und eigenmächtig seyn mögte; sondern ich habe durch die Schwabacher-Buchstaben den eigentlichen Verstand des Hebräischen ausgedrückt. Nicht zwar daß ich meinem Leser die Hebräischen Wörter durch eben so viele Teutsche hätte zuzehlen wollen; (Denn das heist meines Erachtens nicht übersetzen, wenn die Worte in der Uebersetzung gar nicht einmahl einen Verstand haben) sondern daß ich den eigentlichen Sinn der Hebräischen Worte mit guten Teutschen gäbe; da wo die teutschen Redens-Arten mit den Hebräischen übereinkommen, alles eigentlich buchstäblich liesse, hingegen, wo das Hebräische im Teutschen entweder gar keinen oder einen verkehrten Verstand haben würde, andere teutsch-übliche Redens-Arten gleiches Verstandes in die Stelle der Hebräischen setzte. Da aber denn die kurtze und dabey hohe Orientalische Schreib-Art des Buches noch nicht deutlich genug seyn mögte, habe ich, wo es nöthig war, mit Fractur-Buchstaben die Erläuterung eingerückt."

hension of the biblical text. This created a strange and entirely different book under the guise of the conventional exegetical genre of biblical text, paraphrase, and commentary: it consists of two competing translations of the same canonical text, where the second one of them does not try to hide the fact that it corrects the first one; the added notes, which explain these corrections – either out of respect or caution – avoid an open confrontation with the original translation. From Reimarus' own perspective at least, his philological-critical apparatus remains irrefutable, because it is based upon the "tools of rational hermeneutics."[8]

II

That was probably what made the difference: the antiquarian and trained philologist Reimarus on the one hand, and Hoffmann the devout scholar, political philosopher, and diamond vendor on the other, whose *habitus* was characterized by a Baroque combination of scholarly erudition, piety, and commerce; Hoffmann had emancipated himself from the academic realm of scholars.

Hoffmann's biography was certainly atypical even then, but it contains nearly every aspect of a life around the turn of the eighteenth century. What was unusual, though, was that it combined components from two different characters. One of them was the scholarly upstart,[9] the other one was the pious man of the world with some ascetic qualities.[10]

Johann Adolf Hoffmann's origins went also back to the world of the rectory. He was born on 26 August 1676 as the eldest child of Zacharias Hoffmann, a minister from Zarpen in the vicinity of Plön in Holstein, and his wife Anna Magaretha, the daughter of the town's mayor Ehlers; although we cannot say for sure, as it was quite common then there may have been a number of siblings. His early biography appears conventional for its time: he is educated by his father, who discovers that his son "develops an extraordinary propensity for his studies."[11] After private lessons from other

---

[8] Ibid., p. 14*f.: "[...] auf die Hülffs-Mittel die eine vernünftige Hermeneutic an die Hand giebt."

[9] See Albrecht Schöne, *Säkularisation als sprachbildende Kraft. Studien zur Dichtung deutscher Pfarrerssöhne* (Göttingen, 1968).

[10] Representatives of this type of character are the patron of Johann Amos Comenius, De Geer, as well as the anonymous editor of the first Böhme edition, Johann Wilhelm Überfeld.

[11] See "Nachricht von dem Leben und den Schriften des Verfassers," in Johann Adolf Hoffmann, *Zwey Bücher von der Zufriedenheit*, 9th ed. (Hamburg, 1742), p. 606; the Frankfurt

teachers Hoffmann somewhat belatedly at the age of eighteen enters the Academic College in Lübeck; but he gains immediate admission to the highest grade level.

He remains there for four years and acquires the foundations for his extensive skills in classical philology and Hebrew and obtains proficiency in other languages as well. In the end, he acquired skills in Latin, Greek, Hebrew, French, Dutch, Italian, and English. It was not uncommon then to stay at the Academic College for four years. In fact, if skilled philologists were members of its faculty, then it was even possible for students to complete their undergraduate studies there. Reimarus chose the same avenue when he was a student in Hamburg. A logical consequence of course was that Hoffmann decided afterwards in 1698 to study theology at the University of Wittenberg. Naturally, "apart from theology, he eagerly pursued philosophy and philology, but he developed a special interest in the study of antiquities."[12] He was certainly not a student of the unrestrained kind; he was appalled by the "wild and untempered excesses of student life" and by the "ubiquitous spirit of dispute."

He does not seem to have taken any exams, which were not required for a future in the ministry. His career in the Church, however, ended after a few trial sermons. Since philology and antiquities were of little use in the pulpit, Hoffmann chose the career of a scholar. He stayed with his parents for another year and then left to study with Johann Cramm[13] at the University of Copenhagen, where he toyed with the idea of making a living as a tutor at court. His decision to switch from theology to philology probably also included his intention to work as a private tutor for nobles or wealthy citizens until he could eventually secure a post at a university, if he was ever serious about that option. So he first became tutor to the sons of Countess von Friesen and served later as travel companion to the brothers Christian and Friedrich Danneskjöl, Counts of Samsoe, as well as to the Count of Lawig. It remains uncertain how long he held these

---

reprint from 1972 uses the fifth edition, which does not contain the "Nachricht" in the appendix (see also footnote 25): "[...] ein ungemeiner Trieb zum Studiren [...]."

[12] Ibid., p. 607: "[...] und nebst der Theologie auch die Philosophie und Philologie fleißig getrieben, absonderlich aber eine grosse Neigung zur Erkenntniß der Alterthümer bezeuget [...] Anbey gestund er, und has es auch in verschiedenen Stellen seiner Schriften nicht undeutlich zu verstehen gegeben, daß ihm vor dem wilden und freyen Studenten-leben auf unsern Universitäten, und der allda gebräuchlichen Art zu disputiren, ein recht Ekel angekommen sey [...]."

[13] Johann Cramm/Gram: Danish philologist, librarian and historian from Copenhagen (1685–1774).

positions. This period provided ample opportunity for Hoffmann to travel throughout Europe. As evidence of how seriously Hoffmann took his philological career, he journeyed to England in 1716 to work on a critical edition of the writings of Justin Martyr at Oxford. Although he finished the manuscript, it was never published.[14]

This setback appears to have been a turning point in Hoffmann's career – he was by then already forty years old – which had thus far been that of an unsuccessful scholar.[15] As Hoffmann himself recalled, this turning point "became the basis for his book on contentedness and for his choice of a trade in jewels, cut antiquarian stones, and rare coins."[16] Hoffmann thereupon left the conventional career path of a scholar and merchant in return for a life of writing philological works of edification as well as of commerce in valuables. Although this particular literary genre seems pertinent to material wealth, practising both at the same time appears to be unique given the fact that during the early Enlightenment it was still the intellectual and financial domain of Jews.[17]

After his failed publishing venture, Hoffmann stayed on his way back from Oxford in London with a Jewish merchant, both to do business with him and to improve his Hebrew. It remains unclear whether a change of religious belief occurred as a result of this professional connection. The Jewish merchant persuaded Hoffmann to become involved with commerce in valuables. His training in antiquarianism served as the foundation for numismatics, and his extended travels had provided him with important experience as well as with a small collection that he could call his own. His merchandise was now those types of goods which were generally stored in baroque treasure-houses, including impressive and highly valuable arts and crafts, which today are found in the famous Green Vault

---

[14] The manuscript remained until 1750 in the possession of Ebers, professor of logic and metaphysics at the Academic College of Hamburg and one of Reimarus' colleagues. It was auctioned later together with other manuscripts of Hoffmann with Reimarus' library. See Johann Andreas Gottfried Schetelig, ed. *Auktionskatalog der Bibliothek von Hermann Samuel Reimarus* (Hamburg, 1768/70; reprint, Hamburg, 1980).

[15] *Cf.* the biography of the brilliant Johann Jacob Reiske.

[16] See "Nachricht von dem Leben und den Schriften des Verfassers (= 'Nachricht')," p. 612: "Denn es sey diese Begebenheit der Grundstein zur Verfertigung seines Buchs von der Zufriedenheit, und zur Erwählung des Handels mit Juwelen, geschnittenen antiquen Steinen und raren Münzen, gewesen."

[17] According to the model proposed in Hans Joachim Schoeps' *Philosemitismus im Barock. Religions- und geistesgeschichtliche Untersuchungen* (Tübingen, 1952) Hoffmann embodied the utilitarian and liberal-humanitarian type; according to H. R. Trevor-Roper's *Crisis of the Seventeenth-Century: Religion, the Reformation, and Social Change* (London, 1967) he would be an Erasmian.

of Dresden. Hoffmann's London connection worked to his advantage: he became an intermediary of the Jewish-Christian jewellery trade (in his "Büchern von der Zufriedenheit" [Books on Contentedness] he quotes two Jewish prayers, one about the loss of a wife, the other one about the expectation of divine blessing with composure).

Hoffmann frequently had to justify his business ventures, since he was often asked "why he would often deal with Jews and swindlers and thieves of that kind? He would then respond that he had never been cheated by a Jew, since he dealt only with Sephardic Jews and not with Ashkenazi Jews; he also would not lend to Jews, but conduct business only in cash and they liked doing business with him, because they knew that he would take not an exaggeratedly high, but a low and fixed profit; finally they were conscious of the fact that he knew how to impose much trouble and vexation upon a swindler by having him excommunicated from the synagogues of Hamburg, Holland, and England."[18] Hoffmann's life was now shaped by the parallel forces of scholarly erudition, piety, and modest wealth. After each extended business trip, he would spend some time working in Hamburg, which generally resulted in the publication of a book. Still during his Amsterdam years, he published his *Observationum Politicarum sive de Republica Libri decem;*[19] it contained reflections about the state, which were taken from antiquity and which, together with more recent legal concepts from Machiavelli[20] onwards, such as the "De conservatione sui, sive Publica,"[21] tolerance,[22] the early modern concept of martial law,[23] as well as the idea of interest, became part of the Erasmian-Stoic agenda of Hoffmann: "Itaque quod exitus rerum causis liberatus suis, in rebus moralibus habeat vim omnem demonstrationis, Historia in subsidium vocanda fuit, quae eorundem, quales nos sumus, hominum facinoribus, fructum

---

[18] "Nachricht," p. 614: "[…] warum er öfters mit den Juden umgieng, und mit solchen Erzbetrügern und Dieben handelte? Er fügte damals auch dieses hinzu, daß ihn noch kein Jude, weil er nicht mit Hochdeutschen, sondern nur Portugiesen, handele, betrogen habe; so borge er auch keinem Juden, sondern handele nur auf baare Bezahlung, und sie handelten mit ihm gerne, weil sie wüßten, daß er keinen übersetzte, sondern einen billigen und vestgesetzten Profit nehme; und endlich müßten sie sich vor ihm fürchten, weil er die Wege wisse, einen Betrüger durch den Bann in hamburgischen, holländischen und englischen Judenschulen in Angst und Noth zu setzen."

[19] Johann Adolf Hoffmann, *Observationum Politicarum sive de Republica Libri decem* (Utrecht, 1719).

[20] Among the more recent authors, Hoffmann quotes Machiavelli most frequently.

[21] Observationes Politicae, chapter II, title.

[22] See especially Book I, chapter IX, "De Christianorum sectis."

[23] Book X, "De Bello."

partim periculumque exponeret operae, partim illorum, qui fuerunt ante erroribus, nos qui nunc sumus erudiat."[24]

After the manuscript – partly the result of antiquarian-classical erudition, partly the result of applying it to the constancy of virtue – was completed and put into print, Hoffmann went to Hamburg. There, he led a life between wealth and piety: he would always stay for one or two years as a scholar in Hamburg and then return for about half a year to Amsterdam to work as a merchant. During these scholarly interruptions of his merchant life, he completed most of his publications: one of them was his most famous work, the *Zwei Bücher von der Zufriedenheit* [Two Books on Contentedness], which appeared in 1722; it was published in five editions even during Hoffmann's own lifetime, was enlarged in 1741 with the little treatise "Nachricht von dem Leben und Schriften des Verfassers" [An Account of the Life and Writings of the Author], and was reprinted up to its ninth edition.[25]

Although – as far as I can tell – Justus Lipsius is not explicitly mentioned in it, the work itself nonetheless fits perfectly into a neo-Stoic tradition. In regard to the structure of their argumentation, both Lipsius's *De Constantia* (1584) and Hoffmann's *Bücher von der Zufriedenheit* converge. Hoffmann would probably have shared Lipsius' idea that external misfortunes and their internal causes might be overcome by an "equilibrium or genuine strength of one's constitution, which is neither elevated nor suppressed by external or random matters."[26] He would, however, have added piety to it. His concept of contentedness then looks as follows: "If our soul has divine origins, then nothing but divine and intellectually stimulating matter can cure it. Just as bodily ailments are treated partly through physical strength, partly through proven medicine, so God prescribes to those suffering from a heavy temper a twofold treatment: I. the use of common

---

[24] "Observationes Politicae, Lectori benevolo," *4.

[25] Johann Adolf Hoffmann, *Zwei Bücher von der Zufriedenheit nach Anleitung der Vernunft- und Glaubensgründe verfasst* (Hamburg, 1721) (5ed 1731; reprint 1972); 9th ed.(1741) contains in the appendix the "Nachricht von dem Leben und den Schriften des Verfassers" [Account of the Life and the Writings of the Author]; I am indebted to this "Account" for my own account of Hoffmann's life.

[26] Justus Lipsius, *Von der Bestaendigkeit* (De constantia). *Faksimiledruck der deutschen Übersetzung des Andreas Viritius nach der zweiten Auflage von c. 1601 mit den wichtigsten Lesarten der ersten Auflage von 1599*, ed. L. Forster (Stuttgart, 1965), p. 4; on the meaning of the term "Beständigkeit", see afterword by Forster. On "Constantia"/"Beständigkeit", see entry "Beharrlichkeit" in *Historisches Wörterbuch der Philosophie*, vol. 1, pp. 814–816. A conceptual metamorphosis in historical terminology leads during the nineteenth century Master Lämpel to exclaim: "Ach, spricht er, die größte Freud/ist doch die Zufriedenheit."

sense, II. his Word. The two converge harmoniously to the benefit of the contentedness and peace of the soul to such an extent that they lead to a recovery of the temperament, whose deficiency had caused such grief; it is just as it is with the sick, who do not quite know from what exactly they suffer."[27] The arguments of both Hoffmann and Lipsius originate from the same sources: from Cicero and Seneca, from Epictetus, Marcus Aurelius and Boethius. The reason for using these sources might stem from the fact that when *De constantia* was published in the Netherlands in 1584, it was not as easy to talk about an edifying and interdenominational biblical interpretation as it was one hundred and forty years later in the Patriotic Society of Hamburg, in the circle of Brockes and Fabricius, Johann Christoph Wolf and Rutger Ruland. Lipsius's solution was profane Stoicism; Hoffmann on the other hand manages to combine biblical interpretation with his own piety, which he had probably adopted from R. Cudworth and Stillingfleet,[28] perhaps also from Johann Arndt's *Wahrem Christentumb* [True Christianity].[29]

Hoffmann's book went perfectly well with the programme of the Patriotic Society, which tried to combine the *Irdische Vergnügen in Gott* [Earthly delights in God][30] with the scholarly study of nature[31] and pious

---

[27] See *Zwei Bücher von der Zufriedenheit* (5th), p. 5f.: "Ist unsere Seele himmlischer Abkunft, so kan auch nichts sie heilen als was Göttlich und geistreich ist. Dannenhero, gleichwie man denen leiblichen Gebrechen, theils durch die Stärcke der Natur, theils durch bewährte Artzneien zu Hülffe kömmt, also hat Gott denen beschwerten Gemüthern einen doppelten Grund der Erleichterung verordnet: I. Den Gebrauch der Vernunft, II. und sein Wort. Diese beyde vereinigen sich wunderbar, zur Beförderung der Zufriedenheit und Ruhe der Seele, dergestalt, daß sie die Gesundheit des Gemüths befördern, deren Ermangelung dich bisher winseln macht; wie die Krancken, die da fühlen, daß ihnen nicht wohl ist, ohne recht zu wissen, was ihnen fehlt."

[28] Hoffmann quotes from Cudworth's *True Intellectual System* as well as from Stillingfleet's *Variis Tractatibus, contra Lockium de intellectu Humano* on page 2 of his *Observationes Politicae*.

[29] Johann Arndt, *Vier Bücher vom wahren Christentumb* (Frankfurt, 1609); see especially Book 4 on natural piety.

[30] Barthold Hinrich Brockes, *Irdisches Vergnügen in Gott bestehend in verschiedenen aus der Natur- und Sitten-Lehre hergenommenen Gedichte*, 9 vols. (Hamburg, 1721–1748).

[31] Johann Albert Fabricius, *Pyrrhotheologie, oder Versuch, durch nähere Betrachtung des Feuers die Menschen zur Liebe und Bewunderung ihres gütigsten, weisesten, mächtigsten Schöpfers anzuflammen* (Hamburg, 1732); id. *Hydrotheologie, oder der Versuch, durch aufmerksame Betrachtung der Eigenschaften, reichen Austheilung und Bewegung der Wasser, die Menschen zur Liebe und Bewunderung des gütigsten, weisesten und mächtigsten Schöpfers zu ermuntern* (Hamburg, 1734); Friedrich Christian Lesser, *Lithotheologie, das ist, natürliche Historie und geistige Betrachtung derer Steine, also abgefaßt, daß daraus die Allmacht, Weisheit, Güte und Gerechtigkeit des großen Schöpfers gezeiget wird*, ed. and intr. by Johann Albert Fabricius (Hamburg, 1735). See also footnote 86.

apologetics.[32] In 1723 he was made a formal member of the Patriotic Society. Subsequent publications of Hoffmann, which all drew on his erudition and which were written during his years of idleness that were financed by his business ventures, went well with the tendency that the Patriotic Society shared with other large linguistic societies from the Baroque period: a rejection of Antiquity out of national and Christian motivations. To his edition of Marcus Aurelius' *Meditations*, which appeared in German as *Erbauliche Betrachtungen*,[33] Hoffmann added a long introduction and emended in his apologetic annotations everything that could not be interpreted from a Christian perspective: "He changed in his annotations those passages in the otherwise golden words of [Marcus] Antonius [Aurelius], where some pagan thought crept in that has embarrassed many thousands of Christians."[34]

After this publication, he made another business trip to Holland. Only two years later, in 1725, Hoffmann published an enlarged German translation of his *Observationes Politicae* under the title *Politische Anmerkungen über die wahre und falsche Staatskunst* [Political Observations about true and false Statecraft].[35] This work was bolstered by Hoffmann's translation of Cicero's *De Officiis* into German. The standard translation until it was replaced by the famous version of Christian Garve,[36] it became together with the *Zwei Bücher von der Zufriedenheit* the pinnacle of Hoffmann's fame: *Des ehemaligen römischen Bürgermeisters Marcus Tullius Cicero drey Bücher über die menschliche Pflicht* [Three Books on Human Duty by the Former Roman Mayor Marcus Tullius Cicero] was published at the same time as Brockes' *Irdisches Vergnügen in Gott* [Earthly Delights in God]

---

[32] Johann Albert Fabricius, *Delectus Argumentorum et Syllabus Scriptorum qui Veritatem Religionis Christianae adversus Atheos, Epicureos, Deistas seu Naturalistas, Idolatras, Judaeos & Muhammedanos lucubrationibus suis assuerunt* (Hamburg, 1724). On this subject, see also Wolfgang Philipp, *Das Werden der Aufklärung in theologiegeschichtlicher Sicht* (Göttingen, 1957); also Hans Martin Barth, *Atheismus und Orthodoxie. Analysen und Modelle christlicher Apologetik im 17. Jahrhundert* (Göttingen, 1971). Surprisingly, neither of these two authors makes a reference to Hoffmann.

[33] The complete title reads *Des Römischen Kaisers Marcus Aurelius erbauliche Betrachtungen* (Hamburg, 1723).

[34] See "Nachricht," p. 618: "Wo etwas in den sonst güldenen Worten des Antonius, welche viele tausend Christen beschämen, eine heidnische Meynung mit eingeschlichen ist, die hat er in den Anmerkungen geändert."

[35] Johann Adolf Hoffmann, *Politische Anmerkungen über die wahre und falsche Staatskunst* (Hamburg, 1725).

[36] Cicero, *Von den menschlichen Pflichten. Übersetzt und mit Anmerkungen versehen von Christian Garve* (Breslau, 1783). Frederick II in factsuggested this project.

in 1727,[37] two years after the publication of the *Politische Anmerkungen* [Political Observations]. This publication fitted equally well into the Baroque tradition of a Christian adaptation of pagan antiquity. The prologue, which is just about as long as the main body of Cicero's work, not only introduces Cicero's life and writings, but attempts above all to "stress the main purpose, which is a natural morality aiming to foster Christian morality and to expound the agreement of common sense with the loftiness and strength of Christian religion."[38] Hoffmann further promoted this agenda in his final scholarly endeavour, his translation of the Book of Job. This time, however, not everything went as smoothly as before. This private man of learning, who did not strive for public posts, who did not drink alcohol, who ate only a few meals of mostly poor quality, who generally used up his profit fairly quickly, who did not amass any riches, who had a distaste for women, and who was a visitor to the coffee house daily from five to seven in the afternoon, this man was otherwise unbalanced and led a reclusive existence, since he was always dependent on his business travels. When in 1727 at the age of fifty he planned on giving up his secure life in Hamburg and stayed one and a half years in Amsterdam, only the pleas of Johann Albrecht Fabricius were able to convince him to return to Hamburg. In 1729 Hoffmann announced his translation of the Book of Job.[39] He went then on another business trip together with two aristocrats. In the summer of 1731, he returned with the intention of completing his Job, which he had already finished translating and which up to chapter ten was already in its final draft. But things did not turn out as planned. He was no longer able to publish his edition of a biblical book that was suitable to illustrate his concept of an agreement of poetry and faith, theodicy and physical world, Stoa and Christianity, and which represented from Hoffmann's own point of view the embodiment of what an edifying work should be.[40] A lung disease, which he developed on his last

---

[37] Johann Adolf Hoffmann, *Des ehemaligen Römischen Bürgermeisters Marcus Tullius Cicero drey Bücher über die Pflicht. Übersetzt und bevorwortet von Johann Adolf Hoffmann* (Hamburg, 1727).

[38] "Nachricht," p. 621f.: "[...] Endzwecke, die natürliche Sittenlehre zur Beförderung der christlichen in ein desto helleres Licht zu stellen, auch die Uebereinstimmung der gesunden Vernunft mit der Höhe und Stärke christlicher Religion kräftig darzulegen."

[39] Ibid., p. 623: "Nunmehr zog er wiederum, so bald der Cicero die Presse verlassen hatte, seinem Handel nach, und verfügte sich gen Amsterdam woselbst er ganzer anderthalb Jahre blieb, und das Versprechen hinterließ, daß er seine gesammelten Anmerkungen über den Hiob nunmehro in Ordnung bringen und samt dessen Uebersetzung ins Deutsche der Welt mittheilen wollte."

[40] See Wolfgang Philipp, pp. 117–123.

journey led to a rapid deterioration of his health. On 17 November 1731, about six months after his return to Hamburg, Johann Adolf Hoffmann died at the age of fifty-four. Michael Richey expressed his condolences on behalf of the Patriotic Society:

"O Mann! Den wir sowol, als Welt und Vaterland,
Für einen Ehrenmann, für eine Zier erkannt.
Die Weisheit wählte Dich zu ihrem liebsten Sohne:
Jedoch der Edelstein, der Deines Hauptes Krone,
Gedoppelt schätzbar macht, war reine Redlichkeit,
Ein Wunder unsrer Welt, der Zeiten Seltenheit."[41]

[My Dear Friend! Whom We, like Cosmos and Native Land,
As Man of Honour and Decorum learned to Understand,
Wisdom selected You as Her Dearest Son,
But the most Precious Stone on your Head's Crown,
Making it twice as Esteemed, was Pure Probity,
This Time's Marvel, this Age's Rarity]

III

Hoffmann's unfinished Job[42] was now edited by Hermann Samuel Reimarus, son-in-law of Johann Albert Fabricius, the secretary of the Patriotic Society, who had brought Hoffmann back to Hamburg. In his capacity as Professor of Oriental Languages at the Academic College in Hamburg, Reimarus seemed particularly suited for this endeavor. But Reimarus struggled with the project. The anonymous author of Hoffmann's biography, notably irritated, remarks: "The famous Professor Reimarus, as it is widely known, took up the arduous task of preparing the work for publication. What the late Hoffmann has accomplished with diligence and what his intention was, as well as what additions and changes the editor thought to be helpful, all of that he describes in detail in his extensive preface [...] Meanwhile everybody believes that this edition of Job would have had a different shape if its author had finished it himself."[43]

---

[41] The poem is printed as an appendix to the "Nachricht".

[42] The third volume of Hoffmann's manuscript (chapters 19–42), including some traces of Reimarus' changes, remains preserved in the State- and University Library of Hamburg as Cod. Theol. 1295; see also Hermann Samuel Reimarus, *Handschriftenverzeichnis und Bibliographie*, p. 51f., Nr. 23 as well as *Preface*, p. 13*.

[43] "Nachricht," p. 639f.: "Der berühmte Herr Professor Reimarus hat, bekanntermaassen, die mühsame Veranstaltungen des Abdruck über sich genommen. Was sowohl der selige Herr Hoffmann durch seinen Fleiß bey dieser Erklärung geleistet habe, und seine

Indeed, Reimarus deprived the work of its edifying component. Although Reimarus did not change those parts in which Hoffmann "assiduously explains the order of salvation through a redeemer, the trinity of the divine persons, divine providence, the immortality of souls, and the resurrection (not to mention the often interspersed statements of quaint morality"),[44] his paraphrase and commentary nonetheless paralyze these parts. He was not concerned about the incorporation of natural into biblical theology[45] (as the jeweller imagined it), nor about the speculation that "the philosophy of the Ancients was much more solid and profound than today's" so that, as Reimarus points out, Hoffmann "on occasions comments on the hieroglyphics and symbolic images of the Egyptians and of other Oriental people and connects them to the meaning of the Book of Job."[46] Edifying remarks of this kind are dropped. In their place appears what Hoffmann after his unsuccessful edition of Justin Martyr left behind himself: antiquarian scholarship and philology.

Partly also to separate his own parallel translation from Hoffmann's, Reimarus introduces those authors who serve him well to execute a "sophisticated hermeneutical analysis."[47] In the forefront we encounter here the famous Calvinist antiquarian Samuel Bochart, whose main body of work was dictionaries and publications on biblical biography, flora, and fauna;[48] all of these eminently erudite, but also eminently untheological works attempted to identify biblical terminology by linking it to specific geographical locations or specific animal and plant species. Besides Bochart, Reimarus lists some other works that he used both for his

---

Absicht gewesen sey; als auch, was gedachter Herr Editor durch seine eigene Zusätze und Veränderungen für Nutzen zu schaffen gemeynt habe, solches gibt er in seiner gründlichen Vorrede zu diesem Buche ausführlich zu erkennen [...]. Unterdessen glaubt ein jeder, daß der Hiob, wenn ihn der Verfasser selbts vollendet hätte, in einer ganz andern Gestalt würde hervorgetreten seyn."

[44] *Preface*, p. 9*: "[...] die Ordnung des Heils durch den Erlöser, die Dreyfaltigkeit der göttlichen Personen, die göttliche Providentz, die Unsterblichkeit der Seelen, und die Auferstehung der Todten fleissig darthut; (daß ich der hin und wieder eingestreuten artigen Moral nicht einmahl erwehne.)"

[45] Reimarus quotes here (page 8* of "Vorrede") J. J. Scheuchzer (see also "Vorbericht," p. 123*), which is a reference to Scheuchzer's *Jobi physica sacra, oder Hiobs Natur-Wissenschaft verglichen mit der heutigen* (Zurich, 1721).

[46] See *Preface*, p. 8*: "[...] daß der Alten ihre Philosophie weit gründlicher und tieffer gewesen sey als die heutige; wesfals Er hin und wieder der Egyptier und andrer Morgenländischen Völcker ihre Hieroglyphische und Symbolische Bilder erläutert und mit dem Sinn des Buches Hiob zusammen hält."

[47] Ibid., p. 14*.

[48] On the writings of Bochart, see footnote 64.

commentary and notes, which are all exclusively philological in nature: the Job commentary of Sebastian Schmid,[49] a theologian from Strassbourg, the *Animadversiones philologicae*[50] of Reimarus' benefactor from Groningen, Albert Schultens,[51] the *Notae selectae criticae in [...] loca dubia ac difficiliora Jobi* by Heinrich Benedikt Starck,[52] Johann Heinrich Michaelis' large critical edition of the hagiographical books of the Bible,[53] and finally the recently published commentary by Jean LeClerc to the poetical and hagiographical books.[54]

The philological reduction of the biblical text did not remain unchallenged. There seem to have been even plans for an edition of the real Job commentary by Hoffmann which would have left out Reimarus' commentary and would have been different from the present edition in "very few, but still fitting observations."[55] The reviewer of the book in the *Hamburgische Berichte von gelehrten Sachen*, for which Reimarus on occasion also reviewed theological works, suggests the following theory for the divergences between the different Job translations: "Since nonetheless some of the proposed explanations and observations may not be received favourably, due to their novelty (as frequently happens), Professor Reimarus thought it necessary to introduce them already in his prologue so that he did not have to adduce any new explanations in his commentary, because

---

[49] Sebastian Schmid, *Commentarius in Jobum* (Strasbourg, 1670), see "Vorbericht," p. 116*.

[50] Albert Schultens, *Animaderveriones Philologicae in Jobum, in quibus plurima hactenus ab Interpretibus male accepta ope linguae Arabicae & affinin illustrantur* (Utrecht, 1708), see "Vorbericht," p. 123*.

[51] See "Vorbericht" (Prologue), p. 78*.

[52] Heinrich Benedikt Starck, *Notae selectae criticae, philologicae exegeticae, in loca dubia ac difficiliora Jobi. Psalm. Prov. Eccles. & Cantici* (Leipzig, 1717), see "Vorbericht," p. 123*.

[53] Johann Heinrich Michaelis, *Uberiorum adnotationum philologico-exegeticarum in Hagiographis Vet. Testamenti libros continens in quibus textus Hebraeus cum cura expendiur [...]*, 3 vols., (Halle, 1720), see also *Prologue*, p. 116*.

[54] Jean LeClerc, *Vetris Testamenti Libri hagiographi Jobus, Davidis Psalmi, Salomonis Proverbis, Concionatrix & Canticum Canticorum, ex translatione Johannis Clericis, cum ejusdem commentario philologico in omnes numeratos Libros, et Paraphrasi in Jobum ac Psalmos* (Amsterdam, 1731).

[55] "Caspari und Schmid haben von dort aus, folgendes einzurücken, zugesendet: Nachdem die Frau Wittwe Felginers des sel. Herrn Hoffmanns unausgearbeiteten Tractat über das Buch Hiob, durch Herrn Professor Reimarus vollends zu Stande bringen lassen, nun aber einen etwas hohen Preiß darauf schläget, welches das Buch aus vieler Menschen Händen gleichsam reisset; so haben sich ein paar Freunde des sel. Herrn Hoffmanns zusammen gethan, daß Buch, mit kurtzen neuen Anmerckungen verbessert, in den Buchdruckereyen gleich wieder drucken zu lassen, jedoch so, daß Pagina auf Pagina stehen bleibet, folglich von jener nicht anders als in wenigen, doch guten Anmerckungen unterschieden seyn soll. Es soll dieses Buch noch diese Michaelis Messe in Leipzig ausgegeben, und vor 1 Thrl. verkaufft werden." See *Neue Zeitungen von Gelehrten Sachen* (Leipzig), October 1733, p. 712.

he had already presented the findings of scholars in advance."[56] Reimarus may indeed have had such a thing in mind; in the meantime and as his later work proves, he continued to quarrel secretly with prevalent theological scholarship.

Reimarus himself writes that "for the sake of completeness I thought it necessary for the work to introduce it with a prologue about the life and work of Job."[57] It may have been above all this "prologue" which provoked the noticeably aggravated biographer of Hoffmann to suggest that "the Job edition would have looked different if the author had had a chance to finish it himself."[58] This prologue contains clean, cold, and dry philology as it was then predominantly practised in the Netherlands. Reimarus makes no distinction between Calvinist and Lutheran theology. His prologue focuses almost entirely upon realia: the question whether Job really existed is answered in the affirmative and ample space is devoted to a description of the book's geography and chronology; the wisdom and virtue of the main character are presented by briefly touching upon his knowledge of God (§ 1–6) and virtue (§ 7–8), but then by elaborating on his cosmology (§ 9, p. 69*f.), his extensive expertise in zoology (§ 10), his erudition, especially in mineralogy (§ 11), physics, and mathematics (§ 12); this portion of the prologue then ends with a description of the political conditions at the time of Job and of the then prevalent form of warfare.

Philological and linguistic problems are identified as the main reason for the pronounced philological considerations, the link between Job's Hebrew and Arabic, as well as the heroic style of the story. Even the final part of Reimarus' prologue, which presents the canonical tradition of the Book of Job as well as in part its history of interpretation, contains a core that is opposed to an edificatory reading of the work: "Whoever does not use his own taste as a guideline for the Prophetical Books, but instead reads attentively and with reverence what had been revealed to God's people and how [this people] interpreted it over time, [this person] will

---

[56] *Hamburgische Berichte von gelehrten Sachen*, 1733 (83), p. 608: "Da aber nichts destoweniger verschiedene darin vorkommende Meyn-und Erklärungen ihrer Neuigkeit wegen, (so wie es zu geschehen pfleget) nicht gleichen Beyfall erlangen mögten: so hat der Herr Professor Reimarus für nötig gefunden, in der Vorrede deßfalls die Vorerinnerung zu thun, wie er sothanen neuen Erklärungen nicht weiter theilnehme, als insofern er sie derer Herren Gottes-Gelehrten fernerer Untersuchungen anheim gegeben."

[57] *Preface*, p. 15*: "[…] vor nöthig erachtet zur Volständigkeit dieses Werckes eine Vorbericht von dem Leben und Buch Hiobs zu geben."

[58] "Nachricht," p. 640*: "[…] daß der Hiob, wenn ihn der Verfasser selbst vollendet hätte, in einer ganz andern Gestalt würde hervorgetreten seyn."

encounter in the Book of Job the most beneficial teachings and divine wisdom."[59] The prologue then ends in a strictly scholarly fashion with an extensive bibliography.[60]

IV

In general, this conflict may be the simple result of an encounter between a philologist and an edifying author. Reimarus' type of biblical exegesis was not at allunique. The authors whose works Reimarus quotes and who appear in his bibliography treat their Job no differently. Friedrich Spanheim equally introduces his work with a question about the real Job[61] – a question, which Franz Delitzsch would later in his own commentary mock as a complete lack of understanding.[62] Georg Serpelius, Jacob Longius, and Martin Lipenius are even more detailed in their treatment of the biography, lexicography, bibliography, and the study of the realia of Job.[63] The encyclopaedia of Samuel Bochart, which Reimarus used, merely served the purpose of providing a detailed account of all the animals and plants that occur in the Bible as well as of all of its geographical, ethnological, and mineralogical information.[64] Again, in 1762, Bochart's books

---

[59] *Prologue*, p. 94*: " Wer nicht seinen Geschmack zur Richtschnur Prophetischer Bücher machet, sondern was dem Volck Gottes als ein solches anvertrauet, und von demselben allezeit davor gehalten worden, mit Aufmercksamkeit und Ehrfurcht lieset, der wird auch in dem Buche Hiobs die heilsamste Lehren und Göttliche Weißheit finden."

[60] The main source of this bibliography (*Prologue*, pp. 95*–130*) was the famous library of Fabricius, for which Reimarus composed the auction catalogue after the death of his father-in-law and which sold for a total of 8, 496 Reichstaler. See also *Preface*, p. 16*.

[61] Friedrich Spanheim, *Historia Jobi* (Geneva, 1670). Reimarus probably used the Regensburg (and Leipzig) edition from 1710, which G. Serpelius printed in his *Lebens-Beschreibungen der Biblischen Scribenten*.

[62] Franz Delitzsch, *Biblischer Commentar über die poetischen Bücher des Alten Testaments*, vol. 2: *Das Buch Job* (Leipzig, 1864 and 1876).

[63] Georg Serpelius, *Lebens-Beschreibungen der Biblischen Scribenten. Davon der VII. Theil praesentieret Personalia Jobi* (Leipzig, 1710); Jacques le Long, *Bibliotheca sacrae scripturae editionum ac versionum secundum seriem linguarum quibus vulgatae sunt notis historicis et criticis illustratis ... Totum opus cum additamentis, suo loco in nova hac editione collocatis, recensuit & castigavit ... notisque auxit Fridericus Boernerus* (Antwerp and Leipzig, 1709); Martin Lipenius, *Bibliotheca realis theologica omnium materiarum, rerum et titulorum in universae sacro sancto theologicae studio occurentium* (Frankfurt/M., 1685); Joanes Gotofredus Sidelbastius, *Historia omnium scripturarum tum sacrarum tum profanarum in ordinem redacta et ad lucem veritatis protracta*, vols. 1–4 (Leipzig and Amsterdam, 1697–1700).

[64] Of the work of Bochart, whom Pierre Bayle called "un des plus savans hommes du monde" (see entry "Bochart" in Bayle's *Dictionnaire*), Reimarus owned apart from some of his minor works also the extensive encyclopedia, Bochart's *Geographia Sacra*, which are the *Hierozoicon* (edition by David Clodius; see footnote 14 for *Auktionskatalog*, Pars. I, Nr.

were part of the expedition to Arabia Felix which Johann David Michaelis organized, with the goal of making – ideally in accordance with Linné – a definite compilation of all biblical realia.[65] It was simply not out of the ordinary to consult the Bible about realia, whose existence it both naturally presumes and describes. Reimarus lectured on Conrad Iken's work about biblical antiquities throughout almost his entire life without being ever criticized for it.[66] No other work was used more frequently in his lectures. Since the publication of Johann Buxtorf's *Lexicon Chaldaicum* and his *Synagoga Judaica*, training in Jewish antiquities had become a normal part of the philological curriculum.[67]

Hugo Grotius in the true fashion of the polyhistors, and dogmatically certainly different from Buxtorf, had linked the philology of the Old Testament with antiquarian and sententious history, which left its mark on the entire classical philology of the seventeenth century. In his commentary on the Old Testament for example, Grotius correlates biblical sagacity with the wisdom of ancient philosophers. "He treats biblical books like works of profane literature and expounds the words of Jesus and the apostolic epistles with the help of passages from ancient Greek and Latin authors. In his commentary to the Old Testament, he always strives to describe the life of the Israelites."[68] This kind of incorporation of classical texts into the history of ideas of antiquity was the norm among the philology of the

2349) as well as the *Phaleg & Chanaan* (Caen, 1646) (see again *Auktionskatalog*, Pars II, Nr. 969).

[65] Johann David Michaelis, *Fragen an eine Gesellschaft gelehrter Männer, die auf Befehl ihrer Majestät des Königs von Dänemark nach Arabien reisen* (Frankfurt/M., 1762; see also Carsten Niebuhr, *Reisebeschreibung nach Arabien und anderen umliegenden Ländern* (Copenhagen, 1774).

[66] Conrad Iken, *Antiquitates Hebraica* (Bremen, 1732). Reimarus' own copy was sold at the auction of his library on 5 February 1770. It contained numerous notes. See *Auktionskatalog*, Pars II, Nr. 374. The same page of the catalogue (Nr. 373) lists the second important book, Hadrian Reland's *Antiquitates sacrae veterorum Hebraeorum* (Leipzig, 1715), upon which Reimarus based his lectures before he switched to Iken. The copy in the catalogue, "cui multa adscripsit Reimarus" [in which Reimarus wrote many notes], contained "Chartae distinctae" [various charts]. See also Reimarus, *Handschriftenverzeichnus und Bibliographie*, pp. 28–34.

[67] Reimarus owned Johann Buxtorf the Elder's *Lexicon Chaldaicum, Talmudicum et Rabbinicum* (Basel, 1639), see *Auktionskatalog*, Pars I, Nr. 120; also id., *Synagoga Judaica*, ed. Johann Buxtorf the Younger (Basel, 1661), see *Auktionskatalog*, Pars II, Nr. 1304a.

[68] H. C. Rogge, "Hugo Grotius," in *Realencyclopädie für protestantische Theologie und Kirche*, 1307, p. 201: "Er behandelte die biblischen Bücher als literarische Schriften und erklärte die Worte Jesu und die Briefe der Apostel dirch Stellen aus den alten griechischen und lateinischen Schriftstellern. In seiner Erklärung des Alten Testaments trachtete er stets danach das Leben des israelitischen Volkes darzulegen." Hugo Grotius, *Annotationes in Vetus et Novum Testamentum* (Paris, 1644). Reimarus owned a copy of this edition of Grotius' work. See *Auktionskatalog*, Pars II, Designation ff. 310–312.

polyhistors. Johann Georg Graevius, for example, prepared the text of his famous edition of Cicero[69] with a lesser focus on textual criticism than Richard Bentley a few decades later. Instead, he placed in the notes *dicta probantia* from earlier editions of corresponding authors. In the case of Cicero, they were from Plato, Seneca, Aristotle, and Plutarch.

Hermeneutics, which treats the Bible just like any text of profane literature, does not focus on biblical revelation alone. It places biblical revelation next to a natural counterpart, which it presents as a rational reconstruction of creation, such as in natural theology as espoused in R. Fludd's *Physica Moysaica*,[70] as in the biblical and Old Testament physics of J. A. Comenius,[71] as in W. Derham's *Astrotheology* and his *Physico-theology*,[72] which Reimarus' father-in-law Fabricius both translated and embraced, and finally as in Brockes' *Irdisches Vergnügen in Gott*.[73] Revelation in nature provided as much of an opportunity to discover the footprints of God as the Old Testament. Through the efficiency and harmony of nature, natural history illustrated the rational nature of both creation and creator, and human reason was endowed with a claim to truth by this rationality of natural theology. Experience was then not reduced to nature alone, but became applicable to historical and natural themes; historical themes touched predominantly on ethics and politics, whereas natural themes focused on natural history and natural theology. This type of reason manifested itself in the scholarly investigation of nature and history; although the light of natural revelation and of human recognition was ranked between divine and human reason, they were basically identical.[74] This

---

[69] Marci Tullii Ciceronis, *de Officiis Libri Tres, Cato Maior. Laelius Paradoxa, Somnium Scipionis. Ex recensione Joannes Georgii Graevii cum ejusdem notis, ut & integris animadversionibus Dionysii Lambini, Poulvii Ursini, Caroli Langii, Francisci Fabritii Marcodurani, Aldi Manutii, nec non selectis aliorum. Accessit Favonii Eulogii Rhetoris Catarginensis in Ciceronis Somnium Scipionis disputatio, nec decisiones contra Calcaginum. Jacobi Griffoli defensiones Ciceronis contra eundem* (Amsterdam, 1680).

[70] Robert Fludd, *Physica Moysaica, in qua sapientia et scientia creationis et creaturam sacra veraque christiana ad amussim et enucleate explicatur* (Gouda, 1638).

[71] Johann Amos Comenius, *Physicae ad lumen divinum reformatae synopsis* (Leipzig, 1633).

[72] William Derham, *Astrotheologie oder Anweisung zu der Erkenntniß Gottes aus Betrachtungen der Himmlischen Cörper*...Trans. Johann Albert Fabricius (Hamburg, 1728).

[73] See footnote 30 as well as Hans Georg Kemper, *Gottebenbildlichkeit und Naturnachahmung* (Tübingen, 1978).

[74] Johann Heinrich Alsted, *Philosophia digne restituta: Libros Quatuor praecognitorum Philosophicorum complectens* (Herborn, 1612), p. 6: "Nam aut absoluta est (sapientia), aut secundum quid, quae dicitur sapientia in subjecto: Quae est illa eadem sapientia absolute dicta, modificata pro ratione eorum hominum, quibus inest, & ex qua sapientes appellantur."

type of empowerment of reason – the same as Leibniz had done pragmati-
cally in his *Theodicée*– consolidates natural reason. Only then can a concept of nature be developed which is identical to a systematic application
of reason, because it reveals every detail of God as creator; this constituted
the theological precondition for the perfunctory work of the polyhistors
in natural, biblical, and profane history. At the same time and in conjunction with the stabilization of reason, it was a precondition for the
interpretation of natural and historical reason as the measuring stick for
biblical revelation.[75] Once both traditions became equals, they could then
legitimately also be compared with each other. This was the tradition of
Reimarus, who had stayed some time in Leiden,[76] where Albert Schultens,[77]
the philologist from Groningen was his mentor, and both the prologue
and annotations to Hoffmann's *Neue Erklärungen des Buches Hiob* bear
the mark of this tradition.

At about the same time as Reimarus was working on Hoffmann's Job
manuscript (1731), he was lecturing at the Academic Collegeon the *Vindicatio Dictorum Veteris Testamenti in Novo allegatorum*.[78] Using the dictum *sola scriptura* as a precondition, this lecture focuses on inner biblical
hermeneutics. Of course, the new role of natural theology had already led
to a loss of the exclusive nature of the *sola scriptura* principle. The specific
Lutheran *Philologia sacra*, which Rambach called "Hermeneutica Sacra"[79]
and which was practised by scholars from Matthias Flacius via Salomon
Glassius[80] to August Pfeiffer, on whose work Reimarus based his lecture,

---

[75] See for example "Leibniz's Interpretation der biblischen Bileam-Geschichte," in
Wilhelm Brambach, *Leibniz, Verfasser der Histoire de Bileam* (Leipzig, 1887).

[76] See Reimarus, *Handschriftenverzeichnis*, p. 10.

[77] *Prologue*, p. 78*.

[78] See Reimarus, *Handschriftenverzeichnis*, p. 35, Nr. LII. Also Hermann Samuel Reimarus,
Vindicatio dictorum Veteris Testamenti in Novo allegatorum, 1731, ed. and intr. by Peter
Stemmer (Göttingen, 1983). Stemmer based his dissertation on this lecture, which was
published as Peter Stemmer, *Weissagung und Kritik: Eine Studie zur Hermeneutik bei Hermann Samuel Reimarus* (Göttingen, 1983). I shall apply Stemmer's work in regard to the
connection between *Hermeneutica sacra* and *Hermeneutica universalis*.

[79] Johann Jacob Rambach, *Institutiones Hermeneuticae sacrae, variis observationibus
copiosissimisque exemplis biblicis illustratae, cum praefatione J. F. Buddei*, 4th ed. (Jena,
1733). See also Stemmer, *Weissagung und Kritik*, pp. 52–56.

[80] Matthias Flacius Illyricus, *Clavis Scriptura Sacrae, seu de Sermone Sacrarum Litter-
arum*, 2 vols. (Basel, 1567). Salomon Glassius, *Philologia Sacra, qua totius sacrosanctae,
Veteris et Novi Testamenti Scripturae, tum stilus et litteratura, tum sensus et genuinae interpretationis ratio expenditur*, 3d ed. (Frankfurt and Hamburg, 1633). See also Stemmer, *Weissagung und Kritik*, pp. 33–58.

complements an antiquarian approach to the Bible.[81] Although Scripture justifies an antiquarian treatment of any presented *historia* through salvation history, it does not justify this *historia* through natural theology, but through biblical revelation. The *Philologia sacra* provides a justification of the entire antiquarian spectrum through the promise of salvation in the New Testament. The *sola scriptura* principle, namely the claim to the exclusiveness of written revelation, served as a point of departure for both *Philologia* and *Hermeneutica sacra*. This argumentation presents biblical revelation as reason, and ultimately – as it was argued against natural revelation – reason in general.[82] This Christian inner biblical form of reason receives justification in the Old Testament by typologically making Christ the centre of any natural and political *historia*.[83] The exegesis of the Old

---

[81] August Pfeiffer, *Critica Sacra*, 6th ed. (Dresden and Leipzig, 1721). See Reimarus, *Handschriftenverzeichnis*, pp. 28ff., Nr. XLVIa.

[82] Michael Walther, *Harmonia totius S. Scripturae sive brevis & plana conciliatio locorum Veteris et Novi Testamenti apparenter sibi contradicentium*, 2nd ed. (Strassbourg, 1630). Reimarus owned a copy of the Nuremberg edition from 1696 (see *Auktionskatalog*, Pars II, Nr. 378). Walther states from the outset that "verum contradictionem in Scriptura locum habere non posse (Chapter I)," which helps him present contradictions as only apparent ones. August Pfeiffer in his *Dubia vexata Scriptura Sacrae sive loca difficiliora Vet. Test. circa quae autores dissident vel haerent, adductisset modeste expensis aliorum sententiis, succinte decisa, tamque dilucide expedita, ut cuivis de vero sensu et diversis interpretamentis constare facile queat.* (Dresden, Leipzig, and Wittenberg, 1713) is no longer as convinced as Walther about the agreement of biblical and hermeneutical reason; he stresses the *imbecillitas* and suggests leaving conflicting passages unresolved and ultimately granting priority to the Bible as the highest authority (see "Ad lectorem", especially Csr.). Both Walther and Pfeiffer, however, view hermeneutical reason as capable of solving difficulties internally, within the biblical narrative; this approach extracts the component of criticism from reason and introduces it into the Bible. As potential sources of mistakes, Walther is aware of a lack of language proficiency, equivocation, unfamiliarity with both causes and consequences as well as historical circumstances, and also of the "deliratio humanae rationis." Yet, neither Walther nor Pfeiffer separates philological and rational criticism. On the question of "rational hermeneutics" see Oliver R. Scholz, "Der Niederschlag der allgemeinen Hermeneutik in Nachschlagwerken des 17. und 18 Jahrhunderts," in *Aufklärung* 8 (1993). Also, Axel Blüher, ed., *Unzeitgemäße Hermeneutik: Verstehen und Interpretation im Denken der Aufklärung* (Frankfurt/M., 1994).

[83] A typological exegesis works only with the *sola scriptura* principle. The lecture *Vindicatio dictorum Veteris Testamentis in Novo allegatorum* represents an important key point in the development of Reimarus' hermeneutics. Nonetheless, this lecture alone does not offer any possibility of moving from biblical hermeneutics to religious criticism. In his *Weissagung und Kritik* (see footnote 78), Peter Stemmer therefore stresses the significance of the Bible translator and Wolffian Johann Lorenz Schmidt, whose translation broke the connection between Old and New Testament. The critical function of Schmidt's translation can still be reinforced through the critical role of natural theology against revealed theology.

Testament by means of the New was based upon a christologically justified primacy of the New Testament.

This precondition leads to two consequences. Despite the typological inclusion of the Old Testament in the New, it remained genuine Lutheran practice to place the New Testament at the centre as opposed to a strong emphasis on the Old Testament in natural theology, with its emphasis on creation and on fact a from natural history. This means that the Old Testament does not speak for itself. Instead, the interpretation of the entire biblical text, including the philology of the Old Testament, is dominated by Christology. The relationship between the Old Testament and the New made this type of philology irrefutable due to its dogmatic justification; this creates a primacy of theology, a primacy of biblical revelation that was concerned only with Christian doctrine.

At odds with this was a second tradition of biblical theology, the predominantly Arminian-Grotian tradition, which accommodated natural revelation as well. The authors whom Reimarus consulted for his work on Job were almost exclusively not part of the Lutheran *Philologia sacra* or of the Calvinist federal theology. Instead, they were part of the Arminian tradition of hermeneutics, represented by Hugo Grotius, which referred back to the *Consensus veterum sapientium* and thus absorbed in a humanist sense a pre-Christian "natural" theology. It avoided the narrow perspective of a Christological interpretation and justified the veracity of the Bible by the natural rationality of its account. All of this created tension among exegetical possibilities: Calvinist interpretation, as long as it stressed in an Arminian fashion natural theology and the *Consensus veterum*, presented the teachings of the Old Testament as words of wisdom and faith; Lutheran *Philologia sacra* stressed the typological and thus also the historical link between Old and New Testament.

The combination of both approaches created tension between the interpretation of the Old and the New Testament on the one hand, and natural theology on the other. Natural theology leaned towards a connection with the Old Testament: while accepting the teachings of the New Testament it established no connection with salvation history and at the same time it minimised Christology.[84] *Philologia sacra*, on the other hand, did not use certain eternal truths as its point of departure but used

---

[84] Already Duplessis-Mornay in chapter XXX of his *Verité de la religion chrestienne* does not put forward a doctrine of sin or salvation while still maintaining prophecy and miracles. Equally, Grotius' concise christology does without a doctrine of salvation (*De Veritate religionis christianae*, Lib. II, § 6).

history itself and connected Old and New Testament in regard to the salvation history of Christ. Yet, it minimised natural theology and was at the same time unable to define theologically general philological and natural truths. These tensions appear in Reimarus' preface to Job, but the conflict between natural theology and *Philologia sacra* remains unresolved there. When Reimarus for example avoided categorizing Job as a type of Christ, then he "drains the Old Testament of its typological figures, but this by no means represents a contrast with established orthodoxy."[85] Only the reason of natural theology played that particular role in the antiquarian approach, which it exercised due to natural revelation.

This is how "rational hermeneutics", which Reimarus adopted, legitimated itself. Although contrary to strict Lutheran hermeneutics it used the internal agreement and relationship between the Old and New Testament as its point of departure, but at the same time it recognized natural revelation. Even when Christianity remained the norm of exegesis, it was possible despite some tensions to render the broad reason of nature and history compatible with biblical revelation; that was true for the natural history of the Old Testament as well as for New Testament morality. In this way, ancient wisdom, morality, and physiology exercised the same exegetical role. For biblical physiology this implied a legitimation of Grotius' approach of making the Bible part of the body of ancient wisdom literature; as a consequence, this meant for biblical antiquarianism the utilization of the realia of biblical learning for the study of the Old Testament. The dissolution of biblical unity, which was caused by the perception of the Bible as a revealed encyclopaedia of universal learning of some kind and as a manual of wisdom and nature rather than as a salvation narrative of humanity, paved the way to an understanding of the Bible as a testing ground of physics and morality, and vice versa.

The compatibility of natural and biblical theology disarmed christology without destroying it. The internal relationship of the Bible lost its significance whenever the focus was not on salvation history but on the truths of religion and nature, which were knowledge that supported at the same time Christian apologetics. Part of this natural theology of the *Consensus veterum* was definitely antiquarian philology, whose natural and theological foundations could be found not only in Hugo Grotius' *De Veritate Religionis Christianae* (1629), but following Raimundus Sabundus and

---

[85] Peter Stemmer, *Weissagung und Kritik*, p. 65: "[...] Entleerung des Alten Testaments von typologischen Figuren, aber noch lange keinen Gegensatz zur Orthodoxie."

Vives, also in Ramus' *De Religione Christiana* (1577), Duplessis-Mornay's *De la Verité de la Religion Chrestienne* (1581), as well as in Johann Heinrich Alsted's *Theologia Naturalis* (1623) and in R. Cudworth's *Intellectual System* (1678).[86]

So to sum up, the apologetics of natural religion enabled biblical philology to relinquish the Christological focus of the Bible. Therefore, it was possible to isolate biblical realia in exegesis. This was the basis for the incredibly erudite encyclopaedia of Samuel Bochart, the basis for the compendia in comparative religion by Gerard Joannes Vossius, and the basis for Friedrich Spanheim's almost exclusively philological *Historia Jobi*. Biblical philology in the Arminian-Grotian tradition stood opposed to the Lutheran *Philologia sacra* insofar as it gave up Christology and justified instead by means of scholarly erudition the reverence of nature. This was no pure, secularized, profane biblical philology, but instead it was capable of treating the Bible as profane text only because natural theology promulgated the traces of God as reason; this reason manifested itself historically in the wisdom of the ancients – a tradition to which Johann Adolf Hoffmann belonged – and in the harmonious order of the natural universe.[87] This created the following constellation of biblical philology: Lutheran *Philologia sacra* was different from its Calvinist counterpart in that it took an inner biblical and Christological position; Calvinist theology treated natural and biblical revelation as equals, because natural theology was capable of capturing the presence of God in the wisdom of

---

[86] Calvin remains ambiguous in this respect. Nonetheless, the early privileged position of natural theology in Calvinism is unmistakable. This is already evident in the argumentation of the *Institutio*, where Book I, 3 states that knowledge of God is implanted into human beings by nature; this theory is supported by Cicero in his *De Natura Deorum* and by Plato's *Phaidon* and *Theaitetos*. It is probably difficult to achieve an agreement between this theory and Calvin's Christology. But this provides for the existence of a *Physica sacra* next to the *Philologia sacra*, which complements on an equal level Aristotelian physics and occasionally also Paracelsian physics. See Johann Heinrich Alsted, *Physica Harmonica, quattuor libellis methodice proponens. I. Physicam Mosaicam, II. Physicam Hebraeorum, III. Physicam Peripateticam, IV. Physicam Chemicam* (Herborn, 1616); Johann Amos Comenius, *Physicae ad Lumen Divinum synopsis, Philodidactorum et Theodidactorum censurae exposita... Nos igitur in lumine tuo, DEUS, videbimus lumen. Psalm 36, 10* (Leipzig, 1633); William Derham, *Physico-Theology. Or a Demonstration of the Being and Attributes of God, from a survey of the Heavens* (London, 1713).

[87] See in this regard very early the edition of the *Theologia Naturalis* by Raimundus Sabundus, which Comenius published as *Via Lucis* (Amsterdam, 1668); see especially Comenius' preface. More generally on this subject see Wolfgang Philip, *Das Werden der Aufklärung in theologiegeschichtlicher Sicht* (Göttingen, 1957).

history and in the harmony of nature. Natural and biblical revelation were thus on an equal level both sacred and at the same time profane.[88]

If then Reimarus in his preface calls the central chapter "Über Hiobs Weisheit und Tugend" [About Job's Wisdom and Virtue] and describes in it a natural and unrevealed faith in God, together with knowledge of politics, mineralogy, and mining, this means that he uses a string of arguments that links natural and biblical theology, which brings natural reason and biblical revelation into agreement. Whenever he relates the teachings he encounters in Job to the New Testament, he follows the tradition of the *Philologia sacra*. However, he has already reduced the typological element to a bare minimum. His prologue to the Job commentary only faintly hints at the possibilities of an interpretation of the Old Testament through the New; the framework for a typological interpretation remains, its dogmatic content, however, is reduced. "If man sins," Reimarus suggests in Chapter VI. § 5 of the prologue, "then an angel on God's side as intercessor on man's behalf becomes the means of reconciliation, reminding God of his atoning justice towards man and that man found redemption. Job calls him his friend, the Son of Man, and at the same time his witness in Heaven with God, who becomes an intermediary on his behalf with God and his *goel* or redeemer. In short, the cognizance of the messiah and of his expiation is more pronounced in this Book than in any other. Nonetheless, it is not necessary to make Job himself into a type of Christ, since there is not enough evidence for that in either the Old or the New Testament. But it is also evident from what has been said above that Job possessed knowledge about the different persons of the deity, although the doctrine of the Trinity does not appear very clearly in this Book [of the Bible]."[89]

---

[88] Corresponding to it is the different treatment of metaphysics: Lutherans preferred the *Metaphysica generalis de ente qua ente*, whereas Calvinist promoted the *Metaphysica specialis*, which is at the same time a *Theologia naturalis*.

[89] *Prologue*, p. 66*: "Wenn nun der Mensch sündiget, so ist an Gottes Seiten das Mittel zur Versöhnung der Vorsprech-Engel, welcher bey Gott seine genugthuende Gerechtigkeit für den Menschen anzeiget, und saget, daß er eine Erlösung funden habe. Hiob nennet ihn seinen Freund, des Menschen Sohn, und zugleich seinen Zeugen im Himmel bey Gott, denjenigen der für ihn bey Gott Bürge wird, und seinen Goel oder Erlöser. Mit einem Worte, das Erkenntniß von dem Meßia und dessen Genugthuung liegt so deutlich in diesem Buche, als in irgend einem andern. Doch brauchen wir den Hiob nicht selbst zum Vorbilde Christi machen, denn wir findem im Alten und Neuen Testamente keinen genugsamen Grund dazu. Es ist aber auch aus Obigem zu schliessen, daß Hiob von verschiedenen Personen der Gottheit gewust habe, obgleich die Dreyheit derselben in dem Buche nicht so deutlich enthalten ist."

V

When he wrote his prologue, Reimarus apparently did not yet perceive any irreconcilable differences between biblical hermeneutics and natural theology. The increase of knowledge about the rationality of the world, the cognizance of the laws of natural revelation as theodicy presented them, all this contributed to a substantial solidification of reason. As we shall see, this involved certain risks for the exegesis of biblical revelation. A codified concept of rationality had to measure up to the demands of logic and only if the biblical text stood in accordance with reason could it be taken seriously. It no longer came down to a connection between biblical religion and nature, but instead it was also possible to render natural religion the measuring stick of religion in general, because the agreement of these two could be validated. In his "vernünftige Gedanken" [reasonable thoughts] about all aspects of natural science and ethics, the German philosopher Christian Wolff had supplied the remaining key parts for this solidification. If biblical revelation wanted to prevail in the face of natural reason, then it needed to be able to appear as a witness of nature and history as long as they were in agreement with the criteria of reason. It was necessary to detect the presence of eternal truths, physical facts, and a course of history that could be reconstructed. Initially, these criteria appeared definitely ambiguous. It was possible to use them apologetically as is the case in Reimarus' prologue, which attempts a historical reconstruction of the figure of Job, documents his wisdom, and praises his knowledge of geography and physics. Job then represents a case where it was possible to tone down inconveniences in order to avoid open conflict. In case of a conflict, however, the transmitted text needed to serve as witness of the facts that were to be reconstructed, and then it was essential, as is always the case with testimony, for the facts to be extracted from the accounts of the witnesses without any contradictions. The premised rationality could then – as it was ingrained in the logic of the witness accounts – also be applied to determine the credibility of the testimony.

This was not yet the case when Reimarus worked on his Job commentary. But a conflict scenario developed already in early versions of his main religious-critical work, the *Apologie oder Schutzschrift für die vernünftigen Verehrer Gottes* [Apology or Defence of the Reasonable Worshippers of God]. Once a decision between natural theology and biblical theology needed to be made, textual criticism of biblical theology became a criticism of the rationality of biblical theology. Between 1733 and 1736, which constitutes the period from Reimarus' completion of his Job commentary

to the first version of the *Apology*, the explosive potential of a consolida-
tion of the authority of natural reason at the expense of the Bible became
apparent. When the spread of natural reason to all areas of scholarship
proved natural reason to be a more potent and stable measuring stick
than biblical revelation,[90] revelation became accountable to natural reason: the relationship between nature and revelation became in legal terminology one of justification.

As a result, about three years after completing his Job commentary,
Reimarus pondered on what "was reason and reasonable."[91] In order to
determine the legal relationship between nature and revelation and to
reflect on the possibility of a justification of revelation in accordance with
reason and within the context of a natural theology, Reimarus attempted
a comprehensive description of the relationship between nature, reason,
and revelation. Reimarus devised this plan as *Gedanken von der Freyheit
eines vernünftigen Gottesdienstes* [Thoughts on the Freedom of a Reasonable Worship of God] even before he had arrived at the crossroads
of critical and apologetic theology.[92] The outcome in the end was not an
apology of biblical revelation, but an attack on it, which claims the title
of an "apology" not for religion, but for reason as *Apology or Defence of
the Reasonable Worshippers of God*. The originally contrived connection
of reason, nature, and revelation dissolves into the individual components
again in the end. Although Reimarus published his natural theology as *Die
vornehmsten Wahrheiten der natürlichen Religion* [The Principal Truths of
Natural Religion] (1756) and his *Vernunftlehre* [On Logic] (1756), he kept
the main religious-critical body of the work a secret. It was published only
in 1972.

The Reimarus papers in Hamburg still contain portions of the original plan of the work, which attempted to prove the unity of revelation,
nature, and reason. The justification of Scripture is presented here to the
court of reason as the legal logic of a witness account, which renders the
factually reconstructed case a critical measuring stick for the transmitted
biblical account.

---

[90] Reimarus' encounter with the Wertheim Bible, which receives treatment in Stem-
mer's *Weissagung und Kritik* (see footnote 78) attests just that. In this context, see
Lutz Danneberg, "Probabilitas hermeneutica. Zu einem Aspekt der Interpretations-
Methodologie in der ersten Hälfte des 18. Jahrhunderts," in *Aufklärung* 8,2 (1994), pp. 28–48.

[91] See Reimarus, *Handschriftenverzeichnis*, p. 19, Nr. IV.

[92] The plan appears in the introduction to Reimarus' *Apologie oder Schutzschrift für die
vernünftigen Verehrer Gottes*, ed. Gerhard Alexander (Frankfurt, 1972), p. 11f.

For his criticism, Reimarus used the common principle of contradiction as his point of departure, which according to him must serve as the basis for any reasonable judgment: "In making a judgment, human reason is by nature incapable of permitting a constellation of mutually contradictory aspects, if the contradiction is clearly evident: at the same time, it must view those things as mutually necessary, if it clearly determines that they are one and the same."[93] The portrayal of reason as capacity of judgment becomes for Reimarus not only a mere potentiality, but also its active application: "If then," as one particular passage from *Gedanken von der Freyheit eines vernünftigen Gottesdienstes* reads, "it is not possible to view the use of reason as anything but the use or application of the rules of contradiction or unanimity to a particular case, then the use of reason is proper and good, since it has been established according to the same rules; and reason itself then determines the rules of its own workings."[94]

Under the premise that reason, based upon its own structure, is responsible for the entire internal and external spectrum of experience, the rule of contradiction or unanimity becomes always valid and everywhere applicable. Since this rule is part of the process of understanding, there is no alternative to these rules for what constitutes reasonable thought. Reason is then in regard to experience and faith both rule and judge. This premise is also valid for "accounts from others, which bear the name of *belief.*"[95]

The definition of belief as experience based on reasonable external accounts, which can also be made subject to the rules of unanimity and contradiction leads Reimarus to a problem that comes from the tradition of natural theology: it is the attempt to judge the transmitted text according to the rules of reason, whose ability is viewed as competent in every respect; this amounts to invoking the criteria of a credible testimony in treating the biblical text, which represents a document for the knowledge

---

[93] See Reimarus, *Kleine gelehrte Schriften: Vorstufen zur Apologie oder Schutzschrift für die vernünftigen Verehrer Gottes*, ed. Wilhelm Schmidt-Biggemann (Göttingen, 1994), p. 437: "Der menschliche Verstand ist nach seiner Urtheilungs-Kraft von Natur so geartet, daß er sich wiedersprechende Dinge unmöglich zusammen vorstellen kann, wenn er den Wiederspruch klar oder auch deutlich einsiehet daß dieselben einerley sind."

[94] Ibid., p. 455: "Wenn man nun durch den Gebrauch der Vernunft nichts anders verstehen kann, als die Anwendung oder Application der Einsicht in die algemeine Reguln des Widerspruchs und der Einstimmung auf jeden besonderen Fall, so wird auch der Gebrauch der Vernunft richtig und gut seyn, welcher nach diesen Reguln selbst eingerichtet ist: und sodann schreibet sich die Vernunft selbst die Reguln von ihrem Gebrauche vor."

[95] Ibid., p. 462: "[...] aus dem Zeugnisse eines andern, welches den Nahmen Glaube führet."

of eternal truths that could be validated by reason. Reimarus had trouble combining the philological and critical rules for this procedure. So he first set out to describe the rules of rationality and then the rules that determine the credibility of a testimony. Although he was able to draw on forensic logic, rhetoric, and textual criticism,[96] a rigorous application of forensic logic to textual testimonies or even to the entire biblical revelation was entirely new and definitely also an experiment with uncertain results.

Reimarus began the most important part of his argument with the application of his logic to hermeneutics: "1. If we consider what the usage of words implies after putting them together and taking account of the intention of their author and the circumstances, then we have a mental picture of what comes from the mind of a credible witness; in other words, we understand what he means or have arrived at a correct interpretation of his words."[97]

Under these conditions it becomes possible to view the logic of a rational argument as a criterion of credibility. Of course, depending on the subject that needs to be judged, distinctions need to be made. First, a careful examination of the written testimony itself helps to determine whether it internally agrees with logical criteria. Second, it is possible to survey the testimony's history of transmission, and third – which leads us from the credibility of the written testimony to the credibility of the testifier or witness – it is necessary to evaluate the reliability of the author of a source. In the process of the first step, the evaluation of the testimony's internal logic, the reader must adhere to the following rules: 2. a witness who advances undeniably contradictory facts or who differs from otherwise generally accepted truths, is not credible. 3. If a witness presents matters in such a manner that they appear impossible and does not explain

---

[96] Already Hugo Grotius (*De Veritate religionis Christianae* II, 6) emphasized the role of the witnesses for the resurrection account; this is already a central topos from early Christianity: the Easter Gospel is dependent on the reliability of the witnesses. Christian Thomasius writes on the problems of witness and witness account in chapter 10 of his *Einleitung in die Vernunftlehre* (1691; reprint, Hildesheim, 1968) (see especially pp. 229–233) and in his *De fide juridica* (Halle, 1699). This topos appears already in Aristotle's *Rhetoric* III, 16, 17. It seems only natural to the philologist Reimarus that the reliability of a testimony is also an issue in textual criticism.

[97] See Reimarus, *Kleine gelehrte Schriften*, p. 467: "1. Wenn wir uns dasjenige bey den Worten gedencken, was der Gebrauch der Worte, nach ihrer Verknüpfung und Absicht des Schreibers auch Umständen der Sache giebt: so gedencken wir eben das bey den Worten was ein glaubwürdiger Zeuge gedacht hat: das ist wir verstehen ihn recht, oder haben den wahren Verstand seiner Worte."

how these matters may nonetheless be possible, such a witness loses his inner credibility. 4. If it is not possible to explain the plausibility of matters, but if these matters are not clearly impossible, then we should not discard the account, even if it has only a certain extent of credibility on the surface.

Since it is possible to determine whatever is contradictory or not, or whatever is impossible or not, only through a knowledge of the rules of contradiction and unanimity, it is once again clear that reason can also determine the truth of our faith: on the one hand, it can shield us from gullibility and superstition, and on the other hand, it can prevent us from falling into unbelief.[98]

Reimarus' second set of rules is philological by nature; imprinted on them is already the direction which the history of biblical criticism took under the successful and controversial leadership of figures such as Richard Simon. Reimarus summarizes his text-critical reflections on the veracity of texts as follows: "5. If an author of a written work that is undoubtedly his own also identifies another written work as his own; or some of his contemporaries do not have any reservations about classifying it as belonging to him, since both content and style agree with the writer's time, his own personality, circumstances, opinions, and technique; in that case, it is not necessary to question whether the written work indeed comes from the person claiming to be its author; the credit for the believability of the claim then goes to the author. 6. If, however, the testimony of the author himself or of those living at his time or shortly thereafter contradicts the claim that the work comes from the particular writer; or if certain aspects and especially the work's style do not agree with the supposed author's time, his personality, circumstances, opinions, and technique; then it is not possible to assign the work to the person, nor its content to the judgment which the supposed author would have deserved. 7. If a passage in

---

[98] Ibid., p. 470: "[…] entstehen daher für den Leser die Reguln: 2. Ein Zeuge der klärlich wiedersprechende Dinge vorbringt, oder sich selbst, oder andern klar erkannten Wahrheiten wiederspricht, ist nicht glaubwürdig. 3. Wenn ein Zeuge die Sachen so vorbringt, daß sie den Schein der Unmöglichkeit haben, und doch die Möglichkeit nicht erklärt in Sachen da es sich thun läßet, der verliert die inner Glaubwürdigkeit. 4. Wenn sich die Möglichkeit der Sachen nicht erklären läßet, jedoch auch nicht klar unmöglich ist, so können wir deswegen das Zeugnis, wenn es nur sonst seine äußere Glaubwürdigkeit hat, nicth verwerffen. Da sich nun, was wiedersprechend sey oder nicht, was möglich oder unmöglich sey, nicht anders als durch die Einsicht in die Reguln des Wiederspruchs und der Einstimmung ausmachen läßet: so ist abermahls klar, daß die Vernunft auch in so ferne die Richtigkeit unsers Glaubens bestimme und auf der einen Seite der Leichtgläubigkeit und dem Aberglauben, auf der andern dem Unglauben vorbeuge."

the work is quoted verbatim by the author somewhere else or from others who lived either at the time of the author or shortly thereafter or if this passage is confirmed by old, carefully composed manuscripts; or if it is otherwise coherent and does not contain anything contradictory; then there is no need to doubt its candour: and its credibility is attributed to the author. 8. If however, the said passage is missing or quoted differently by the author himself somewhere else or by anybody else living at his time or shortly thereafter, or if it does not appear in reliable manuscripts where it ought to appear or appears there in a slightly different form; or if it is in any way incoherent and contains anything contradictory: then it is not from that particular author or has been corrupted; and it then deserves no credibility. Since it is important in this process to determine whether the written work and passages thereof correspond to testimonies, manuscripts, and to the author's personality, his time, circumstances, opinions, and style, and whether it is coherent or contains anything contradictory, it is once again up to reason to judge the veracity of a belief in regard to authorship."[99]

---

[99] Ibid., pp. 471–473: "Wenn ein Schriftsteller in einer Schrift die ungezweiffelt seine ist, die andere auch für seine erkennet; oder diejenigen so zugleich und kurz hernach Leben nimmer Bedencken gefunden ihm die andere Schrifft beyzulegen, auch die darin enthaltene Sachen sowohl als die Schreibart mit des Schriftstellers Zeiten, Personen, Umstände und Meynungen und Schreibart übereinstimmen: so hat man nich Ursache zu zweiffeln, daß die Schrifft des vorgegebenen Verfassers in der That sey; und beruhet aldenn die Glaubwürdigkeit derselben auf des Verfassers Verdienste. 6. Wenn hergegen des Schriftstellers eigenes, oder anderer zugleich und kurtz hernach lebenden Zeugnis dem Vorgeben daß die Schrifft des Verfaßers sey wiedersprechen: oder auch die Sachen und besondere Schreibart mit des vorgegebenen Verfassers Zeiten, Person, Umständen, Meynungen und Schreibart nicht übereinstimmen: so kann man die Schrifft nicht für des Verfassers annehmen, noch ihrem Inhalt den Lgauben, welchen der vorgegebene Verfasser verdient hätte, zufließen lassen. 7. Wenn eine Stelle der Schrifft von dem Verfasser selbst anderwerts oder von anderen zugleich oder kurtz hernach lebenden wörtlich angeführet, oder durch alte mit Sorgfalt verfertigte Handschrifften bestättiget wird: oder sonst guten Zusammenhang hat, und nicht wiedersprechendes in sich hält: so ist and derselben Aufrichtigkeit nicht zu zweifeln: und beruhet aldenn die Glaubwürdigkeit derselben auf des Verfassers Verdienste. 8. Wenn hergegen die Stelle der Schrifft von dem Verfasser selbst anderwerts, oder von andern zugleich oder kurtz hernach lebenden, oder in alten guten handschrifften da sie angeführet werden sollte, ausgelassen oder anders angeführet wird; oder sonst übelen Zusammenhang und etwa wiedersprechendes in sich hat: so ist sie nicht des Verfassers oder verdorben: und verdient so ferne keinen Glauben. Da es nun bey diesem Urtheile darauf ankommt, ob die Schrifft und deren Stelle mit den Zeugnissen, Handschrifften, und mit des Verfassers Person, Zeiten, Umständen, Meynungen und Schreibart, und mit dem Zusammenhange übereinstimmen oder denselben wiedersprechen, so ist es abermahl ein Werck der Vernunft der Richtigkeit des Glaubens, so ferne er sich auf den Verfasser selbst beziehet zu bestimmen."

This philological and text-critical delineation of a credibility pattern pre-supposes a dogmatic shift which had not yet occurred in Reimarus' Job commentary: the idea that the biblical text was not dictated directly into the mind of the scribe or that every word was divinely inspired, but that the scribes themselves may have manipulated the text. This is where the most delicate part of Reimarus' outline of the credibility of texts in general and of the biblical narrative in particular starts. How would it be possible to evaluate the credibility of the authors? "Could they have known the truth and did they want to speak it?"[100] This gave rise to the suspicion, generated by a contextualisation of the Bible which constituted the secret guiding principle of Enlightenment criticism of biblical revelation: the insinuation of using religion for political purposes. This is where Reimarus' set of principles of rational hermeneutics dissolves. These problems are even reflected in the respective part of the extant manuscript, which is over-flowing with numerous deleted portions and changes. Reimarus' first version of the relationship between religion, nature, and reason closes with those delicate critical rules about the credibility of the author of the biblical text, which could covertly progress from textual criticism to a polemic against revelation.

"9. If an author claims that he himself experienced what he wrote, that he is trained in the skill of interpreting it correctly and that he applied the proper scholarship, care, and precision; then it becomes clear that he could have experienced what he testifies and his own experience thus conforms to our own or to any other true experience, and therefore it becomes the same as if we experienced it ourselves. Once a matter or instance becomes specific and requires more than general experience, scholarship, care, precision as well as impartiality and honesty; or if it lacks credibility: then we cannot rely on an author who does not build on his own experience or on general knowledge and belief. 10. If an author tells us that he based his narrative on genuine documents, primary sources, or on filed catalogues of occurrences: then this means that he knew what he was writing about, and therefore it is possible to put his sources in place of our own or any other true experience; hence, it is just as if we experienced it ourselves. 11. If an author neither experienced himself what he is writing about nor can cite his primary sources, but instead has to rely on secondary sources: then he gradually loses his credibility in relation to the suggested distance of the location and times, about which one is even less informed due to

---

[100] Ibid., p. 473: "[...] die Wahrheit wissen können und sagen wollen?"

the lack of alternative historical accounts and less so even based upon the credibility of the quoted sources, unless a first-hand reliable eye-witness determines whether everything is mere rumour or fiction or partly fiction. If the accounts of many different eye-witnesses who were unable to consult each other confirm one particular matter, then its credibility becomes even stronger; if, however, many confirm it, but they base their information upon the same rumour or they contradict each other or they were perhaps even able to consult each other: then the credibility does not become stronger, but even disappears.

If an author shows that he is a knowledgeable friend of truth and that he was not motivated by pleasure, awe, or advantage to tell anything but the truth, and that neither fear nor displeasure, neither shame nor damage, induced him to remain silent or to distort what he thought to be true: then this means that his words conform with his thoughts and that he writes what he thinks to be true.

If an author derives from his account not only no advantage, but even loses all of his advantages and instead is burdened with displeasure, shame or damage: then this proves even more that he said or wrote what he believed to be true. If an author provides no indications that anything may have induced him to provide an untrue account or not to speak the truth, then we do not know whether he wanted to write what he thought to be true."[101]

---

[101] Ibid., pp. 475–477: "9. Wenn ein Schriftsteller darthut, daß er es selber erfahren was er bezeugt, daß er die Erfahrungs-Kunst verstehe, und bey dieser Erfahrung die nöthige Wissenschaft, Achtsamkeit und Behutsamkeit gebraucht habe: so erhellet, daß er es habe wissen können was er bezeugt und demnach lässet sich seine Erfahrung in die Stelle der unsrigen oder einer jedweden richtigen Erfahrung setzen, folglich ist es einerley, als ob wir es selbst aufs richtigste erfahren hätten. Sobald eine Sache oder Begebenheit ins besondere hineingehet, oder mehr als gemeine Erfahrung, Wissenschaft, Achtsamkeit, Behutsamkeit, oder auch Unparteylichkeit und Ehrlichkeit erfordert: oder keine innere Glaubwürdigkeit hat: so können wir einem Zeugen, der nicht von seiner oder das Gerüchte und Tradition gebauet hat, nicht trauen. 10. Wenn ein Schriftsteller uns überführet, daß er seine Erzehlung aus echten Urkunden, aus ersten Quellen, oder Actenmäßigen Verzeichnißen der Begebenheiten, genommen habe: so erhellet, daß er es habe wissen können was er schreibt, und demnach lassen sich seine Urkunden in die Stelle unser eigenen oder einer jeden richtigen Erfahrung setzen: folglich ist es einerley als ob wir es selbst aufs richtigste erfahren hätten. 11. Wenn ein Schriftsteller es weder selber erfahren noch die ersten echten Urkunden anführen kann, sondern sich auf andere beziehen muß: so verlieret seine Glaubwürdigkeit stuffenweise nach Masgebung der Entfernung der Oerter oder Zeiten, nach welchen man wegen Mangel anderer historischer Nachrichten um so vielweniger von der Glaubwürdigkeit seiner angeführten Zeugen unterrichtet seyn, oder ihm den ersten zuverläßigen Augenzeugen noch ob es ein bloßes Geruchte oder Getichte sey, oder wenigstens dazu getichtet worden herausbringen kann. Wenn viele bewehrte Augenzeugen die sich nicht zusammen bereden konnten einerley Dinge bekräftigen, so wird derselben

The last set of rules severs the links to the field of apologetic hermeneutics; if these criteria are applied to the Bible, then its accounts lose their credibility.

Reimarus' exegetical criteria in this particular fragment, which dates from around three years after his Job commentary, are not the final and definite application of inalienable natural criteria to religion, which, confronted with such criteria, is put on the defensive. Rather, the claims of reason on nature, which emancipate themselves from the Bible, were theological in their origin and received their respective legitimation by imparting their rationality to nature. Only this theological legitimation of natural rationality honed the criteria of authenticity by presenting itself as both a natural and rational legitimation. Against these new criteria, biblical reality could no longer legitimate itself in the face of natural theology. This then made it possible for a professor from Hamburg to summon it before the court of reason.

Glaubwürdigkeit desto stärker, dagegen wenn es zwar viele bekraftigen, oder sie haben es alle von dem Gerüchte, oder sie wiedersprächen sich ein ander, oder sie haben sich vielleicht bereden können: so wächst die Glaubwürdigkeit nicht alleine nicht, sondern sie verschwindet gar. Wenn ein Schriftsteller zeiget, daß er ein verständiger Liebhaber der Wahrheit sey, und daß er keine Bewegungs Gründe der Lust, der Ehrfurcht, oder des Vortheils gehabt noch haben können warum er etwas anders hatte sagen sollen als er für wahr gehalten noch daß ihn Furcht und Unlust, und Schande oder Schaden abgehalten das zu verschweigen oder zu verstellen was er für wahr gehalten: so erhellet daß seine Rede mit seinen Gedancken übereinstimme, oder daß er eben das schreibe was er für wahr gehalten. Wenn sich ein Zeuge von seinem Zeugnisse nicht allein keine Vortheile vorstellen können, sondern auch alle Vortheile daruber verlohren und sich Unlust, Schande oder Schaden dadurch zugezogen: so erhellet noch stärcker daß er eben das gesagt oder geschrieben was er fur wahr gehalten. Wenn ein Schriftsteller nicht darthut daß ihn nichts zum falschen Bericht anreitzen noch von der Wahrheit abhalten können, so können wir nicht wissen ob er eben das habe sagen wollen, was er für wahr gehalten."

THE PUBLIC DISCOURSE OF HERMANN SAMUEL REIMARUS AND JOHANN LORENZ SCHMIDT IN THE *HAMBURGISCHE BERICHTE VON GELEHRTEN SACHEN* IN 1736

Ursula Goldenbaum

It is the aim of my paper to challenge the mainstream narrative of German intellectual history of the 18th century, which does not know about public discourse in early 18th century Germany in general, or about Reimarus as a participant in a particular public debate. While it was generally accepted from Hegel to Habermas[1] to see German enlightenment as backward and developing its own public sphere only during the last third of the century, Hermann Samuel Reimarus is considered as strictly avoiding almost any public performance. Wilhelm Schmidt-Biggemann emphasizes: "It happened only once that he stepped out of philosophical-theological existence in the shades: with his two very cautious reviews of the *Wertheim Bible* in the *Hamburgische Berichte*."[2]

However, these two little reviews are not marginal texts within the work of Reimarus. As demonstrated by Peter Stemmer, in his profound intellectual biography of Reimarus, these two German texts from 1736 are central for any explanation of Reimarus' seemingly sudden change from an orthodox Lutheran scholar to a more and more critical reader of the Bible, culminating as the author of a systematic foundation of Deism.[3] This

---

[1] Cf. Goldenbaum, „Das traditionelle Bild der deutschen Aufklärung als Ergebnis der Kanonisierung von Parteiurteilen", in: Goldenbaum, *Appell an das Publikum. Die öffentliche Debatte in der deutschen Aufklärung 1687–1796*. 2 parts. (Berlin: Akademie Verlag, 2004), pp. 13–32.

[2] Actually, only the first review discusses the *Wertheim Bible*. Reimarus' second review is on Schmidt's *Beantwortung*, see below. – „Nur einmal ist er aus dem philosophisch-theologischen Schattendasein mehr nolens als volens wohl herausgetreten: in zwei sehr vorsichtigen Rezensionen der ‚Wertheimer Bibel' in den Hamburgischen Berichten von Gelehrten Sachen." (Wilhelm Schmidt-Biggemann: „Einleitung", in: Hermann Samuel Reimarus, *Kleine gelehrte Schriften. Vorstufen zur Apologie oder Schutzschrift für die vernünftigen Verehrer Gottes*, ed. by Schmidt-Biggemann (Veröffentlichungen der Jungius-Gesellschaft, 79) (Göttingen: Vandenhoeck & Ruprecht, 1994), pp. 57–58) – See also Peter Stemmer, *Weissagung und Kritik. Eine Studie zur Hermeneutik bei Hermann Samuel Reimarus* (Veröffentlichungen der Jungius-Gesellschaft, 48) (Göttingen: Vandenhoeck & Ruprecht, 1983), pp. 92–146.

[3] Cf. Stemmer (see footnote 2), p. 137.

evolution was initiated between these two reviews in the *Hamburgische Berichte von gelehrten Sachen*, published on January 6, and on October 23, 1736.

THE PLACE OF THESE PUBLICATIONS

The *Hamburgische Berichte von gelehrten Sachen* was not a learned journal, written and read by scholars. Rather, it was a new kind of newspaper, appearing twice a week as cheap, thin booklets readable in half an hour, offering news of the learned and scientific world to an interested and educated but non-academic audience. As in political newspapers, all news was labelled after the place from where it was sent. The editor of such a "Gelehrte Zeitung" obtained news in the same way as the editor of any other newspaper at that time by an extensive correspondence[4] with educated or even learned people in Europe, especially in London, Paris or Amsterdam, Leipzig and Göttingen, and even smaller places. They also received unsolicited information and contributions. These newspapers were not supported by the state, church or universities and no one was under any obligation to buy them. Because of their focus on academic news, they also enjoyed a very relaxed or complete lack of any censor-

---

[4] „Die gelehrte Correspondentz ist demnach, so wie auch bey politischen Gazetten, die Haupt-Quelle aller Nachrichten, und so zusagen, die Seele einer gelehrten Zeitung. Fehlet es an der, so fehlts auch gantz gewiß an täglichen Neuigkeiten, mangelt es aber darann, und kommt man bloß mit solchen Sachen, die etwa nur in demselben gantzen Jahr sich zugetragen, oder mit unaufhörlicher Erzehlung, der darinn nach und nach herausgegebenen Bücher aufgezogen [!], so mangelt es an einem wesentlichen Stücke des Journals, und dasjenige, was ein Tag-Buch seyn solte, wird zu einem Jahr-Buch oder Chronic." (Notification. An die Herrn Gelehrten und Liebhaber der gelehrten Sachen. Einlagblatt vom 24.10.1733 [advertisement]. Quoted after: Holger Böning, *Deutsche Presse. Biobibliographische Handbücher zur Geschichte der deutschsprachigen periodischen Presse von den Anfängen bis 1815*. Bd. 1.1: H. Böning/Emmy Moepps, *Hamburg. Kommentierte Bibliographie der Zeitungen, Zeitschriften, Intelligenzblätter, Kalender und Almanache sowie biographische Hinweise zu Herausgebern, Verlegern und Druckern periodischer Schriften. Von den Anfängen bis 1765* (Stuttgart: Frommann-Holzboog, 1996), col. 412. – The editor of the *Hamburgische Berichte*, Johann Peter Kohl, explains already in the long subtitle of his newspaper that it is based on an extended correspondence: „Hamburgische Berichte von neuen Gelehrten Sachen, Auf das Jahr 1732. aus einer täglichen beglaubten Correspondentz mit den berühmt- und gelehrtesten Männern in Deutschland, Schweden und Dänemarck, und mit Beyhülffe verschiedenen vornehmen Gönner und Freunde zu Paris, Londen und Amsterdam, Zum Aufnehmen der Gelehrsamkeit, und zur beliebigen Unterhaltung, mit unpartheyischer Feder ans Licht gestellet, und mit einem zureichenden Register versehen", ibid., col. 409. See also col. 416–418)

ship. They existed only as long as enough copies could be sold to an interested audience, at least as many as 500.[5] The Leipziger *Neue Zeitungen von gelehrten Sachen* appeared first in 1715 and continued up to the 19th century. The *Hamburgische Berichte von Gelehrten Sachen* was published between 1732 and 1757. Given the rather short existence of the "Moralische Wochenschriften," averaging two or three years, which are nowadays known mainly to scholars of the Enlightenment, the long lasting existence of the "Gelehrte Zeitungen" can be evaluated as a sign of the great interest of a sufficiently large audience in news about the learned world. This is particularly true of the time of the public debate about the *Wertheim Bible* from 1735 till 1737, in which both the mentioned newspapers played an important role. Two of the issues of the *Hamburgische Berichte von Gelehrten Sachen* in 1736 make the disputed *Wertheim Bible* the lead, on June 8 and on October 23, the latter with the review of Reimarus.[6] The journalists of both newspapers were a kind of Wolffian and in contact with Gottsched.[7]

Having characterized these newspapers as directed to a broad public audience, the question arises, why did the scholar Reimarus, known for avoiding public attention, place both reviews, which became a turning point in his intellectual development, in such a newspaper? The first step in answering this question is easy, at least for the publication of the first review. Reimarus was simply asked to write this review by the editor of the *Hamburgische Berichte*, Johann Peter Kohl. But this raises the next question: why would Kohl ask the famous scholar for such a popular review? The answer is because of his need for a critical counter piece to another paper he already intended to publish in his newspaper. Kohl wanted to publish an article which was openly in favor of the *Wertheim Bible* and its author, both of which had been under heavy theological attack since September 1735. In order to justify the publication of a partisan of the *Wertheim Bible* he had to balance this publication by another critical article. He had done this once before in the autumn of 1735, publishing one positive review of Joachim Lange's polemical refutation of the *Wertheim*

---

[5] Cf. Joachim Kirchner, *Die Grundlagen des deutschen Zeitschriftenwesens mit einer Gesamtbibliographie der deutschen Zeitschriften bis zum Jahr 1790. 1. part: Bibliographische und buchhandelsgeschichtliche Untersuchungen* (Leipzig: Hiersemann, 1928), pp. 100–102.

[6] Cf. *Hamburgische Berichte*. Nr. 46. June 8th 1736, pp. 417–424 (!).

[7] Cf. Goldenbaum, „Der Skandal der Wertheimer Bibel. Die philosophisch-theologische Entscheidungsschlacht zwischen Pietisten und Wolffianern", in: Goldenbaum, *Appell an das Publikum* (footnote 1) chap. 8, pp. 243–253, see especially footnote 207.

Bible, the *Religionsspötter*, and one positive review of the *Wertheim Bible* itself.[8]

The other "hot" paper had been sent directly from Wertheim and was written by an anonymous author: Alethaeus Eusebius.[9] It is still not known who shielded his identity under this pseudonym, but the name suggests the Wolffian society of the Alethophiles. However, this author was openly in favour of the *Wertheim Bible*, presented the whole project of a new translation of the Bible, and defended its methods with good reasons against its critics, especially against its particularly hostile enemy Joachim Lange, the head of the Pietist theologians at Halle. Eusebius argued particularly against the suspicion that the author of the *Wertheim Bible* wished *intentionally* to destroy the Christian religion and its very foundation, the text of the Bible, though pretending to defend it. That this was indeed the goal of Lange becomes evident already by the title of his work, *Religionsspötter*, which means: "Mocker of Religion". According to the Elenchus, the procedure of admonition within the Protestant Church at that time, one needed particularly to prove the bad intentions of an author in order to initiate any persecution by state power. I shall come back to that.

Whereas Lange attacked the introduction of the *Wertheim Bible* because of its merely rational explanation of the successful history of Christianity, neglecting its miraculous character, Eusebius argued it would serve only to antagonize the enemies of Christian truth. Therefore one should rely solely on clear concepts and logical conclusions. In order to engage with the Deists, one needed to accept their demand for proof of everything, because nobody should believe without having reason for faith. The introduction is even praised as helping to refute the Deists.[10] The translation

---

[8] „Da uns vor wenigen Stunden eine zwifache, die neue wertheimische Bibelüberset-zung betreffende Nachricht, deren die eine wieder, die zweite aber für sie ist, durch die Post eingeliefert worden: so halten wir es unserer Pflicht am gemässesten zu seyn, beide nacheinander, unverändert einzuschalten, und den unparteiisch richtenden das Urteil davon zu überlassen." (*Hamburgische Berichte von gelehrten Sachen*. N. 90, November 11th, 1735, pp. 729–732, quotation on p. 729)

[9] *Hamburgische Berichte von gelehrten Sachen*. N. II, January 6th 1736, pp. 9–12. It is not unlikely that Johann Wilhelm Höflein, the chancellor of the Counts of Löwenstein-Wertheim and the supporter of Schmidt, wrote this article. But there are other candidates as well.

[10] „So wolle die Vorrede nur sagen, sie [die Deisten etc.] hätten allerdings Recht, Beweis zu fordern, weil man von niemand etwas ohne Grund glauben solte. Es werde aber hierauf gezeiget, wie der Beweis zu führen sey. Summa die Vorrede bestehe aus lauter abgesonderten Begriffen, weil sie um der Feinde der Wahrheit willen geschrieben sey, und wer die Art Leute kenne, werde dergleichen Schreibart nicht tadeln." (*Hamburgische Berichte von gelehrten Sachen*. N. II, January 6th 1736, pp. 12–18)

itself is presented as conveying the sense of the divine scribes in a far stronger light than many extensive interpretations. Concerning the disturbing lack of any prophecies of Jesus Christ, the readers are asked to await patiently the end of this translation before making a final judgment of the whole enterprise, instead of blocking it by persecution.

Given the "general theological mobilization"[11] against the *Wertheim Bible* since the appearance of Lange's *Religionsspötter* in September 1735, it was courageous of Kohl to publish this article at all. Although at first glance it appears as an anxious action by him, wishing to be balanced, it is actually a strategic attempt to find a way to get it published at all. He was absolutely right to be cautious and his great efforts to publish as much as was possible were even acknowledged by Schmidt himself in a letter to Kohl.[12] About the same time, on February 1st, 1736, the other "Gelehrte Zeitung" at Leipzig was placed under a renewed theological censorship because of its blunt and non-diplomatic position in favour of the *Wertheim Bible*.[13] The denunciation of that newspaper was sent to the Court at Dresden by the theologians of Leipzig, but was initiated by the urgings of Joachim Lange. The editor of the newspaper at Leipzig reacted with a promise not to publish any more news from Wertheim (if it could not happen without censorship). Thus the "Wertheimer" lost one important public medium.

Johann Peter Kohl at Hamburg got "his" letter from Joachim Lange too, very likely in February. In his answer to Lange on March 7, 1736, Kohl tries very hard to be diplomatic and balanced in order to maintain the ability to publish. He makes great efforts to justify his publication policy

---

[11] Hirsch called the wave of refutations against Schmidt "allgemeine Mobilmachung" in the military sense. (Emmanuel Hirsch *Geschichte der neuern evangelischen Theologie im Zusammenhang mit den allgemeinen Bewegungen des europäischen Denkens.* Vol. 2. [Gütersloh: Bertelsmann, 1951], p. 432)

[12] „Die unpartheiische Gewogenheit, welche e.H. gegen mich so wol als meine Gegner, in dero Berichten blicken lassen, und die Willfährigkeit, nach welcher sie meine Schriften darin bekant machen, verbindet mich, ihnen hiemit meine gehorsamste Dankbarkeit dafür zu bezeugen. Ich kene die Absicht der Berichte, und lobe die Unparteilichkeit derselben. Dahero wundere ich mich gar nicht, daß ich manchmal die giftigsten Ausdrücke meiner Feinde darin antreffe, zumal da ich sie öfters als Nachbarn von mir daselbst erblicke. Mein Trost bei allen den heftigen Lästerungen und Verfolgungen ist die Unschuld meiner Sache. Ich hoffe, meine Herren, Sie werden mich nirgends auf Betrug und unrichtigem Verfahren in meinen Schriften angetroffen haben, oder befinden, daß ich gegen meine Feinde unbillig bin. Ich gedencke gar oft an ienes: Sie wissen nicht, was sie thun. Ob aber ihr Verfahren, auch in dem Fal eines irrigen Gewissens mit den Regeln der Gottseligkeit überein komme, das werden erleuchtete Personen gar leicht sehen." (Schmidt to Kohl. *Hamburgische Berichte von gelehrten Sachen.* N. 46. June 8th 1736, pp. 417–418)

[13] Cf. Goldenbaum, „Der Skandal der Wertheimer Bibel" (see footnote 7), chap. 10, pp. 255–270.

in the Wertheim affair.[14] While he sounds humble and respectful, his answer is still somewhat ambivalent and certainly would be perceived by Lange as insufficient. Kohl mentions the remarkable number of defences of the *Wertheim Bible* sent to his newspaper that he rejected, using them as justifications for the few he did publish.[15] Also, while he regrets the whole enterprise of the *Wertheim Bible*, he does not agree with Lange's slandering of the author and his bad intentions. Rather, he expresses compassion and regret when he speaks of him. He promises to maintain absolute impartiality. However, he also promises not to give any place to the partisans of the *Wertheim Bible*.[16] This ambivalence, due to political pressure, becomes even more evident if we look at the publications in this newspaper during 1735 and 1736. In fact, Kohl published more articles in favour of the *Wertheim Bible*. He adapts very smoothly to the development of the political situation concerning the Wolffian philosophy and the *Wertheim Bible*. Fortunately, his true opinion can be found in a letter he wrote at about the same time, on February 20, 1736, to the chancellor of Löwenstein-Wertheim, a committed supporter of the *Wertheim Bible*, Johann Wilhelm Höflein, where he is very outspoken:

> It is more than well known how cautious one has to be in these years and how one has to put almost each word and thought on the scale in order to not give any opportunity to theologians to make innocent intentions suspicious or even to cause public damage. We live here in a place where it is quite easy to get into trouble and under the censorship of theologians. If anybody loves truth and impartiality, the authors of the [Hamburgische] 'Berichte' certainly do. *And they wished nothing more than to place everything which is sent to it, pro and con, in the weekly sheets* in order to improve on discovering the truth. But this cannot be done as things stand now.[17]

---

[14] Archive of the Franckesche Stiftungen Halle, A 188b:372, 1r–2v.

[15] „Es sind zwar schon mehr, als einmal Vertheidigungen für die Wertheimische Übersetzung eingesandt worden. Man hat sie aber beständig abgewiesen, weil wir uns fest vorgenommen haben, nicht das geringste in defensionem einzusetzen, sondern die dahingehörige Schriften zur Historie, (damit [...] die Historie dieser Controverse in ihrer Connexion bleibe) zu berühren." (Ibid., 2r–v)

[16] Ibid., 2r.

[17] „Ew. etc. ist mehr als zu bekannt, wie behutsam man in diesen Jahren verfahren und wie man fast alle Worte und Gedanken auf die Wagschale legen müsse, damit man den Herrn Theologis nicht Gelegenheit gebe, die sonst unschuldige Absicht verdächtig zu machen, ja oftmals öffentlich zu schaden. Wir leben hier an einem Orte, da man es in diesem Stücke gar leicht versehen und in die Censur der Herren Theologorum verfallen kann. Wo sonst irgend einer die Wahrheit und Unparteilichkeit liebet und hochschätzet, so sind es die bisherigen Verfasser der 'Berichte', und wünschten sie dahero nichts mehr, als daß sie alles, was pro und contra eingesandt wird, zu desto besserer Entdeckung der Wahrheit, ihren Wochenblättern einfügen könnten, allein dieses läßt sich rebus sic stanti-

There was no need or even pressure to please Höflein, as Kohl had done with the influential and dangerous Joachim Lange. Therefore I take this letter as clearly indicative of Kohl's true opinion. This does not mean that Kohl agreed with the "Wertheimer" about everything, but that he was certainly committed to publishing texts in favour of and against the *Wertheim Bible* and to keep the discussion going. However, he does appear to be sympathetic to the whole project of the *Wertheim Bible*.

But the question arises whether Reimarus shared the opinion of Johann Peter Kohl or whether he was simply asked for a complementary paper because the editor needed a critical paper for his balancing strategy. The latter would mean that Kohl knew about Reimarus' rejection of the *Wertheim Bible*. Given the content of the first review of Reimarus, I am certainly inclined to believe the latter. Nevertheless, Kohl did not ask just any polemical theologian who could have served to balance the pro-Wertheim article. He had specific reasons for asking Reimarus. There exists a letter of the editor of the German *Acta eruditorum*, Christian Gottlieb Jöcher in Leipzig, to Wertheim, where he explains the particular difficulty of an editor in finding an author who is sufficiently critical about the subject in order to satisfy the censorship, but can still be accepted by the readers of his journal. Kohl had to deal with exactly the same difficulty, and I therefore quote this letter of Jöcher:

> So far, I am an unchanged friend of truth and will gratefully accept it wherever I find it; also, by careful and long standing exercise of reason, I tried to enable myself to see with my own eyes and to distinguish right and wrong.... Concerning the review you don't approve, I affirm sincerely *that I did not write it myself but engaged with great care a certain personality.*[18]

If he had chosen a polemicist who did not engage the readers of his journal, an important part of them could become frustrated and begin to disrespect him. The editor belonged more or less to the same intellectual community as his readers, and he wanted to please them. But if the review was too much in favour of the work, it could mean the end of the journal.

Johann Peter Kohl was not one of those common journalists of the time who came directly from university, earning a living by writing a

bus nicht thun." (Kohl to Höflein on February 20, 1736. In: Gustav Frank, „Die Wertheimer Bibelübersetzung vor dem Reichshofrat in Wien", in: *Zeitschrift für Kirchengeschichte* XII (1890), 2nd issue, Gotha, pp. 279–302, here pp. 291–292 (My emphasis – U.G.)).

[18] Jöcher to Schmidt on April 22, 1736, in: Goldenbaum, „Der Skandal der Wertheimer Bibel" (see footnote 7), p. 279.

newspaper. He was a former professor of church history and *Belles Lettres* at, and a member of, the Academy at St. Petersburg. He still retained a pension from this Academy and was a citizen of Hamburg with a very good reputation. He was a learned man himself, a great admirer of Leibniz, and certainly inclined to the work of Christian Wolff. It does not come as a surprise that we find him well acquainted with the circle of Hagedorn, Brockes, and Zinck, the editor of the great political newspaper *Der Hamburgische Unpartheyische Correspondent*. That is exactly the circle to which Reimarus belonged as well. This might clarify how the first review originated. Reimarus was an ideal candidate for Kohl. According to the content of his first review, he obviously rejected the translation as well as the method of translation used in the *Wertheim Bible*. But neither did he go along with the polemical attacks of Joachim Lange, which lacked any argument, and whose only goal was to obtain a ban on this work, together with the philosophy of Christian Wolff, and the persecution of the author. Reimarus must have at least agreed with Kohl's intention to publish the pro and con arguments. He certainly possessed an advance copy of Eusebius' paper, as is clear from his review. Furthermore, he must have known in advance that his review would be published together with Eusebius'. Having established that, it is undoubtable that Reimarus consciously entered an ongoing public debate in a newspaper late in 1735 (given the publication on January 6th, 1736). That was before any ban had yet hit the *Wertheim Bible*. Nevertheless, the ongoing public debate was already at its peak and was only to a small extent an exchange of arguments. For the most part it was determined by theological denunciation and simultaneously threatened by theological calls for a ban.

THE *WERTHEIM BIBLE*

At this point something has to be said about the *Wertheim Bible* itself, because it is almost forgotten today. Actually, it was deliberately forgotten by the great heroes of German idealism and classics, such as Herder and Hegel, whose judgments were then canonized by professional intellectual history in Germany.[19] If mentioned at all, such as in dictionaries, it is usually seen as the work of a radical Wolffian, a rationalist who was not able

---

[19] Cf. Goldenbaum, „Das traditionelle Bild der deutschen Aufklärung als Ergebnis der Kanonisierung von Parteiurteilen", in: Goldenbaum, *Appell an das Publikum* (see footnote 1), pp. 13–32.

to recognize the beauty and the sublimity of biblical language translated from poetic Hebrew into Wolffian abstract philosophical language. His work is seen as completely worthless and rightly forgotten, although most authors of the articles do not even present the historical facts correctly, to say nothing of their knowledge of the translation itself.[20]

The book appeared at Easter 1735 in a well designed edition of 1600 copies, with beautiful copperplates and at a large format, under the long title *Die göttlichen Schriften vor den Zeiten des Messie Jesus Der erste Theil worinnen Die Gesetze der Israelen enthalten sind nach einer freyen Übersetzung welche durch und durch mit Anmerkungen erläutert und bestätiget wird*. It was printed at the printing-office of the Counts of Löwenstein-Wertheim, by "Johann Georg Nehr, Hof- und Canzley-Buchdrucker". The introduction mentioned its approval by some well known, but not mentioned, scholars, as well as the sponsorship of some highly ranked personalities, unnamed as well. The book was announced in some newspapers and journals in advance and soon received both praise and critical reviews in the *Leipziger Zeitungen von gelehrten Sachen* and the *Hamburgische Berichte von gelehrten Sachen*. Both these "Gelehrte Zeitungen" in Leipzig and Hamburg then published still more positive reviews of the translation during 1735 and 1736. In fact, what is called the *Wertheim Bible* is only the first part, the Pentateuch, of the project of a new translation of the Bible, which was supposed to be accomplished, but could not be finished because of the immediate persecution. The translation was made and printed in Wertheim and that is why it is called the *Wertheim Bible*.

The author was Johann Lorenz Schmidt, who is almost completely unknown today.[21] If mentioned at all in German intellectual history,

---

[20] See e.g. „Schmidt, Johann Lorenz". In: *Deutsches Literatur-Lexikon. Biographisch-bibliographisches Handbuch*. Founded by Wilhelm Kosch. 3rd, completely new edition, vol. 15. Ed. H. Rupp and Carl Ludwig Lang (Bern: Saur, 1993), col. 384–385; „Schmidt, Johann Lorenz" (Author: Winfried Schröder). In: *Literaturlexikon*. Ed. Walther Killy. Vol. 10 (Gütersloh and Munich: Bertelsmann, 1991), p. 313; „Bibelübersetzungen" (Author: D. Hölscher). In: *Realencyklopädie für protestantische Theologie und Kirche*. 3rd edition (Leipzig: Hinrich, 1897), p. 80; „Bibelübersetzungen". In: *Die Religion in Geschichte und Gegenwart. Handwörterbuch in gemeinverständlicher Darstellung*. Vol. 1 (Tübingen: Mohr, 1909), col. 1166; „Schmidt, Johann Lorenz". In: *Die Religion in Geschichte und Gegenwart. Handwörterbuch in gemeinverständlicher Darstellung*. 2nd edition. Vol. 5 (Tübingen: Mohr, 1931), col. 207–208; „Schmidt, Johann Lorenz" (Autor: I. Ludolphy). In: *Die Religion in Geschichte und Gegenwart. Handwörterbuch in gemeinverständlicher Darstellung*. 3rd edition. Vol. 5 (Tübingen: Mohr, 1961), col. 1458.

[21] The newest and most instructive biography, based on new research in the archives, is by Paul S. Spalding, *Seize the Book, Jail the Author. Johann Lorenz Schmidt and Censorship in Eighteenth-Century Germany* (West-Lafayette: Purdue University Press, 1998). Up to

Schmidt is generally seen as an outsider, a radical Wolffian beyond the mainstream of the moderate Wolffians, let down by Wolff and his disciples after the persecution had begun. This is recently proven as completely wrong.[22] Born in 1702, Johann Lorenz Schmidt was eight years younger than Reimarus. He studied philosophy, mathematics and theology at the University of Jena 1720–1724, where Reimarus had studied a few years before, from 1714–1716. In 1725, Schmidt received an appointment as a tutor at the Court of Löwenstein-Wertheim, in a small Protestant Country in the middle of large Catholic territories such as the Archbishopric of Mainz and the Bishopric of Würzburg. Supported by the Counts of Löwenstein-Wertheim and their chancellor Johann Wilhelm Höflein, he began to work on a completely new translation of the Hebrew Bible. After receiving an informal approval of some parts of the work by Reinbeck, Mosheim and Wolff, he published its first part, the Pentateuch, at Easter 1735, again supported financially and morally by the Counts and the chancellor. Also, the book was authorized and printed in the printing-office of the Counts.

All contemporary critics of good will (e.g. Mosheim, Reinbeck, Reimarus) acknowledged in general the great Hebrew and German language skills which enabled Schmidt to make a very correct, understandable and readable (!) German translation. Nevertheless, they all saw problems too. The main problem with the translation was clearly seen in the total lack of any prophecy of Jesus Christ in these books of the Old Testament. Schmidt justified this outcome by the lack of any words that implied these prophecies. Claiming to translate only what is given in the text itself and which could be understood only in that way by the audience it was addressed to at the time of its origin, Schmidt rejected the use of any later text, such as e.g. the New Testament, for the authentic understanding of the texts of the Old Testament: "The first author has to be understood by himself, and it would be wrong to look for the concepts of his words in the subsequent writings appearing only long after him."[23] The words were directed to the

---

then we had only two short presentations: Paul Friedrich Schattenmann, *Johann Lorenz Schmidt, der Verfasser der Wertheimer Bibelübersetzung* (Programm der kgl. bayer. Studienanstalt Schweinfurt für das Schuljahr 1877/78) (Schweinfurt, 1878), and Frank, *Die Wertheimer Bibelübersetzung* (see footnote 17), pp. 279–302.

[22] Spalding has shown that Schmidt was supported by many Wolffians, see Paul S. Spalding, „Im Untergrund der Aufklärung: Johann Lorenz Schmidt auf der Flucht", in: *Europa in der Frühen Neuzeit. Festschrift für Günter Mühlpfordt.* Vol. 4: Deutsche Aufklärung, ed. by Erich Donnert (Weimar-Köln-Wien: Böhlau, 1997), pp. 135–154.

[23] „der erste Verfasser muß für sich verstanden werden, und es würde eine verkehrte Sache seyn, wenn man die Begriffe von seinen Worten in den folgenden Schriften suchen

Jews of those ancient times and were meant to be understood by them. Therefore, the words cannot be understood except by taking their own original context into account. Whereas it was common in Christian tradition to understand the divine sentence about Adam (and Eve) and the snake as one about the constant battle between the devil (appearing as the snake) and the saviour (*the* seed of Adam) on behalf of human beings, the story was now told as one about the constant hostility between humans and snakes and their offspring that was then starting, because this was the literal meaning of the words. The consequence was a complete lack of prophecies of Jesus Christ in the whole Pentateuch, thus questioning the meaning of the Old Testament for the Christian religion in general.

Nevertheless, it was the intention of Johann Lorenz Schmidt to defend the Christian religion against the powerful criticism of Deists and atheists who had started to dispute the inner truth of the Bible, citing its inner contradictions and questioning the likelihood of the described events. Schmidt wanted to provide a new translation in order to remove all vague or misleading passages of the Bible and present a clear and unambivalent text on which Christian dogma could be rebuilt. Questioned during the public debate by more objective critics on how to avoid the obviously negative consequences of his translation, he finally tried to argue in favour of an oral tradition. What the ancient Jews did not receive through the words of the text as it came down to us they must have learned by oral teachings which were still known at the time of Jesus Christ. But that was highly speculative because we know nothing about that, and it would re-open the doors to criticism by the Deists. But Schmidt insisted throughout the whole debate on his principle that it would not make sense to translate the Old Testament using knowledge of the New Testament. By doing so, he rejected the dogma of divine inspiration according to which both Testaments were written by God and were therefore beyond any time and rules of humans. He treated the Holy Scriptures according to the hermeneutics of any given human writing.

In addition, everything was translated into understandable common expressions of contemporary German that took away all the magic gloss of religious language and even of proper names. For example, "Apostle" became a simple messenger, the Latin "Paulus" became simply Paul, and

---

wolte, welche erst lange nach ihm verfertiget worden." (*Die göttlichen Schriften vor den Zeiten des Messie Jesus Der erste Theil worinnen Die Gesetze der Israelen enthalten sind nach einer freyen Übersetzung welche durch und durch mit Anmerkungen erläutert und bestätiget wird* [Wertheim. Gedruckt durch Johann Georg Nehr, Hof- und Canzley-Buchdrucker 1735] (*Wertheimer Bibel*), p. 44).

thus the then still used German vocative appeared as "Messenger Paule!"
It sounded as if somebody in your own neighbourhood was being called.
The Bible no longer looked very marvellous. Thus, it should not come as a
surprise that this new translation caused huge alarm among theologians.
Joachim Lange, the head of the Pietist theologians at Halle University,
started a general mobilization and almost no department of theology of
any university within the Protestant area of the Empire dared to refrain
from attacking the "Wertheimer" and his work.

But what indeed comes as a great surprise is the mere fact of this
very long lasting and extended public debate about the *Wertheim Bible*.
This became possible because of the complicated political structure of
the Empire and the rights of censorship after the Westphalian Peace in
1648. Built on the acknowledgment of the three large Christian denomina-
tions, Catholics, Lutherans, and Calvinists, the censorship, mostly directed
towards religion, was no longer executed by the Catholic Emperor in
Vienna but was given to the rulers of the territories. Thus the Counts of
Löwenstein-Wertheim were in charge of censorship in their small territory
and could print whatever they wanted to publish.[24] Likewise, whatever
Joachim Lange and his allies wrote and published against the *Wertheim
Bible* could prompt the rulers in Saxony and Prussia and other states or
Freie Reichsstädte, such as Frankfurt or Nürnberg, to forbid the book and
discussion about it and to punish the selling or owning of the book. But
they could not completely stop the "Wertheimer" from answering the
critiques and constantly publishing in the printing-office of the Counts
of Wertheim. And as long as he published his writings they had to be
answered by his enemies according to the rule of the "Elenchus". Otherwise they would be perceived as running out of arguments. Also, as long
as his writings could be sold elsewhere and be reviewed or even discussed
somewhere, the public debate would continue.

The way to forbid a book and to punish the author within the Protestant
area usually worked in the following way. Somebody had to criticize the
author or the work for having violated religion, giving evidence by nam-
ing passages that made the violation clear. The author did not necessarily

---

[24] It was a little more complicated because the printing-office was also used by the
Prince of Löwenstein-Wertheim, who was Catholic and lived at the same place. He did not
agree to print the *Wertheim Bible* at first but was calmed down by the Counts later on. Also,
the Lutheran pastor in Wertheim tried to stop the printing and got in touch with Lange in
the end. Nevertheless, the Counts enforced the continuation of the printing. See Spalding,
Seize the Book (footnote 21), pp. 74–95.

have to be named. But the author, being a member of the Christian community as well, had – according to the practice of the Elenchus – the right to justify his opinion and to show his agreement with true doctrine. That could be answered again by the theologians and could continue indefinitely. Only, if it could be shown or at least be pretended to be shown, that somebody did refuse to answer the concerns of the theologians and was resistant to their admonishment, could a bad intention be attested, and no further discussion was necessary. The state power had to stop such an enemy of the Christian Commonwealth.

With state and church working in close connection, there had seldom been much opportunity for a long standing public discourse between an alleged heretic and the theologians of the dominant church. But the political structure of the Empire made it almost impossible to stop the author of the *Wertheim Bible* once and for all. Lange had to go the long way of threatening single editors of journals and newspapers in letters, by denouncing them to their governments, by working constantly to get the rulers of one state after another to forbid the work and to persecute the author. But, above all, he had to secure a ban across the whole Empire in order to stop the printing-office in Wertheim. Lange's correspondence stored in the archives at the Franckesche Stiftungen in Halle shows the huge efforts of Lange in all these fields. He must have worked with incredible energy and patience. And ultimately, he would persuade the Prussian Court to send a denunciation of Johann Lorenz Schmidt and his book and a complaint about the lack of responsibility of the Counts of Löwenstein-Wertheim to the Court of the Emperor in Vienna.[25] Lange's overwhelming efforts to ban the *Wertheim Bible* and with it the Wolffian philosophy as a direct and necessary consequence of it can serve as an example for Spinoza's saying that there is no greater hatred than theological hatred.

The first ban on the *Wertheim Bible* occurred in Saxonia at the end of January 1736. This ban came together with the renewed censorship of the *Neue Zeitungen von gelehrten Sachen* in Leipzig. The next ban within a larger territory was announced in June 1736 in Prussia, after a long battle at the Prussian Court. Joachim Lange wanted to make the *Wertheim Bible* appear as a necessary consequence of the Wolffian Philosophy; however, he failed in that respect. The Royal Commission, named in spring 1736, did not determine that this philosophy violated religion. Wolff's logic was

---

[25] That it was the action of the Prussian Court could finally be shown in: Cf. Goldenbaum, "Der Skandal der Wertheimer Bibel" (footnote 7), p. 325.

even made an obligatory teaching book at all Prussian universities. But, on the other hand, the *Wertheim Bible* was forbidden in Prussia. Moreover, the Prussian Court agreed to sue the author and to press for a ban on the book from the Court in Vienna. After these two large Protestant territories, other states and Freie Reichsstädte followed their example, and the space for a public debate shrank more and more.

When the Court in Vienna banned the book and filed suit against Johann Lorenz Schmidt, he was arrested in February 1737. But he was still allowed to publish and could even send 500 copies of his *Öffentliche Erklärung* [Public declaration] to the Diet in Regensburg, asking the Corpus Evangelicorum to support a Lutheran and his freedom to interpret the Holy Scriptures according to his own mind. He also discussed the legal rights of a citizen of the Empire after the Westphalian Peace. This move, to appeal to the political institution of the Corpus Evangelicorum, was successful in stirring up the authorities and their lawyers and initiating a dispute about the legality of filing suit over religion against a Lutheran in a Catholic court. Even the Prussian king became reluctant at that point.[26] When the Catholic and Protestant estates of the area finally, in 1738, overcame the stalemate concerning the legal institution of the process, Schmidt was supposed to be delivered to a prison in Bamberg within a Catholic territory. But then, he escaped arrest in spring 1738, supported again by his Counts. Contrary to a widespread rumour, which can still be found in the dictionaries, he did not go to the Netherlands but to Altona, via some Protestant territories, passing through Leipzig, Helmstedt and Lüneburg. At all the places he passed through he was supported by the members of the largely underestimated Deutsche Gesellschaften.[27] Arriving in Altona after some weeks, he had to live thereafter his whole life under cover, as Schröder, at first in Altona, in close proximity to Reimarus at Hamburg, then in 1747 in Wolfenbüttel until his early death in 1749.

REIMARUS' FIRST CONTRIBUTION

Looking at Reimarus' first review in the *Hamburgische Berichte*, which discussed the *Wertheim Bible*, the translation, the methods and the introduction, it becomes clear that he argues in clear awareness of the Elenchus.

---

[26] Cf. Goldenbaum, „Der Skandal der Wertheimer Bibel" (footnote 7), chap. 23, p. 395.

[27] This was discovered and convincingly shown in: Paul S. Spalding, "Im Untergrund der Aufklärung" (see footnote 22), pp. 135–154.

What makes his first review appear orthodox is not so much his critique of the translation and its details, which are not even the subject of this review, but rather the question or rather the suspicion about the true intentions of the author. Reimarus comes directly to the main point of the Elenchus. He wants to know whether the translator had a negative opinion of the divine character of the Biblical Books. Only then does he ask the second question, whether the translator had a reason for his translation and for his introduction to it.[28] The first question is answered with a clear and blunt yes. Reimarus pretends not to see at all how this could not have been written by a disguised Collin, Woolston or Tindal as well.[29] According to him, the translator presented the divine character of the Bible through the mere fact that it indeed received a divine acknowledgment. However, this could also have been gained by natural causes as well. Thus, he in fact weakens the argument for a divine source. The same was true of the translator's failure to include the significance of the Messiah for the foundation of Christianity. Leaving it up to a mere natural development, it could have happened otherwise just as well, given different circumstances. The review also includes many suspicions of the author's being arrogant towards his critics, being unwilling to listen to their arguments, and being convinced of his superiority. He is also supposed to be a co-conspirator of Alethaeus Eusebius, the author of the defence. That was already enough to serve as a clear denunciation of Schmidt to the state power to be persecuted, as it showed him as an unwilling and resistant heretic who intended to destroy the foundation of the Christian religion.[30]

Given the clear suspicion about the hostile intentions of the translator presented by the famous scholar Reimarus, it does not come as a surprise that it was immediately used by Joachim Lange. He included it in his

---

[28] „1. ob der wertheimische Dolmetscher von der Göttlichkeit der biblischen Bücher, und der geoffenbarten Religion eine schlimme Meynung geheget habe oder nicht? 2. wie viel Grund er zu seiner Übersetzung und zu den Sätzen seiner Vorrede gehabt habe?" ([H. S. Reimarus:] „Anmerkung zu der vorigen Rechtfertigung", in: *Hamburgische Berichte von gelehrten Sachen*, N. II, January 6th, 1736, pp. 12–18, quotation on p. 12)

[29] „nicht einsehen kan, warum nicht ein verkapter Collin, Woolston und Tindal eben dieses schreiben könnte?" (Ibid.)

[30] „Nun wil wol weiter kein rechtfertigen helfen, daß man nicht offenbar sehen solte, wie sich eins zum andern schicke, wie eins mit Fleis um des andern Willen gesetzet, und deswegen schwach vorgestellet sey, damit das andere desto stärker scheine. Folglich ist offenbar, welche Meinung der Wertheimische Dolmetscher von den biblischen Büchern und deren Inhalt hege. Und brauche ich daher nicht, solches aus besondern Stellen seiner Übersetzung noch weiter zu erhärten." (Ibid., p. 15)

second edition of his polemical booklet *Religionsspötter*,[31] which was sent
to theologians as well as to rulers and chancellors in order to convince
them all of the danger of the translation and the urgent need to suppress
it. That Lange succeeded becomes clear from the files on the *Wertheim
Bible* at the court of Saxonia[32] and at the Court of Vienna,[33] which include
the *Religionsspötter*. The documents in the appendix to the second edition
include the papers that gave evidence and justified the ban on the book
and the persecution of the author. This was very likely the case as well in
the Court of Berlin. Thus, Reimarus' first review became not only a part
of the public debate, but also a part of the call for banning the *Wertheim
Bible* and persecuting the author, simply because he declared the bad and
hostile intentions of the author's translation.

Reimarus answers his second question about the reasons for the whole
enterprise of a new translation even more harshly: "In the whole thing
there is no proof at all."[34] Continuing at first to question the character of
the author,[35] he admits at least that the correctness of the opinion of the
translator would need to be more fully examined. Then he touches on a
crucial point of the whole discussion, saying: If the translator should hold
the opinion that he is not obliged to believe anybody about anything he
could not conceive as possible and which could not be proved from the
truths known to him, such a principle has to be rejected.

Nevertheless, concerning the translation itself (except the problematic
passages), Reimarus praises its quite good German language and also adds
the remark that an expert could well see in particular passages how the
translator had approached his translation. But the still orthodox scholar
denies that the translator had given any proof for his translation, in spite

---

[31] Joachim Lange, *Der philosophische Religionsspötter* (Halle, 2nd. ed. 1736).

[32] Cf. Sächsisches Hauptstaatsarchiv Dresden. *Acta, Die Übersetzung einer teutschen
Bibel, welche zu Wertheim herausgekommen und was dem anhängig betr. Oberconsistorium,
anno 1736.* Confisc. 10742, No. 7, 13r–45v. – See also 46r–51r.

[33] The Prussian deputies Graeve and Brand on June 27th, 1736 from Vienna to King
Friedrich Wilhelm I., presented to him on July 4th 1736. In: Geheimes Staatsarchiv Preußis-
che Kulturbesitz Berlin-Dahlem: HA I, Rep. 13, Nr. 29, Fasz. 19, d. 14. Martii 1738. *Acta betref-
fend die sogen. Wertheimische Biblische Übersetzung* [this file is not paginated].

[34] „Beweis ist in diesen allem gar nicht." ([H. S. Reimarus:] „Anmerkung zu der vorigen
Rechtfertigung", in: *Hamburgische Berichte von gelehrten Sachen*, N. II, January 6th, 1736,
pp. 12–18, quotation on p. 15)

[35] „wir sind scharfsinnige Gelehrte, unsere Wiedersacher können uns nicht antworten,
wir haben schon den Sieg." (Ibid., p. 16)

of more than 1600 footnotes, to say nothing of the problematic and disputed passages traditionally read as prophecies.[36]

REIMARUS' SECOND CONTRIBUTION

The second review of Reimarus in the *Hamburgische Berichte* appears on October 23, 1736. It is the leading article of that issue and discusses Schmidt's *Beantwortung verschiedener Einwürfe, welche von einigen Gottesgelehrten gegen die freie Übersetzung der götlichen Schriften sind gemacht worden* [Answer to various objections made by some theologians against his translation].[37] A footnote by the editor makes it clear that the author of this review is the same as that of the earlier review of the translation itself. But what a different approach! This time it is an objective discussion of the arguments of Schmidt, sometimes highly critical, but with no suspicion of any hostile intention.

Reimarus begins the review with a quite objective presentation of the first paragraphs of Schmidt's *Beantwortung*, though still annoyed about the self-confidence of the translator.[38] When he comes to discuss the attempt of Schmidt to save the prophecies of Jesus Christ by metaphorical interpretation of the written words according to an oral tradition, he asks why the translator can now take the word of Jesus Christ in the New Testament for granted.[39] According to him, taking Schmidt's preconditions seriously can only make it probable and not at all certain. Then he discusses the Wolffian terminology as used by Schmidt: the concepts of being necessary, possible, certain, uncertain, probable. Thus, taking up Schmidt's own approach, he criticises him from an immanent point of view. At first he objects that the significance of a word is not necessary simply because of its context. Therefore, the use of a word could not be an inevitable reason for a certain translation, as another use remains always possible. That would be particularly true in the case of a dead language where the particular use of a word could no longer be shown. Beyond that, it is the constellation of words which points to each determined use of the word

---

[36] The continuation of Reimarus' review in: *Hamburgische Berichte von Gelehrten Sachen auf das Jahr 1736*, January 10th 1736, N. III, pp. 17–18.

[37] *Hamburgische Berichte von gelehrten Sachen*. October 23rd 1736. Nr. 85, pp. 761–773.

[38] The objective presentation of the first six paragraphes of the *Beantwortung* can be found ibid., pp. 761–764.

[39] Ibid., p. 764.

and therefore to the concepts. Reimarus discusses this explicitly by means
of the example of the snake in Genesis 3,1–15. He comes to the conclusion that the snake in that passage could not have been a common snake,
simply because it spoke. Being already adult, Adam and Eve must have
realized the uncommon character of that snake. Reimarus concludes that
this allows the translation of the passage to go beyond the understanding
of a mere natural snake and justifies a metaphorical interpretation.

Concerning the oral tradition, which was rejected and criticized by
many theologians during this public debate, Reimarus is very open and
declares explicitly:

> I am not one who disputes the claim of the author according to which an
> oral explanation took place *or was even necessary* in order to get a distinct
> knowledge of what they [the Jews] could see themselves, although rather
> obscure because the concepts are not sufficiently determined by the words.
> But how could they themselves determine and restrict the concepts which
> lay in undetermined words, if they had not either got in advance by means
> of oral teachings, concepts capable of determining the meaning of the unde-
> termined words, or if they had not received some more oral teachings from
> Moses, and from the priests and Levites?[40]

Thus, Reimarus appeals, as Schmidt had already done, to various authorities to justify this oral tradition, although he presents his explanation in
itself as quite evident.

But the most interesting expression of Reimarus' change of mind, con-
fronting the intentions of the translator as well as the acknowledgment
of the main principle of the whole translation, is the following sentence:
"Thus, if Mr. Wertheimer [sic!] writes for those who do not yet believe in
the Scriptures I do not reprove him for not expressing more than the words
themselves say."[41] By saying that, Reimarus declares clearly his agreement
with the general approach of the translation of the *Wertheim Bible*. When
writing for non-believers one is justified in maintaining the literal meaning of the words and in disregarding the power of faith. And he did so in

---

[40] „Ich bin dahero nicht derienige, der dem Hn. Verfasser streitig machet, daß bei
diesem allen eine mündliche Erklärung stat gefunden, *ja nöthig gewesen sey*, zum deutli-
chern Erkentnis dessen, was sie mit einiger Dunkelheit in den Worten selbst sehen konten.
Dan die Begriffe sind durch diese Worte nicht genug bestimt. Wie wäre es aber möglich,
daß sie die Begriffe, so in unbestimten Worten liegen, selber bestimmen und einschränken
könten, wan sie nicht entweder vorher schon bestimte Begriffe durch mündlichen Unterricht bekommen hätten, welche aufzuwecken unbestimte Wörter zureichten, oder wan sie
nicht nach dem Lesen hätte mehrern mündlichen Unterricht bei Mose, bei den Priestern
und Leviten einziehen können." (Ibid., my emphasis – U.G.)

[41] Ibid., pp. 771–772.

a public newspaper in late October 1736, when the most important territories had already banned the book! He openly admits that the words of the Pentateuch do not include in themselves any prophecy of Jesus Christ.

Reimarus continues, though, by criticizing the inconsistency that he sees in the strict application of this principle on the one hand and on the other hand of the justification of the prophecies by oral tradition alone. Although he agrees with the assumption of an oral tradition in general, he finds the solution of Schmidt insufficient to bear the whole burden of the prophecies. It seems to be arbitrary to justify them:

> But beside that which is wrong in itself I reject what follows. The translator determines and restricts the concepts in his interpretation and translation in such a way that they no longer mean what they indeed mean in themselves. He takes away all the light of the Gospel from the words, because they lack clarity and distinctness, and takes away all the light from the oral teachings, because we cannot do without it. I reject his claim that the words could not at all mean what Christian doctrine says. Therefore he begins by making out Christ and the Apostles to be liars who [wrongly] refer to the words of Moses, and then does not know any other way to present the Christian doctrine than to presuppose the testimony of Christ and the Apostles to be sacrosanct. But this will not be admitted by any mocker [of religion]. And what will the mockers think of the Old Testament itself when they hear of Moses introducing a naturally talking snake as the cause of all the evil in the world? Nobody thinks that way of Aesop, but are we willing to represent Moses in such a way?[42]

Although this sounds highly critical, the review tackles substantial problems of the translation and of Christian theology in general. Reimarus acknowledges the sincere motives of Schmidt and comes to see the real problems of the translation. He discusses the argument of "Mr. Wertheimer" and takes him to be a serious scholar. It is ironic that

---

[42] „Aber das tadele ich, ausser dem, was an sich falsch ist, daß er die Begriffe auf der andern Seite in seiner Auslegung und Übersetzung so bestimt und einschränket, daß sie nunmehr das nicht bedeuten, was sie in der Taht in sich fassen: daß er den Worten alles Licht des Evangelii abspricht, weil sie nicht alle Klarheit und Deutlichkeit haben; hingegen alles von dem mündlichen Unterricht herholet, weil derselbe nicht gänzlich zu entbehren war. Daß er behauptet, die Worte könten das, was die christliche Lehre sagt, unmöglich bedeuten; folglich Christum und die Apostel, die sich auf Mosis Worte berufen, erst zu Lügnern macht, und darnach doch keinen andern Weg weis die christliche Lehre darzutuhn; als Christi und der Apostel Zeugnis als unverwerflich vorauszusetzen, welches ihm ia kein Spötter zugestehen wird. Und was sollen Spötter vom alten Testament selbst denken, wan sie hören Moses führe eine natürliche Schlange redend ein, und die sey der Grund alles bösen in der Welt gewesen? Niemand denkt so von Aesopo, und wir wollen Mosen so vorstellen?" (Ibid., pp. 771–772)

the critical questions he raises here are just those which he will soon have to answer himself. Actually, these questions, raised to Johann Lorenz Schmidt, might even have started his complete change of mind at that time. Peter Stemmer has already pointed to the fact: "Reimarus entered the critical field in 1736 at the latest and put himself on the side of the 'Wertheimer' by throwing away the principles of his 1731 lecture. There he still followed the orthodox tradition and outlined a hermeneutics which was valid for the Biblical books alone."[43]

What Caused His Change of Mind?

Something changed Reimarus' mind. It is very likely that this was due to the great efforts of Johann Lorenz Schmidt and his supporters at Wertheim to refute the accusation of Lange concerning his hostile intentions. Realizing the great danger of Lange's raised suspicions about his allegedly bad intention within the framework of the Elenchus, enabling his enemies to cause his persecution by the state and to sue him, Schmidt had already made a trustworthy confession in his *Vestgefügte Wahrheit* [The well-founded Truth] in the spring of 1736 that he was a true Lutheran according to the Confession of Augsburg. But together with his supporters at Wertheim, he also explored the opportunity to gain support from the political institution of the Corpus Evangelicorum at the Diet in Regensburg, delivering his *Öffentliche Erklärung* [Public Declaration] to all the deputies. This again included a great Lutheran confession. He even asked the deputies for the protection of his right as a Lutheran according to the Westphalian Peace guaranteeing his freedom to interpret the Holy Scriptures according to the best of his knowledge and conscience. Both writings were very convincing to contemporaries who were open-minded enough to look at them. They also made a great emotional impression.

Whereas the *Vestgefügte Wahrheit* appeared early enough to get reviews and to become known among interested people (and they were many more than just scholars), the *Öffentliche Erklärung* was delivered only to the deputies of the Diet. Nevertheless, it became well known

---

[43] „Reimarus hat spätestens 1736 kritischen Boden betreten und sich mit der Verwerfung grundlegender Prinzipien seiner Vorlesung von 1731, in der er der orthodoxen Tradition gefolgt war und eine nur für die biblischen Bücher gültige Hermeneutik entworfen hatte, auf die Seite des Wertheimers gestellt." (Stemmer, *Weissagung und Kritik* (see footnote 2), p. 137; see also pp. 102–146)

through another new form of public media, the "Historical Reports" of the *Wertheim Bible* and its author. As had already been argued by Johann Peter Kohl to Joachim Lange, the authors of these "Historical Reports" wanted simply to report about the ongoing events within the academic arena without taking sides. That kind of report was acknowledged as legitimate and possible without producing the troubles caused by censorship. About four kinds of such "Historical Reports" of the public debate on the *Wertheim Bible* and the fate of its author started to appear in the very end of 1736, clearly signalling the great and continuing public interest in this ongoing debate.[44] Although the authors all expressed their distance from the work and its author, they reviewed the recent writings about it, counted the bans, reported the situation of Johann Lorenz Schmidt and the ongoing negotiations about the process, and finally about his escape. Also, they repeatedly presented his confession as a Lutheran and reported the struggles between the Catholic and Protestant Courts regarding the place of the process. Counting on the solidarity of fellow Lutherans and the Protestant suspicion of Catholics in general, these "Historical Reports" raised a kind of regret and compassion for Schmidt that then raised an even more intense interest in the whole development of the *Wertheim Bible* itself than before. The *Öffentliche Erklärung*, as well as other published writings of Schmidt and his opponents, were reported in detail or even presented as excerpts.

Reimarus was definitely not the only contemporary who finally became convinced of the sincere intention of Schmidt concerning the Christian religion during the public debate on the *Wertheim Bible* in 1736. Mosheim,[45]

---

[44] See Goldenbaum, "Der Skandal der Wertheimer Bibel" (see footnote 7), chap. 29 on the „Historical News" i.e. the reports about the development of the affair, pp. 451–482; *Acta historico-ecclesiastica, oder gesammlete Nachrichten von den neuesten Kirchenberichten.* Weimar 1736 ff. [Editor: Johann C. Colerus, since 1736 Wilhelm Ernst and Johann Christian Bartholomaei] – Part 1, Appendix to vol. 1, 1736, pp. 1–105; vol. 2. Part 7 (1737), pp. 145–172; part 8 (1737), pp. 281–310; part 9 (1737), pp. 480–496; part 10 (1738), pp. 608–663; part 11 (1738), pp. 835–849; part 12 (1738), pp. 1000–1015; 2. vol.: *Anhang zu den Actis historico-ecclesiasticis.* 1738, pp. 1038–1152; 3. vol., part 13 (1738): „Weitere Nachricht von den itzigen Streitigkeiten wegen der wertheimischen Bibel", pp. 136–156; part 16, 1739, pp. 620–631; part 17 (1739), pp. 781–795; 4. vol. Appendix. Weimar 1740, pp. 1140–1144. – Johann Nicolaus Sinnhold, *Ausführliche Historie der verruffenen sogenannten Wertheimischen Bibel, oder derjenigen freyen Übersetzung der fünf Bücher Mosis, welche unter dem Titel: Die Göttlichen Schriften vor den Zeiten des Messie Jesus: Der erste Theil: worinne die Gesetze der Jisraelen enthalten sind; im Jahr 1735. zu Wertheim gedruckt worden* (Erfurt: Nonne, 1739).

[45] „Was Derselbe zur Erklärung der Vorrede und des darin gefälleten Urtheils über das Schicksal der heil. Schrift sowohl in der Vertheidigung gegen Hn. D. Langen, als in der Schrift an das hochlöbl. evangelische Corpus beygebracht haben, benimmt mir allen bösen

Reinbeck,[46] Fröreisen,[47] and later on even Siegmund Jacob Baumgarten expressed explicitly their conviction that the translator might have been in error about some or many points, but was driven by a sincere intention to save the Christian religion. That all these expert theologians recognized the sincere intentions of the "Wertheimer," although aware of the difficulties and dangerous consequences of the translation, is certainly an expression of the convincing character of the public confessions of Johann Lorenz Schmidt during the years 1735 and 1736. If their opinion had been acknowledged by the rulers, no persecution would have been justified at all, according to the rules of the Elenchus! But none of these experts dared to express this conviction to the public, except in private letters to the "Wertheimer" or much later. We have a very late testimony of regret and a feeling of guilt from Jacob Siegmund Baumgarten who wrote much later about the persecution of Schmidt:

> Comparison of the writings and counter-writings makes it clear that I went much too far in respect of the author, especially with the accusation of mockery of the Christian religion [this goes against Lange's *Religionsspötter*!]. He speaks with great awe and respect of the Bible and restricts his interpretation to the determined meaning of the words, after the prejudices [sic! – earlier judgments?] of Grotius and others, rather than being suspicious of them. Therefore, his intention may have been better than his writing actually turned out to be.[48]

Argwohn." (Mosheim to Schmidt on April 26, 1736. In: Johann Rudolph Schlegel, *Johann Lorenz von Mosheims Kirchengeschichte des Neuen Testaments aus desselben gesammten grössern Werken [...] bis auf die neuesten Zeiten fotgesetzet. Sechster und letzter Bd., welcher den Rest der Geschichte des achtzehnten Jahrhunderts enthält* (Heilbronn: Eckebrechtsche Buchhandlung, 1788), p. XXII)

[46] Reinbeck demands still in his Introduction to the Third Part of the *Betrachtungen zur Augsburger Confession* that it is "appropriate to listen to him [Schmidt] [billig, daß wir ihn hören]." (Cf. *Sammlung*, p. 266)

[47] Fröreisen's objective though critical letter to Schmidt on the *Wertheim Bible* was published as an excerpt within the *Gründliche Vorstellung* [Profound Presentation (cf. *Acta historio-ecclesiastica*. Vol. 2, Part 10, pp. 608–663, esp. p. 655). It can also be found in full in Schmidt's introduction to his *Samlung* (without page numbering) which caused some troubles for the theologian at the university of Straßburg. He had to recant. Cf. the chap. 26 on Fröreisen in: Goldenbaum, "Der Skandal der Wertheimer Bibel" (see footnote 7), pp. 421–434.

[48] „Aus Vergleichung dieser Schriften und Gegenschriften erhellet augenscheinlich, daß man dem Verfasser in einigen Stücken zu viel gethan habe, sonderlich durch Beschuldigung seiner Arbeit einer Religionsspötterey. Er redet mit zu vieler Ehrfurcht und Achtung von der Bibel, und schrenket seine Auslegung blos allein auf den, nach Grotii und anderer Vorurtheilen, bestimten Wortverstand ein, als daß er in diesen Verdacht fallen solte. Seine Absicht kan daher besser gewesen seyn, als seine Schrift wirklich geraten". ([Siegmund Jacob Baumgarten:] *Nachricht von einer Hallischen Bibliothek*. Vol. 1ff. Gebauer: Halle 1748ff.,

While published after the deaths of Joachim Lange and Johann Lorenz Schmidt, it remains cautious because it was written for publication. Baumgarten had been one of the earliest, though rather moderate and objective critics of Schmidt, especially when compared with Joachim Lange, his chair at Halle.[49] Nevertheless, he had signed the denunciation the theologians of the University of Halle, together with all the other Faculty members, sent to the Court in Berlin to ban the book and to persecute the author in early 1736.[50] Mosheim, Reinbeck, Wolff, and Fröreisen expressed their acknowledgement of his good intentions toward Schmidt or Höflein but did not dare to publish it. Only against this background can one measure the great significance of the publication of the second review by Reimarus of Schmidt's *Beantwortung*.

But as mentioned above, the year 1736 was also the year of a great public debate about the Wolffian philosophy. Joachim Lange was trying very hard to connect the persecution of the *Wertheim Bible* with that of his arch-enemy, arguing that the translation would be the necessary result of the Wolffian philosophy, which had to be forbidden as well. The *Royal Commission* was installed at the Court in Berlin, at the request of Joachim Lange, designed to prove his accusations against the Wolffian philosophy. The announcement of the Commission by the King was celebrated by Lange in his newspaper at Halle as the approaching final victory over his arch-enemy Wolff. It was rather a surprise when the names of the members of the Commission became known to the public. They were all quite moderate theologians, among them Reinbeck. With the rising expectation of their positive judgment, Kohl at the *Hamburgische Berichte* seems to have anticipated the beginning of a thaw. He published a full issue of the newspaper in favour of the *Wertheim Bible* and its author on June 8th 1736.[51] Nothing but the *Wertheim Bible!* It was like a celebration of the first anniversary of the publication of the book.

In early June, the Royal Commission concluded that the Wolffian philosophy did not involve any violation or danger for the Christian religion and even recommended Wolff's *German Logic* to all Prussian universities, constituting a triumph for the Wolffians and a total defeat for

---

vol. 8 (1751), pp. 1–10 (Die göttlichen Schriften) as well as pp. 10–18 (Samlung derienigen Schriften), quotation on pp. 17–18)

[49] Cf. Siegmund Jacob Baumgarten, *Diss. de dictis Scripturae Sacrae probantibus* (Halle Nov. 1735).

[50] Cf. Archive of the Franckesche Stiftungen at Halle, C 722:14–18.

[51] Cf. *Hamburgische Berichte*. Nr. 46. June 8th 1736, pp. 417–424 (!).

Joachim Lange's party. Nevertheless, at the same time, the King banned the *Wertheim Bible* and delivered the denunciation of Johann Lorenz Schmidt to the Court in Vienna, initiating the persecution of Schmidt by the Emperor. The public space for debate on the book shrank again and threatened to disappear entirely very soon. But it was in October of 1736 that the review by Reimarus of Schmidt's *Beantwortung* appeared in the *Hamburgische Berichte*. No thaw anymore for the "Wertheimer" at all!

Nevertheless, Reimarus discusses the arguments of Schmidt against his critics as if no persecution was occurring at all. He had definitely worked through the whole book and was honouring the scholarly behaviour of "Mr. Wertheimer" by taking his arguments seriously, although criticizing them. It is indeed admirable to see how Schmidt, even under the threat of persecution, was committed to his scholarly project, answering the criticisms seriously and ignoring all slander. His *Beantwortung* appeared in the early autumn of 1736. Although the public debate became smaller and smaller since the first ban in Saxonia, his book brought together again all the meaningful arguments that had come up during the public debate after the publication of Reimarus' first review. Thus, it gave surprising evidence that, although most of the published writings were simply slanders and suspicions of the author and his hostile intentions, many serious statements of critical but reasonable theologians and scholars had appeared, as single booklets, as a chapter in a book, or in articles, such as within the Deutsche *Acta eruditorum*. Although nobody within the realm of the influence of Joachim Lange was eager to be seen as a supporter of the disputed book and its translator but rather glad to criticize, there was some serious and meaningful criticism among them, i.e. including argument. Given the ocean of slanderous writings denouncing Schmidt, he was obviously glad to answer these meaningful criticisms of his methods and his approach to the translation. The book still deserves to be read for its many interesting arguments concerning language in general and translation in particular. Schmidt also added and answered an unpublished manuscript he had received from the members of the German Society in Leipzig. It concerned the translation of texts from dead languages.[52] In his introduction, he informed the readers of the many letters he had received from learned scholars discussing his translation critically but respectfully.

---

[52] Cf. also Goldenbaum, „Der Skandal der Wertheimer Bibel" (see footnote 7), chap. 22 on the extended discussion of translation in the *Beyträge zu einer Critischen Historie der deutschen Sprache, Poesie und Beredsamkeit*, edited by the Deutsche Gesellschaft at Leipzig, pp. 371–385.

Although he did not want to drag them into his own case of persecution, this information was convincing evidence for the existence of other learned men who took the project of Schmidt seriously and cared about the problems and their solution.

If we ask for the cause of Reimarus' total change of mind we will have to consider all these events and publications together: the wave of persecution because of the allegedly hostile intentions, the serious declaration by the "Wertheimer" of adherence to the Confession of Augsburg, the restricted though still ongoing discussion of the issues of the translation, the courageous behaviour and committed striving after truth by the "Wertheimer", and last but not least the newspapers and the Historical Reports that reported all these events.

The publication of Reimarus' second review in the *Hamburgische Berichte* at this time required personal courage. He might have been impressed by the strong behaviour and striving after truth of Schmidt himself, once he had realised his sincere intentions. Also, I think it is not an exaggeration to assume that he felt a kind of guilt about his first review. It was known to everybody that it had become a part of the second edition of Lange's *Religionsspötter*, thus directly serving the persecution of Schmidt. His second review demonstrated to the educated community within the Protestant area of the Empire that Reimarus did not belong to the party of Joachim Lange and no longer demanded persecution. But above all, it seems at this point that Reimarus was definitely caught by the questions and problems raised by the public discussion of the *Wertheim Bible*. He was infected by the fever of a new investigation and was on his own journey to seek a solution in order to avoid a catastrophe – the falling apart of the Old and New Testament.

Reimarus' review is the last extended statement on that topic which appears in any newspaper. The response of Schmidt to Reimarus, sent to Hamburg on November 28, 1736, was not published in this newspaper. It is likely that the ban of the Emperor had already occurred when Kohl was still debating how to justify its publication. After that ban it became impossible to write explicitly in favour of the *Wertheim Bible* within the Empire. Schmidt's answer appeared within his final collection of critical papers and his answers to them in the *Sammlung*, also published in Wertheim, in 1738, and then sold by a bookstore in Hamburg.[53] It is

---

[53] Cf. Spalding, *Seize the Book* (see footnote 21), pp. 182–184.

listed in the library of Reimarus, as are the *Wertheim Bible* itself and the *Beantwortung*.

Not much is written or known about Johann Lorenz Schmidt. There exists an old rumour in the literature about a personal encounter or even a continuing relationship between Schmidt and Reimarus during Schmidt's stay in Altona from 1738 to 1747.[54] Recently, Almut and Paul Spalding made personal contact between the two men highly probable.[55] Given the learned interest or even obsession of these two men with the very same theoretical problems, their rare familiarity with the Hebrew text of the Old Testament, their general theological scholarship as well as their studies of the English Deists (and very likely of Spinoza), such a contact seems to me indeed inevitable. It would rather be surprising if they had not got into contact, living so close together in Hamburg and Altona. Such a contact could easily be mediated by Johann Peter Kohl, who was already in correspondence with the chancellor Höflein at Wertheim, and who took care as much as possible to support Schmidt even in his exile.[56] But above all, it is proven by Spalding that Schmidt could not have obtained a position at the Court of Wolfenbüttel without the support of some influential personalities in Hamburg.[57]

However, the encounter of the famous scholar Reimarus with the young but learned and committed "Mr. Wertheimer", Johann Lorenz Schmidt, became a turning point in the intellectual development of Reimarus, even if the two men never met in person. But it was not the mere reading of the *Wertheim Bible* that changed the mind of Reimarus. Otherwise his first review would have looked different. His fundamental change of mind can be understood only by taking into account the whole public debate between 1735 and 1736, including scholarly publication, as well as

---

[54] Cf. David Friedrich Strauss has – according to Stemmer (see the following footnote) – at first discussed the possibility of a personal contact. Cf. Strauss, *Hermann Samuel Reimarus und seine Schutzschrift für die vernünftigen Verehrer Gottes* (Leipzig, 1862), p. 26; Mönckeberg takes it for granted without giving evidence, but might have known of papers in the private archive of the family of Reimarus. Cf. C. Mönckeberg, *Hermann Samuel Reimarus und Johann Christian Edelmann* (Hamburg, 1867), p. 58. Stemmer, *Weissagung und Kritik* (see footnote 2) mentions in a long footnote these sources and the way the rumour circulated. See footnote 3 on pp. 144–145.

[55] Cf. Almut and Paul Spalding, „Der rätselhafte Tutor bei Hermann Samuel Reimarus: Begegnung zweier radikaler Aufklärer in Hamburg", *Zeitschrift des Vereins für Hamburgische Geschichte* 87 (2001), pp. 49–64.

[56] A. and P. Spalding also name other people who, very likely or even definitely, supported Schmidt in finding a permanent position. See pp. 51–54.

[57] Cf. Spalding, *Seize the Book* (see footnote 21), pp. 194–212.

the development of the persecution and the public "Historical reports" about it. Only when Reimarus started to believe in the sincere intentions of the "Wertheimer" to save the Christian religion within the development of this public debate did he open his mind and become committed to the project initiated by Schmidt. By taking up and working on this project he eventually transcended it in order to found Deism.

REIMARUS, THE CARDINAL, AND THE REMAKING OF CASSIUS DIO'S *ROMAN HISTORY*[1]

Ulrich Groetsch

In December 1746, a notably exasperated Reimarus wrote a disgruntled letter to his longtime correspondent and benefactor Cardinal Angelo Maria Querini,[2] Archbishop of Brescia and head of the *Bibliotheca Vaticana*. Querini had just informed him that Nicolaus Carminius Falco,[3] who was then Archbishop of Naples, was planning to publish his new edition of Cassius Dio's *Roman History* – a project, Reimarus thought, that Falco had long abandoned:

> I admit that nothing has caught me more by surprise than that after twenty-two years of silence this famous man has set out to fulfil his promise [...]. For more than three years now, if I am not mistaken, you have not only publicly made mention of my Dio project, but you have even presented yourself thus far as a great supporter of it, if I may not even say eulogist of the cause: why did [Falco] not approach you? Why did he not revive [in public] the already nearly extinct and buried awareness of his work?[4]

But why did this matter spark such indignation in Reimarus?

In order to grasp the depth and significance of this issue, we need to change the entire scene back to an earlier point in Reimarus' life, when on 30 April 1736, at the age of sixty-eight, Reimarus' famous mentor,

---

[1] I am grateful to Anthony Grafton, Donald R. Kelley, Robin Ladrach, Karl F. Morrison, Martin Mulsow, Gary Rendsburg, Wilhelm Schmidt-Biggemann, Azzan Yadin, and Leon Wash for their comments and suggestions.

[2] On Querini see Alfred Breithaupt, *De Cardinalis Querini Vita et Operibus* (Paris, 1889); Gino Benzoni, ed., *Cultura Religione e Politica nell'età di Angelo Maria Querini* (Brescia, 1980); recently also Ennio Ferraglio, *Libri, biblioteche e raro sapere: carteggio tra Angelo Maria Querini e Girolamo Tartarotti, 1745–1755* (Verona, 2003).

[3] On Falco see *Archivio Biografico Italiano*, I 390, pp. 50–60.

[4] *Fondazione Querini Stampalia* (VQS). Ms. 257, Reimarus to Angelo Maria Querini, 10 December 1746: "Fateor, nihil magis praeter expectationem meam accidisse, quam hoc, quod post duorum et viginti annorum silentium, Vir Clarissimus exequi promissa instituerit [...]. Quando enim iam ante triennium, ni fallor, Dionis mei non tantum mentionem publice fecisti, sed patronum Te adeo magnum et adiutorem, ne dicam laudatorem, causae praebuisti: cur non scripsit ad Te? cur memoriam suae operae iam prope extinctam et sepultam, non renovavit?"

benefactor, and father-in-law, the humanist Johann Albert Fabricius died.[5]
While the entire scholarly community mourned this loss, learned Europe's
gaze remained focused intently on Hamburg. As quickly as the news of
his death spread, so did also the interest in what would happen to the
treasure of books, manuscripts, and papers that the learned man had so
diligently gathered, and that was now for sale. The task of compiling the
auction catalogue and of responding to unanswered correspondence fell
to his trusted son-in-law Reimarus.

The practical and psychological effects of Fabricius' death upon Reimarus were profound. As Anne Goldgar has noted in her splendid portrayal of the Republic of Letters, "the scattered residence of scholars, the
unavailability of books, the difficulty of travel, and the sometimes mystify-
ing nature of the book trade" were substantial factors in determining the
success or failure of its citizens, depending on location and to whomever
they were connected.[6] Reimarus thus lost in 1736 not only a mentor and
friend, but also an important resource. No longer would he be able to
venture across the street of the *Gymnasium illustre* where he worked and
drop by Fabricius' house to borrow a copy of a book or a manuscript,
receive an update on recent publications and gossip, or be introduced to
some famous scholar passing through Hamburg. Nonetheless, Fabricius'
death also presented a new opportunity. Since he was entrusted with both
compiling the auction catalogue and answering unfulfilled requests, Reimarus was able to remain at an important intersection within the Republic of Letters, and as we shall see, following in the footsteps of his famous
father-in-law, establish his own learned network. So in October 1736 we
find Reimarus writing a response to an earlier letter by Cardinal Querini.
The Cardinal, who as Archbishop of Brescia was still very connected with
his city's history, was at that time working on a series of editions of the
ancient fathers of the Brescian church. Already in 1721, Fabricius himself
had published an edition of a work by one of them, Philastrius' *De Haeresibus liber*,[7] and the Cardinal was asking whether, since the publication

---

[5] Johann Albert Fabricius (1668–1736); see Erik Petersen, *Johann Albert Fabricius: En
Humanist I Europa*, 2 vols. (Copenhagen, 1998).

[6] Anne Goldgar, *Impolite Learning: Conduct and Community in the Republic of Letters,
1680–1750* (New Haven, 1995), p. 13.

[7] Philastrius, *De Haeresibus liber cum emendationibus et notis J. A. Fabricii* (Hamburg,
1721); see Letter Querini to Fabricius, 19 July 1736, Royal Library Copenhagen, Fabr. 104–123:
"Peto preaterea ab humanitas tua, ut mecum communicare dignetur secundas curas, si
quas in promptu habet, ad locus petandam Editionem S. Philatrii, quam Brixia adorniamus
una cum Editione SS. Gaudentiis Adelmannis et Lamperti, quippe qui in animum induxi,

of this edition, Fabricius had subsequently added notes in the margins of his own copy that he might be willing to share with a new edition.[8] Reimarus found little among Fabricius' papers to satisfy this particular request, but he was able to send Querini a number of references and some Syriac excerpts by the fourth-century Syrian Christian writer St. Ephrem, also a former Bishop of the Cardinal's native city.[9] The Cardinal was apparently so pleased with Reimarus' response that in return he offered him the Vatican Library as a resource for the future. This offer, however innocently it may have been scribbled down then, was the beginning of an intensive correspondence between both men that spanned a period of almost twenty years. None of these letters have been known thus far or have been evaluated vis-à-vis Reimarus' work or intellectual development. But they prove incredibly revealing and full of insights. As a result of this correspondence, Reimarus established himself as a scholar par excellence and first-class Graecist, whose work left a mark on the map of the *Respublica literaria* and who no longer stood in the shadow of his famous mentor Fabricius.[10]

While sifting through the papers of the deceased, Reimarus came across extensive notes on Cassius Dio's *Historia Romana*, which he must have remembered from the time when Fabricius was still alive. Aware of their value but also of their need for revision and with the Cardinal's offer fresh in his mind, Reimarus jumped at the opportunity and sent another letter

---

eum eximium Ecclesia mea decas sit, quatuor ex antiquis episcopis suis tam doctrina quam sanctitate florentes ostendare, eorum Opera unico volumine, eoque satis magnifico complecti."

[8] VQS. Ms. 257, Reimarus to Angelo Maria Querini, 15 October 1736: "Litterae ab Eminentia Tua scriptae ad Fabricium, mihi genero post eius obitum, quamquam serius, redditae sunt; in quibus video desiderari posteriores Fabricii ad Philastrium curas, et quae ille de textu Syriaco S. Ephraimi recens competa habeat [...]."

[9] According to his letter, Reimarus was able to make these excerpts from the Slavonic Codex, which the famous polyhistor and former professor of church history at the Imperial Academy of St. Petersburg, Johann Peter Kohl (1698–1778) provided. Following a rumour of his secret relationship with the future Empress Elizabeth, Kohl was dismissed in 1728, but granted a pension. He spent the rest of his life in both Hamburg and Altona. According to Erik Petersen's records, Kohl was already corresponding with Fabricius and, though no records exist, Reimarus may have made Kohl's acquaintance through his father-in-law. On Kohl, see ADB, vol. 16, p. 425; see also Petersen, *Johann Albert Fabricius*, vol. 2, p. 932.

[10] The first footnote in the unabridged version of Gibbon's monumental *The History of the Decline and Fall of the Roman Empire* for example reads: "Dion Cassius [...] with the annotations of Reimar, who has collected all that Roman vanity has left upon the subject [...]," see Edward Gibbon, *The History of the Decline and Fall of the Roman Empire*," ed. J. B. Bury, vol. 1 (London, 1905), p. 2. I am particularly grateful to Martin Mulsow for pointing this out to me.

to the Vatican, asking for help in this undertaking and more specifically for collations from two Dio manuscripts that were stored in the Vatican library:

> [...] I shall ask from You, Most Eminent Cardinal, boldly and openly, that you undertake without any hesitation the collation of these Vatican codices, which the revered Nicolaus Carminius Falco mentions. Just as friends have informed me that a new edition of Dio could hardly be expected from him anymore, I have at the same time the extensive and learned notes of my father-in-law on the same author in my hands, which are assuredly not unworthy of publication, if by your kindness it is granted to me to polish this same author by relying on old manuscripts. I would then have almost everything to whichever edition a collation might be made, since I own all [editions] that exist.[11]

A new critical edition of Dio's work was highly desirable, especially since the *editio princeps* of 1548 by Robert Estienne[12] was based upon a single, faulty codex, and the Latin translations by Wilhelm Xylander[13] and

---

[11] VQS. Ms. 257, Letter Reimarus to Querini, 29 February 1737: "[...] Ipse, Amplissime Cardinalis, petam abs Te audacter et libere, Dionis nimicrum Cassii ut collationem ad Codices Vaticanos institui haud gravatim cures, quos memorat Rev. Nicolaus Carminius Falco. Nam ut Dionis editionem novam ab illo vix sperandam esse retulerunt amici, ita Soceri mei notas in eundem Scriptorem amplas et eruditas habeo in manibus, luce profecto non indignas, si ipsum auctorem fide veterum membranarum expolire Tuo beneficio daretur. Perinde autem mihi fuerit, ad quam editionem collatio instituat[a], quoniam eas quae extant possideo propemodum omn[ia]."

[12] ΤΩΝ ΔΙΟΝΟΣ ΡΟΜΑΙΚΩΝ ΙΣΤΟΡΙΩΝ ΕΙΚΟΣΙΤΡΙΑ ΒΙΒΛΙΑ. *Dionis Romanarum historiarum libri XXIII, à XXXVI ad LVIII usque.* Ex Bibliotheca Regia (Paris, 1548); on Robert Estienne see Elizabeth Armstrong, *Robert Estienne Royal Printer: An Historical Study of the Elder Stephanus* (Cambridge, 1954); also Fred Schreiber, *The Estiennes: An Annotated Catalogue of 300 Highlights of their Various Presses* (New York, 1982); on Estienne's famous type designs see Hendrik D. L. Vervliet, "Robert Estienne's Printing Types," *The Library* 5 (2004), pp. 107–175.

[13] Wilhelm Xylander (1532–1576) [Wilhelm Holtzman]; see ADB 44 (1898), pp. 582–593; see also Jill Kraye, " 'Ethnicorum omnium sanctissimus': Marcus Aurelius and his Meditations from Xylander to Diderot," in Jill Kraye and M. W. F. Stone, *Humanism and Early Modern Philosophy* (London, 2000), pp. 107–110; *Dionis Cassii Nicaei historiae libri (tot enim hodie extant) XXV. nimrum à XXXVI ad LXI.* [sic]... *Additum est Ioannis Xiphilini è Dione Compendium, Guil. Blanco Albiensi interprete: quae versio ab eodem Xylandro diligenter est, ubi oportuit, castigata* (Basel, 1558); Xylander himself in his dedication to his benefactor Johann Heinrich Herward humbly admits his own shortcomings: "I do not even mention the feebleness of my intellect, the ignorance of my age, the deficiency of my training as well as the brevity of time involved (as you know, notwithstanding how much I have also been busy with elsewhere, I have completed this entire work in only seven months); only the experts know how difficult it is to render good Greek editions into proper Latin ones. [Omitto ingenii imbecillitatem, aetatis imprudentiam, exercitationis defectum, temporis quoque (nam totus hic labor nobis, quod nosti, intra septimum mensem desudatus est, utcunque aliunde etiam impeditis) angustiam: ex bonis Graecis bonos Latinos libros facere, quantae sit difficulatis, sciunt qui sunt experti." Reprinted in *Cassii Dionis Cocceiani*

Johannes Leunclavius[14] needed to be emended as well.[15] In the meantime, other potential sources with which to expand the existing corpus of twenty-five books from the original eighty had surfaced. Among them was a collection of previously unknown fragments published by the Roman humanist Fulvio Orsini[16] in 1582. Unfortunately, Orsini's bookbinder had by accident cut off the outer section from the Greek manuscript, and since Orsini could no longer make much sense of portions of the mutilated text, he dotted it with asterisks.[17] What was basically needed was a new critical Greek-Latin edition, which would incorporate recently discovered fragments and epitomes, touch up the translation and – what none of the previous editions had done so far – offer both a historical and philological commentary. Not surprisingly, between 1712 and 1736 numerous projects of a new edition of Dio were begun, discontinued, or taken up again. In 1701 for example, the *Acta Eruditorum* announced that the Amsterdam printing press owned by the Huguetan brothers was preparing a new Greek-Latin edition and the same journal announced eleven years later that a Greek-Latin edition with the learned notes of a certain Obadiah Oddey, an Englishman, was under way.[18] None of these projected editions ever reached the printing press. New hope had especially grown out of the announcement by the aforementioned Vatican *Protonotarius* Nicolaus Carminius Falco, who published a little work in 1724 under the title *Cassii Dionis ultimi libri tres reperti restituque.*[19] In his preface, Falco claimed that

---

Historiae Romanae quae supersunt...cum annotationibus Hermanni Samuelis Reimari, vol. II (Hamburg, 1752), p. 1387.

[14] *Dionis Cassii Cocceiani Historiae Romanae libri XLVI partim integri, partim mutili, partim excerpti: Ioannis Leunclavii studio tam aucti quam expoliti* (Frankfurt, 1592); on Johannes Leunclavius (1541–1593) see ADB 18 (1883), pp. 488–493; also M.-P. Burtin, "Un apôtre de la tolérance: l'humaniste allemand Johannes Löwenklau dit Leunclavius (1541–1593?), *Bibliothèque d'Humanisme et Renaissance* 52 (1990), pp. 561–570.

[15] Fabricius calls the fifteenth-century codex "mendosus, nec satis castigatus," whereas Estienne himself admits that "cum unico exemplari, eoque valde mendoso usi essemus, de iis locis te admonere, quos adhibita coniectura, similiumve locuru collatione emendatu iri speraremus, non incommodum fore putavimus [...]." See Fabricius, *Bibliotheca Graeca,* p. 145; for Estienne's account, see TON ΔΙΟΝΟΣ, p. 474.

[16] On Fulvio Orsini see Giuseppina Cellini, *Il contributo di Fulvio Orsini alla ricerca antiquaria* (Rome, 2004); more specifically on his library Pierre de Nolhac, *La Bibliothèque de Fulvio Orsini: Contributions à l'Histoire des Collections d'Italie et à l'Étude de la Renaissance* (Paris, 1887); Giovanni Beltrani, *I libri di Fulvio Orsini nella Biblioteca Vaticana* (Rome, 1886).

[17] *Ex libris Polybii, selecta de legationibus* (Antwerp, 1582).

[18] See *Acta Eruditorum* 2 (1701), p. 430 and *Acta Eruditorum* 5 (1712), p. 528.

[19] ΚΑΣΣΙΟΥ ΔΙΩΝΟΣ ΡΩΜΑΙΚΗΣ ΙΣΤΟΡΙΑΣ ΤΑ ΤΕΛΕΥΤΑΙΑ ΒΙΒΛΙΑ ΤΡΙΑ ΕΥΡΙΣΚΟΜΕΝΑ ΚΑΙ ΑΠΟΚΑΘΙΣΤΑΜΕΝΑ. *Cassii Dionis Romanae Historiae Ultimi Libri Tres Reperti Restitutique. Studio ac Labore Nic. Carminii Falconis Presbyteri* (Rome, 1724).

he had reexamined Orsini's mutilated codex and fully restored the last three books from Dio's work and that he would soon be able to publish the entire *Historia Romana* in all its glamour again. But the years went by without another word from him. We do not know exactly how far the project had already progressed in Fabricius' hands or, more importantly, what Fabricius' initial plan in regard to Dio was, but in order to assess Reimarus' contribution, it would be helpful to have some idea about it. From the famous Italian man of letters Scipione Maffei we learn that in 1727 he himself had originally planned to work on a new edition of Cassius Dio, but that he had "discarded the idea," once he had learned that "the renowned Albert Fabricius, who would be much more successful in such an undertaking and to whom [I] was much indebted" was in the process of preparing such an edition.[20] So does this mean then that Falco's discovery from 1724 may have served as a trigger for other scholars such as Fabricius or Maffei to cast their eyes on this particular classical author and reawaken their interest in him? The idea sounds certainly tempting, since Fabricius, as one of the foremost Greek scholars in the world, undoubtedly monitored these types of events, but it does not hold in this case. According to the noted Hebraist Johann Christoph Wolf,[21] a close friend of Fabricius, the edition was already well under way before 1724 when Falco made his discovery[22] and Reimarus himself explains that most of Fabricius' work was complete by September 1726, but:

> [Fabricius] put them aside thereafter, because the printers with whom he had dealt did not want to begin publication unless every single part of it, from beginning to end, was absolutely perfect [...] when he handed it over to [them]; but for this kind of work he never had the patience, so that he seemed to receive my pleas and encouragements, which were reiterated constantly in regard to what still needed to be done, with some annoyance.[23]

---

[20] "[...] ma l'intendere come ha gia preso in Amburgo quest'Autor per mano il rinomato Alberto Fabricio, il quale può tanto meglio riuscire in sì fatta impresa, e cui molto debbo per avermi con tanta gentilezza voluto indirizzare il Volume duodecimo dell'eruditissima sua Biblioteca Greca, mi ha fatto desistere da tal pensiero." Scipione Maffei, *Istoria Diplomatica* (Mantua, 1727), p. 18.

[21] Johann Christoph Wolf (1683–1739); see ADB 44, pp. 545–548; also Johann Heinrich von Seelen, *Commentatio de Vita, Scriptis et Meritis in Rempublicam Literariam Viri Summe Venerandi, Excellentissimi Eruditissimique Ioan. Christoph. Wolfii* [...] (Stade, 1717).

[22] See Letter from Johann Christoph Wolf to Eric Benzelius, 3 December 1722: "Cl. amicissimusque Fabricius noster in recognoscendo Dione Cassio totus est. Illius imprimendi initium Lipsiae fiet vere imminente, sumtibus Fritschii." Alvar Erikson, ed., *Letters to Erik Benzelius the Younger from Learned Foreigners*, ed. vol. 1: 1697–1722 (Goteborg, 1979), p. 249.

[23] *Cassii Dionis Cocceiani Historiae Romanae*, vol. 1 (1750), p. xxviii, § 21: "Superest ut de *Annotationibus* aliquid addam [...]. Plurimae & potissimae hic sunt a B. Socero meo

The image of Reimarus pressing Fabricius about his notes on Dio, and Fabricius' choice to put them aside, makes me in fact believe that many aspects of the new Dio edition – the nature of the critical apparatus with a meticulous recording of Greek variants, the correction of the Latin translations of Xylander and Leunclavius, the appendices with the extended biographical sketch, and the inclusion of the castigationes and emendationes from the pens of previous and contemporary scholars – are based more on Reimarus' own decision than on that of his father-in-law. These methods, in fact, reflect rather the classical scholarship prevalent at that time in Holland, where Richard Bentley's revolutionary work[24] had undoubtedly already had a huge impact. German classical scholarship, however, had remained much more faithful to the framework of a *historia literaria* that was principally concerned with printed editions. Even a cursory look at Reimarus' finished edition, in contrast, reveals its striking similarities to the philological work that was then practised by Dutch advocates of Bentley's work such as Tiberius Hemsterhuys[25] or Petrus Wesseling,[26] who rigorously attacked the Vulgate text with a combination of conjecture and manuscript readings.[27]

Clearly, those assuming that Fabricius' previous work needed only some polishing, which his gifted son-in-law could finish in just a few months, are mistaken. The exchange with the Cardinal reveals that Reimarus laboured almost continuously for close to fifteen years on what would become an

---

Jo. Alb. Fabricio, quas inde a libro XXXV. usque ad finem libri LX. jam anno 1726. d.7. Septembris absolutas habuit: seposuit tamen postea temporis, quod bibliopolae, cum quibus egerat, editionem aggredi nollent, nisi omnia & singula quae ad eam pertinerent, a capite ad calcem absoluta & perfecta simul semelque in manus ipsis tradidisset, cuius laboris patientiam impetrare a se numquam potuit, sic ut preces meas & cohortationes, praesertim iteratas, de addendis reliquis, postremo molestius ferre videretur. Cur igitur graeca, cur versionem, cur indices, cur fragmenta & reliquos XX. libros nulla parte attigerit, ex ratione modeo dicta facile intellegitur. Eo vita functo, indignum facinus visum est, si annotationes ejus affectas perire sinerem: tanta enim conscriptae sunt diligentia, eruditione, copia, & mentis acie, [...]."

[24] See Kristine L. Haugen, *Richard Bentley: Scholarship and Criticism in Eighteenth-Century England* (Ph. D. diss., Princeton University, 2001), p. 259f.

[25] A good example of Bentley's influence on Hemsterhuys would be the 1706 edition of Pollux. See Julius Pollux, *Onomasticum: Graece & Latine: post egregiam illam Wolfgangi Seberi editionem denuo immane quantum emendatum, suppletum, & illustratum, ut docebunt praefationes ... et post eum reliquis Tiberius Hemsterhuis*, 2 vols. (Amsterdam, 1706); on this subject see John E. Sandys, *A History of Classical Scholarship*, vol. 2 (Cambridge, 1908), p. 449f.

[26] See for example Wesseling's magnificent edition of Diodorus Siculus' *Bibliothecae Historicae Libri qui supersunt* [...] 2 vols. (Amsterdam, 1745).

[27] See Lucian Müller, *Geschichte der Klassischen Philologie in den Niederlanden* (Leipzig, 1869), p. 79.

imposing two-volume masterpiece of classical scholarship. So how did Reimarus proceed? The letters, in conjunction with Reimarus' notes, provide
valuable clues to this journey,[28] marked as much by set-backs and frustrations as by bursts of enthusiasm, scholarly passion, and friendship. The
most obvious task ahead was to go over Fabricius' notes on the core text
of Dio, which chronicles events from the fall of the Republic to the death
of Claudius in 54 CE, and with the help of collated manuscripts, improve
the faulty Greek text wherever necessary. Aside from the Vatican codex,
Reimarus mentions in his edition also two manuscript codices from the
Medicean Library in Florence,[29] which he labels as *praestantissimi* [most
excellent],[30] but it remains unclear how or through which channels he
was able to acquire them. Given that we know for certain that Reimarus
never made an attempt to conquer the serpentines and peaks of the Alps –
conscious as he was of his weak physique[31] – there was also the technical problem of conveying the information in the Greek manuscripts from
Rome to Hamburg. Although the Vatican Library had a policy of lending
out books and possibly even manuscripts from its collection,[32] we know
that the medieval manuscript did not leave the sacred halls for a trip to
Hamburg. So what exactly was it that Reimarus received from the Cardinal through various book-dealers? Did the Cardinal have his copyists sim-

---

[28] Reimarus admits in the *Epistola* that it struck him as "it happens to travellers,
who, when they are close enough to see the summit to which they strive, may not see
the walkways and roughness of the road in between; although the greatest distance had
already been overcome, they nonetheless do not appear to be closer, but further away from
the goal (Accidit mihi quod viatoribus, qui arcem, quo tendunt, velut propinquam satis
prospectant semper, ambages et salebras interiectas non prospiciunt; et profligato iam
maximo spatio, non propius sibi, sed longius abesse a scopo videntur) [...]," see *Epistola
ad Eminentissimum ac Reverendissimum D.D. Angelum Mariam Tituli S. Marci Cardinalem
Quirinum* [...] *Occasione Edendi Dionis Cassii ad Nicolai Carminii Falconis* [...] *Submittit
Hermannus Samuel Reimarus* (Hamburg, 1746), p. 5.

[29] See "Explicatio notarum in Variis Lectionibus," *Cassii Dionis Cocceiani Historiae
Romanae*, vol. 1 (1750), p. xxx.

[30] Ibid., p. 636, note r.

[31] In one of his letters to Querini Reimarus complains about his periodic, migraine-like
attacks of headaches that prevent him from getting any rest and weaken him to such an
extent that he is unable to get any work done: "Recte autem suspicaris, obsuisse mihi
valitudinem, qua scilicet iam per triennium adeo dubia et fragili utor, ut ex frequenti
insomnia et capitis doloribus imparem me literis et seriae meditationi esse sentiam:
praesertim, cum ea sit suscepti muneris prope dixerim miserrima conditio, ut instituendae
iuventuti senas quotidie horas tribuere, et reliquum fere omne tempus in recuperandis
viribus exhaustis conterere necesse sit [...]," Letter Reimarus to Querini, 4 July 1743, VQS.
Ms. 257.

[32] See for this purpose Christine Maria Grafinger, *Die Ausleihe Vatikanischer Handschriften
und Druckwerke (1563–1700)* (Rome, 1993).

ply duplicate the entire Greek text? That would have been a possibility, but not a likely one. Copying the entire text would have been extremely tedious and not very time-efficient, and since Reimarus asks for a collation to any existing edition, it is more likely that only variants were noted. In September 1737, after expressing his gratitude to the Cardinal for his support, he writes:

> Although you had been taking care of these excellent codices, from which these passages were requested, as a skilful scholar, yet, since they are the only source from which Dio could be polished and supplemented and since the sample already furnishes a number of useful notes, I expect more and more extensive ones from the remaining portions. Therefore, please do not be concerned about irritating me, Your Eminence, in case you do not order as spontaneously as I ask from you shamelessly what you granted with kindness, namely to have the Vatican copyists also collate the remaining sections from page thirty and page thirty-eight of Estienne's edition to codices 993 and 144 (since that is where we left off).[33]

A year later, the order was well under way and almost complete, because on 5 November 1738, Reimarus informs the Cardinal that he has received six sheets of collated notes covering Estienne's edition from pages one to four hundred and ninety-four.[34] Since we know that the Vatican copyists must have collated the manuscripts either to Henri Estienne's edition of 1591 or the revised edition of 1592,[35] we may conclude that Reimarus probably had the entire collation in his hands no later than the spring of 1739. This process of sending the collation piecemeal and the reference to the

---

[33] Letter Reimarus to Querini, 19 August 1737, VQS. Ms. 257: "Quanquam enim Codices, ex quibus lectiones petitae sunt, praestantiones exspectaverans Ipse, peritissimus harum rerum judex; tamen cum ii fere soli sint unde emaculari aut suppleri Dio queat, cumque jam Specimen istud videatur, quasdam bonae notae lectiones exhibere, plura etiam mihi et majora ex sequentibus promitto. Quare succensere mihi noli, Domine Eminentissime, si non tam libere, quod pro Tua Clementia concessisti, quam impudentius rogo, ut reliqua etiam a pag. 30 et 38 editionis Stephani, (nam eo usque ventum erat) ad Codices 993 et 144 conferri Vaticanis Scriptoribus jubeas.

[34] Letter Reimarus to Querini, 5 November 1738: "[…] tum variarum lectionum ad Dionem Cassium plagulas VI. ut nunc Codicis 144. Vaticani, collationem teneam a pp. 1–494. A. editionis Stephani, Codicis autem 993 a pp. 1–37. B. eiusdem editionis […]," VQS. Ms. 257.

[35] In his preface to the first volume, Reimarus writes: "[…] hanc Ille [Quirinus] statim insignem mihi gratiam retulit, ut Vaticanae Bibliothecae usum non offeret tantum per literas, sed praebet etiam re ipsa, duorum Dionis codicum lectiones cum Henrici Stephani editione collatas transmittens." See *Cassii Dionis Cocceiani Historiae Romanae*, vol. 1 (1750), p. xxiii § 15. Page 494 in Estienne's edition of 1592 stops in the middle of Book fifty. Since codex 144 contains Books thirty-six to fifty-four and codex 993 contains Books thirty-six to fifty-eight, we can safely assume that the completion of the collation to the remaining four to eight Books did not take more than six months.

six separate sheets of collated notes also imply that most likely the Vatican
Library's copy was used for the collation and that Reimarus did not send
his own copy to have the collation made in the margins.[36] The collated
material was crucial to the major task ahead, namely to emend the *editio princeps* and provide a running commentary of variant readings. The
Reimarus papers in Hamburg contain a few sheets of corrections, which
Reimarus labeled as *Xylandri et Leunclavii errores* in reference to the sixteenth-century Latin translators.[37] It is a testimony to Reimarus' scrupulous
examination of previous editions and to his brief and concise emendations. So, in the context of the war between Pompey and Caesar, when
fellow Romans were fighting each other, Reimarus proposes to change
Leunclavius' translation of κατὰ τῆς τῶν Ῥωμαίων δουλείας from *adversus
servitutem Romam* [against Roman slavery] to *pro servitute Romana* [for
Roman slavery]. A later note in the list suggests that the sense of ἡ ἀπιστία
in the phrase ἡ δὲ δὴ πρὸς τοὺς οὐκ ὁμοήθεις ἀπιστία [distrust against those
of their fellow citizens who were not of the same character] would be
better expressed by *dissidentia* [contrariety, diversity], which would be
a more neutral reading than by the already negative *perfidia* [falsehood,
dishonesty]. Another note rejects Xylander's translation of ἐθάρσησε μέν
πως τὸν Καίσαρα into *nonnihil Caesari fidens* [Cleopatra trusted Caesar to
some degree], but judges Leunclavius's correction to *Caesari animum quodammodo addidit* [Cleopatra was to some degree well-inclined towards
Caesar] as much worse, so that Reimarus would eventually opt for *quod
in Caesarem fiduciam quodammodo collocasset* [because she had placed
a certain degree of confidence in Caesar]. Another sheet among these
pages is labelled *loca biblica non observata Fabricio*, which suggests that
Reimarus was not blindly taking Fabricius' commentary at face-value,
but made his own adjustments to the historical commentary wherever
he felt that they were necessary. Many of these notes were incorporated
into the edition, and as the note from above suggests, among them was

---

[36] The catalogue of the Vatican Library lists both editions. The edition of 1591 appears
under the call number "Stampati, R.I.I.545" and the edition of 1592 is listed under "Stampati,
Barberini. J.IX.42".

[37] Staatsarchiv Hamburg, 622–1 Reimarus, A 6: "Xylandri et Leunclavii errores"; Reimarus
refers to these examples as follows (page numbers correspond always to the Frankfurt
edition of 1606, which Reimarus apparently used): "p. 181. C. κατὰ τῆς τῶν Ῥωμαίων δουλείας
adversus servitutem (imo pro servitutem)"; "p. 198. A. ἀπιστία non perfidia sed dissidentia";
"p. 450. C. ἐθάρσησε μέν πως τὸν Καίσαρα Xyl. nonnihil Caesari fidens: Leunclavius peius:
Caesari animum quodammodo addidit"; see also *Cassii Dionis Cocceiani Historiae Romanae*,
vol. 1 (1750), p. 641, l. 3–4.

a substantial amount of both biblical references and works on Jewish antiquities. A page-by-page glance at the variant readings in Reimarus' edition reveals the meticulous and masterly correction of both Greek and Latin text. Although many of the changes often do not go beyond simply a case change or the insertion of an additional καί, hardly a single one of the close to fourteen hundred pages remains unaffected by Reimarus' scholarly hand and attentive eye. A good example of Reimarus' use of the Vatican material occurs in the context of Dio's account of Antony's and Cleopatra's escape during the sea battle of Actium on 2 September 31 BC, when both abandoned their fleet. The edition by Henri Estienne of 1592, based on the *editio princeps*, puts the key passage as follows:

ὡς γὰρ τότε ἐκ τῆς ναυμαχίας ἔφυγον,
μέχρι μὲν τῆς Πελοποννήσου ὁμοῦ ἀφίκοντο,
ἐντεῦθεν δὲ καὶ ἀκόντων αὐτῶν ἀπεχώρησαν,
Κλεοπάτρα μὲν ἐς τὴν Ἄιγυπτον, μή τι, τῆς συμφορᾶς σφῶν προπυθόμενοι,
νεωτερίσωσιν, ἠπείχθη.[38]

(they [Antony and Cleopatra] escaped the sea battle until they together reached the Peloponnese; there, *they departed from those who were unwilling*; Cleopatra then hurried to Egypt so that they who had heard beforehand about their defeat would not cause any uprising)

The problematic part of the passage sounds most awkward in translation, namely the phrase ἀκόντων αὐτῶν ἀπεχώρησαν [they departed from those who were unwilling]. There seems to be little doubt that the subject of ἀπεχώρησαν [they departed] is Antony and Cleopatra, but what about the ἀκόντων [those being unwilling]? When Xylander initially translated Dio into Latin in 1557, his emendations do not make any particular mention of this passage, which suggests that the humanist did not find anything wrong with it. Instead of wondering about the identity of the ἀκόντων αὐτῶν [those being unwilling] and with no other subject occurring within the segment, Xylander interprets it as a reference to Antony and Cleopatra as well, which makes it into a reflexive clause:

Hi a pugna navali fuga elapsi, usque ad Peloponnesum simul quum pervenissent, ibi *praeter animi sui sententiam divulsi invicem sunt*, Cleopatra in Aegyptum condentente, ne clades audita novos ibi tumultus concitaret.[39]

---

[38] *Dionis Cassii Romanarum Historiam Libri XXV*. Excudebat Henricus Stephanus (1592), p. 510 C.
[39] I am using here the aforementioned bilingual edition of 1592 by Henri Estienne. Ibid., p. 510 C.

> (After they [Antony and Cleopatra] escaped in their flight from the sea bat-
> tle, they reached the Peloponnese together; there, *they were separated from
> one another against their will*, since Cleopatra hurried to Egypt lest the news
> of the defeat cause new rebellions there.)

Xylander's decision against a partitive genitive implies that he did not
assume that the Greek text could be faulty here and that it was complete
as such. Reimarus, on the other hand, criticizes the decision as inappro-
priate to both the Greek text and the historical context:

> if you related it [αὐτῶν] back to Antony and Cleopatra, you would stray from
> the true meaning and you would go against the force of the Greek text. This
> is what Xylander has done [...]. Nor did Leunclavius notice this gap, which
> is certainly not easy without the manuscript codex.[40]

Indeed, not even Leunclavius' improved Latin translation makes any mention of the passage, but leaves it reflexive, as Xylander had done before
him. In spite of justified criticism, because the passage should have war-
ranted a little remark in Xylander's emendations, Reimarus was in no position to be overly harsh on a still plausible interpretation of the passage.
Having the collation of the Vatican codices in front of him, he was able to
provide a rich and marvellously elucidatory addition to the text that none
of the previous humanists could have guessed. After comparing the faulty
text with his collation, Reimarus changed the segment as follows:

> ὡς γὰρ τότε ἐκ τῆς ναυμαχίας ἔφυγον,
> μέχρι μὲν τῆς Πελοποννήσου ὁμοῦ ἀφίκοντο· ἐντεῦθεν δὲ τῶν συνόντων
> τινὰς ὅσους ὑπώπτευον ἀποπέμψαντες, (πολλοὶ δὲ καὶ ἀκόντων αὐτῶν ἀπεχώρησαν)
> Κλεοπάτρα μὲν ἐς τὴν Αἴγυπτον, μή τι,
> τῆς συμφορᾶς σφῶν προ-πυθόμενοι, νεωτερίσωσιν, ἠπείχθη·[41]

Upon realizing that the Vatican manuscript yields a combination of words
that fits perfectly into the apparent gap, Reimarus concludes that "the string
of words [from ἐντεῦθεν] up to πολλοί, was as a common mistake of the
copyists, left out of Dio."[42] The addition not only renders the passage into
better Greek from a grammatical point of view, but also changes its meaning by identifying the ἀκόντων αὐτῶν as τῶν συνόντων τινὰς [some of those

---

[40] "ad Antonium vero & Cleopatram si retuleris, a veritate aberraveris, & Greacis vim
inferas, sicut fecit Xylander [...]. Neque sensit lacunam Leunclavius, quod certe nec facile
est sine codice MS." see *Cassii Dionis Cocceiani Historiae Romanae*, vol. 1 (1750), p. xxiii, § 15.

[41] Ibid., p. 636, l. 74–80.

[42] Ibid., p. 636, footnote "r": "verba quae sequuntur usque ad πολλοὶ δὲ, faltu consueto
librariorum Dioni detracta erant [...]."

with them]. The relative clause ὅσους ὑπώπτευον [whom they suspected] basically serves as an additional piece of information, which may have served as the premise of why these men were sent away [ἀποπέμψαντες]. The initially puzzling segment ἀκόντων αὐτῶν appears in parentheses as a partitive genitive with πολλοί [many], followed by the verb ἀπεχώρησαν. Reimarus is thus able to render the entire passage into a much more lucid and elegant Latin translation:

> Hi a pugna navali fuga elapsi, usque ad Peloponnesym quum una pervenis- sent, ibi *quosdam sociorum itineris, quos suspectos habebant, dimiserunt, multis etiam contra ipsorum voluntatem discendentibus.* Hinc Cleopatra in Aegyptum celeriter contendit, ne clades ante audita novos ibi tumultus concitaret.[43]

> (Having escaped the sea battle, [Antony and Cleopatra] reached the Pelo- ponnese together; thereupon *they sent those of their associates away whom they suspected, with many also departing against their will.* Hence Cleopatra rushed to Egypt fearing that news beforehand of their destruction could cause uprisings there.)

A glance at the polished Latin translation also reveals some minor changes that make the text much more readable. Starting a new sentence after *discendentibus* and replacing Xylander's ablativus absolutus *Cleopatra in Aegyptum contendente* with the finite construction *Cleopatra in Aegyptum celeriter contendit* removes any remaining ambiguity from the text and at the same time sets the stage for a sharper focus on Cleopatra in what follows. Although these types of changes undoubtedly testify both to Rei- marus' sensitivity to Dio's style and to his mastery of Greek, his decisions were often facilitated by the excellent resources he had at hand. These resources were not only the collated manuscripts from the Vatican and the Medicean Library, but also commentaries and notes from other scholars,[44] who had suggested alternative readings or translations of the Greek text or, as I have suggested earlier, had published additional fragments[45] that should ultimately be part of an enlarged and updated new edition. Virtu- ally all of these published texts had been part of Fabricius' collection and

---

[43] Ibid., p. 636, l. 74–80.

[44] Jacob Paulmier, *Exercitationes in optimos auctores greacos* (Leyden, 1668); Lambert Bos, *Animadversiones ad Scriptores quosdam Graecos* (Franeker, 1715); Jacob Gronov, *Supplementa Lacunarum in Aenea Tactico, Dione Cassio, et Arriano* (Leyden, 1675).

[45] For example the fragments published by the French humanist Henri de Valois (1603– 1676) as *Polybii Diodori Siculi Nicolai Damasceni Dionysii Halicar. Appiani Aledand. Dionis et Iaonnis Antiocheni Excerepta ex Collectaneis Constantini Augusti Porphyrogenetae Henricus Valesius nunc primum Graece edidit, Latine vertit, Notisque illustravit* (Paris, 1584).

Reimarus did not have to worry about purchasing copies through various bookdealers.[46] A high priority was of course Falco's discovery from 1724, where the latter had enthusiastically announced that he had completely restored the last three books of Cassius Dio. On the assumption that Falco's new edition had fallen through, it seems surprising that Reimarus did not approach Falco, as Querini had done with his *Philastrius*, and request any potentially helpful material. What Reimarus, however, had in mind becomes clear from a letter he sent to Querini in January 1746, in which he suggested a review of Falco's publication from 1724 in the form of a public letter to the Cardinal. Reimarus attached already the first sheet of the proposed letter for Querini to look over.[47] He would also ask the Cardinal to compare Falco's little book with the actual codex from which the sixteenth-century humanist Orsini had published his fragments and which was stored in the Vatican library. The idea was that the Cardinal would write a public reply to Reimarus' piece, including an assessment of Reimarus' comments on Falco's work. Querini must have approved of the proposal, because as early as February Reimarus asked the Cardinal if he had received five copies of the letter with whose dispatch he had commissioned a bookseller from Augsburg.[48] Although formally addressed to Querini, the category "epistle" seems deceptive. After introducing his own project, the circumstances of his inheriting it from Fabricius, and complimenting Falco for his efforts, Reimarus produced a very detailed line-by-line dismantling of Falco's philological work, exposing grave errors both in his Greek conjectures and Latin translations, which, mixed with often pointed remarks, borders on ridicule. Reimarus' emendations are peppered with phrases such as "which Falco has changed against the nature of the Greek language;" "his Latin translation here reverses everything;" or

---

[46] Many of these works also contained marginalia by Fabricius; one entry in the auction catalogue of Reimarus' library reads: "*Polybii, Diodori Sic. Nicolai Damasceni, Dionysii Halic. Appiani Alex Dionis & Io Antiocheni excerpta ex Collectaneis Constantini Porphyrogenetae, gr. lat. cum notis Henr. Valesii . Paris.* [1]634. Ad Dionis Cassii excerpta pauculae leguntur Fabricii observationes," see *Johann* Andreas Schetelig, *Auktionskatalog der Bibliothek von Hermann Samuel Reimarus* (Hamburg, 1769 and 1770; reprint 1980), pars II, p. 201, 35.

[47] "[...] ausus nunc sum, quod aequi bonique, rogo, interpreteris, de ultimis libris Dionis a Cl. Falcone editis nonunnulla, per modum epistolae ad Te datae, commentari. Mitto hic eius primam plagulam [...]." Letter Reimarus to Querini, 01 January 1746, VQS. Ms. 257.

[48] "Spero iam reliqua epistolae folia, cum quinque eius exemplis integris, quae Augustam Vind[elicorum] missa bibliopolae cuidam commendaveram, recte Tibi reddita esse.[...] Rogo nempe, ut Viro cuidam docto, extrema Dionis a Falcone edita, denuo cum codice illo antiquisssimo conferenda committas." Letter Reimarus to Querini, 19 February 1746, VQS. Ms. 257.

"Falco often blames Orsini for having misread something which is actually correct." These phrases, however, are only a small element in what frequently amounts to a lengthy, sophisticated, often heavily annotated, but above all, meticulous analysis. To give some idea of the nature of Reimarus' criticism, let us take a look at one of the fragments which Falco published from Book seventy-eight, where Dio recounts the eccentric sense of fashion of the emperor Caracalla (188–217 CE), both on and off the battlefield. Among these garments was apparently an Oriental tunic, which Dio describes in greater detail:

χλαμύδα τε τότε μὲν ὁλοπόρφυρον, τότε δὲ μεσόλευκον, ἔστι δ'ὅτε καὶ μεσοπόρφυρον, ὥσπερ καὶ ἐρυθρὸν ἐφόρει·

(he [Caracalla] wore at times a cloak that was all-purple, at times shot with white, at times shot with purple, just as it was also plain red)

Falco, evidently not satisfied with Leunclavius' Latin version,[49] translates the passage as follows:

chlamydemque ex integro purpuream aliquando, aliquando vero albam ex parte, quod est nempe semipurpuream, sicuti quoque rubram gestabat.[50]

(he wore a cloak that was sometimes all-purple, sometimes to a certain degree white, which means of course half-purple, in the same way as it was also red).

Even for a Latin beginner, the passage looks and sounds confusing. Why would Dio have taken pains to explain with a relative clause – *quod est nempe semipurpuream* [which is of course half-purple] – what seems abundantly clear on its own – *aliquando vero albam ex parte* [mostly white], thus making the passage almost incomprehensible, especially since *albam ex parte* [to a large extent white] and *semipurpuream* [half-purple] seem to be two different things? Obviously Falco's correction misfired, because it converted what was a straightforward passage in Greek into obscure Latin. Reimarus easily picked up on what he interpreted as an amateurish mistake:

---

[49] *Dionis Cassii Cocceiani Historiae Romanae* [...] *Io Leunclavii studio tam aucti, quam expoliti* (Frankfurt, 1592), p. 901: "Chlamydem aliquando totam purpuream, aliquando semialbam, aliquando semipurpuream, sicut & rubram, gestabat."

[50] *Cassii Dionis Romanae Historiae ultimi libri tres reperti restitutique studio ac labore Nic. Carminii Falconis Presbyteri* (Rome, 1724), p. 5.

Our Falco wanted to correct Leunclavius and translates ἔστι δ' ὅτε καὶ μεσοπόρφυρον as *quod est nempe semipurpuream* [which is half-purple]. This is indeed as if ἔστι δ'ὅτε [at times] was the same as τοῦτ' ἔστι [which means] [...]. Who would not know that in Greek instead of *interdum* [at one time], *modo* [at another time], or *aliquando* [yet another time] ἔστι μὲν ὅτε ἔστι δ' ὅτε [sometimes] or τότε [at times] or τότε μέν, τότε δέ [at one time... at another] and at the third instance [in a list] ἔστι δ' ὅτε [sometimes] are used?[51]

Indeed, just as μὲν [on the one hand] and δὲ [on the other hand] usually mark a contrast in Greek between two things or people, they can be supplemented by particles such as τότε [then; at one time] either for matters of emphasis or to determine the nature of the contrast such as temporal or spatial. As Reimarus pointed out, since μὲν and δὲ are used only to contrast two groups, in this case ἔστι δ' ὅτε [sometimes] is used as an enumerative conjunct in reference to a third group in what is a simple parallel construction. Reimarus, however, did not leave it at just demonstrating Falco's shortcomings as a linguist, but since Falco had apparently misunderstood the passage's true meaning, he meticulously expounded it, thereby showing off his tremendous learning and familiarity with ancient antiquities and custom:

> I believe that what needs to be observed above all is that this *chlamys* [cloak, mantle] which is called μεσόλευκος [shot with white], is generally designated by the addition πορφυροῦς [purple-clad, in purple]. So the clothing of the Medes and Persians, which is called *sarapis*, is described in Pollux VII.61 as πορφυροῦς μεσόλευκος χιτών, *vestis purpurea medio albo colore distincta* [a purple garment with white in the middle] and Cyrus in Book VIII on page 215. B. of Xenophon's *Cyropaedia* is said to have worn χιτῶνα πορφυροῦν μεσόλευκον [a tunic in purple shot with white in the middle]. Nor is the sense any different in Book XII. p. 537. E. of Athenaeus [Deipnosophistae] where Alexander was, according to Persian custom, dressed in χλαμύδα πορφυρᾶν καὶ χιτῶνα μεσόλευκον [a purple mantle and a tunic shot with white], where πορφυρᾶν [purple-coloured] means the same as ὁλόπορφυρον [all-purple] and μεσόλευκον [shot with white] is the same as πορφυρᾶν μεσόλευκον [purple shot with white]. For the same Athenaeus writes in Book V. p. 215. G. about the Epicurean Lysias, tyrant of Tarsus, πορφυροῦν μὲν μεσόλευκον χιτῶνα ἐνδεδυκώς, χλαμύδα δὲ ἐφεστρίδα περιβεβλημένος πολυτελή [he put on a purple garment that was shot with white, after having wrapped himself in an expensive upper garment].[52]

---

[51] *Epistola*, p. 11f.: "Noster [Falco] corrigere Leunclavium voluit, ἔστι δ'ὅτε καὶ μεσόπορφυρον, interpretatus, *quod est nempe semipurpuream.* Quasi vero ἔστι δ' ὅτε idem esset ac τοῦτ' ἔστι [...]. Quis enim nescit, pro *interdum, modo,* aut *aliquando* Graecis dici ἔστι μὲν ὅτε ἔστι δ' ὅτε, aut τοτὲ vel τοτὲ μὲν, τότε δὲ, et tertio fere loco, ἔστι δ' ὅτε?

[52] Ibid., p. 11f.: "[...] Puto autem ante omnia observandum esse, quod ea chlamys, quae μεσόλευκος vocatur, simul addito πορφυροῦς soleat designari. Sic vestis Medorum

This head-spinning survey shows in an impressive way that Reimarus knew what he was talking about. As a Professor of Hebrew and Oriental Languages, who would almost every year teach a course in Jewish antiquities, the customs of Mediterranean and Oriental civilizations were not unfamiliar turf for him. Though scholarship on Persians, Parthians, and Medes was, unless it touched upon the always popular field of religion or idolatry, far less vibrant than that on Greeks, Hebrews, or Romans, Reimarus could nonetheless draw on an exquisite core of helpful works. In this particular case of ancient vestment, the foremost ones were probably Ottavio Ferrari's *De re vestiaria libri septem* (1654) or Albertus Rubenius's *De re vestaria veterum*, both of which were conveniently available in the sixth volume of Graevius's *Thesaurus antiquitatum romanarum* (1694–99). Whereas Reimarus would eventually quote them in his own Dio edition, none of these scholarly works made it into his review of Falco's edition. Given the length of the letter, space did not seem to have been a matter of concern. A more plausible explanation is that referencing scholarly works was not on top of the priority list of an incredibly talented, but still relatively unknown scholar, who had not yet established himself in the Republic of Learning through his own works and needed to show just how well-skilled a linguist he was. How could he have done this any better than by showing his acute sense of the Greek language in pulling out similar instances of usage from various other Greek authors or in drawing analogous conclusions, as he does in the case of the example mentioned above, where he notes that πορφυρᾶ μεσόλευκος must be "purple that is white in the middle or is encircled by a white border" since "μεσόγαιος means in the middle of the land, μεσεντέριον refers to the part in the middle of the intestines, μεσοκράνιον is the part in the middle of the skull, μεσονύκτιον refers to the middle of the night and μεσοναῦται are the people in the middle between seamen and ordinary travellers"?[53]

---

et Persarum, *Sarapis* dicta, πορφυροῦς μεσόλευκος χιτών, *vestis purpurea medio albo colore distincta*, (sic Interpres) definitur ap. Pollucem VII. 61. et Cyrus ap. Xenophontem lib. VIII. Cyrop. p. 215.B. getasse dicitur χιτῶνα πορφυροῦν μεσόλευκον. Nec alio sensu ap. Athenaeum lib. XII. p. 537. E. Alexander Persico more indutus erat χλαμύδα πορφυρᾶν καὶ χιτῶνα μεσόλευκον, ubi πορφυρᾶν idem est quod ὁλοπόρφυρον, et μεσόλευκον idem quod πορφυρᾶν μεσόλευκον. Nam sic idem Athenaeus lib. V. p. 215. G. de Lysia Epicureo, Tarsi Tyranno, πορφυροῦν μὲν μεσόλευκον χιτῶνα ἐνδεδυκώς, χλαμύδα δὲ ἐφεστρίδα περιβεβλημένος πολυτελῆ [...]."

[53] Ibid., p. 12: "Nam ita μεσόγαιος, quod medium est terra, μεσεντέριον, quod medium est intestinorum, μεσοκράνιον, quod media est cranii pars, μεσονύκτιον, quod medium est noctis, μεσοναῦται, qui medii sunt inter nautas et vectores. Ergo et πορφυρᾶ μεσόλευκος erit purpura, quae medium tenet albi, seu fimbriam habet in circuitu albam [...]."

Given the fact that this epistle is basically a long review of Falco's scholarship on Cassius Dio and given the slightly polemical tone whenever he
exposed his fellow humanist's mistakes, it becomes clear that Reimarus
believed that Falco had not only misunderstood individual passages, but
that he lacked the skill to complete an edition which he once must have
had in mind and which Reimarus himself was just about to finish. His con-
descending tone did not remain unnoticed. Despite Reimarus' deceptively
polite tone towards Falco in the beginning of the letter, Querini in his public response to Reimarus characterized the *Epistola* as "a beautiful woman
in the upper part, which ends in an ugly fish in the lower."[54] But Reimarus'
publicity stunt did not miss its target, both in a negative and a positive
sense. Given the project's past history and Reimarus' relative obscurity, it
seemed invaluable to publicize his project so that other scholars not only
knew about the planned Hamburg edition, but could also provide possible
assistance. This is why Reimarus had ended his *Epistola* with a plea to
the Cardinal to inquire whether other scholars in the field would kindly
volunteer any possibly helpful information for the project.[55] Undoubtedly,
Reimarus had been in an exceptional position. On the one hand, before
1739, which is when Johann Christoph Wolf died, he could still count on
the latter's support to promote his project, and on the other hand, while
preparing the auction catalogue for Fabricius' library, he remained in
contact with other scholars such as Eric Benzelius, head of the library of
Uppsala, and – just as he established his contact with Querini – when he
answered their requests, he could drop a casual note about his Dio.[56] So
by word-of-mouth news about this project had spread throughout Europe

---

[54] The quotation is from Horace, *Art. Poet.* 4: "Turpiter atrum definit in piscem mulier
formosa superne;" Letter Querini to Reimarus, 23 August 1746: "[...] attamen in medium
afferens Animadversiones illas tuas, Falconis effigiem iis coloribus pingis, ut de eadem
jure ac merito dici possit ... *Turpiter atrium Definit in piscem mulier formosa superne* [...].,"
reprinted in *Epistolae Eminentiss. et Reverendiss. D. D. Angeli Mariae Querini*, ed. Nicolaus
Coleti (Venice, 1756), p. 284.

[55] *Epistola*, p. 43: Liceat autem hic sub Tuis auspiciis implorare Viros eruditos, ut si
quid adhuc lectionum in primis variarum ex codicibus MSS. tum & emendationum aut
observationum ad Dionem habeant in promptu, id conferre ad proximam editionem ne
dedignentur."

[56] Eric Benzelius (1675–1743); On 3 December 1737, Reimarus wrote to Benzelius:
"Confecto Catalogo, quod spero proxima aestate futurum, Dioni Cassio manus admovebo,
flagitantibus cum Viris doctis magni nominis, tum Wetstenio et Smitho Bibliopolis
Amstelodamensibus. Accepi ad ornandam editionem ab eminentissimo Cardinali Quirino
specimen variarum lectionum ex duplici Codice Dionis Vaticano, idemque sequentia
etiam pollicitus est." See Erikson, ed., *Letters to Erik Benzelius* (2), p. 401.

and scholars acquainted with the late Fabricius offered their services to his gifted son-in-law.[57]

These informal efforts had already produced some results. Even before the publication of the *Epistola*, Reimarus had received some additional, previously unpublished emendations by Jacob Gronov from his son Abraham, who was then librarian in Leiden, and Friedrich Mentz, Professor of Philosophy at the University of Leipzig, had sent him a copy of Estienne's *editio princeps*, which he believed the French humanist Adrian Turnebe had previously owned and which contained a large number of scholarly *marginalia*.[58] The public letter to the Cardinal, however, boosted the publicity level of his project. Already in February 1746 the reviewer of the *Epistola* in the local newspaper, the *Staats- und Gelehrten Zeitung des hamburgischen unparteyischen Correspondenten*, had observed that its author's "diligence, learning, apt conclusions, and mature judgment come across equally strongly"[59] and having already received comments by the brilliant Graecist from Utrecht Petrus Wesseling in July 1746, Reimarus enthusiastically informed Querini in February 1748 that he was expecting still more material from Tiberius Hemsterhuys and Richard Mead.[60]

---

[57] The librarian of the Royal Library in Copenhagen for example wrote to Reimarus on 30 September 1738: "Equidem salleris, Vir doctissime, si hunc hominem esse opiniaris, qui idonens aptusque ad continuandos magni viri labores vel suo vel aliorum judicio aestimari queat." See Staatsarchiv Hamburg, 622–1 Reimarus, A 23, Letter Hans Gram to Reimarus.

[58] *Epistola*, p. 43f.: "Misit etiam mihi benevole Vir Politissimus, Fridericus Mentzius, Professor Lipsiensis, editionem Robertinam, quae fuerat quondam Adriani Turnebi, non paucis elegantibus in margine emendationibus insignem, praesertim in principio: nam quo magis penetro ad medium, eo magis omnia cum Xylandri emendationibus conveniunt. Nuper etiam Abrahamus Gronovius, Vir non Majorum magis quam suis in literas meritis clarissimus, qua solet esse humanitate, mecum communicare coepit varias leciones ex codice Medico, qua in Parentis Jacobi supplementis lacunarum praeteritae sunt: neque dubito, eum reliqua etiam, quae servat, Dioni ornando idonea, id quod publice nunc precibus ad eo contendo, suppeditaturum."

[59] "Die Probe, welche der Hr. Verfasser von dieser letztern der Welt gegenwärtig mitgetheilet hat, ist unvergleichlich, und je mehr wir dieselbe in Betrachtung ziehen, je mehr werden wir überzeugt, daß der Fleiß, Gelehrsamkeit, glückliche Erfindungen und reife Beurtheilungskraft auf allen Seiten in gleicher Stärke hervorleuchten [...]. Wir erkühnen uns denselben hermit zum Besten der gelehrten Welt inständig zu ersuchen, seinen Schatz aus gar zu grosser Sorgfalt nicht länger zurück zu haltern, und wünschen, daß er die Früchte seiner rühmlichen Bemühung baldigst, und viele Jahre reichlich geniessen möge." See *Staats- und Gelehrten Zeitung des hamburgischen unparteyischen Correspondenten* 18 (1 February 1746).

[60] "Promisit Rich[ard] Meadius codicem Oddianum, promisit Burgius Codicem Breslaviensem Xiphilini, promisit Hemsterhusius observationes suas." Letter Reimarus to Querini, 5 February 1748, VQS. Ms. 257.

But as we already know, the damper came in December 1746, when we learn from Reimarus' notably angry response to Querini that Falco had taken up his Dio project again. Reimarus may in fact just have overestimated the impact of his elucidations on Falco.[61] Some of his comments were quite humiliating and they may very easily have been the trigger for Falco to resume his work, both to rehabilitate himself and, in the spirit of true gamesmanship, spoil Reimarus' day. Almost instantly, however, the entire episode took a few more positive turns in Reimarus' favour. Within the same month, the Cardinal was able to get back to Reimarus about the ancient codex in the Vatican Library from which Falco's publication had sprung. Having compared the parchment with both Orsini's earlier publication and with Falco's publication from 1724, Querini reported that Falco had completely exaggerated his claim and that his negligible additions by no means held up to his boastful announcement of a recovery of the last three books of Cassius Dio.[62] The news energized Reimarus, and not without some malice he expressed his surprise in a letter to Querini about "how far Falco had wandered from the correct reading of his codex."[63] At the same time, while continuing his own work, Reimarus wanted to wait for Falco's edition so that he could incorporate it into his own. He was certain that his public letter to the Cardinal had put the learned world into the "right mindset" of what it could expect from a man like

---

[61] On 17 September 1746, for example, an overly confident Reimarus wrote to Querini: "[...] ut Vir iste optimus facilius sibi exprobari aliquid jactantiae, quam calcar ad respondendum addi, existima verit. Neque tamen ego intercedo, quominus respondeat, si non se tantum erroris suspicione liberare, sed et meo scripto refellendo lucem Dione afferre norit. Neque mirabor, si sapere iam me plus possit, postquam duos et viginti annos, atque adeo amplius, in uno Dione limando collocarit [...]. Ceterum, Tu etiam auctoritate, imperterritus coepto labori insisto, itaque mihi persuasi, nihil responderi a Falcone posse, quin id vel honeste vertatur in rem meam [...]," see VQS. Ms. 257.

[62] Letter Querini to Reimarus, 14 December 1746: "Codicem illum Vaticanum per integrum mensem Octobrem diurna, nocturnaque manu a me versatum fuisse primo loco affirmare possum, adhibitis ad eam rem non oculis tantum, & diligentia, sed, pro tenuitate ingenii mei, eruditione, judicio, sagacitate, ac ferme divinatione [...]," in *Epistolae Eminentiss. et Reverendiss. D.D. Angeli Mariae Querini*, (Venice, 1756), pp. 291–297.

[63] Letter Reimarus to Querini, 24 December 1746, VQS. Ms. 257: "Equidem sic acquiescebam in Tua sollicitudine et cura pro mea Dionis editione, ut nunciatus Cl. Falconis ausus meam alacritatem non frangeret sed intenderet, neque novo mihi incitamento ad perficiendum laborem opus esse videretur [...] Verum, quod significabam proxime, cupio prius, neque id quidem leviter, videre quae edidit Falco: atque hoc magis magisque non tam opus mihi, sed prope necesse esse, perspicio. Dedi quidem id negotii amico cuidam, qui cum bibliopola Italo commcercium exercet literarum [...]. Etiam ex Epistola Tua novissima perspexi, Falconem sapiuscule a vera lectione illius ipsius codicis aberrasse."

Falco.[64] The Cardinal on his part was able to pull some strings and already in early April 1747, Reimarus was able to take a look at some samples from Falco's newly restored Dio. But what he saw on those loose sheets barely resembled what he had in fact expected. It seemed eerily familiar and nothing like Dio at all.[65]

> It came into my mind to take a look at Plutarch's *Poplicola* [...] and I immediately caught the man in the act: I recognize that every single part, with the exception of the defects of the edition or the excerpts from the Latin edition, has been copied from Plutarch p. 101. section F onwards [...]. It makes me wonder how any scholar who takes up the task of reviewing the edition could fail to discover this villainy?[66]

What Reimarus describes here as villainy may not have been a result of ill-intentions. It was a conscious, but bad decision based upon the argument that Dio may have plagiarized Plutarch. Henri de Valois had already raised this possibility, when he published his fragments in 1583,[67] and even modern scholarship has recognized Plutarch as a potential source for Dio.[68] Valois' reference, however, served as Falco's pretext for looking at various segments in Plutarch and inserting them in chronological order into Dio's *History*.[69] Although Reimarus was even prepared to acknowledge

---

[64] Ibid.: "Interim oportune mihi videor, in epistola mea, Viros Eruditos, quibus ultimorum librorum editio Romana non ad manus erat, iis instruxisse argumentis, ex quibus iam de futura integri Dionis editione Neapolitana judicium queant capere."

[65] Letter Reimarus to Querini, 8 April 1747, VQS. MS. 257: "Pergratum mihi fuit, Tuo, Cardinalis Eminentissime, beneficio oculis usurpare specimen restituti Dionis Falconiani; quo perlecto intellexi statim, non facile esse, si erratis typographorum vel librariorum discesseris, quod in Graecis queat desiderari, quae mihi, ut Falconis verbo utar, non Dionem quidem, sed tamen antiquum scriptorem Graecum olebant."

[66] Ibid.: "Venit igitur in mentem Plutarchi Poplicolam consulere [...]. Statim deprehendo hominem ipso in furto: nam omnia et singula, ne ipsis quidem vitiis editionis, aut versione latina excerptis, ex Plutarcho p. 101. F. sq. video esse huc translata [...]. Quemadmodum vero mirari subit, Virum eruditum, qui recensendae editionis curam in se suscepit, haec latrocinia non animadvertisse [...]."

[67] See for example appendix to *Polybii Diodori Siculi* [...]. *Dionis* [...] *Henricus Valesius nunc primum Graece edidit, Latine vertit, Notisque illustravit* (Paris, 1584), p. 91, where de Valois writes in regard to a particular segment: "Sic in codice nostro exaratum est, cum tamen τῶν ἔργων legendum sit ex Plutarcho in Sulla. ex quo haec & sequentia quatuor capita ad verbum transcribit Dio. Sed & caput 34. & 37. legationum ex Dionis historia Excerptarum, similiter exscripta sunt ex eiusdem Plutarchi Sulla. Adeo furaces & plagiarij Graeci fere omnes deprehenduntur [...]."

[68] Fergus Millar, *A Study of Cassius Dio* (Oxford, 1964), p. 34.

[69] "Sed magna adhuc lumina & incrementa Dionis deerant, eaque forte fortuna in Plutarcho detego, dum Valesii verba lego [...]. Nam confestim Plutarchum sumo, & cum, ne dum allegata a Valesio ibi invenio, sed omnem propemodum Sullae vitam, inde exscriptam

the potential usefulness of other classical authors besides the two Byzantine epitomators Xiphilinus and Zonaras to patch the gaps in Dio, he was outraged about Falco's uncritical and exaggerated use of this technique, especially since the latter inserted large chunks from both Plutarch and Zonaras into Dio without explicitly indicating his sources, thus trying to sell these parts as genuinely recovered segments from the *Roman History*.[70] There was no need for Reimarus to worry that Falco's clumsy restoration would remain undetected. After Scipione Maffei reviewed the first volume, containing the first twenty-one books of Falco's Cassius Dio in November 1748, it became clear that it would remain the only volume.[71] Just as Reimarus suspected, Maffei had no problem exposing the fraud. "How surprised," he writes, "is one once one encounters after Falco's much trumpeted *Quod felix, faustumque sit, Cassii Dionis Historiae habemus libros* [What a great fortune to have the books of Cassius Dio's *Roman History*!] works of Zonaras and Plutarch presented as works of Dio."[72] Four years later, the brilliant Graecist Johann Jacob Reiske would express this sentiment in less flattering terms when, after telling a friend that he had finally had a chance to look at the notorious Falco edition, he marvelled "how [this man] could have sold these quite lousily patched holes from Zonaras and Plutarch as the work of Dio!"[73]

---

video a Dione; Excerpta statim loco moveo, quem obtinebant, & ad calcem paginarum, de more meo, rejicio: restituoque hoc pacto, ad duos ferme libros, Dionem. Interim, quod suapte evenire natura, in ejusmodi solet, occasionibus; hinc mihi animus excitatur, ad explorandum, num & alibi quoque Plutarchus apud Dionem lateat: ut sic restitui satius Dio queat." See "Prolegomena," in *Q. Cassii Dionis Coccejani Romanae Historiae ex ejus octoginta libris tomus primus...studio et labore Nic. Carminii Falconii* (Naples, 1747), p. a 4.

[70] See Letter Reimarus to Querini, 8 April 1747, VQS. MS. 257: "Verum, inquiet Falco, male nos haec Plutarcho vindicare, cum et Dio soleat (v.g. in fragmentis prioribus) Plutarchum excribere. Solet, scio, idque animadverti in locis quibusdam, de quibus silet Ursinus atque Leunclavius; sed nullo in loco, praesertim tam longo, qualis de Poplicola est, ita omnia ad amussim cum editis Plutarchi conspirant, quin subinde corrigendi et supplendi Dionis ex Plutarcho, aut vicissim Plutarchi ex Dione detur materia. [...] Quae in Zonara uncis circumscripsit Falco, ipsa sunt Plutarchi verba, vel ut ille nugatur, Dionis."

[71] Scipione Maffei, *Tre Lettere del Signor Marchese Scipione Maffei* (Verona, 1748), pp. 5–25.

[72] Ibid., p. 16.: "Ma quanto rimane attonito chi dopo la trompa festiva, *Quod felix, faustumque sit, Cassii Dionis Romanae Historiae habemus libros*, si vede presentare come di Dione scritti di Zonara, e di Plutarco?"

[73] Letter Reiske to Johann Stephan Bernard, 9 May 1752: "Mirum est qui potuerit homo ille lacinias Zonarae et Plutarchi miserabilem in modum consutas pro Dionis opere venditare." See *Johann Jacob Reiske's Briefe*, ed Richard Foerster (*Abhandlungen der philologisch-historischen Classe der Königl. Sächsischen Gesellschaft der Wissenschaften*) (Leipzig, 1897), p. 455.

The stage had thus been appropriately set for the publication of Reimarus' edition. But before it reached the press, history almost seemed to repeat itself. Just like his father-in-law, Reimarus initially experienced frustrations in finding a printer. Already in October 1744, Reimarus had complained to Querini about the excessive stipulations of the Dutch printer Jean Neaulme,[74] and when the French invaded the Dutch Republic in April 1747 and civil unrest increased, Reimarus' search for a publisher seemed to reach a dead end, because all of the prestigious Dutch printing houses – Neaulme, Wettstein, Langerak – with the spectre of revolution looming over them, expressed their regrets at being unable to take on Reimarus' project.[75] With his options greatly diminished, Reimarus was eventually able to convince the local printer Christian Herold to publish his work.[76] Given the outcome, probably neither printer nor author regretted this decision. Finally, in September 1749 and approximately one year later than anticipated, Reimarus was able to send Querini two copies of page proofs.[77] Still in the same year, the *Göttingische Zeitungen von Gelehrten Sachen* announced the imminent publication of the Hamburg Dio edition and numbered it among the gems of Germany and its times.[78] When the first volume was officially published in 1750, both national and international receptions were unanimously positive and it was no different two years later when the second volume appeared. Practically all reviewers were very pleased with Reimarus' efforts to correct Leunclavius'

---

[74] Letter Reimarus to Querini, 8 October 1744, VQS. MS. 257: "Habes autem hic Neaulmii ipsius epistolam, qua suam in rescribendo tarditatem excusat, sed duram hanc mihi legem imponit, *de mettre tout dans sa perfection et derniere perfection.*"

[75] Letter Reimarus to Querini, 22 November 1747, VQS. MS. 257: "Nam dum bibliopolae meo in Belgio auctor sum, ut iam iam omnia in vernum tempus anni proximi ad editionem Dionis comparet, ille tergiversari, metumque belli imminentis causari ncipit. Ago rursus per D'Orvillum cum aliis, Wetstenio, Langerakio, ut ipsi alias vel maxime pares negotio, operam suam instituto commodent: omnes vero, Hannibalem ante portas suas esse Musis infestum, quasi compacto, respondent."

[76] Letter Reimarus to Querini, 5. February 1748, VQS. MS. 257: "Nunc quoniam Heroldus mutavit consilium, et fortunam libelli expecandam sibi duxit, illud quoque nequicquam à me scriptum sit."

[77] Letter Reimarus to Querini, 8 October 1749, VQS. MS. 257: "Duo nempe exempla ligata, alterum charta majori, alterum vulgari, capsula lignea inclusa, et linteo cerato probe munita contra tempestatis injurias, die xxvii. Septembris Lipsam ad Jo. Henr. Wolfium, mercatorem, ut jusseras, misi."

[78] *Göttingische Zeitungen von Gelehrten Sachen*, 29 December 1749 (129), p. 1027: "Wir tragen wenigstens kein Bedenken dieses Werk unter die größten Zierraihen [sic] Deutschlands und dieser Zeiten zu rechnen, man mag es auf einer Seite betrachten auf welcher man will."

Latin translation and restore the Greek text.[79] One reviewer noted particularly Reimarus' discreet bracketing of insertions into the text from outside
sources such as Xiphilinus or Zonaras.[80] The German press praised the
work – even from an aesthetic point of view – as testimony that "not only
Holland and England were able to produce skilled scholars and excellent
editions of ancient writers"[81] And even twenty years later and entirely
unprejudiced by nationalist enthusiasm, the English scholar Edward Harwood in his classical bibliographical study noted that, after reading Reimarus' edition twice, he had come to the conclusion that it was "one of
the most correct and valuable Greek books ever published."[82]

The publication of Cassius Dio serves as a landmark in Reimarus' career.
It represents his first major publication on a grand international scale. It
not only placed him on the map of international scholarship, but provided
admittance into the pantheon of German classical scholarship, populated
by such outstanding figures as his famous father-in-law, Johann Matthias
Gesner, or Johann Jacob Reiske, and the offer to replace the deceased
Gesner in Göttinger is no small proof of that.[83] Reimarus' approach and
the nature of his work, however, represent a form of classical scholarship
that no longer fell into the philological tradition of a *historia literaria* that
had been so widespread in Germany during the seventeenth-century.
Long before many of his contemporaries, Fabricius had taken notice of
the pioneering work of Richard Bentley, but his demise may have pre-

---

[79] *Journal des Sçavans*, August 1751, p. 522: "Après cette digression M. Reimar rend
compte de tout ce qu'il a fait pour rétablissement du texte & our la correction de lar
traduction Latine de Dion. Il paroît n'avoir négligé aucun secours pour rendre son édition
parfaite."

[80] *Zuverläßige Nachrichten von dem gegenwärtigen Zustande Veränderung und Wachsthum
der Wissenschaften* 1752 (154), p. 515: "Die einzeln Stücken die sich in den sogenannten
Excerptis peirescianis und Legationum, oder Fulvii Ursini fanden, and gehörigen Orte und
Stelle eingerückt, dabey aber die wohlangebrachte Vorsicht gebraucht, die eingerückten
Fragmenta mit Klammern einzufassen, damit man sogleich wissen könne, was in den
gemeinen Ausgaben des Xiphilini zu finden sey oder nicht." The anonymous reviewer was
Johann Jacob Reiske, who wrote on 20 December 1749 in a letter to his friend Johann
Stephan Bernard in Amsterdam: "Nuper recensui in Actis Germanicis novum Dionem
Cassii Reimari. Mittam ubi prodierit et occasio fuerit oblata. Splendida et bona est editio,
[...]." See *Johann Jacob Reiske's Briefe* (Leipzig, 1897), p. 365.

[81] Ibid., p. 513f.: "Wir freuen uns, daß Deutschland ein Werk zu Stande gebracht,
welches ihm Ehre macht, und zu einem Beweise dienen wird, daß nicht allein Holl-und
Engelland fähig sind, geschichte Criticos und düchtige Ausgaben alter Schriftsteller hervor
zu bringen."

[82] Edward Harwood, *A View of the Various Editions of the Greek and Roman Classics*
(London, 1778), p. 81.

[83] Carl Mönckeberg, *Hermann Samuel Reimarus und Johann Christian Edelmann*
(Hamburg, 1867), p. 125.

vented him from following Bentley's example and putting these principles into practice.[84] Whereas Bentley's work had fallen onto fruitful soil in the Dutch Republic, German classical scholars seemed much more reserved about challenging the Vulgate. By aggressively attacking Estienne's *editio princeps* and working extensively with the Vatican and Medicean manuscripts, Reimarus displayed already symptoms of the cold textual criticism that would become more prominent among some of his younger peers such as Reiske[85], ultimately culminating in the work of Lachmann.[86] Arguably then, the publication of Reimarus' Dio also marked the end of another journey, namely his "Fabrician tutelage". Up to that point – with the exception of some smaller pieces – every publication of his had been produced under the supervision of, or in direct relationship to Fabricius. With the completion of his Dio, Reimarus had finally managed to establish himself as a major figure in his own right, and at the age of fifty-eight, it was just about time.

An Afterthought

It seems almost blasphemous to write about Reimarus without touching in one way or another on his other life or his secret self. In my study of Reimarus' classical scholarship as exemplified in his edition of Cassius Dio, I wanted to avoid reading the *Apology*[87] into Cassius Dio or reading Cassius Dio into the *Apology*. In fact, the latter attempt would not yield too many results. But are there parallels or even intersections? Since I am neither philosopher nor theologian by training, my approaches as a historian are limited and constrained and I have to resort to merely practical, possibly even self-evident observations.

In a later draft of his *Apology*, Reimarus himself claimed that he had been working on his project for just about thirty years. Peter Stemmer has provided plausible evidence that Reimarus did indeed start his secret work some time during the 1730s.[88] From purely practical considerations

---

[84] Petersen, *Johann Albert Fabricius*, vol. 2, p. 887.

[85] Hans-Georg Ebert, ed., *Johann Jacob Reiske – Leben und Wirkung: ein Leipziger Byzantinist und Begründer der Orientalistik im 18. Jahrhundert* (Leipzig, 2005).

[86] Sebastiano Timpanaro, *The Genesis of Lachmann's Method*, ed. and trans. by Glenn W. Most (Chicago, 2005).

[87] Hermann Samuel Reimarus, *Apologie oder Schutzschrift für die vernünftigen Verehrer Gottes*, 2 vols., ed. Gerhard Alexander (Frankfurt, 1972).

[88] Peter Stemmer, *Weissagung und Kritik* (Göttingen, 1983), pp. 92–102.

alone we can then assume that for quite some time, Reimarus pursued both the *Apology* and his Cassius Dio project simultaneously, and apart from some minor funeral eulogies, speeches, or treatises, not much else. A glance at Reimarus' publication record during the period he was involved in the Dio project seems bleak, to put it mildly. All of his major works were published after his Dio edition: the *Vornehmsten Wahrheiten der natürlichen Religion* was published in 1754, the *Vernunftlehre* was published in 1755 and the *Allgemeine Betrachtungen über die Triebe der Thiere* was published in 1760.[89] That obviously does not mean that he may not have worked on some or any of these works, nor does it mean that these works need to be considered separately from the *Apology*. However, it is nonetheless probably safe to assume that Reimarus was engrossed mainly in his Dio edition during this period and the little time he had at his disposal may very well have been spent on his secret work.

One should also not discount the fact that Reimarus' physical condition was by no means as strong as Fabricius'.[90] The letters to the Cardinal contain frequent references to Reimarus' ailing physical condition, which included tormenting headaches and insomnia, and by his own account incapacitated Reimarus to such an extent that he was virtually unable to accomplish any work besides some domestic duties, as he calls them, and the daily six hours of teaching or tutoring.[91]

If we may then assume that his literary efforts were to a large extent concentrated upon his Cassius Dio and the *Apology*, is it not possible that working with a classical author and elucidating his text had some impact on Reimarus' approach to the classical authors of the Hebrew Bible and the New Testament? Might it not then happen that any classical text, in no matter what language, would be approached and examined with sim-

---

[89] Hermann Samuel Reimarus, *Die vornehmsten Wahrheiten der natürlichen Religion*, ed. Günter Gawlick et al., 2 vols. (reprint; Göttingen, 1985); id., *Vernunftlehre*, ed. Friedrich Lötzsch, 2 vols. (reprint; Munich, 1979); id., *Allgemeine Betrachtungen uber die Triebe der Thiere, hauptsächlich über ihre Kunsttriebe*, ed. Jürgen von Kempski, 2 vols. (reprint; Göttingen, 1982).

[90] Reimarus writes about Fabricius' physical condition: "Nam gaudebat primum per naturam valetudine corporis adeo inconcussa, ut prope intra triginta vitae postremos annos eum aegrotasse non meminerim" See Hermann Samuel Reimarus, *De Vita et Scriptis Joannis Albertii Fabricii comentarius* (Hamburg, 1737), p. 41.

[91] See Letter Reimarus to Cardinal Querini, 4 July 1743, VQS. Ms. 257: "Recte autem suspicaris, obscisse mihi valetudinem, qua scilicet iam per triennium adeo dubia et fragili utor, ut ex frequenti insomnia et capitis doloribus imparem me literis et seriae meditationi esse sentiam: praesertim, cum ea sit suscepti muneris prope dixerim miserrima conditio, ut instituendae iuventuti senas quotidie horas tribuere, et reliquum fere omne tempus in recuperandis viribus exhaustis conterere necese sit [...]."

ilar tools and materials? As many scholars probably know, Cassius Dio
describes close to one thousand years of Roman history, or to put it in
more vivid terms, Roman history from village to empire. At its height,
the empire stretched from Spain to parts of Armenia and from Britain
to Egypt. Dio's *Roman History* then inevitably describes many instances
of encounters between Romans and other cultures. Among them were
also those in the cradle of civilization and the lands of the Bible. From a
text-critical point of view, this leads inevitably to some overlap between
philologia profana and *philologia sacra*. I have already hinted before that the
historical commentary includes numerous references to biblical passages
as well as references to many works on Jewish antiquities, and the note
Loca biblica non observata Fabricio suggests[92] that this was a conscious decision. A glance at the sources used in both the *Apology* and the Dio edition
reveals striking coincidences: besides the heavy use of classical authors we
find in both cases voluminous works by Samuel Bochart, Salomon Deyling,
Ezechiel and Friedrich Spanheim, as well as more specifically, references to
Hadrian Reland, Pierre Daniel Huet, John Marsham, and John Selden.

An indication of this coincidence of *philologia sacra* and *philologia
profana* is also the case when theoretical works for the analysis of one
type of texts are used as a guide for the other. For instance, Dio describes
a rebellion during the reign of Nero under the leadership of a charismatic
female figure referred to as Boadicea. As Dio reports, the Queen gave a
rousing speech in which she likened the Romans to foxes and hares trying to rule over dogs and wolves, and once she had finished, she let a hare
escape from a fold of her dress.[93] Reimarus puts this gesture into the context of the prophets of the Old Testament and refers the reader to Salomon
Glassius' *Philologia Sacra*, a standard theoretical text of Lutheran exegesis,
which served as an instructive work for a philologically correct reading of
Scripture.[94] Glassius explains that prophets "often through the Holy Spirit
utter and indicate by means of external objects hidden meanings about
present or future."[95] Ironically, Reimarus also makes a reference to Jean

---

[92] See footnote 29.
[93] See *Cassii Dionis Cocceiani Historiae Romanae*, vol. 2 (1752), Lib. LXII, 703 B–C, pp.
1006–1007: "ταῦτα εἰποῦσα, λαγὼν μὲν ἐκ τοῦ κόλπου προήκατο μεντείᾳ τινὶ χρωμένη, καὶ
ἐπειδὴ ἐν αἰσίῳ σφίσιν ἔδραμε [. . .]."
[94] Ibid., see footnote § 32.
[95] Salomon Glassius, *Philologia Sacra* (Leipzig, 1713), p. 453: "Typus Prophetiae
seu propheticus est, quo Prophetae divinitus inspirati, suis in concionibus, partim
commonitoriis, partim vaticinatoriis, crebro utuntur, quando videlicet symbolis externis
res occultas, sive praesentes sive futuras, per Spiritum sanctum figurant & significant."

Le Clerc's commentary on Genesis 32.24, where Jacob wrestles with an angel. In a lengthy note, Le Clerc explains that the people of the Orient often expressed themselves not only through words, but also by means of symbolic actions.[96] Why is the reference to Le Clerc ironic? Because just about twenty years earlier, when a young Reimarus recounted in his travel journal his meeting with the famous Le Clerc, he expressed his irritation with the latter's too profane study of the Bible.[97]

Another example occurs in Book 69, where Dio describes the Jewish revolt and explains its cause as the Emperor Hadrian's decision to make Jerusalem into a pagan city. Here, Reimarus agrees with Dio and rejects the other potential cause stated in the *Historia Augusta*, which blames a ban on circumcision for the unrest. Reimarus suggests that Dio's argument seems more convincing, since the reconstruction of the temple was a necessary prerequisite for the coming of the messiah, and the notorious pseudo-messiah Simon bar Kosiba was spearheading the uprising.[98] Reimarus then quotes numerous authors who, starting with Eusebius, have written about bar Kosiba. Tillemont for example in his *Histoire des Empereurs* adopted Scaliger's theory that bar Kosiba's name was originally Cozeb, which he translates as *menteur*, but that he later took the name Coquebas and then Barcoquebas, which means *fils de l'étoile* [descended from the star] in order to "rally the Jews and to present himself as having descended from heaven to rescue them."[99] And Reland, a frequent source in the Apology, provides an equally lengthy discussion of him in his *Palaestina*.[100] But Simon bar Kosiba appears in the *Apology* as well,

---

[96] See Jean Le Clerc, *Genesis sive Mosis Prophetae Liber Primus* (Tübingen, 1733) p. 249: "Orientales solitos esse quod vellent, non modo verbis, sed actionibus exprimere, ex pluribus Scriptorum Sacrorum locis constat."

[97] Staats- und Universitätsbibliothek Hamburg Carl von Ossietzky (StUBH), Reimarus Nachlaß III b4, "Tagebuch Notiz aus Holland": "Le Clerc [...] schiene mir ein wenig profan, daß er sagte, er critisirte die Bibel nicht anders, als ob er den Aristophanen vor sich hatte."

[98] See *Cassii Dionis Cocceiani Historiae Romanae*, vol. 2 (1752) p. 1161, footnote § 108:" [...] Dionis igitur causa unice vera est. Accedebar dux seditionis & Pseudo-Messias Barcochebas, de quo *Scaliger* ad Euseb. p. 216. *Wagenseilius* ad Misnam Sota VIII. I. not. 12. alii apud *Wofium* Bibl. Hebr. P. I. & III. num. 1336. Nec ab hac ratione dissentiunt, qui Judaeos dicunt voluisse priorem Politiam & templum restaurare. Hoc enim consilium cum Messiae venientis opinione necessario conjunctum fuit."

[99] Tillemont, *Histoire des Empereurs*, vol. 2 (1691), p. 306: "Scaliger remarque sur l'autorité des Rabbins qu'il s'appelloit en son nom Cozeb, c'est à dire *menteur* [...] il prit celuy de Coquebas qui signifie *étoile* ou Barcoquebas *fils de l'étoile*, pour tromper les Juifs, & se faire considerer comme un astre favorable descendu du ciel pour secourir."

[100] Hadrian Reland, *Palaestina: ex monumentis veteribus illustrata* (Nuremberg, 1716), p. 696f.

when Reimarus expounds on the role of charlatanry in Jewish messianism. We learn from Reimarus that Simon bar Kosiba, not Jesus, was the
most notorious of all these impostors, since he caused "a great deal of
unrest." He "acquired the reputation of a miracle worker by breathing fire
(just as travelling entertainers do these days)"[101] and Reimarus explains
that people like him tried to incorporate the then widespread expectation of a messiah into their scheme to gain power through charlatanry
and deception.

Of course, I do not claim that these sources cannot be used in both
contexts without automatically serving the purpose of undermining revelation. But what I would like to suggest is that they can serve as tools
simply to explain the miraculous or supernatural away by treating it
within the history of ancient cultures and antiquities. As a consequence,
the sacrificial practices among Jews become no different from what the
Greeks, Romans, Phoenicians, or Parthians did, as outlined in the works
of Graevius, Pfeiffer, or Ugolino. So when Dio for example mentions the
battle cry of Roman soldiers under Pompey in their fight against Mithri-
dates, Reimarus adds a reference to Jacob Lydius' *Syntagma de re militari
et de iure iurando Hebraeorum* as well as to Gideon's campaign against the
Midianites in Judges 6–8 to those by Lipsius or Thomas Hutchins.[102] What
many of these works have in common is that they are heavily philological
and require often not only proficiency in Greek and Hebrew, but also in
Syriac, Aramaic, and even Arabic. Proficiency in these languages was even
in Reimarus' day and era no longer or not yet the norm (Michaelis, Lowth,
etc.). Reimarus' own proficiency in Arabic seems either non-existent or
rudimentary at best and his course in Chaldaic and Hebrew at the *Gymnasium illustre* was often cancelled due to a lack of interested students.[103]
The period from the sixteenth to the eighteenth century had seen the
publication of encyclopedic works such as Bochart's, Old Testament projects such as Johann Heinrich Michaelis' or Benjamin Kennicott's, and

---

[101] Reimarus, *Apologie oder Schutzschrift für die vernünftigen Verehrer Gottes*, ed. Gerhard
Alexander, vol. 2 (Frankfurt, 1978), p. 19f.: "Keiner aber ist desfals berühmter, als der
Barcochebas, welcher bey den gelehrtesten Juden von Bitter, insonderheit von dem Rabbi
Akibha, für den wirklichen wahren Messias gehalten ward, und große Unruhen anrichtete.
Man sieht aus den Nachrichten von ihm daß er sich bey den Seinigen das Ansehen eines
Wunderthäters erworben, indem er zwischen seinem Reden (wie die Gaukler jetzt thun)
Feuer aus dem Munde gehen lassen; daß er sich, wie sein Name lautet, für eine Sohn der
Sterne ausgegeben, (quasi sidus e coelo delapsum, wie Eusebius sagt.) [...]."

[102] See *Dionis Cocceiani Historiae Romanae*, vol. 1 (1750), p. 105, § 105.

[103] See Wilhelm Schmidt-Biggemann, *Hermann Samuel Reimarus: Handschriftenverzeichnis
und Bibliographie* (Göttingen, 1979), p. 30ff., see entries for 1738/39, 1758/59, 1762/63.

convenient compilations such as the Protestant *Philologici Sacri* or Blasius Ugolini's *Thesaurus Antiquitatum Sacrum*, from which Reimarus benefited both in his secret and non-secret work (see here especially Fabricius' *Bibliographia Antiquaria*). This has therefore led me to believe that one could potentially argue that Reimarus was able to harvest the seeds that had been sown by humanists and reformers with their plea to study the sacred languages.

APPENDIX

Selection of letters from the Reimarus-Querini correspondence illustrating the nature of Reimarus' work as well as his controversy with Falco.[104]
(VQS: Fondazione Querini Stampalia; PBN: Paris, Bibliothèque Nationale)

Letter 1
[Hamburg, 29 January 1737: Reimarus requests collations of two Dio manuscripts from the Vatican Library].[105]

Eminentissimo Reverendissimoque Domino
Angelo Mariae Cardinali Quirino
Episcopo Brixiensi et S. R. C.
Bibliothecario
S. P. D. Hermannus Sam. Reimarus

Immortali me beneficio affecisti, Domine Eminentissime, qui non tantum respondere ad levidenses literas meas dignatus es, sed et ex Bibliotheca Vaticana quae mihi opportuna et utilia esse possint, ultro ac liberaliter offers. Fateor, venerationem illam virtutum Tuarum, quas et aliunde novam, et mirifice mihi praedicabat amicus meus Conradus Widovius, Senator Hamburgensis, multum Tecum in aedibus Longuerueianis Lutetiae versatus, haud mediocriter apud me auctam esse isto Magnis Viris proprio studio bene merendi de omnibus iisdemque ignotis et immerentibus. Quare haud aegre feres, si quod iusisti Ipse, Amplissime Cardinalis, petam abs Te audacter et libere, Dionis nimirum Cassii ut collationem ad Codices Vaticanos institui haud gravatim cures, quos memorat Rev. Nicolaus Carminius Falco. Nam ut Dionis editionem novam ab illo vix sperandam esse retulerunt amici, ita Soceri mei notas in eundem Scriptorem amplas et eruditas habeo in manibus, luce profecto indignas, si ipsum auctorem fide veterum membranarum expolire Tuo beneficio daretur. Perinde autem mihi fuerit, ad quam editionem collatio instituati quoniam eas quae exstant possideo propemodum omnes. Utinam placeret Tibi, Eminentissime Cardinalis, aliquid oneris mihi imponere, non

---

[104] I am grateful to Ennio Ferraglio from the *Biblioteca Queriniana*, Brescia for bringing these letters to my attention and to Barbara Poli from the *Fondazione Querini Stampalia*, Venice for providing me with reproductions.

[105] VQS. Ms. 257.

quod compensare me ullo pacto Tuam in me voluntatem posse arbitrer, aut quod minus libenter sim in aere Tuo, sed ut intelligas, quantopere me insignis Tuae humanitatis admiratio incenderit, modo quid proficisci a virium mearum tenuitate queat, desideriis Tuis vel etiam meis respondens. Accipe interim benevole geminum Philastrii Fabriciani exemplum, et nugas quasdam meas iis adiunctas. Vale. Dabam Hamburgi IV. Kal. Febr. CVVCCXXXVII.

Letter 2

[Hamburg, 4 July 1743: Reimarus requests a response from Querini about a Dio fragment published by Henri de Valois in 1634,[106] which recounts the attempt of the Roman Tribune Licinius Stolo to convince the Roman people of the validity of all three of his proposed bills (most importantly access to the Consulate)].[107]

Reverendissimo et Eminentissimo
ANGELO MARIAE Cardinali QUERINO
Bibliothecario Vaticano et Episcopo
Brixiensi
S. P. D.
Hermannus Samuel Reimarus

Credidi quidem semper facilius posse accidere, ut scriptione mea inficeta, quam ut silentio cuiquam essem molestus; tamen quatenus Summorum Virorum singularis humanitas verecundiam meam interdum vincit exactione debitae responsionis, nemo est, qui vel magis meam in scribendo tarditatem, vel prior accuset, me ipso; nemo, cui hoc officium debeam impatientius quam Tibi, Cardinalis Eminentissime, ad cuius me favorem studiosissime amplectendum non magis purpurae et gentis splendor, quam doctrinae eximiae, ingenii, industriae et comitatis admiratio rapit.

---

[106] *Polybii Diodori Siculi Nicolai Damasceni Dionysii Halicar. Appiani Alexand. Dionis et Iaonnis Antiocheni Excerepta ex Collectaneis Constantini Augusti Porphyrogenetae Henricus Valesius nunc primum Graece edidit, Latine vertit, Notisque illustravit* (Paris, 1634), p. 585; Reimarus would later acknowledge in his commentary the response he received in this particular case from Querini; see *Cassii Dionis Cocceiani Historiae Romanae*, vol. 1 (1750), p. 16, § 51: "[...] attamen nolo placere mihi, & lubens cogitata submittam iudicio doctiorum, atque in his praesertim Eminentissimi Cardinalis *Querini*, cui & alias Dio hicce plurimum debet. Ei enim, forte per literas, quid ageret Dio noster, quaerenti, cum hanc inter alia emendatiunculam perscripsissem, respondit [...]."

[107] VQS. Ms. 257.

Recte autem suspicaris, obfuisse mihĭ valetudinem, qua scilicet iam per triennium adeo dubia et fragili utor, ut ex frequenti insomnia et capitis doloribus imparem me literis et seriae meditationi esse sententiam: praesertim, cum ea sit suscepti muneris prope dixerim miserrima conditio, ut instituendae iuventuti senas quotidie horas tribuere, et reliquum fere omne tempus in recuperandis viribus exhaustis conterre necesse sit; nisi etiam domesticae vitae rationes hanc debilitati meae necessariam medicinam intervertant. Recreo me tamen interdum lectis Tuis epistolis, cum iis quas ad Viros doctissimos datas typis exprimi curasti, varia eruditione iucundas, tum iis, quas geminas nuper manu Tua ad me scripsisti, significatione prolixa Tuae in me voluntatis suavissimas; nisi quod hoc unum aegre me habet, quod nondum potui desiderio Tuo videndi Dionis, partim ob rationes commemoratas partim ob bibliopolae ipsius occupatam adhuc in aliis operam, satisfacere. Interim dum Scriptorem lectu dignissimum extrema quasi lima per otium pro viribus polio, placet Tecum, Cardinalis Eminentissime, emendationum mearum specimen communicare, et iudicio Tuo exercitato submittere. Nuper excerpta ex Dione a Valesio edita in Peirescianis retractans incidi in locum p. 585. ubi Licinius Stolo Tribunus turbulenta oratione reconciliationem plebis cum patribus impedire non veretur. Populus enim ex duabus eius rogationibus alteram de foenore et agro iusserat, alteram de plebeio consulatu antiquaverat. At Stolo: *aut omnia*, inquit, *accipite, aut nihil fero*; teste Livio VI.40. τοιοῦτόν τι εἰπὼν, ὡς οὐκ ἀπίοιεν εἰ μὴ φάγοιεν, teste Dione l.c. Haec mirum in modum obscura sunt, inquit Valesius; ipse, ut si legeretur ἢ μὴ φάγοιεν, interpretatur: *potius a cibo quam à perferendis rotationibus abstinere*. Sed ne sic quidem is sensus erui potest. Mihi legendum videtur: ὡς οὐκ ἂν πίοιεν εἰ μὴ φάγοιεν. Proverbiali enim locutione negat Stolo, bibendum esse ei qui esse nolit, h. e. negat concedendam plebi alteram rogationem sine altera, cum utraque coniungi debeat perinde ut potus et cibus. Intemperantia enim habebatur apud Veteres, bibere ante sumtum cibum; οὐδὲ γὰρ ὕδωρ οἱ παλαιοὶ πρὶν ἐντραγεῖν ἔπινον, ut ait Plut[archus] Sympos[ium] p. 734. A. et iudice Seneca ep[istola] 122. *isti videntur contra naturam vivere, qui ieiuni bibunt, qui vinum recipiunt inanibus venis*: quae intemperantia seriore demum aetate sub Tiberio Claudio invaluit, ut Plinius auctor est. XIV. 22. Eiusmodi quid, τοιοῦτόν τι, per proverbium populo dixisse Stolonem, colligas etiam ex responsione Appii Claudii, quae est apud Livium, eadem metaphora, sed in aliam partem versa: *ut si quis ei quem urgeat fames venenum ponat cum cibo, et aut abstinere eo quod vitale sit iubeat, aut mortiferum vitali admisceat*. Aut igitur vehementer fallor, aut proverbio locutus antea erat Stolo, ὡς οὐκ ἂν πίοιεν εἰ μὴ φάγοιεν, quod simpliciter apud Livium effertur: aut omnia accipite, aut nihil fero. Sed falsum me esse in hac coniectura fatebor lubens, si Tibi, Cardinalis Eminentissime, displiceat, quippe summo harum rerum iudici et arbitro; gratulabor contra mihi, si Tuum merebitur assensum, et plures emendationes in posterum Tibi sistere non verebor. Ceterum ne inanis prorsus haec ad Te veniat epistola, adjunxi *M. Jo. Henr. Leichii, Lipsiensis Diatriben de Diptychis Veterum et de Diptycho Emin. Quirino*, Lips. 1743. 4. Agit Sect. 1. de Diptychis Consularibus II. de Brixiano Boetii Consulis et de Ecclesiasticis Diptychis. III. de Diptycho Tuo. Ad Consularia ille referendum negat, aut ad amantium tabulas, denique nihil habere dicit commune cum veterum diptychis; suspicatur pertinere ad aetatem Pauli II. P.M. qui remascentes literas et artes praesidio suo fovit. Vult autem a sculptore Meleagrum et Atalantam, Paridem et Helenam, duo amantium paria afficta esse, et Meleagrum in veteri gemma apud Maffei *Gemone antiche* T. IV. 19. cum hoc confert: habitum, quem Sculpator largitus est suis, ab antiquo esse alienum, nec exstare in monumentis vetustatis exemplum modestiae eiusmodi, qua sine membro vir repraesentetur. Haec paucis praemonere volui, quia forte libellus epistolam hanc tardius sequentur. Interim alteram Tuarum epistolarum Decadem, quam huc deferendam Te curasse scribis, avide exspecto, enixe rogitans ut proxima occasione quoque imaginem Tuam aeri incisam, cuius ectypon huc allatum vidi, mihi ne invideas; cum habere identidem ante oculos optem corporis simulacrum cuius hospes est animus tot monumentis diffusae eruditionis, tanto virtutum et comitatis decore dudum mihi cognitus. Vale. Dabam. D. IV. Jul. CVVCCXLIII.

P.S. Cl. Siberi de Melodis Graecis plenior commentarius, quod sciam, non prodiit in lucem, digitur tamen elaboratus ab eo relictus esse, quod Menckenius optime docebit.

Letter 3
[Hamburg, 30 August 1743: Reimarus expresses his wish to dedicate his future edition of Dio to the Cardinal; he makes a few more suggestions for the interpretation of the passage about the Licinian laws (see previous letter) and provides a list of samples from Dio published by Henri de Valois, for which he proposes changes].[108]

---

[108] VQS. Ms. 257.

Eminentissimo ac Reverendissimo
ANGELO MARIAE Cardinali QUIRINO
Bibliotheca Vaticano
S. P. D.
Hermannus Sam. Reimarus

Quanquam eo mihi videbar animo erga Te, Eminentissime Cardinalis, esse affectus, ut ad Tuarum admirationem virtutum nihil putarem posse accedere; tamen ut eas et perspicerem et suspicerem magis, effecit missum nuper ad promovendam editionem Dionis Cassii munus duplex, alterum nummarium, literarium alterum. Quidni enim opem, quam tulisti loco difficili, pariter pro munere, et auro contra habendam existimem?

In illa quidem liberalitate nummaria, praeter expectationem in me derivata, studium inusitatum, in hac literaria, vires et ingenium iuvandi bonas artes, admiratus sum vehementer: in utraque iuxta Tuam in me benivolentiam agnovi venerabundus. Ego vero vel maxime nunc collecto animo in maturandam Dionis editionem incumbo, postquam Tibi id tantopere placere, et spem aliquam in mea qualicunque opera positam esse intellexi. Quin addidisti fiduciam, ut Dionem illum, quem tot modis ornasti et fovisti, modo hanc a Te veniam imetravero, sub Tuis auspiciis, Illustri Tuo nomini dedicandum prodire iubeam in lucem. Neque enim circumspicienti mihi succurrit nomen illustrius in republica literaria, aut melius vel de eruditione universa, vel de Dione, meque adeo ipso meritum; cuius ego et decora singularia et praestita mihi beneficia publice praedicandi occasionem dari mihi serio optem. Interea dum hanc abs Te veniam mihi concedi intellexero, suppeditare liceat materiem novis Tuis in ipsum hunc Auctorem observationibus. Ac primum quae pro erudita Tua interpretatione loci proposini facere visa sint dicam. *comedere* eo sensu Plautus adhibet: Aul[ularia] III. VI. 1. *nimium libenter edi sermonem tuum*, quod interpres editionis in usum Delphini exponit: devoravi auribus. et ipse Plautus Asin[aria] III. III. 59. *auscultate, atque operam date et mea dicta devorate*, i.e. accipite avide. denique Cist[ellaria] IV. II. 54. *istuc mihi cibus est*, inquit, quae me docuit Cl. Burmannus ad Quintil[ianus] Decl[amationes] CCLXVIII. p. 508 ubi pro verbis: *nomen sapientiae avide dederunt*, legi posse censet *avide ederunt*. Chaldaeorum quoque phrasis est Dan[iel] III. 8. אֲכַלוּ קַרְצֵיהוֹן *ederunt exitium eorum* i.e. avide captarunt; qua ratione et Syrus interpres novi Testamenti τὸν διάβολον captantem vel *edentem exitium*, solet describere. Poterat etiam Stolo, apud Livium certe, videri rogationem duplicem instar duplicis *ferculi* proponere, si eo referas verba: aut omnia accipite, aut nihil *fero*. Neque tamen potui adhuc in graecis scriptoribus similia exempla verbi φάγειν, pro *avide accipere*, expiscari, quae Tua forte amplissima lectio suppeditabit. Succurres etiam quaeso haesitanti in eo, quod Stolo nihil addit, quid debeant φάγειν, cum videatur dicendum fuisse, εἰ μὴ ἑκάτερον φάγοιεν, aut πάντα φάγοιεν; quae si essent, nihil posset ad evidentiam tuae interpretationis accedere, cuius et ego ut par est, honoroficam in Dione faciam mentionem. Interim nihil in textu mutare certum est, quod nec alias soleo facere, nisi ubi sphalmata sunt admodum manifesta, aut praeiverunt Codices Tui, vel etiam interdum Zonaras, qui Dionea plerumque ad verbum exscripta exhibet. Dabo hic, pace Tua, quaedam exempla Excerptorum Valesii, ubi in contextu aliquid mutavi, praemonito tamen Lectore, ut iudicare possis, fuerrimne ea in re nimis audax.

p. 770. Ἰανὸν διὰ τὴν τοῦ χρόνου ξένισιν. Scribo: *Κρόνου*. Ianum, eo quod Saturnum hospitio exceperit, futurorum ac praeteritorum notitia donatum.

p. 771. med. ἐπὶ τὸ ἀπ᾽ αὐτοῦ ὠνομασμένον Ἀλβανὸν ὄρος. Scribo cum Pottero: ἀπ᾽ αὐτῆς, scil. Χοίρον λευκῆς ab alba porca Albanum appellavit.

p. 774. καὶ ἐδικαιολογήθησαν ἐν τῷ συνεδρίῳ. Scribo: ἐδικαιώθησαν ex Suida, et res docet; Campanos actores Marcelli male mulctatos esse. Liv[ius] XXVI.34.

p. 775. Δίων ἐν κθ᾽. Deleo totum fragmentum, est enim in editis Dionis Lib. XXXIX. p. III. A. edit. Leunclavii, et Suidas recte laudat librum λθ.

p. 602. fin. ἔσεσθαι αὐτὸς ἐν ἔρωτι. Scribo: αὐτῆς ἐν ἔρωτι ex Zonara p. 430 C. edit[io] Cangii.

p. 605. init. ἐγγύηται. Scribo: ἐγγεγύηται, ut est apud Zonar. ibid.

p. 610. καὶ τὰ ἐκείνων ἐπήυξετο. Scribo ἐκείνου, nempe Persei, ut rectius Zonaras p. 457. B.

p. 613. τῇ γυναικὶ προῖκα ἀποδοῦναι. Scribo ἀποδοθῆναι ex Zonara p. 460. B. et sensus requirit passivum.

p. 617. Συλάββους Ταλάτας. Scribo Σασλάββους. Ita cum alii tum Dio ipse constanter. p. 412. A. 414. D. 513. D. E.

p. 637. Χωρίον ἐνερκὲς τειχιβάριενος. Scribo εὐερκὲς. Illud inusitatum Graecis, hoc praeter ceteros Dio habet p. 463. B. εὐερκέσατον τεῖχος et p. 579. E. ἐπ᾽ εὐερκοῖς πέτρας ἐπετετείχιστο.

Iam alia rurus specimina accipe benevole, quae minus nimirum certa, intacto textu, in notas reieci.

p. 773.   ἔνθα νῦν ἡ *Ρώμη* ἐστὶ, χωρίον ἦν πρῶτον λεγόμενον Οἰνωτρία. Romam in Oenotria non reperio. Forte *Χώνη* legendum. Steph[anus] Byz[antinus] Χώνη, πόλις Ὀινότρων ἧς στράνων [sic] μέμνηται [sic] ἐν ἑρδόμῃ, καὶ τὴν γῆν ὠνόμασε Χώνην. Philoctetes, de quo hic sermo, Chonin habuit sedem, teste Strab[o] VI. p. 254.

p. 582.   ἐπείπερ οὗτος ὠνομάζετο. Videtur legendum, *οὕτως*

p. 589.   *Φίλιππος* ὁ Μακεδῶν. Nullus ea aetate in Macedonia Philippus. Viderint doctiores, an sit scribendum: *ἀλέξανδρος* ὁ Μακεδὼν, intellige Alexandrum Cassandri Filium, quem frater Major. Antipater pellere instituerat. Is enim Pyrrhum arcessivet, eique auxilii mercedem Nymphaeam, Ambraciam, Acarnaniam, Amphilochiam dedit, atque ab eo restitutus est, ut refert Plut[archus] in Pyrrho p. 386.A.B.

p. 590.   ἐπὶ μεῖζον *διαιρούμενοι*. forte rectius *αἱρόμενοι* ut Zonaras habet. ibid *κύντον* Φάβιον, lege *Κύϊντον*, ex Zonara.

p. 593.   τὴν ἀρχὴν ῥαδίως ἐνελῆθαι δι ' αὐτὴν ἀποστῆναι. Valesius legendum censet *διελῆ*, ut propagatum sibi in alterum annum imposium vix tulerit. Ego nihil muto. τὴν ἀρχὴν est omnino, ut saepius apud Dionem, δι' αὐτὴν scil. πενίαν. Sensus est: in tanta paupertate versabatur, ut propter illam omnino aegre domo discesserit. Nam constat vel ex Aurel[io] Vict[ore] de. V.J. c.40. absente eo coniugi ac liberis ob paupertatem sumtus publice datos.

p. 598.   καὶ παραχρῆμα ἀπεστρατοπεδεύβαντο. accuratius Zonaras p. 445. D. ὁ Ροῦφος ἀπεστρατοπεδεύβατο, h.e. ut Plutarchus effert p. 180. C. ἰδία καὶ χωρὶς ἐστρατοπέδευβεν.

p. 613.   fin. συμβαίνειν εἰώθει. videtur legendum *εἴωθε*.

p. 646.   init. *ἐπιλειποῦς* δε ' τῆς ὕλης. *ἐπιλειπούβης* apud Plut. p. 459. A. unde haec petita.

Plura nolo, ne molastus sim. Doleo diatriben de Diptychis nondum ad Te pervenisse; gratias habeo pro honore mihi in epistola Tua tributo; expecto avide Melodos Tuos una cum epistolis editis. Tuum favorem vero, Cardinalis Eminentissime ut mihi perpetuum ferves enixe rogo. Vale. Dabam Hamb. D. XXX Augusti CV VCC XLIII.

Letter 4
[Hamburg, 1 January 1746: Reimarus proposes to Querini a review of Falco's edition of the last three Books of Cassius Dio[109] in the form of a public letter addressed to him].[110]

Eminentissimo ac Reverendissimo
ANGELO MARIAE Cardinali QUIRINO
Episcopo Brixiensi et Bibliothecario Vaticano
S. P. D.
Hermannus Samuel Reimarus

Dum literas Tuas, Cardinalis Eminentissime, iam diu sollicite desidero, magis magisque adducor, ut meas pridem ad Te datas intercidisse credam. Scripseram autem, Tuo me monitu, mercatori Augustano ostendisse viam, qua tuto in posterum fasciculos sibi commendatos transmitteret; id quod fecit, omniaque in integrum restituit. Quodsi me ergo, id quod submisse et vehementer abs Te, Reverendissime Cardinalis peto, beare porro scriptis Tuis exoptatissimis dignaberis, recte ad me curabuntur omnia, quae reddi iusseris *à Messrs Wille, frères, marchands à Nurnberg pour l'adresse de Mr Rudolph Berenberg, Senateur à Hambourg.* Teneo autem adhuc ex tua novissima liberalitate, praeter Epistolas Pastorales, Partem primam epistolarum Cardinalis Poli, in quibus itemque vita eius Cardinalis recensendis usitatam Tuam non tantum accurationem et diligentiam, sed et iudicii vim et historiae omnis scientiam, quin et humanitatem erga adversarios facile agnosco. Schelhornius, ni fallor, ex eo tempore vivis excessit; mihi autem honorem sane meritis meis longe ampliorem tribuisti, quod meam quoque epistolam voluisti illius scripto adiungere. Scio enim, in hoc praesertim genere, nihil à me proficisci posse, quod luce publica dignum sit. Sed quoniam coepisti iam saepius, pro insigni Tuo in me favore, non solum literarum mearum vel particulas vel integras nonnullas immortalibus Tuis scriptis inserere, sed etiam me excitare benignius, ut aliquid ad Te dissertationis eruditae darem in vulgus: ausus nunc sum, quod aequi bonique, rogo, interpreteris, de ultimis libris Dionis a Cl. Falcone editis nonnulla, per modum epistolae ad Te datae, commentari. Mitto hic eius primam plagulam, integra autem ad plagulam F. excurrit: cuius reliqua, una cum initio Bibliothecae latinae medii aevi Fabricianae, à Schoetgenio

---

[109] *Cassii Dionis Romanae Historiae ultimi libri tres reperti restitutique studio ac labore Nic. Carminii Falconis Presbyteri* (Rome, 1724).
[110] VQS. Ms. 257.

Rectore Scholae Dresdensis continuata, cuius ego corrigendae curam suscepi, ad Te per mercatores nostros, forte Rizanium, aut alia, quae primum se offeret, occasione, perferri curabo. Vides iam ex commentationis huius exordio, eam non modo ad excusandam Tibi canetationem meam pertinere, sed et iudicium Tuum de illo meo specimine recensendi Dionis exquire. Quanquam vero nihil mihi gratius accidere possit, quam si quid calculo Tuo favente dignum inveneris; tamen velim existimes, me et monita Tua et reprehensiones, si quas privatim communicare mecum dignaberis, non minus grata mente accepturum. Nam ut Tuo illustri beneficio subsidii non parum Dio accipiet, sic eum ad Tuam quoque mentem quam maxime conformatum, eoque omnibus quoque rerum intelligentibus procul dubio placiturum, velim prodire in lucem. Ceterum vides simul quousque, ne quid celem, processerit mihi negotium, hoc est, graeca pariter et latina omnia Dionis et Xiphilini ad extremum esse recensita, et nihil praeter notas quasdam ad Xiphilinum, quarum iam praecipuam materiam congessi, superesse. Quare et eo amplies rogo benignitatem et patientiam Tuam, donec et has in ordinem redegero. Repeto autem et hic votum pro Tua incolumitate, quod epistolae editae subiunxi, ut Te Deus immortalis servet hoc anno quem novum ingredimur, servet etiam per complures secuturos ad feram aetatem, sic ut rebus undiquaque fecundis crescas ipse gloria, et literas augeas. Vale. Dabam Hamb. Kal. Ian. An. CVVCCXLVI.

Scripseram iam superiora, cum mihi in mentem venit, non potuisse me tuto Partem tuam I. epistolarum Card. Poli bibliopego committere, quoniam Epistolae ipsae incipiunt à p. 381. sed quae praecedit commentatio ad has epistolas desinit in p. 359. sic ut hiatus aliquis intercedere videatur. Quare haud gravatim ea de re certiorem me facies, aut, si placet, quae desunt mittes.

Letter 5
[Hamburg, 1 January 1746: Abbreviated version of the *Epistola*]

Hermann Samuel Reimarus, *Epistola ad Eminentissimum ac*
Reverendissimum
D.D. Angelum Mariam Tituli S. Marci Cardinalem Quirinum Brixiae
Episcopum et Bibliothecarium Vaticanum cet. qua Occasione Edendi Dionis
Cassii ad Nicolai Carminii Falconi J. U. et S. Theol. Doct. et Proton. Ap.
Editionem Trium Ultimorum Dionis Librorum ex Antiquissimo Codice
Restitutorum Animadversiones Nonnullas Summi Viri Judicio Submittit
(Hamburg: Carl Bohn, 1746)

Visus est mihi Nicolaus Carminius Falco, Vir Clarissimus, et de Dionis Cassii historia extrema diligenter meritus, argumentum suppeditare non prorsus indignum, quo Te publice affarer. Nam cum ego superiorem annum in magna parte Xiphilini, et ultimis hisce Dionis libris, quos ille Falco Vester ex antiquissimo Codice vulgavit, recensendis contrivissem, lentiusque mihi adhuc totum negotium processissset, quam vel ipse optarem, vel Tua, Cardinalis Eminentissime, ferre videretur exspectatio: faciendum putavi, ut Tibi de causis constaret, quae editionem, quam paro, Dionis et Xiphilini, per annos iam complusculos moratae sunt; utque intelligeres in primis specimine aliquo, quantum mihi adhuc salebrarum in hoc scriptore, post tot virorum doctissimorum labores, obiectum remanserit. Cui enim hanc cunctationem meam potius excusatum irem, quam Tibi? qui me dudum varietate lectionum ex duobus bibliothecae Vaticanae Codicibus humanissime instruxeras; qui et privatis Tuis literis incitabas subinde, et editis in vulgus semel atque iterum mentionem instituti a me operis adspergere dignabare; imo qui industriam meam munere liberalissimo, et praeterea tot tantisque ex eo tempore transmissis Tui ingenii documentis, Corcyrae Primordiis, Philastrio, literatura Brixiana, Francisci Barbari et Cardinalis Poli vita atque epistolis, itemque Tuis ad eruditos disputationibus bene multis, quasi stimulis, quibusdam, provocasti. Enimvero id primum verecunde et submisse abs Te peto, ne alios, et me quidem vel maxime, tardioris ingenii hominem, ex Tuae non modo doctrinae, sane quam diffusae, copia, sed et mentis mira et sagaci celeritate, atque adeo expedito in tanta negotiorum mole studio, et scribendi facilitate, metiare. Haec praecipua Tibi sunt decora, quibus, haud profecto minus, quam purpura Tua, Eminentissimus, aut natalibus, Illustrissimus merito audis; praesertim cum illa soleas prolixa benignitate erga alios, et iuvandis liberalissime hominum etiam exterorum conatibus, sicut ad communem utilitatem, ita ad Tui singularem admirationem, cultum amoremque convertere. De mea autem tenuitate, si quae unquam profutura, certe pauca, exilia, sera, et multo tamen meo labore quaesita, debes expectare. Memineris etiam, quaeso, veterum querelarum mearum, quarum ne nunc quidem cessat materia, de noctibus multis mihi insomnibus, deque valetudinis debilitate interdum erumpente in morbum. Quae quidem incommoda ita affligunt vigorem mentis, ut suspendere identidem studia literarum, et differre spem mihi aliisque factam cogar; abunde tum contentus, si muneris publice demandati partes quodammodo implere, et expedire domesticas rationes possim. Neque tamen ego naturam unam et tempora mea, quin me potius ipsum haud leviter accuso in eo, quod iam ab initio praecipere cogitatione, et figere iam mente sim ausus terminum suscepti laboris, et eum quidem longe angustiorem, quam amplitudo et difficultas rei, praesertim in tanta virium mearum infirmitate, pateretur. Quare si quid mihi quondam ad Te scribenti eiusmodi verbulum excidit, quod dudum finem operae certum et propinquiorem statueret, non recuso, quominus me praecipiti quadam spe lapsum existimes. Nam initio, cum praestantissimas illas Fabricii τοῦ πάνυ animadversiones ad Dionem, omni refertas eruditione vidissem, persuadebam mihi, eas et Graecis, et Latinae eorum interpretationi, emendandis facile suffecturas; ad Xiphilinum autem et fragmenta Dionis, quae plane non tetigerat socer meus, nullis adeo opus fore annotationibus arbitrabar; operamque meam omnem, et eam non adeo multam, in expoliendis, apteque disponendis et coniungendis iis, quae reperissem satis instructa ab aliis, positam fore; denique, quando ad extremos Dionis libros a Falcone editos ex optimo Codice, et observationibus illustratos, ventum esse, correctionibus meis aut accessionibus vix locum fore existimabam. Verum me in his plerisque spes et opinio mea fefellit; et ita fefellit, ut quo plus iam studii in hoc opere consumsissem, eo plus superesse adhuc intelligerem demum. Accidit mihi quod viatoribus, qui arcem, quo tendunt, velut propinquam satis prospeciant semper, ambages et salebras interiectas non prospiciunt; et profligato iam maximo spatio, non propius sibi, sed longius abesse a scopo videntur. Nolo de singulis dicere, quae iam, ut potui, superavi: vel extrema haec Dionis, quis non existimasset, studio Falconis tam expedita fore, ut cursim et inoffenso pede transiliri possent; praesertim trita iam ante eum vestigiis summorum virorum, Ursini, Leunclavii, Sylburgii? Et est sane diligentia Viri summopere praedicanda, qua Dionem ex vetustissimo Codice, accessionibus nonnullis, Ursino neglectis, auctiorem voluit dare, atque in ea re, quantum iudico, accurate satis et religiose versatus est. Verum non dubito, Cardinalis Eminentissime, Te pro Tua summa in his literis scientia, perspecturum simul ex dicendis, non tam occasionem mihi ab eo relictam fuisse, quam necessitatem impositam, refingendi et rescribendi quam plurima. Quae ego nunc, non tantum ad excusandam Tibi aliquatenus tarditatem meam, indicanda duxi; sed, si Tuo praesertim acuto iudicio stabunt, praeterire etiam silentio in Dione ipso vix possim. Puto enim officii esse eorum, qui ad scriptores veteres curam applicant suam, ut praeter codicum et editionum omnium lectiones, doctorum quoque virorum emendationes, et coniecturas sollicite recenseant, examinent, et causas cur ab iis discesserint, breviter et modeste exponant. Quod argumentum, nunc Tibi propositum, si forte nonnullis, vel propterea, quod Graeca tractat, quod ad literulas et voces adhaerescit, exile et summorum virorum personis minus dignum videbitur, Tibi certe, artifici et aestimatori elegantioris doctrinae

non ingratum fuerit, qui ipse variis in scriptis ex hoc genere studii orna-
menta Tuae purpurae parasti; qui me olim in Dione aliquid emendationis
tentantem scite admonere non gravatus es; qui denique perspicis optime,
quoniam scientia omnis humana literis et vocibus continentur, nos sine
critica arte, pro scriptis veterum, nil nisi imperita librariorum errata, aut
commenta falsariorum, pro Graecis Latinisque leporibus, barbaram et
soloecam striblinginem, pro historia, nugas et fabulas, pro ipsis denique
divinis literis, mera hominum somnia habituros. Quanquam vero in exer-
citationibus huius fori evitari non potest, quin lapsus aliorum, qui certe
nobis videntur, simpliciter prodamus, faciam tamen profecto, ut intelligas,
me a mordaci acerbitate quam maxime abhorrere, tantumque abesse, ut
memet ipsum ab hallucinationibus immunem credam, ut mitibus mihi et
aequis vicissim iudicibus fore opus in posterum arbitrer. Nunc autem vel
maxime memini, me scribere ad Virum, apud quem humanitas omnis et
Musae mansuetiores domicilium habent: cuius ego oculis nolim quicquam
a me indecens, et inurbanum afferri. Igitur serena fronte, Cardinalis Eminentissime, accipies, spero, quae mihi in Falconis libello emendationem
admittere visa sunt; et singula haec ea quoque ex ratione ad Te perscripta
existimabis, ut Tuo potissimum stent cadantve iudicio [...].

Venio nunc ad Graeca: ubi vellem, ad ea recte edenda plus Graecitatis
attulisset; vellem, Dionis stilum sibi ante reddidissent magis familiarem;
vellem codici suo non subscripsisset superstitiosius; vellem in eius lectione
exhibenda plus iudicii adhibuisset, et magis sibi constaret; vellem, Xiphilinum non tam temere et frequenter deseruisset, aut doctas et probas
emendationes virorum eruditorum sprevisset; vellem, non tam multa, sine
ratione et necessitate, ex suo ingenio, praeter indolem linguae Graecae, et
praeter nexum ac scopum Dionis mutasset. Nam omnia haec coniuncta
efficiunt sane, ut quae iam habebamus ante Falconem Graeca Dionis,
multo corruptiora apud eum legantur: quae vero nondum habebamus, vix
confidenter satis ab eius manu accepta usurpemus [...].

En Tibi, Eminentissime Quirine, specimium, credo, satis; ex quibus
intelligas, aliquam certe cunctationis meae culpam conferri debere in
multitudinem mendorum, quibus Dio et Xiphilinus, ubi id vel minime
expectandum erat, foedissime conspurcati et obruti iacebant. Quanquam
vero ea molestia, quae in expurgandis Graecis Latinisque posita est, iam
perfunctus mihi quodammodo (quantula fuit in hac re facultas mea)
videor, sic ut nihil supersit, nisi ut materiam adhuc observationum con-
gestam ad Xiphilinum a pp. 689–880. in ordinem redigam; tamen vix mihi
unquam diligentia et accuratione facio satis, quando in Te et Tua scripta
cogitationem reflecto, aut praestantiam coeptae a Fabricio operae intu-

eor. Nam ut huic rudem plane pannum, crasso filo negligentius velle adsu-
ere, temeritatis et impudentiae foret: ita Tuis vel maxime oculis non nisi
timide et cunctanter subiicere aliquid, huius praesertim generis, possum:
cum legendis Tuis libris intellexerim satis, quantum et quam acute cer-
nas in omni antiquitate, historia, reque literaria; quanta arte et sagacitate
critica examines, expolias, interpreteris, Graecorum Latinorumque monumenta. Atque haec quoque ratio mihi inter ceteras fuit, ad Te scribendi,
ut facto quodam prius periculo Tuum de mea commentandi ratione,
Tuique similium eruditione Virorum, explorarem iudicium: quo possem
monitus adhuc in ceteris vel intendere limam, vel reprimere impetum
ingenii, vel circumferre magis oculos et plus cautionis adhibere. Neque
sane sum nescius, esse in superioribus quaedam ancipitis disputationis;
quorsum inter cetera illud περὶ τοῦ λέοντος συμμαχήσαντος τῷ Ἀντωνίνῳ,
ad p. 4. et de *Gannyde* vel *Gynnide*, ad p. 55. sqq. pertinet: in quibus et
similibus sententiam mutare hoc minus erubescam. In summa, docilem
me velim credas esse, nec a lapsu me immunem arbitrari. Quodsi fuerint in his superioribus, quae Tibi non omnino displiceant, eo certior mihi
spes foret, aliorum vere doctorum calculos meae qualicunque industriae
non prorsus denegatum iri. Liceat autem hic sub Tuis auspiciis implorare
Viros eruditos, ut si quid adhuc lectionum in primis variarum ex codicibus MSS. tum et emendationum aut observationum ad Dionem habeant
in promptu, id conferre ad proximam editionem ne dedignentur. Teneo
quidem adhuc praeter varias lectiones Vaticanas a Te benignissime trans-
missas, et praeter soceri mei elaboratas usque ad p. 689. animadversiones,
Viri quoque cuisdam docti castigationes, Wechelianae editioni adspersas.
Misit etiam mihi benevole Vir Politissimus, Fridericus Mentzius, Professor
Lipsiensis, editionem Dionis Robertinam, quae fuerat quondam Adriani
Turnebi, non paucis elegantibus in margine emendationibus insignem,
praesertim in principio: nam quo magis penetro ad medium, eo magis
omnia cum Xylandri emendationibus conveniunt. Nuper etiam Abrahamus Gronovius, Vir non Maiorum magis quam suis in literas meritis clarissimus, qua solet esse humanitate, mecum communicare coepit varias
lectiones ex codice Mediceo, quae in Parentis Iacobi supplementis lacunarum praeteritae sunt: neque dubito, eum reliqua etiam, quae servat,
Dioni ornando idonea, id quod publice nun multis precibus ab eo contendo, suppeditaturum. Quo plura vero supersunt in Dione et Xiphilino,
vel mutilata vel corrupta: et quo minor hodie codicum MSS. copia sup-
petit, eo gratius fecerint Viri etiam ceteri, promovendis literis idonei, si
quid ex Bibliothecis publicis aut privatis ad integrandum et perficiendum
Scriptorem praeclarum liberalius subministrent. Tibi autem, Cardinalis

Eminentissime, qui promovendis literis nihil non impertire soles, sicut plurima iam debeo, ita non pudet amplius velle debere, si quando Tibi placuerit, codicem illum antiquissimum Vaticanum, a viro non indocto, Te auctore, denuo inspici. Nosti enim, ad recte legenda antiqua, non tantum oculis et diligentia plurium, sed et eruditione, iudicio, sagacitate, ac prope divinatione quadam, in quibus homo homini praestat, opus esse; praesertim in codice mutilato, qui et literis insolentioribus, iisque passim evanescentibus, sine accentuum notis, et sine ulla literis, verbis, sententiis, interposita distinctione aut spacio, exaratus deprehenditur: cuius ideo particulam descriptam subiunxi, ut cures haud gravatim explorari, eum ad exampli similitudine fideliter expressa, atque hinc digna sit, quae in ipsius Dionis praefatione exhibeatur. Ita Tuo memorabili beneficio, Tuaque illustri liberalitate, addito etiam cumulo, antiqui splendioris non parum Dioni restituetur, meque Tibi non tantum, sed omnes eruditos, et posteritatem omnem, immortali munere hoc magis devincies. Quod reliquum est, ut hunc Tibi, quem ingredimur annum, cum longa sequentium serie Deus O. M. fortunet, Teque decus Italiae, praesidium literarum, virtutis et humanitatis exemplum, quam diutissime salvum et florentem servet, sincera mente precor.

Reverendissimi Nominis Tui.
Dabam Hamburgi, Kal. Jan. A. CVVCCXLVI.
observantissimus cultor,
Hermannus Samuel Reimarus

Letter 6

[Hamburg, 17 September 1746: Reimarus expresses his gratitude for Querini's public response to his letter, anticipates further contributions from other (especially Italian) scholars, and voices scepticism about a potential rebuttal or response by Falco].[111]

Eminentissimo ac Reverendissimo
ANGELO MARIAE Cardinali QUIRINO
Bibliothecario Vatic[ano] et Episcopo Brix[iensi]
S. P. D.
Hermannus Samuel Reimarus

Cum alioquin verba mihi desint saepenumero, tum in prasentia vix reperio, qua ratione Tibi, Cardinalis Eminentissime, publice literas ad me mittenti, pro tanti mueras dignitate, respondeam. Nam ut per se valde

---

[111] VQS. Ms. 257.

honorificum mihi ducendum est, quod commercium istud epistolarum,
quas omnibus legendas impertire soles, nunc ad me quoque, hominem
nulla adhuc in luce, nisi forte per Te, positum, demittis: ita nullis ego verbis assequi me posse confido liberalitatem et gratiam plane singularem,
qua studium Tuum operamque multifariam explendis meis desideriis
omnibus navaturum sedulo polliceris. Quidni ego nunc codicem antiquissimum velut praesens intueri videbor, postquam Tu ipse oculis Tuis et
mentis acie, (de cuius sagacitate abunde constat) eundem perscrutatu-
rum recepisti? Vereor tantum, ne graviter impudens fuisse videar haec
Tua legentibus, qui id quod sponte suscepisti, qua es in me benivolen-
tia, onus, à me Tibi audacter impositum iudicent: cum summa votorum
meorum in eo consisteret, ut alium virum doctum, Tibi probatum, ad id
negotii feligere dignarere. Sed mirabor, si in posterum homines poeni-
teat elegantiorum literarum ex vetusto membranarum pulvere erutarum,
posteaquam in huius permolesti laboris societatem venire non erubuisti
Purpuratus, eique Tuo exemplo praeivisti. Pariter et Italiam omnem, quae
una codices Dionis possidet, quaeque eruditissimis omni parte Viris, sicut
ab initio restauratae eruditionis, ita nunc vel maxime abundat, spero iam
confidentius tenui meae opellae non denegaturam auxilium, posteaquam
Tibi placuit, mea desideria non tantum vulgare literis Tuis, sed et principes doctrinae humanioris Viros, Vulpium, Muratorium, Bartolum, Ric-
cium, Mazochium, nominatim ad beneficii huius praestationem evocare.
Quanquam vero Antistitem Venerandum Falconium, cuius ego προράματα
in extremis Dionis perstrinxeram, omni modo in me concitare vicissim,
videri possis; tamen in recensendis speciminibus meis, interlacet iudicium Tuum, tam manifeste pro mea disceptans parte, ut Vir iste optimus
facilius sibi exprobrari aliquid iactantiae, quam calcar ad respondendum
addi, existimaverit. Neque tamen ego intercedo, quominus respondeat,
si non se tantum ab erroris suspicione liberare, sed et meo scripto refellendo lucem Dioni afferre norit. Neque mirabor, si sapere iam me plus
possit, postquam duos et viginti annos, atque adeo amplius, in uno Dio
limando collocarit. Quodsi huius generis observationes utiles, et meliora
me docentes, regesserit, fidem ego meam Tibi adstringo meminem futurum, qui me libentius retractet sententiam, et monita saniora suo acutori
publice in acceptis ferat. Verum pace Tua, Cardinalis Eminentissime, erit
Dio ipse optimum meae in huiusmodi rebus facilitatis monumentum:
ubi et Tuum monitum nuperum non neglectum videbis, quod τῷ εἰπόντι
retineri posse indicat: cui sane assentior, nisi si hoc umum addere liceat,
commodius tum in latina interpretatione pronomen *ei* omitti. Ceterum,
Tua etiam auctoritate, imperterritus coepto labori insisto, itaque mihi
persuasi, nihil responderi à Falcone posse, quin id vel honeste vertatur in

rem meam, usuque publicos, vel si eius generis non sit, velut auctori per se probrosum, negligatur. Vale et immortalia Tua in me beneficia, quoad eius fieri possit, tuere. Dabam Hamb[urgi] D. XVII. Sept. A. CVVCCXLVI.

Letter 7

[Hamburg, 10 December 1746: Reimarus, who has just learned about Falco's intentions of still pursuing his edition of Cassius Dio, expresses his dismay about Falco's ambition and urges Querini upon his return from Rome to provide him with the results of his examination of the *Codices Fulvii Ursini*[112] in the Vatican Library, which, as Falco claimed, would enable him to restore the entire *Historiae Romanae*].[113]

Eminentissimo ac Reverendissimo
ANGELO MARIAE Card. QUIRINO
Ep[iscopo]. Brixiensi et Bibliothecario Vatic[ano]
S. P. D.
Hermannus Samuel Reimarus

Notui Te, Cardinalis Eminentissime, Romam profectum, interpellare meis literis: nunc autem, confecto intinere, Brixia scribenti tanto celerius respondendum duxi, quo magis mira de S. R. Falconis Dione nuncias. Fateor, nihil magis praeter expectationem meam accidisse, quam hoc, quod post duorum et viginti annorum silentium, Vir Clarissimus exequi promissa instituerit. Equidem non disputabo iam, quando rem ipsam in dubium vocare vix licet, de eventu. Mihi tamen certum est, et penitus statutum manet, tueri provinciam, quam desertam dudum à Falcone, et occupatam deinde à B. socero meo, atque ex parte administratam, suscepi, non clam quidem aut subdole, sed praemissa publice significatione, nec sine cohortatione Virorum Eruditorum. Cuius instituti mei famam, si minus illa ex Commentario quem scripsi de vita Fabricii, aut ex Actis Eruditorum, ad ultimam Italiae oram dimanasset, poterat tamen bonus Falco vel ex Tuis literis percepisse, quas vel ignorare, vel non legisse dedecori foret. Quando enim iam ante triennium, ni fallor, Dionis mei non tantum mentionem publice fecisti, sed patronem Te adeo magnum et adiutorem, ne dicam laudatorem, causae praebuisti: cur non scripsit ad

---

[112] This codex had been published by Fulvio Orsini as *Ex libris Polybii, selecta de legationibus* (Antwerp, 1582).

[113] VQS. Ms. 257.

Te? cur memoriam suae operae, iam prope extinctam et sepultam, non renovavit? cur postliminio saltem ius suum vindicare se velle non significavit? Verum, abundet Ille suo sensu, et captet gloriam, quam sibi pollicetur: mihi quidem sunt causae non tantum iustae, sed et boni ominis, cur Tuum, Cardinalis Eminentissime, beneficium in Dione meo collocatum, cur praeclarum Summi Fabricii commentarium in hunc scriptorem, cur meam, quod praefiscini dixerim, qualemcunque opellam Xiphilino praecipue navatam, perire nunquam patiar: praesertim cum prope exploratum mihi fit, Viros doctos, qui tum demum bene sperare de Falcone coeperant, postquam manum de Dione retraxisse videbatur, tanto molestius nunc laturos fatum sinistrum huius Auctoris, quo certius ex speciminibus à me patefactis, iudicium de futuris possunt capere. Haberem non pauca, quae hanc in rem ex epistolis Virorum peritorum ad me datis possem expromere, nisi Tu ipse, Cardinalis Reverendissime, quae Tua eximia est in Criticis perspicacia, intellegeres unus omnium optime, Virum, cetera suis meritis mea defraudandum, his literis natum haud esse, et sibi pariter ae reipublica literariae minus recte consulturum. Quam ob rem mirifice abs Te peto, ut fructum Tui itineris Romani ad me quam primum redire patiaris, et quae ex codice pervetusto extricasti, sicut Te facturum receperas in epistola publice ad me scripta, benevole transmittas: Ego enim nunc ad Caracallum Dionis illustrandum accedo, ut oportune Tua mihi monita et observationes possint subvenire. Interim ardeo cupiditate incredibili, neque ut ego arbitor reprehendenda, videndi quae Falco adhuc edidit: eo praesertim, ut cognoscam, num codicum quorundam forte latentium subsidio sit usus, ut differri propterea editionem meam tantisper necesse sit, donec Dio integer ab eo sit excusus. Cetera nihil me morabuntur. Cum vero idem ut scias Tua putem interesse, magnopere peto, ut folia isthaec, quae iam praela evaserunt, Neapoli cures ad Te perferri, et lecta, una cum iudicio Tuo, quid me velis facere, mecum communices. Ego spem omnem et fiduciam in Tua constanti et saepius declarata benevolentia repositam habeo, cuius et documentum recens dedisti, perscriptis ad me Cl. Bartoli, Viri sane eruditissimi, annotationibus: de quibus utrique Vestrum me multum debere profiteor. Duas tantum nunc attingam. Altera de leone τῷ Ἀντωνίνῳ συμμαχήσαντι, me iam addubitantem, (ut indicabam in epistola p. 48) magis in contrariam inclinavit et prope pertraxit sententiam. Existimaveram quidem, leonem in numis Antonini, posse esse Mithriacum Heliopolitanis non insuctum, qui victoriam Antonino latus gratuletur, nec ad aliquod eiusmodi factum respiciat; putebam in Spartiano, victoriam de leone ante Parthicam expeditionem narrante, ordinem haud magnopere requirendum esse, cum constet, nihil esse perturbatius hoc scriptore eiusque similibus; denique illum locum *de feris bestiis in barbaros immissis* minus huc pertinere opinabar, cum non diserte de leone, sed de pluribus generatim feris, iisque non sponte pro Antonino decertantibus, sed ex cavea in hostes immissis, loquatur. Verum re aequo animo perpensa, fateor, vim tantam inesse praestantissimi Viri argumentis, quae probabilitatis longe maioris speciem eius sententiae conciliet, usu praesertim verbi, συμμαχεῖν τινὶ, confirmatae. Quam ob rem, nisi certiora se prodant argumenta, hanc praeferre et à priori mea discedere non dubitabo. Altera Viri observatio spectat ad milites utrem Vini secantes. *visibilmente*, inquit, *transpare non ludibrio, ma riverenza e stolidezza de' soldati.* Illud vero nondum mihi persuasit. Nam cum id colligeret Vir summus ex verbis Dionis οὕτω γὰρ τὸν αὐτοκράτορα σφῶν ἡδοῦντο, (quae est *riverenza*) et sequentibus καὶ φρονήσει ἐχρῶντο, (quae est *stolidezza*) non attendisse videtur, se alterum proprie, alterum ironice interpretari. Utrumque vero ironice accipiendum videtur, et quemadmodum posterius ἀφροσύνην dicit, ita prius ἀναίδειαν. Vera scilicet affectio animi militum haec fuit: dum uterque integrum vini utrem sibi vindicat, nec alter vult alteri cedere, malunt Imperatorem suum *irreventer* obtundere rixis: et dum eius mandatum sic exequuntur ipso praesente, ut omnia potius effundant sine usu, modo ne adversario quicquam relinquatur, irreverentiam cum *stolida improbitate* coniungunt. Sed quicquid huius sit, stabunt quae dixi, *nisi scripserit Xiphilinus* νείμασθαι τὸν ἀσκὸν, *frigide rem narrasse censendum esse*: nam ut prae stultitia quis mandatum ad literam interpretari solet. Ceterum Tillemontio viro si quis unquam in historia accurato et perspicaci, tribuam utique debitum honorem. De Gynnidos et Comazontis nominibus sic existimo ut de Ciceronis loco pro Cluentio: *Guttam adspersit huic Bulbo*, quae utique nomina propria sunt manentque, sic tamen ut ad significationem appellativam vel maxime respiciatur. Nec dubito interpretem horum verborum quacunque in lingua haesitaturum, quomodo acumen latens velit in suam linguam, retentis nominibus propriis, transfundere. Quod reliquum est, velim existimes, nemini me unquam concessurum esse, qui Tua beneficia vel avidius excipiat vel magis grato animo. Deus Tibi exitum anni cum plurimis sequentibus fortunet. Dabam Hamburgi D. X. Decemb[ris]. A[nno] CVVCCXLVI.

Letter 8

[Hamburg, 24 December 1746: Having just received several sheets of Querini's[114] examination of the *Codices Fulvii Ursini*, Reimarus expresses

---

[114] See "Epistola XL," in Nicolaus Coleti, *Epistolae Eminentiss. et Reverendiss. D. D. Angeli Mariae Querini S. R. E. Cardinalis Bibliothecarii* [...] (Venice, 1756), pp. 291–297.

his surprise at Falco's margin of error in his reading of the parchments and informs Querini that he has made efforts to obtain a copy of Falco's edition as soon as possible in order still to incorporate it into his own work. At the same time, Reimarus expresses his satisfaction that his *Epistola* will provide the *Respublica litteraria* with a "proper" assessment of Falco's work].[115]

Eminentissimo ac Reverendissimo
ANGELO MARIAE Cardinali QUIRINO
S. P. D.
Hermannus Samuel Reimarus

Ex quo tempore scripsi nuper, accepi non tantum Lipsia aliquot exampla epistolae Tuae prioris, in vulgus editae; sed et cum binis manu Tua exaratis proxime per tabellarium publicum mihi reddi coepit initium alterius epistolae, quae itineris Romani fructum exponit. Equidem sic acquiescebam in Tua sollicitudine et cura pro mea Dionis editione, ut nunciatus Cl. Falconis ausus meam alacritatem non frangeret sed intenderet, neque novo mihi incitamento ad perficiendum laborem opus esse videretur. Quare quod placuit Tibi, Cardinalis Eminentissime, denuo munus adiicere exhortationibus Tuis, id abundantis Tuae liberalitatis, prolixaeque in me voluntatis argumentum interpretor: tantoque magis gratus laetusque acccipio, quo magis serio Te cupere et urgere operam meam qualemcunque intellexi. Ego, mihi crede, nihil in me studii aut constantiae patiar desiderari, et ut multum debeo patientiae Tuae nondum deficienti, ita efficiam totis viribus, ne ea abusus esse videar. Verum, quod significabam proxime, cupio prius, neque id quidem leviter, videre quae edidit Falco: atque hoc magis magisque non tam opus mihi, sed prope necesse esse, perspicio. Dedi quidem id negotii amico cuidam, qui cum bibliopola Italo commercium exercet literarum; vereor tamen, ne haec mihi spes in irritum recidat. Quodsi ergo Tua mihi auctoritas et facultas hac in re non subvenerit, ut vel à Falcone ipso impetret, vel à bibliopola Neapolitano extorqueat folia imperfecta, periculum est, ne expectandum mihi sit, donec absolutum opus exierit. Non flagito haec, quod multa mihi et magna de editione Neapolitana pollicear: nam ut probe mones in altera epistola Tua, exiqui momenti sunt, quae in extremis libris praeter Ursinum praestitit, et huic non tantum verum et Leunclavio, ceterisque Viris doctissimis facit iniuriam, non sine iactantia. Attamen certus esse

---

[115] VQS. Ms. 257.

debeo, nec contemntae aemuli, qui forte aliquid membranarum veterum usurpare poterat, ulla parte deteriorem editionem procudere. Interim oportune mihi videor, in epistola mea, Viros eruditos, quibus ultimorum librorum editio Romana non ad manus erat, iis instruxisse argumentis, ex quibus iam de futura integri Dionis editione Neapolitana iudicium queant capere. Etiam ex Epistola Tua novissima perspexi, Falconem saepiuscule à vera lectione illius ipsius codicis aberrasse: et mirari Te, Cardinalis Eminentissime, vix satis possum, qui tam expedite et tuto, sine duce sine comite, in tam obscuris et evanescentibus literarum vestigiis versatus sis. Ornabit et hoc specimen editionem meam, eoque maiori iam desiderio, quae reliqua sunt Tuae epistola exspecto. De Zaluskio Comite, quod scribis, verissimum est. Novi Virum, Hamburgi quondam, cum distraherentur libri Fabriciani, per aliquod tempus morantem. Habet diffusam et accuratam librorum cognitionem, multumque, credo, Fratri, in comparanda et instruenda ishae Bibliotheca publica, fuit eritque adiumento. Est praeterea singulari humanitate, ceterisque virtutibus, quae literis decus conciliant. Quod reliquum est, iterum iterumque opto et voveo, ut instantem annum novum et Tibi, Reverendissime Cardinalis, et Tuis laboribus, hoc est Reipublicae literariae, salutarem et proficuum Deus O. M. esse iubeat. Dabam Hamb. d. 24 Dec. A. CVVCCXLVI.

Letter 9
[Hamburg, 8 April 1747: Through Querini's efforts, Reimarus was able to obtain selections from Falco's newly restored Dio.[116] Even a casual examination of them revealed that large portions had been taken from Plutarch. Reimarus concludes his letter with the good news that he is expecting variant readings from England[117]].[118]

---

[116] *Q. Cassii Dionis Coccejani Romanae Historiae ex ejus octoginta libris tomus primus...* *studio et labore Nic. Carminii Falconii* (Naples, 1747).

[117] In the preface to his first volume, Reimarus writes: "Praeterea cum legissem in Actis Eruditorum 1712. p. 528. Anglum eruditum Obadiam Oddey de nova quadam editione Dionis cogitasse, eiusque adeo specimen edidisse, audissemque, manu eius notatum exemplum esse penes Richardum Meade, Medicum Regis Britanniarum Experientissimum, eumque recondita non minus eruditione quam officiosa comitate celebratissimum, egi cum eo per literas, ut iam & Dioni medicinam, seu materiam certe medicam Oddeyanam, benevole impertiret: quod & mihi gratificatus est transmisso Dionis exemplo editionis Henrici Stephani [...]," in *Cassii Dionis Cocceiani Historiae Romanae*, vol. 1 (1750), p. xxv.

[118] VQS. Ms. 257.

Eminentissimo ac Reverendissimo
ANGELO MARIAE Cardinali QUIRINO
Episcopo Brixiensi
S. D.
Hermannus Samuel Reimarus

Pergratum mihi fuit, Tuo, Cardinalis Eminentissime, beneficio oculis usurpare specimen resituti Dionis Falconiani; quo perlecto intellexi statim, non facile esse, si ab erratis typographorum vel librariorum discesseris, quod in Graecis queat desiderari, quae mihi, ut Falconis verbo utar, non Dionem quidem, sed tamen antiquum scriptorem Graecum olebant. Dum circumspicio eundem, incidi forte iterum in observationem antea negligentius à me perlectam, ubi ait *Dionem haec et sequentia narrasse non hic cum Zonara, sed inferius cum Plutarcho posuisse.* Venit igitur in mentem, Plutarchi Poplicolam consulere. Quid multa? Statim deprehendo hominem ipso in furto: nam omnia et singula, ne ipsis quidem vitiis editionis, aut versione latina exceptis, ex Plutarcho p. 101. F. sq. video esse huc translata; unde et de iis quae hanc narrationem antecedunt aut sequentur, imo de toto ni fallor Dione Falconiano iudicium fieri potest. Quemdadmodum vero mirari subit, Virum eruditum, qui recensendae editionis curam in se suscepit, haec latrocinia non animadvertisse: ita Tua mihi, Cardinalis Eminentissime, εὐστοχία merite praedicanda est, quod recte et vere, etiam nondum viso hoc specimine, coniecisti, centonem nobis ex Xiphilino, Zonara, Cedreno, aliisque ab acutae naris homine datum iri, quippe qui illico quae Dionis sint, possint olfacere. Verum, inquiet Falco, male nos haec Plutarcho vindicare, cum et Dio soleat (v.g. in fragmentis prioribus) Plutarchum exscribere. Solet, scio, idque animadverti in locis quibusdeam, de quibus silet Ursinus atque Leunclavius; sed nullo in loco, praesertim tam longo, qualis hic de Poplicola est, ita omnia ad amussim cum editis Plutarchi conspirant, quin subinde corrigendi et supplendi Dionis ex Plutarcho, aut vicissim Plutarchi ex Dione, detur materia. Multo minus errata librariorum utrinque possunt eadem esse: aut eadem Falconis versio latina, quae interpreti Plutarchi in mentem venire. Neque dubito, si plura per occasionem nancisci folia editionis Falconianae possem, me ab initio totius huius compilatae undique fabulae, pennas alienas, cuius tandem sint aviculae, agniturum; aut si quae forte calcis loco huic arenae de suo adspersit praeclarus Dionis restaurator, à ceteris nullo negotio discreturum. Quae in Zonara uncis circumscripsit Falco, ipsa sunt Plutarchi verba, vel ut ille nugatur, Dionis. Haec liberius, et forte dicacius ad Te scripsi, temperaturus mihi, ubi publice de eo iudicandum fuerit, vel propterea, quod ipsemet se abunde iam ridendum propinavit intelligentibus.

Quod reliquum est, quando me iubes sententiam dicere, sintne illa apud Leunclavium Theodosii, ut vocat, excerpta ab Ursinianis diversa nec ne? infitias equidem ire nolim, me adhuc nondum deprehendisse satis praegnantem rationem, cur diversa statuam. Nam quae apud Leunclavium sub Theodosii nomine leguntur, quia nempe codex Sylburgii eum prodit auctorem, eadem ego omnia apud Ursinum invenio velut à Ioanne quodam Cpolitano collecta. Fidem faciat collatio. Num XLI. p. 710. XLII. p. 712. XLIII. p. 710sq. XLIV. p. 738. sq. et à verbis καὶ ὁ πρῖμος. p. 742. XLV. p. 746. sq. XLVI. p. 761. XLVII. p. 760. XLVIII. p. 761. XLIX. p. 761. L. p. 762. LI. p. 777. vel 774. LII. p. 773.sq LIII. p. 774. LIV. p. 775. LV. p. 777. C. LVI. p. 778 LVII. p. 779. LVIII. p. 780. LIX. p. 780.sq. LX. p. 781. LXI. p. 794. LXII. p. 794. LXIII. p. 807. LXIV. p. 807.sq. LXV. p. 808. LXVI. p. 808. LXVII. p. 808. sq. LXVIII. p. 809. LXIX. p. 809. LXX. p. 809. LXXI. p. 809. sq. LXXII. p. 810. LXXIII. p. 817. LXXIV. p. 817sq. LXXV. p. 848. LXXVI. p. 849. LXXVII. p. 854. Num. LXXVII. omissus à Leunclavio, quia ad Hadriani tempora pertinet, legiturque fere apud Xiphilinum p. 794. D. LXXIX. p. 851. LXXX. p. 888. LXXXI. p. 889. LXXXII. p. 889. Quae deinde sequuntur, certum est ad Excerpta illa referri non amplius debere, quippe petita ex vetusta illa Membrana ut monet Ursinus in notis. Num vero priora illa excerpta à num I–XL. etiam in Sylburgii codice lecta fuerint, aut eidem Theodosio tributa, pro certo non dixerim: nec enim clare satis hae de re Leunclavius.

Ceterum quod ad vocem σφίσιν annotat Falco, *νιπαράλογον utrumque valeat, uti reor*, putem sic intelligi posse: *νιπαράλογον* (seu *παρὰ λόγον, forte*) *utrumque* (nempe σφίσι et κτῆσιν) *valeat* (i.e. locum habeat) *uti reor*. Quam observationem Tibi non ingratam spero fore, qui debitam cuique laudem non soles imminuere, sed pro Tua humanitate adeo augere.

Quodsi adhuc habes, Cardinalis Eminentissime, adnotata quaedam ex antiquissimo codice Vaticano, quae me cum aliis in locis, tum iis praesertim quae indicaveram, meliora et certiora, quam Falco fecerat, edoceant: facies mihi gratissimum, sive publicis ea sive privatis literis mecum placuerit communicare. Celeb. Bartolus Prof. Taurinensis posset me certiorem reddere, num in Bibliotheca Taurinensi asservetur codex Ms. Dionis, quod traditur in Anglicis Memoriis Literariis, *Memoirs of Literature*, J. III. p. 47. aut num is usui esse possit. Sed expecto Tuum nutum, an scribere ad illum hac de re consultum sit. Oddii, Angli, collectas ad Dionem varias lectiones et annotationes spero me ab humanitate Richardi Meadii, Medici Regii, impetraturum, post datas ad eum nuper literas, in quibus id flagitabam. Totus iam sum in percurrendis Criticis, Antiquariis, Nummariis Scriptoribus, ut inde spicilegium aliquod lucrari, et ita hoc anno, Volente Deo, ultimam manum finemque imponere Dioni et Xiphilino possim. Sed finem imponere huic epistolae par est, meam erga Te, Cardinalis Eminentissime, submissam observantiam testando. Vale. Dabam D. VIII. April An. CVVCCXLVII.

Letter 10
[Hamburg, 28 Mai 1748: Having received and examined the first and only volume of Falco's proposed new edition, Reimarus judges it inferior to the works of previous scholars (most notably Leunclavius). Most importantly, however, Reimarus exposes virtually all of Falco's new discoveries as fraud, because they were all passages that he had taken from other well-known classical authors (Plutarch, Dionysius Halicarnassus, Zonaras) and crudely patched into Dio's narrative].[119]

Eminentissimo ac Reverendissimo
ANGELO MARIAE Cardinali QUIRINO
Episcopo Brixiensi et Bibliothecario Vatic[ano]
S. P. D.
Hermannus Samuel Reimarus

Biduum est, ex quo per bibliopolam Heroldum Lipsia reducem accepi V Tuas, Cardinalis Eminentissime, epistolas, una cum Dionis à Falcone restituti Volumine primo. Utriusque autem muneris nomine Tibi debeo plurimum. Nam Tuae quidem epistolae continent scitu digna quam plurima, ut solent quae ex Tuo proficiscuntur ingenio; et quanquam Helvetiis, Suevis, Augustanis invidere coeperam vicinitatem Italiae, qua fit, ut non modo colloqui Tecum per literas, sed et praesentem Te coram adire et venerari possint, tamen legendis hisce, solor quantum licet longinquitatis dolorem, meque benevolentiae Tuae, cuius ubique per scripta spargis vestigia, recordatione sustento. Iucunda pariter mihi fuit Dionis Falconiani perlustratio, quod nunc tam certus sum quam qui maxime, non frustra à me, post huius Viri infelicissimum conatum, in nova Dionis editione paranda elaborari. Patere enim, Reverendissime Cardinalis, ut iudicium meum de hoc opere, requisitum praesertim à Te, libere aperiam. Est quidem diligentia Falconis Historica, quam in Prolegomenis demonstravit,

---

[119] PBN. Ms. Ital. 511.

maximopere laudanda, neque habeo adhuc (quantum percurrendo obser-
vari potuit) quod magnopere in iis desiderem, nisi qua parte suum institutum non sine iactatione et aliorum contemtu commendat, et in Viros
melius de Dione meritos, Leunclavium praesertim, est iniquior. Huic enim
iactantiam exprobrat, editionem eius consarcinationis nomine traducit:
et ab Huetio atque Fabricio, qui Leunclavii interpretationem laudave-
rant, longissime se abesse professus, mediocrem eum appellat interpretem, vix Latinum, et in Romana re Antiquaria infantem. Iam vero ipsum
opus, quanquam id aeternum sibi fore pollicetur, meris constat scopis,
quisquiliis, purgamentis, ut potuisset, periturae parcere chartae. Non iam
urgeo titulum libri, qui Dionis promittit Historiam restitutam ἐκ τῶν αὐτοῦ
ὀκτογίντα βιβλίων, credo, quod iam in fronte latina graecis miscere pul-
chrum ducebat, ut in ipso centone suo graecos inter se auctores miscet:
taceo in eodem titulo audaciam in praenomine *Quinti* Cassio assignando,
licet in Prolegomenis fateatur, de praenomine silere antiquitatem et Cassii
etiam ac Lucii (addo et Marci, Titi, Publii) praenomina in gente Cassia
reperiri. Ipsum vero mehercle institutum tam ieiunum et puerile est, ut
Virum gravem atque ab infula quam gerit Venerabilem, ut Italiam, quae
à renascentibus inde literis habuit habetque Magna Nomina, ut nostram
aetatem, qua luce artium et humanitatis nunc exsplendescit, neutiquam
deceat. Promissum enim restituendi Dionis integri, quo per XXIV annos
suspensum exspectatione tenuit orbem terrarum, eo nunc tandem redit, ut
lacinias ex Dionysio Hal. ex Plutarchi Romulo, Numa, Poplicola, ex Zonara
potissimum, subiectis quibusdeam paucis et vere Dioniis fragmentis, con-
sarcinet, iisque Dionis nomen audacter inscribat, eas digerat per libros et
Decades, summa Capita et temporum seriem ex sua Graecitate praefigat.
Quasi hos auctores Historiae Romanae non iam haberemus, et ordine pos-
semus evolvere atque inter se conferre: aut quasi Dionem servili plagio
totos Dionysii et Plutarchi libros expilasse credendum sit: aut Zonaram
non constet apud omnes, quaedam omnino ex Dione, sed et quamplu-
rima ex aliis mutuatum esse. Non erat profecto, cur hoc consarcinandi
consilium capiens Falco, sacrum sibi per V [?] lustra silentium indiceret,
ne quis in acrana eius penetrans provinciam hanc invaderet. Neque enim
id cuiquam in mentem venisset sano. Hoc non est restituere auctores dep-
erditos, sed facere ut illi quos habemus integros pereant et confundatur:
veluti si quis ad restituendam Praxitelis aut Phidiaε statuam, complures
integras confringens statuas aliorum artificium, ex diversis diversarum
membris coagmentatis unam conficiat, hac usus in speciem ratiuncula,
quasi vel Praxiteles hos artifices, aut illi hunc imitati exacte sint, et alter
alterius opus sic expresserit ut pro uno et eodem debeat haberi. Vide

autem quam egregie novus hic confundendi artifex in divellendi et coniu-
gendis membris antique fabricae versetur. Scripserat iam dudum, se initia
libri primi Dionis alibi nactum esse. Credebant omnes in codice antiquo,
praesertim cum summa capita libri I. Graece etiam, ut solent esse Dionis,
praefigeret. Nihil minus: fatetur nunc se id ex Excerptis Constantini peti-
isse, ubi legitur p. 568. Atque non ibi modo ad tempora Numae refertur, et
ipsum fragmentum nihil aliud loquitur, sed et Cedrenus T. I. p. 148. B. post
Romuli et Numae res verba ex eodem bene multa adducit. Quid Falco, ut
non ἀκέφαλον Dionem suum sistat? Resecat non modo praefatiunculam
de Numa, sed et extrema fragmenti, quae diem navitatis Numae produnt;
eaque in librum usque tertium reiicit, quanquam cum proxime anteced-
entibus arcte cohaerentia. Sicut vero discerpit coniuncta per naturam, et
prorsus alieno collocat loco, ita imprudens disiuncta et diversa in hoc ipso
fragmento conflat in unum. Nec enim animadvertit (quod nec Valesius
fecerat) duplex statim fragmentum Dionis afferri in his collectaneis praemissa formula duplici ὁ δὲ Δίων φησὶν · ὅτι – ἔπειτα καὶ · ὅτι – *deinde ait*:
Quare Dio haec non uno et continuo filo scripsit, sed posterius intervallo
aliquo interiecto, sicut et verba ipsa neutiquam cum prioribus cohaerentia
docent. At Falco ἔπειτα καὶ ὅτι velut ipsius Dionis verba interpretatus, uno
quasi halitu eum ab initio proferre iubet, quae locis et temporibus diversis-
simis scripserat. Praeter hanc auctorum et locorum perturbationem, non
est, quod vel emendationis aliquid in corruptis, aut lucis in obscuris ab eo
expectes. Ego totum perlegi libellum, et sancte testor, si à Prolegomenis
discedam, nihil fuisse a me repertum quod me doceret. Quare in eam iam
prope descendo sententiam, quoniam ipse se Falco ad commiserationem
usque ridendum praebuit, meque praeterea in Prolegomenis quam poterat mollissime tangit, indignum fore mea persona et prope iniquum, si
vellicare amplius Virum publicis in scriptis vellem: statque propositum,
non nisi semel sub initium mei operis paucis indicare, quid sibi de Dione
Falconis, paucis adhuc exteris noto, polliceri debeant eruditi. Quare et
hoc abs Te, Cardinalis Eminentissime, contendo submisse, ut haec quae
iam scripsi, quanquam defendi semper possint, in sinu Tuo conquiescere
patiare. Scripsi enim Tuo iussu potissimum, non pruritu laedendi quen-
quam, sed ex vero et animi sententia. Ceterum, ut iter Germanicum Hel-
veticumque prospere Tibi cedat, et ut feliciter redux Brixiam de Tuo in
me animo nihil unquam remittas, opto, rogo. Vale. Dabam Hamburgi D.
XXVIII. Maii A. CV VCC XLVIII.

REIMARUS, THE HAMBURG JEWS, AND THE MESSIAH

Dietrich Klein

I. Paul and the Jews of Antioch

In his unpublished critical work, the "Apologie oder Schutzschrift für die vernünftigen Verehrer Gottes", Hermann Samuel Reimarus develops an extensive criticism of the Old and the New Testament which can be analyzed from many perspectives. There are some main topics, such as the criticism of miracles or of the priest's illegitimate power in non-religious matters, which can be followed throughout the whole "Apologie". One of these dominant topics is the criticism of Jesus Christ the Messiah as promised in the Old Testament. Of course, Reimarus does not negate Old Testament Messianic belief, but he rejects every attempt to connect it to the New Testament and its belief in Jesus Christ, the son of God, resurrected from the grave. Drawing out his criticism of the Old Testament, he addresses all the Messianic verses which were used in Christian dogmatics to defend the belief in the Messiahship of Jesus Christ. A 'Protevangelium' preached to Adam,[1] a Messianic interpretation of the promise of Abraham,[2] and of his offering of Isaac,[3] are rejected while explaining the patriarchal narratives. And, in a separate chapter, the Messianic passages of the books of the Prophets and of Psalms are shown to be interpretable without drawing lines to the New Testament.[4] In this way, Reimarus tries to reconstruct a history of Messianic belief as it developed during pre-Christian times when the late Old Testament books emerged. Instead of viewing the Old Testament from the perspective of the New, he explains the activities of the historical Jesus and his followers against the background of Old Testament Jewish belief.

Facing the New Testament from this perspective, the biography of Jesus appears to differ totally from the tradition of dogmatics, which would emphasize the humility of the historical Jesus. In Reimarus' view, Jesus

---

[1] Hermann Samuel Reimarus, *Apologie oder Schutzschrift für die vernünftigen Verehrer Gottes*, ed. Gerhard Alexander, vol. 1 (Frankfurt, 1972), pp. 193–194.

[2] Ibid., pp. 224–226.

[3] Ibid., pp. 238–240.

[4] Ibid., pp. 718–755.

now seems to be possessed by the idea of a glorious Davidic king, who is going to rescue Israel from its oppressors in order to restore the old and eternal kingdom. Believing that he will be this Davidic king, he starts a political movement and gains loyal followers who are willing to support his movement, hoping that one day they will take part in his kingdom. But the movement comes to an end when Jesus, the glorious Davidic Messiah, dies on the cross.[5] Now, in order to overcome their disappointment, the disciples of Jesus remember a second, less popular form of the Old Testament Messianic belief, saying that the Messiah, before returning in glory, had to suffer and die in order to fulfil what is written in the book of Isaiah on the suffering of the Servant of God.[6] Using this second form of Messianic belief, the disciples were able to retain their view of Jesus Christ the Messiah and gain new believers among Jews and Gentiles. In this way an independent Christian belief emerged alongside Judaism, and after a short time the apostles were able to look at the Old Testament from their own tradition, claiming the Messianic passages of the Old Testament to be proof of the Messiahship of Jesus.

In the course of the "Apologie", Reimarus' rejection of the Christian reading of the Old Testament Messianic verses becomes more and more aggressive. In the first volume, he discusses the passages in a moderate way, showing that the Christian exegetes' allegorical interpretation is not the only possible way to read the Messianic passages and that a simple and philologically correct reading could lead to a more reasonable understanding. But in the second volume, when it comes to the New Testament and its use of the Messianic verses, Reimarus falls into sharp polemic. In his criticism of the resurrection he discusses the Apostle Paul's attempt to defend it by pointing to the Messiahship of Jesus Christ, which, as Paul believes, is evident from the Old Testament. In the 13th chapter of Acts, Paul preaches to the Jews of Antioch, who are not convinced of the resurrection of Jesus. He explains to them how the Old Testament proof of the Messiahship of Jesus can serve as evidence for his resurrection. At this point Reimarus, as he often does in his "Apologie", offers his readers more than the biblical text. Reimarus supposes that the Jews of Antioch probably did not keep quiet during Paul's speech, and so he presents some possible objections which the Jews might have made to his arguments.[7]

---

[5] Hermann Samuel Reimarus, *Apologie oder Schutzschrift für die vernünftigen Verehrer Gottes*, ed. Gerhard Alexander, vol. 2 (Frankfurt, 1972), pp. 40–170.

[6] Ibid., pp. 274–277.

[7] As the manuscripts show, Reimarus wrote the following passages sometime around the year 1760.

Paul starts his speech by pointing to Israel's history of salvation, culminating in the government of King David. From King David he draws a line to Jesus, the direct descendant of David and Saviour of Israel. But the Jews of Antioch interrupt him in a fictional answer to this explanation:

> My dear Paul, if the latter were to be the main point of your lecture, you might have spared the aforementioned old and known histories, which do not contribute anything to this matter. Whereas you cannot assume that what you so briefly said about your Jesus of Nazareth is known to us. So we ask you for threefold evidence: 1) That this Jesus is descended from King David, since we hear that you people are not quite able to prove his mother's descent from King David (which is the most important thing). 2) That, even if he had been from that lineage, he alone, before many others who were also David's descendants and still are, must be the Saviour of Israel. 3) That the promises of a Saviour from David's descent contain personal marks that all accord with this Jesus and with no one else, because, as we have read and learnt, the Saviour of Israel should sit on the throne of David in Jerusalem as a great Regent, humiliate all the enemies of our people, and set free and collect all dispersed and imprisoned Israelites. How does this square with someone who was crucified?[8]

But Paul goes on in his speech to remind the Jews of John the Baptist's witness of Jesus, and of the prophets' promises in general. Then he turns to the miracle of the Resurrection, using it as evidence for the Messiahship of Jesus, which is still not enough to convince the Jews. They insist on a clear distinction between matters of Resurrection and of Messiahship. But Paul subsequently connects these two matters, and in order to defend the Resurrection, refers to the second Psalm, in which he finds proof of the divinity of Jesus Christ. The Jews answer:

---

[8] Hermann Samuel Reimarus, *Apologie oder Schutzschrift für die vernünftigen Verehrer Gottes*, ed. Gerhard Alexander, vol. 2 (Frankfurt, 1972), p. 255. "Mein guter Paule wenn dieses letztere der Hauptsatz deines Vortrages werden sollte, so hättest du die vorangeschickten alten und bekannten Historien, welche nichts zu dieser Sache beytragen, wohl ersparhen mögen. Dagegen kannstu bey uns nicht so bekannt annehmen, was du von deinem Jesu aus Nazareth in aller Kürtze sagest. Wir verlangen also zuvörderst dreyerley Beweise von dir: 1) Daß dieser Jesus von dem König David entsprossen sey. Denn wir hören, daß ihr Leute die Abstammung seiner Mutter, (auf welche es vornehmlich ankommt) von dem Könige David nicht so recht beweisen könnt. 2) Daß, wenn er auch aus dem Geschlecht gewesen wäre, er allein vor vielen andern, die Davids Nachkommen waren und noch sind, der Heiland Israels seyn müsse. 3) Daß die Verheissungen eines Heilands aus Davids Geschlecht solche persönliche Merkmaale enthalten, die sämtlich auf diesen Jesum, und sonst auf niemand passen. Denn, soviel wir gelesen und gelernet haben, so sollte ja der Erlöser Israels auf dem Thron Davids zu Jerusalem als ein großer Regente sitzen, alle Feinde unsers Volks demühtigen, alle zerstreute und gefangene Israeliten befreyen und sammlen. Wie reimt sich das zusammen mit einem der gekreutziget ist?"

So you, Paul and Barnabas, want to prove now in our presence neither from
your own experience, as someone who has seen Jesus resurrected, nor from
the other disciples' witness, but mainly from Scripture, that God raised Jesus
from the dead and that therefore in him the promises are fulfilled. Now we
would like to know how this is contained in the second Psalm. *You* (David)
are my son, today I have begotten you, should mean as much as: *In future
I am going to raise Jesus of Nazareth, Joseph's son, from the grave.* Heavens!
who can comprehend and understand such an explanation, since no single
word, no subject, no predicate, and no circumstances retain their natural
meaning? Even supposing that this Psalm was about the Messiah, how is it
indicated that it will be Jesus of Nazareth?[9]

II. Two Examples of Judaica Used by Reimarus

It is not pure coincidence that Reimarus puts the enlightened criticism of
the Christian reading of the Old Testament into a Jewish mouth. In treating the Messianic passages, he often refers to the rabbinic tradition, available to him in new editions mostly with a Latin translation. He quotes
the Talmud, Saadiah Gaon, David Kimḥi, Joseph Albo, Asarja de Rubeis,
Manasseh ben Israel and (not only while discussing Messianic verses)
Maimonides.[10] In addition to this list of rabbinic thinkers from antiquity
to the late Middle Ages, Reimarus' footnotes and manuscripts contain
a broad spectrum of Christian literature on Jewish writings, mostly by
Protestant scholars of the 17th century such as John Lightfoot, Johannes
Coccejus, Theodor Hackspan, Johann Christoph Wagenseil, Johann Jacob
Schudt and Johann Christian Schöttgen. The list could be extended by
many exegetical books which do not exclusively deal with the rabbinic
tradition. In his interest in Jewish literature, Reimarus follows his teacher,

---

9 Ibid., pp. 257–258. "So wollet ihr denn, Paulus und Barnabas, jetzt, vor uns, weder aus
eigener Erfahrung, als die Jesum auferstanden gesehen hätten noch auf der andern Jünger
Zeugniß, sondern hauptsächlich aus der Schrifft beweisen, daß Gott Jesum von den Todten
erweckt habe, und daß folglich in ihm die Verheissungen erfüllet sind. Nun mögen wir
doch gerne wissen, wie das im zweyten Psalm enthalten sey. *Du* (David) *bist mein Sohn,
heute hab ich dich gezeuget,* soll so viel heissen: *ich will Jesum von Nazareth, des Josephs
Sohn, künftig vom Tode erwecken.* Himmel! wer kann solche Erklärungs-Art begreiffen oder
verstehen, da kein eintzig Wort, nicht Subjectum, nicht Prädicatum nicht Umstände, in
ihrer natürlichen Bedeutung bleiben? Gesetzt, die Rede sey auch in dem Psalm von dem
Messia. Wodurch wird doch angedeutet, daß es Jesus von Nazareth seyn werde?"
10 Reimarus cites Maimonides in his discussion of a Jewish theory of tolerance based on
the seven Commandments revealed to Noah. In this context Reimarus has the opportunity
to take notice of Maimonides' position on Messianic belief as well, which is fundamental
for an understanding of medieval Jewish debate on this topic.

Johann Christoph Wolf. But Reimarus is not among the pioneers of Protestant Jewish studies, of which his teacher Wolf could be named as one
of the last. The main work on Jewish literature had been done during the
16th and 17th centuries, and so Reimarus is able to obtain a broad knowledge without the burden of working with pure Hebrew texts himself.[11] The
literature available to him offers philological material which often goes
into details of the Old and New Testament's single words, as well as general theological reflections on the rabbinic studies' results. One example
is Theodor Hackspan's "De scriptorum Judaicorum in Theologia usu vario
& multiplici Tractatus", another, Rabbi David Kimḥi's commentary on the
second Psalm. The list could easily be extended by some other writings,
for example Rabbi Isaac Troki's "Hizzuq Emunah" or the famous "Toldoth
Jeshu" denying Jesus' Davidic descent. Both writings were available to
Reimarus in Johann Christoph Wagenseil's compilation of anti-Christian
Jewish writings "Tela ignea satanae".[12]

Theodor Hackspan's "De scriptorum Judaicorum in Theologia usu vario
& multiplici Tractatus" was published in 1644 together with an edition of
Rabbi Yom Tov Lipmann Mühlhausen's "Liber Nizzachon", which circulated in secret amongst Jews until Hackspan and his pupils managed to
steal it from a Rabbi in Schnaittach near Nürnberg.[13] Theodor Hackspan
was one of the first Lutheran theologians in Germany to introduce oriental languages like Syriac and Arabic into the *philologia sacra*. Having
studied at the Lutheran faculties of Jena and Helmstedt, he became a professor of Hebrew in Altdorf and published many books and shorter dis-
sertations, mostly on matters of philology but also on Judaism, on Islam
and a few on exegetical matters.[14] His "Tractatus" on the use of Jewish
literature was broadly accepted amongst Lutheran theologians, who felt
a need to find an authorized way of dealing with Jewish writings, and

---

[11] Heinz Mosche Graupe, *Juden und Judentum im Zeitalter der Aufklärung*: Hermann
Samuel Reimarus (1694–1768) ein "bekannter Unbekannter" der Aufklärung in Hamburg
(Göttingen, 1973), pp. 113–127, p. 116. Graupe points out that Reimarus' Jewish studies
did not reach the level of his teacher Wolf. His conclusion that this reveals his general
indifference towards the Jews and their intellectual tradition is to be rejected.

[12] Johann Christoph Wagenseil, *Tela ignea satanae* (Altdorfi Noricorum, 1681).

[13] On the "Tractatus" in general Samuel Kraus, *The Jewish-Christian Controversy from the
earliest times to 1789*, vol. 1, ed. William Horbury, (Tübingen, 1996), pp. 223–225 and Martin
Friedrich, *Zwischen Abwehr und Bekehrung. Die Stellung der deutschen evangelischen
Theologie zum Judentum im 17. Jahrhundert* (Tübingen, 1988), pp. 67–68.

[14] *Hackspan* (*Theodorus*): Jöcher, Allgemeines Gelehrtenlexikon 2 (1750, repr. 1961),
pp. 1305–1306.

Hackspan offered what they were looking for.[15] The point of Hackspan's "Tractatus" is an analysis of the competing Jewish parties of the Pharisees and the Sadducees, who later lived on as the Karaite movement. Since Lippmann in his "Liber Nizzachon" defends the Pharisees' allegorical use of the Old Testament against the Sadducees' criticism, Hackspan is sure that the "Liber Nizzachon" can serve as a defence of Christian dogmatics, though it was written with polemical intention.[16] The tradition of Jewish polemical writings against internal criticism pursued by the Karaites is as old as the Karaite movement itself, and the Christians often took up these polemics, as illustrated by the history of Judah ha-Levi's medieval book "KitÁb al-ËazarÐ", which circulated amongst Christian theologians as the "Liber Cosri" or "Kuzari". It is written not only against Christianity and Islam but against the Karaites as well, and in some passages it offers arguments which could easily be taken as proof of the pre-existence of Jesus Christ the Messiah.[17] Hackspan holds anti-Karaite writings like this to be valuable and is proud to present a new one of the same kind. In his eyes, the Karaites' or Sadducees' spiteful criticism obviously seems equivalent to the Socinian criticism of dogmatics. His analysis of the Sadducees' history and their use of the Bible is explicitly based on Socinian writings.[18] Indeed, the Socinians had to face Jewish and Karaite criticism in 16th century Poland.[19] Karaite-Socinian contact was of a polemical nature, but they still shared a common interest: the criticism of dogmatics and unreasonable interpretations of Scripture. One could imagine that Socinians somehow felt attracted to the Sadducees' heirs, who kept the true biblical religion free of new precepts and in this way offered a reasonable belief. That Hackspan took notice of an alliance of Jewish criticism and Socinianism is evident from a fictional religious dialogue entitled "Assertio Passionis Dominicae Adversus Judaeos & Turcas Dialogo inclusa" and

---

[15] Martin Friedrich, *Zwischen Abwehr und Bekehrung. Die Stellung der deutschen evangelischen Theologie zum Judentum im 17. Jahrhundert* (Tübingen, 1988), pp. 67–68.

[16] Theodor Hackspan, *De scriptorum Judaicorum in Theologia usu vario & multiplici Tractatus:* Lippmann (von Mühlhausen), Liber Nizzachon (Norimbergae, 1644), pp. 215–512, p. 512.

[17] Hartwig Hirschfeld, Einleitung: Abu-l-Hasan Jehuda Hallewi, Das Buch Al-Chazari (Breslau 1885, repr. 2000), pp. XXXII–L and Abu-l-Hasan Jehuda Hallewi, Das Buch Al-Chazari (Breslau 1885, repr. 2000), p. 181.

[18] Theodor Hackspan, *De scriptorum Judaicorum in Theologia usu vario & multiplici Tractatus:* Lippmann (von Mühlhausen), Liber Nizzachon (Norimbergae, 1644), pp. 215–512, pp. 224–236.

[19] Samuel Kraus, *The Jewish-Christian Controversy from the earliest times to 1789*, vol. 1, ed. William Horbury, (Tübingen, 1996), pp. 124–125.

published in 1642. The Jew refers to Socinus while explaining his position to the Catholic, the Lutheran and the Muslim.[20] However, be it Sadducean-Karaite, Socinian or both, as a Lutheran theologian Hackspan feels a need to fight this kind of criticism.[21] He suggests following the Pharisees' path when using Jewish literature in matters of theology, hoping that this will help him to defend orthodox Christian belief in Jesus Christ the Messiah and Son of God. Additionally, he refers to the Qur'anic belief in Abraham and his original monotheistic religion, which after being distorted must be restored by the mission of Moses, Jesus and Muhammad.[22] Since in this regard the Messiahship of Jesus is an important aspect of Qur'anic belief, Hackspan does not hesitate to present the letter of an anonymous Muslim theologian which he quotes from a Catholic disputation held in Rome during the 1630s, and which in 1637 was adopted by Philipp Guadagnoli in a "Responsio" to a Persian theologian from Isfahan.[23] The letter contains an explanation of some passages in the books of the prophets which support Christian Messianic belief. This Arabic letter might illustrate once again the general idea of Hackspan's "Tractatus" and its Lutheran readers: to use the writings of foreign religions as evidence for the truth of Christian belief, no matter in which context and for whom they were once written. Reimarus does not discuss this bizarre Jewish-Muslim defence of Christianity. He respects Islam for its tolerance towards other religions, and he admits that its revelation contains less unreasonable doctrines. But he accuses the Qur'an of being a source of blind obedience and holding back reason. (No 1) So in Reimarus' view it does not make any sense to call a Muslim as witness for the truth of Christianity. Both revelations have their weak points and so one cannot serve as a defence of the other. Regarding Judaism, one is faced with nearly the same problem. Judaism offers no

---

[20] Theodor Hackspan 1642, *Assertio Passionis Dominicae Adversus Judaeos & Turcas Dialogo inclusa* (Altdorphi, 1642). Without page numbers.

[21] In Altdorf the Socinian threat was particularly present. In 1616 a couple of Socinian students from Poland caused a scandal in Altdorf, which the government of Nürnberg silenced by official persecutions. Altdorf theologians had to show that they had undoubtedly got rid of Socinianism. Zbigniew Ogonowski, *Der Sozinianismus*: (Friedrich Ueberweg) ed., Grundriss der Geschichte der Philosophie, vol. 4: Das Heilige Römische Reich Deutscher Nation. Nord- und Ostmitteleuropa (Basel, 2001), pp. 871–881, pp. 876–878.

[22] Theodor Hackspan, *De scriptorum Judaicorum in Theologia usu vario & multiplici Tractatus:* Lippmann (von Mühlhausen), Liber Nizzachon (Norimbergae, 1644), pp. 215–512, pp. 237–238. Hackspan quotes Sura 3,50 but the text he gives is in fact a shortening of Sura 3,65 and 67.

[23] *Antitheses fidei ventilabuntur in conventu S. Petri Montis Aurei fratrum Minorum S. P. Francisci* [...] (Romae, 1638) and Philippo Guadagnoli, *Pro Christiana Religione responsio ad objectiones Ahmed filii Zin Alabedin* (Romae, 1637).

support for Christian belief in revelation. It rather helps to get rid of it. Reimarus skips over Hackspan's whole superstructure of dogmatic apologetics and takes up only the historical results. From Hackspan he adopts his analysis of the Pharisees and Sadducees, deciding himself to follow the Sadducees.[24]

The second example is a "Commentarius in aliquot Psalmos Davidicos" written by Rabbi David Kimḥi, a 13th century grammarian and exegete of Narbonne in the south of France. In his exegetical works, Kimḥi follows his father Joseph Kimḥi's and Ibn Ezra's methodology in order to establish a non-mystical and purely historical understanding of the biblical text.[25] His commentary on the Psalms was published with a Latin translation in 1723 in Adrian Reland's "Analecta Rabbinica", a collection in which Reland tries to enable a large circle of readers to use the rabbinic commentaries in matters of exegesis. The use of Kimḥi's exegetical works was nothing unusual amongst humanist exegetes interested in a historical understanding of the Old Testament. Hugo Grotius was one of the first. Many others followed.[26] Reimarus obviously took particular notice of Kimḥi's explanation of the second Psalm. Kimḥi starts with some general words about the arrangement of the Psalter.[27] After that, he first defines the second Psalm's reference to the biography of King David. King David sang this Psalm when he was under Philistine pressure, after he had been anointed king over Israel. The raging of heathens and peoples in verse 1 is a poetic description of the Philistines' actions, known from 2 Sam 5, where the riots that started after King David's anointing are described.[28] And so the Lord's "anointed" mentioned in verse 2 can be none other than King David, who in verse 7 is called the "son" because of his obedience to God, and the "today begotten" son because the Psalm here alludes to the time of the anointing, when David was accepted as the obedient son of God.[29]

---

[24] Hermann Samuel Reimarus, *Apologie oder Schutzschrift für die vernünftigen Verehrer Gottes*, ed. Gerhard Alexander, vol. 1 (Frankfurt, 1972), p. 929 and vol. 2 (Frankfurt, 1972), pp. 267–270.

[25] Frank Talmage, *Kimḥi, David*: Encyclopaedia Judaica 10 (1971), pp. 1001–1004.

[26] Henning Graf Reventlow, *Epochen der Bibelauslegung*, vol. 3 (München, 1997), p. 216.

[27] David Kimḥi, *Commentarius Rabbi Davidis Kimchi in aliquot Psalmos Davidicos*: Adrian Reland, Analecta Rabbinica, 2nd ed. (Trajecti ad Rhenum, 1723), p. 26.

[28] Ibid., pp. 26–28.

[29] Ibid., pp. 34–36. "...ac si diceret, Rex iste, meus est, & filius meus, & servus meus qui mihi obtemperat: omnis enim qui ita mihi obedit, ut Deo serviat, vocabitur filius, sicut filius qui patri obtemperat, & illi servire paratus est. [...] *Ego hodie genui te*, dies quo in regem unctus fuit, ipse est quo Deus eum suscepit in filium, ut supra dictum fuit, *Providi mihi in regem*."

Assuming this basic hermeneutical insight, Kimḥi develops a clear and non-mystical understanding of the Psalm's remaining verses. Everything refers to the second book of Samuel and its narratives about King David. At the very end of his explanation Kimḥi makes a surprising comment. He admits that his explanation is not the only acceptable way to read the second Psalm. The Psalm could also be read in reference to Ez 38, where Gog and Magog's eschatological raging is described.[30] This would enable the reader to use the Psalm as proof of a future coming of the Messiah. The explanation would then be less clear and scientific but more acceptable.

This latter remark in Kimḥi's commentary on the second Psalm points to a general debate inside Judaism about the Messianic passages' meaning. As the footnotes to the "Apologie oder Schutzschrift" show, Reimarus was quite aware of this Jewish debate. Of course, the idea of a Messiah and his Salvation is not totally alien to Judaism, since in some verses the Old Testament mentions a Messiah of Israel. But how this indistinct Old Testament Messianic belief should be developed in terms of a Jewish doctrine was discussed throughout the whole history of Judaism, because if a Messianic time was expected, it is not clear whether it should be simply a restoration in time of King David's glorious kingdom, or a future utopia often expressed in terms of eschatological imagination, as was widely present in medieval folk apocalyptic belief. A second question regarded the Messiah's person – whether he should be described as the glorious Messiah ben David restoring the Israelite kingdom, or as the suffering Messiah ben Joseph, bearing the apocalyptic threat at the end of time.[31] Since the medieval apocalyptic Messianic belief often turned into antinomianism, the rabbinic tradition considered it to be dangerous to Judaism, and many of the medieval rabbinic authorities tried to set limits to the common Messianic belief. The greatest exponent of this more negative position on Messianism is Maimonides. He stresses the Messianic belief's restorative dimension and rejects the idea of an eschatological Messianic Salvation, replacing it with the idea of a constant rational renovation of Judaism's complete contents. Future Salvation can be reached by philosophical contemplation and there is no need for an eschatological coming

---

[30] Ibid., p. 42. "Sunt porro qui hunc Psalmum exponant de (f) Gog & Magog, & de Meia, hoc est de Rege Messia, & sic ipse interpretati sunt Magistri nostri piae memoriae. Et si hac ratione exponatur hic Psalus, sensus ejus erit dilucidus: sed verovidetur similius Davidem hunc Psalmum de seipso composuisse sicut nos explicuimus."

[31] Gershom Scholem, *Judaica*, vol. 1 (Frankfurt am Main, 1963), pp. 10–14 and 39–40.

of the Messiah.[32] Reimarus discusses Maimonides while describing a Jewish theory of tolerance, and regarding the history of Jewish Messianism, he takes up the post-maimonidean medieval debate on the "ikkarim": the most fundamental principles of Jewish religion. Reimarus assumes that after Maimonides the Messianic belief was not regarded as an "ikkar" anymore. He points to Joseph Albo, a 15th century Spanish philosopher and preacher, who made a distinction between the most fundamental "ikkarim" and their less important branches called "emunot". Albo says that Messianic belief is part of the "emunot" but not of the "ikkarim", and Reimarus regards this decision as originally Jewish.[33]

Despite all this rational restraint, folk apocalyptic Messianic belief never ceased, and in fact flourished whenever the situation of the Jews became worse. After the expulsion from Spain in 1492, it gained new power and found its expression in the writings of the New Cabbala, which allowed the idea of the Messiah to be understood as the outward appearance of cosmological actions within God.[34] This new Messianic enthusiasm reached its zenith in the 17th century when Shabbetai Ñevi proclaimed himself the Messiah and founded a Messianic movement inside Judaism based on the ideas of the New Cabbala. When the Turkish Sultan stopped Shabbetai's activities by forcing him to convert to Islam, the Sabbatian movement reached a crisis. It was Nathan of Gaza who revived the weakened movement, stressing the idea that conversion to Islam was a necessary part of the Messiah's eschatological activities. He interpreted Islam as a realm empty of God by depicting it as analogous to the New Cabbala's cosmological teaching of a realm left empty by God after the Creation. In this view, the Messiah's conversion to Islam is necessary to release the last trapped sparks of divinity left in that empty realm, which otherwise would stay separated from God. In this way the Sabbatian movement formed a valid doctrine which spread to many Jewish parishes even after Shabbetai's scandalous conversion.[35] In the 18th century a couple of Jewish and

---

[32] Ibid., pp. 41–47 and 50–65.

[33] Hermann Samuel Reimarus, *Apologie oder Schutzschrift für die vernünftigen Verehrer Gottes*, ed. Gerhard Alexander, vol. 1 (Frankfurt, 1972), p. 725 and Alexander Altmann, *Albo, Joseph*: Encyclopaedia Judaica 2 (1972), pp. 535–537.

[34] Gershom Scholem, *Sabbatai Ñevi. The Mystical Messiah 1626–1676* (Princeton, 1973), pp. 15–22.

[35] Ibid., pp. 668–814 or William Scott Green / Jed Silverstein, *Messiah*: Encyclopaedia of Judaism 2 (1999), pp. 874–888, p. 883.

Christian works inspired by Sabbatian ideas would have been available.[36] But Reimarus does not show any interest in this Jewish Messianic movement, although it was obviously much more open-minded towards other religions and towards the idea of a Messiah than the more traditional authorities Reimarus prefers. In his view the Jews represent a negative position on the Christian belief in a Messiah, and allow him to refuse the Christian Messianic reading of the Old Testament.

III. The Rabbinate Struggle in Hamburg

But why does Reimarus stress the Jewish contribution to the enlightened debate on the Christian use of the Old Testament Messianic verses? Since the discussion of Jewish exegetical literature had already led to some insights during the late 17th century, Reimarus could have used them for his criticism without showing so plainly its dependence on Jewish traditions. Is it a subtle kind of anti-Judaism to make the Jews responsible for the breakdown of the Christian belief in Jesus Christ the promised Messiah? To avoid a misunderstanding of Reimarus' thought here it can be useful to remember what happened in the Jewish community in his native town immediately before he wrote the passage quoted at the beginning.[37] During the 1750s a struggle took place in the Triple Community of Altona, Hamburg and Wandsbeck that affected Jews from Poland to the Netherlands.[38] It was the struggle from 1750 for the office of Chief Rabbi of the Triple Community waged by Rabbi Jonatan Eybeschütz, who was, it seems, a quite educated Rabbi of excellent descent, popular among both Jews and Christians.[39] In April 1751 Eybeschütz was publicly

---

[36] Martin Friedrich, *Zwischen Abwehr und Bekehrung. Die Stellung der deutschen evangelischen Theologie zum Judentum im 17. Jahrhundert* (Tübingen, 1988), pp. 95–96 and 102–105. Christian missionaries took aim at disappointed Sabbatians and produced literature on Sabbatianism.

[37] As the handwritten preparations to the "Apologie" show, Reimarus started to write his criticism of the New Testament in the 1760s.

[38] For the most detailed description of the Rabbinate Struggle see Bernhard Brilling, *Der Hamburger Rabbinerstreit im 18. Jahrhundert*: Zeitschrift für Hamburgische Geschichte 55 (1969), pp. 216–244.

[39] Gutmann Klemperer, *Rabbi Jonathan Eibenschütz. Eine biographische Skizze*, ed. Wolf Pascheles (Prag, 1858). A poem of praise to Eybeschütz was published in 1752. It was the first in the German language dedicated to a Jew. Bernhard Brilling, *Das erste Gedicht auf einen deutschen Rabbiner aus dem Jahre 1752. Ein Beitrag zum Emden-Eibenschütz-Streit*: Bulletin des Leo Baeck Instituts 41 (1968), pp. 38–47, p. 39.

accused of being a follower of the Sabbatian movement because of some suspect amulets he had given to sick women. His accuser was an equally well-educated Rabbi of excellent descent named Jacob Emden.[40] Rabbi Emden had lived in Altona since 1732, made some money as a merchant and spent it on a system of financial support for the poor and on a small printing-house. He ran this printing-house under licence from the Danish King in order to print his Hebrew writings without having to depend on the approval of other Rabbis. In his house he set up a private synagogue, where he was allowed to hold services for his followers.[41] In one of these private services the scandalous accusation against the official Chief Rabbi Eybeschütz came up. In this way Rabbi Emden started a struggle which soon spread throughout the whole Triple Community, and in which the parties of Emden and Eybeschütz fought each other, sometimes leading to street brawls. The Government of Hamburg treated the struggle as an internal Jewish affair, which the Jews should clear up by themselves in order to avoid external punishment.[42] The Danish Government in contrast used the struggle as an opportunity to narrow the autonomy of the Triple Community, obviously with the intention of using the Jews living in Hamburg and Wandsbeck to gain power inside these administrative realms. Eybeschütz knew about this Danish interest and consequently took care to gain the sympathy of the Danish Government, which soon started to support him. Here the theological righteousness of the Chief Rabbi was regarded as one of the most important points in this affair, so Eybeschütz was asked for proof of his innocence. While refuting the accusation of Sabbatianism before the Jewish community, he managed to take advantage of Lutheran theological interest in the Sabbatian movement when he explained his position to the Danish Government. In 1752 one of his disciples, who had converted to Christianity and become baptized as Karl Anton, wrote a theological report on Eybeschütz praising his great secular erudition and generally refuting the accusation.[43] In 1755 followed an

---

[40] Jacob Joseph Schacter, *Rabbi Jacob Emden: Life and Major Works* (Harvard, 1988) and Moshe Shraga Samet, *Emden, Jacob*: Encyclopaedia Judaica 6 (1971), pp. 721–724.

[41] Jacob Joseph Schacter, *Rabbi Jacob Emden: Life and Major Works* (Harvard, 1988), pp. 178 and 182–184.

[42] The senate of Hamburg published two mandates in this affair in May 1752 and in October 1753. Staatsarchiv Hamburg 522–1 Jüdische Gemeinde 88b = 741–4 Fotoarchiv Sa 928, pp. 31–33 also printed in the senate's Book of Mandates 1751–1762.

[43] Heinrich Graetz, *Geschichte der Juden von den ältesten Zeiten bis auf die Gegenwart*, vol. 10 (Leipzig, 1897, repr. 1998), pp. 379–380.

official comment on the accusations written by the Chief Rabbi himself.[44] The theological defence of Eybeschütz culminated in 1756 when a Pietist theologian named David Friedrich Megerlin analyzed the suspect amulets, insisting that they showed a secret reference to Jesus Christ.[45] The latter report might not be regarded as an extraordinary opinion. It rather shows a common position on Judaism among Lutheran theologians, which often saw the Jews – and particularly Sabbatian Jews – as a missionary object.[46]

Eybeschütz knew about this Lutheran interest. Playing a double role towards Jews and Christians, he gained Danish support and soon was able to vindicate his authority against his enemies, stressing his appointment by the Danish King, as a letter written in October 1753 (probably by a member of the Jewish community of Hamburg) reveals. (No 2) Eybeschütz was able to keep his office with Danish support, although the Government of Hamburg rejected him. In 1756 the Danish Government arranged pseudo-democratic elections and in this way silenced the enemies of the Chief Rabbi. In a letter from the Government of Altona to the Danish King we find a detailed description of how the elections were arranged. The elders were to come to the town hall of Altona in order to decide under the supervision of the Danish Government on the question: "Whether the Chief Rabbi Eybeschütz' office is to be relinquished or whether the vocation given to him may be renewed for the usual period..." (No 3) The Triple Community was allowed neither to organize the elections by itself nor to set up an opponent, as was the practice before the Rabbinate Struggle. And the worst thing: the Jews not living in Altona were forced to accept the supervision of a Christian Government they probably did not think highly of, being citizens of Hamburg or Wandsbeck. Eybeschütz won the struggle with Danish support, leaving a couple of enemies among the Jews and in the Government of Hamburg, which finally had to accept the decision forced on it by Altona.

Regarding Reimarus' use of Jewish criticism, it may be of interest to focus on Eybeschütz' opponent, Rabbi Jacob Emden. What kind of Jewish intellectual could this obscure private Rabbi have been to start so easily one of the worst struggles among German Jews during the 18th century? We shall pass over the details of his exciting biography, which led him to

---

[44] Ibid., p. 383.

[45] Ibid., pp. 384–385. On Megerlin see *Megerlin (David Friedrich)*: Jöcher, *Allgemeines Gelehrtenlexikon* 4 (1750, repr. 1961), p. 1186.

[46] Martin Friedrich, *Zwischen Abwehr und Bekehrung. Die Stellung der deutschen evangelischen Theologie zum Judentum im 17. Jahrhundert* (Tübingen, 1988), pp. 145–149.

many Jewish communities from Prague to Amsterdam to London. Early in his life he gained some influential friends during his travels who afterwards supported him in his struggle against Eybeschütz. But what are the characteristics of Emden's thought? As his writings show, his special area of interest was the tradition of Halakha, in which he tried to find a conservative mode of exegesis avoiding all mystical or philosophical additions.[47] He always showed an interest in philosophy, even of gentile origin, but he subsequently refuted its authority in matters of religious practice.[48] When it came to the struggle against Eybeschütz and Sabbatianism in general, Emden's philological work turned into a sharp criticism of the Cabbala, which he considered to be one of the main sources of the Sabbatian heresy. In 1768 he presented a broad critique of the Zohar, showing by philological evidence that it contains many words and grammatical characteristics that sometimes date from the late Middle Ages. The authority of the Zohar cannot be justified by its age any more.[49] In this way, by stressing the necessity of a non-mystical reading of the biblical tradition and analyzing the history of Hebrew literature critically, he represents a mode of thought which to Reimarus might have seemed quite familiar. His teacher Wolf in his "Bibliotheca Hebraea"[50] pursued the same kind of literary criticism, and in 1717 he had already suspected the Cabbala generally of being an obscure mixture of old, new, gentile and Hebrew ideas (No 4), as Emden demonstrated in detail during the 1760s. The paths of conservative Jewish thought and of radical enlightenment seem quietly to converge here.[51] In addition, a friendly attitude toward the opponent of Eybeschütz might have been appropriate for Reimarus as a resident of Hamburg. The Rabbinate Struggle merely confirmed Reimarus in his rejection of Jews who were willing to support orthodox theologians in their unreasonable belief. Already in 1744 he had expressed his disappointment with the Christian delusion of converting more Jews to Christianity. (No 5) And after Eybeschütz' appearance in the Triple Community he expressed this rejection more aggressively.

---

[47] Jacob Joseph Schacter, *Rabbi Jacob Emden: Life and Major Works* (Harvard, 1988), pp. 159–177.

[48] Ibid., pp. 507–511, 548 and 550–570.

[49] Ibid., pp. 520–527.

[50] The method Wolf pursued in his "Bibliotheca Hebraea" is described in early reviews: *Deutsche Acta Eruditorum* 41 (1716), pp. 343–354, *Deutsche Acta Eruditorum* 77 (1722), S. 323–341 and *Deutsche Acta Eruditorum* 129 (1727), pp. 664–679.

[51] We do not know whether Reimarus ever came into contact with Rabbi Emden. There are only a few pieces of evidence for Reimarus' contact with Jews, mentioned in Almut and Paul Spalding's contribution to this volume.

IV. Conclusion

The criticism of Jesus Christ the Messiah promised in the Old Testament is one of the main topics in both parts of the "Apologie oder Schutzschrift". In some late passages of the second part of the "Apologie" a radicalization of this criticism is obvious. The reason for this radicalization is Reimarus' disdain for the Lutheran theologians' position on Judaism. Since Lutheran theologians like Theodor Hackspan are not able to see Judaism as an independent religion alongside Christianity but merely as a not yet Christian community which may add some dogmatic evidence to the debate on Jesus Christ's Messiahship before it finally converts, they are also not able to see the differences regarding the view of Jesus Christ and the great critical potential of Jewish thought. Reimarus' goal is to set free this critical potential. He cites many medieval Jewish writings written by conservative Jewish exegetes who tried to restrain the Jewish Messianic belief and demanded a pure historical understanding of the Old Testament Messianic passages. In this way Reimarus shows how to dismantle the Christian dogma of Christ's divinity by using the Jewish tradition, while at the same time giving up the Pauline idea of the Jews' eschatological conversion to Christianity. During the Rabbinate Struggle in the 1750s Reimarus has to witness that his idea of dealing with the Jews as an independent religion was unrealistic. Playing with the Christian Government's hope of converting Jews, Rabbi Eybeschütz gambled the Triple Community's independence away and made it a puppet of Danish policy inside the administrative realm of Hamburg. The struggle reveals that both Christians and Jews are still far away from real tolerance. Reimarus reacts with mockery of the Christians' foolish attempt to convert Jews, and implicitly with mockery of the Jews as well, inasmuch as they are not able to resist this Christian attempt.

Regarding Messianic belief Reimarus sees two differing modes of Jewish thought, the first capable of accepting the Christian belief in Jesus Christ the Messiah in the hope that any approach to Christianity will accelerate the coming of the true Messiah. The other mode is to keep a critical distance from any Messianic enthusiasm, hoping for Christian tolerance towards a tradition which will always reject the fundamental doctrines of Christianity. Reimarus prefers the latter. He stresses Jewish criticism of the Messianic belief of Christian dogmatics and in this way shows that Judaism should be seen as an independent religion alongside Christianity which is quite capable of encouraging the Enlightenment in its own way.

APPENDIX

No 1

A comment on Islam and on missionary possibilities in the Ottoman Empire written by Reimarus in 1744; Staatsarchiv Hamburg 622–1 Familie Reimarus A 13f., pp. 39–40

Text

Dies ist der Zustand im gantzen Türckischen Reiche. Es würde da einem ein kurtzer Proceß gemacht werden, wenn er sich des Vorhabens äusserte, die Muselmänner in ihrem Glauben irre zu machen, und sie zum Christenthum als einer besseren Religion zu bewegen. Ich entsinne mich auch nicht jemahls von Missionarien in der Türckey etwas gelesen oder gehört zu haben. Es würde dieses auch bey den Türcken selbst, wegen ihres blinden Gehorsams und Eiffers für ihren Glauben und Alcoran, nicht angehen. Denn eben das bringt ihre Religion mit sich, nicht zu raisonieren, nicht zu zweiffeln, fremde zu hassen und zu verfolgen. Sie sind so ernste von der göttlichen Sendung des Mahomet, und von der Wahrheit seiner Wunder, von der göttlichen Eingebung und Vorzügen ihres Alcorans überredet, sie haben aus dem Alcoran selbst so starken Haß wieder das Christentum als eine Vielgötterey und Abgötterey eingesogen, daß es keiner Gesetze und Straffen bräuchte sie davon abzuhalten. Es ist wahr, sie dulden Christen unter sich, und man muß es der Christenheit zur Schande nachsagen, daß Christen unter türckischer Regierung ihren Gottesdienst ungehinderter treiben als unter christlicher. Es ist auch nicht zu leugnen, daß die Türcken nach dem Alcoran selbst Mosen und Christum für grosse Propheten halten: Aber sie glauben daß die Bücher Altes Testaments von den Juden heßlich verdorben sind und deswegen der Alcoran gegeben sey; daß von Juden so wohl als Christen viel falsche Lehren, und insonderheit von diesen die Abgötterey und Vielgötterey eingeführet worden. Denn daß Christen drey Götter haben ist einem Türcken so klar, als daß er drey zehlen kann. Und daß ein Mensch zugleich Gott sey ist bey ihnen offenbahre Abgötterey. Dieses ihnen anders zu bedeuten und aus dem Sinn zu reden, ist schwer. Dieses macht daß sie so wenig Lust haben Christen zu werden, als Christen Lust haben Juden zu werden, ungeachtet die Juden unter ihnen wohnen, und das alte Testament beiden gemein ist: genug sie verwerfe Christum.

Translation

This is the situation in the whole Turkish Empire. They make short work of anyone who announces that he wants to confuse Muslims in their creed and convert them to Christianity as a better religion. And I do not remember reading or hearing of any missionary activities in Turkey. In fact it would not work with the Turks because of their blind obedience and zeal for their creed and their Qur'an, since this is what their religion actually entails, not to reason, and not to doubt, while hating and pursuing foreigners. They are so honestly persuaded of the divine mission of Mohammed, of the truth of his miracles and of the divine inspiration and merits of the Qur'an, and from the Qur'an itself they have imbibed such a hatred for Christianity, a hatred as strong as for polytheism or idolatry, that no law or punishment would be needed to keep them away from it. It is true, they tolerate Christians amongst themselves, and as a disgrace to Christendom it is to be said that Christians hold their services more freely under Turkish government than under Christian. Also, it is not to be denied that the Turks according to the Qur'an consider Moses and Christ to be great prophets. But they believe that the Old Testament books have been badly distorted by the Jews and that for this reason the Qur'an has been given, and that by both Jews and Christians many false doctrines have been invented, especially polytheism and idolatry, because to a Turk it is as clear that Christians have three Gods as is counting to three. And that a man should be God at the same time is plain idolatry to them. It is difficult to explain this to them in a different way and to talk it out of them. For this reason they no more feel like becoming Christians than Christians feel like becoming Jews, although Jews live amongst them and the Old Testament is common to both of them. However, they reject Christ.

No 2

Staatsarchiv Hamburg 522–1 Jüdische Gemeinde = 741–4 Fotoarchiv Sa 928, p. 18

Text

Demnach ich unter <   >, <   > und heutiges dato unser zwey zahl bediente Nahmens Samuel Susman und Wulh< > Spiro nach Altona gesandet, umb an dem dortigen Ober Rabiner Jonatan Eybeschitz in Nahmen unser hiesiger gemeine, Sein Ober Rabiner Schaft, von unser Hamburger gemeine ab zu Sagen und loß zu kündigen, weillen aber die Bedienten diverse mahl vor dem Ober Rabiners tühr geweßen, und sie zurück und abgewießen worden, und nicht im Hauße gelaßen, noch viel weniger den Ober Rabiner zu sprechen bekomen < >, also habe mir Selbst, heute Nachmittag gegen 6 uhr nach Altona begeben und nach gedachtes Ober Rabiners Hauße gelaßen, ihm auch durch gute Worte Selbst zu sprechen bekome, und im Nahme unßer hiesige gemeine Seine Ober Rabinerschaft von unser Hamburger gemeine abgesaget und loß gekündiget Wurauf der Ober Rabiner mir Antwortet, Er kenet diese Loßkündigung ganß und gar Nicht an, da unser Hamburger gemeine nicht imstandt und Mächtig wehre ihn ab zu Sagen und Loß zu kündigen weille Er von 28 Männern gewählet, und von Ihro maystad Der König zu Dannimarck eingesezet ist.

Translation

After I under < >, < > and today sent two servants named Samuel Susman and Wulh< > Spiro to Altona in order to cancel and in the name of our parish here to the Chief Rabbi Jonatan Eybeschitz there give notice to his being Chief Rabbi of our parish in Hamburg, since the servants standing in front of his door having been refused and not let into his house several times and not in the least able talk to him, I did myself proceed to Altona at about six o'clock in the afternoon and went to the Chief Rabbi's aforementioned house and by gentle words came to talk to him and did in the name of our parish here cancel and give notice to his being Chief Rabbi, to which the Chief Rabbi replied to me, that he did not at all accept this giving notice since our parish of Hamburg was not able and empowered enough to cancel and give notice to him, because he had been elected by 28 men and appointed by his majesty the King of Denmark.

No 3

Staatsarchiv Hamburg 522–1 Jüdische Gemeinde 88b = 741–4 Fotoarchiv Sa 928, pp 27–28

Text

[…] ob dem Ober Rabbiner Eybeschütz sein Amt aufzusagen, oder die ihm ertheilte vocation auf die gewöhnliche Zeit zu erneuren [ist] damit nach

denen Majoribus ein Conclusum formiret werden könne, [und die Älte-
sten] ihr votum geben sollen, und zwar solchergestalt, daß ein jeder von
zwene ihm zuzustellenden Zetteln, wovon der eine auf die Entlaßung und
der andere auf die Beybehaltung des Ober Rabbiners lautet, einen unter
der Aufsicht des Commissarii und der ihm zu geordneten Assistenten in
eine Büchse lege, mithin von seinem voto, wenn er es geheim zu halten
wünschet, niemand etwas bekannt werde, und daß weile die Hamburgische und Wandsbeckische Gemeinen bey dem vorseyendem Geschäfte
mit interessiret sind, in <   > Intimation annoch hinzu zufügen, daß die
Altonaische Gemeine von dem an sie von mir zu ertheilenden Befehl auf
Art und Weise wie sie mit denselben sonsten zu correspondiren pfleget,
Nachricht ertheilen und bey ihnen darauf anfragen solle, daß sie ebenfalls
durch ihre contribuierende Hausväter an dem von mir zu bestimmenden
Tage hieselbsten erscheinen und über die Beybehaltung oder Dimission
des Ober Rabbiners mit votiren.

Translation

[...] whether the Chief Rabbi Eybeschütz should have his appointment
cancelled or if the vocation given to him should be renewed for the usual
time, so that a majority decision may be reached and [the elders] give
their vote, in such a way that each should put into a can one of two papers
being given to him, one for the dismissal, the other for the Chief Rabbi's
retention in office, whereby, if he wishes to keep it secret, no one shall
know about his voting, and that, if the parishes of Hamburg and Wandsbeck are interested in the aforementioned proceedings, they should be
added to them by agreement, so that the parish of Altona may inform
them about the order which will be given by me as [the parish of Altona]
is normally used to correspond with them, and may invite them, so that
they, represented by their contributing elders, may appear here on a day
defined by me, and that they also may vote on the retention in office or
dismissal of the Chief Rabbi.

No 4

Johann Christoph Wolf on the idea of using the Cabbala as an old and
undistorted philosophy in Johann Christoph Wolf, Atheismi falso suspec-
tos [...], Vitembergae: Prelo Gerdesiano 1717, pp. 21–22

Text

Cum autem Kabbala illa vel omnis, vel saltem maxima sui parte recentior sit, et ex impuris Philosophorum lacunis deducta, quod nemo temere negaverit, consequitur, ex ea de veterum Hebraeorum mente iudicari minime omnium posse. Misturam autem antiquae illius, si qua fuit, de quo nunc non disputabimus, et recentioris Cabbalae agnoverunt illi, qui in ea interpretanda et excutienda prae ceteris occupati fuerunt. Sic Io. Georg. Wachterus non solum in eo libro, quem Spinosismum in Iudaismo inscripsit, et eo comparatum esse voluit, ut improbanda Cabbalae dogmata in luce ponerentur, sed et in Elucidario Kabbalistico, in quo priore sententia mutata, benignius, sed praeter rationem, de Cabbala sentire coepit, ex Gentili Philosophia multa in Cabbalisticum Systema translata esse agnoscit ultro, nec invitus profitetur. Vide librum priorem pag. 69. sq. et p. 221. ubi diserte ait, Cabbalam esse telam, a recentioribus Rabbinis pertextam, ex Philosophia veterum Barbarica, idque olim se per partes demonstraturum esse pollicetur. Nec minus in libello posteriore passim, v. c. p. 66. Cabbalae antiquissimas quidem traditiones, sed multis tamen modis adulteratas tribuit. Idem agnoverunt Henr. Morus, Th. Burnetus in Archaeologia lib. I. cap. 7. p. 336. Abrah. Hinckelmannus in Detectione Fundamenti Böhmiani, Celeb. Buddeus in Introduct. ad Histor. Philosophiae Hebraeorum p. 321 ut alios taceam. Nihil nisi nova, et ex alienis fontibus deducta, inventa in Cabbala animadvertit Auctor Bilibrae veritatis pag. 122. et Clericus Tomo VII. Biblioth. Universalis p. 367. ac prior quidem statuit, nihil nec futilius nec vanius occurrere in omni Scriptorum turba, quam secretiores Kabbalistas: quicquid enim promant de suis Sephiroth vel Numerationibus, de Azilot sive Emanationibus, non nisi putidissima esse otiosorum hominum commenta vel deliria.

Translation

But since the Cabbala in whole or at least for the most part is more recent and derived from philosophers' dirty swamps, which no one will idly deny, it follows that the ancient Hebrews' mind can be judged least of all on account of it. Those who were concerned with interpreting and scrutinizing the Cabbala prior to others were aware of that mixture of ancient (Cabbala), if it ever existed – about that we won't say anything now –, and more recent Cabbala. Thus Io. Georg. Wachterus (= Johann Georg Wachter), in his book entitled 'Spinozism in Judaism'[52] not only wanted [Spinozism] to be compared with it, in order to illuminate the Cabbala's reprehensible doctrines, but further in the 'Elucidarius Cabbalisticus',[53] in which, changing his mind, he started to think about the Cabbala in a friendlier, but irrational way, became aware that much of pagan philosophy had been transferred to the Cabbalistic system, and freely acknowledged it. See the former book on p. 69ff. and p. 221, where he eloquently says, that the Cabbala is a texture woven by younger Rabbis out of older barbaric philosophy, and where he promises to prove it eventually in part. And not less in the latter book in various places, for instance p. 66, where he concedes to the Cabbala the oldest, though in many ways garbled traditions. Henr. Morus (= Henry More), Th. Burnetus (= Thomas Burnet) in the 'Archaeologia'[54] book I, chapter 7, p. 336, Abrah. Hinckelmannus (= Abraham Hinckelmann) in 'Detectio Fundamenti Böhmiani',[55] and the celebrated Buddeus (= Johann Franz Budde) in the 'Introduct[io] ad Histor[iam] Philosophiae Hebraeorum',[56] p. 321, were aware of the same, to leave others aside. That nothing but late [things], derived from foreign sources, were found written in the Cabbala, the author of 'Bilibra veritatis'[57] p. 122, and Clericus (= Jean Le Clerc), tome VII of the 'Biblioth[eca] Universalis'[58] observed, and the former stated that nothing more futile and vain is found in the whole of Scripture than the more recondite Cabbalists; that is, whatever they uttered on their Sephiroth or Numerations, on the Aziroth or Emanations, was nothing but idle people's most affected comments or deliriums.

No 5

A comment on Judaism written by Reimarus in 1744; Staatsarchiv Hamburg 622–1 Familie Reimarus A 13f., pp. 41–43

---

[52] Johann Georg Wachter, *Der Spinozismus im Jüdenthumb / Oder / die von dem heütigen Jüdenthumb / und dessen Geheimen Kabbala vergötterte Welt* (Amsterdam, 1699).

[53] Johann Georg Wachter, *Elucidarius cabalisticus, Sive Reconditae Hebraeorum Philosophiae Brevis & Succincta Recensio* (Rome, 1706).

[54] Thomas Burnet, *Archaeologia philosophica* (London, 1692).

[55] Abraham Hinckelmann, *Detectio Fundamenti Böhmiani, Untersuchung und Widerlegung Der Grund-Lehre / Die In Jacob Böhmens Schrifften verhanden* (Hamburg, 1692).

[56] Johann Franz Budde, *Introductio ad Historiam Philosophiae Ebraeorum. Accedit Dissertatio De Haeresi Valentiniana* (Halle, 1702).

[57] Jonas Schlichting, *Bilibra veritatis et rationis de Memera de-Yeya seu verbo Dei librae Joh. Stephani Rittangelii et appendix Josepho de Voisin Raymundoque Martini* (Freistadii, 1700).

[58] Jean Le Clerc, *Bibliothèque universelle et historique* (Amsterdam, 1686–1693).

Text

Ich könnte noch von den Juden besonders handeln, warum davon nicht mehrere zum Christentum treten; da sie doch mitten unter denselben leben, ihre Bücher, die oft genug bey ihnen versetzet werden, lesen können, oft genug zum Christenthum gereitzet werden, und einerley Grundsätze mit denen Christen annehmen. Der Pöbel schilt nur auf die grausame Verstockung und Boßheit der Juden. Allein, lieben Leute, es will niemand gerne zum Teuffel fahren: Könnte das Volck einsehen, daß ihnen Heil in Christo offen stünde, sie würden gewiß zugreiffen. Es ist ihnen aber so leichte nicht einzusehen wie ihr wohl dencket. Der Jude hat von seinen Vorfahren gantz andere Zeugnisse und Nachrichten von Jesus als die Evangelisten und Apostel davon gegeben. Da sich nun diese Zeugnisse von dem höchsten Raht in Jerusalem, von 70 angesehenen obrigkeitlichen Personen, herschreibet, und selbst das Neue Testament bestättiget, daß die Vorfahren der heutigen Juden gantz andere Meinung von Christi Absicht und Thaten gehabt: so trauet der Jude seinen Vorfahren, und dem gantzen hohen Rathe mehr als dem Zeugnisse eintzeler Jünger Jesu. Es ist im Gesetze Mosis aufs schärfste gemahnet er soll nicht mehrere Götter anerkennen, es sey nur ein Gott: er kann aber doch die Lehre daß Jesus sowohl Gott sey, wie der Vater, und der Heilige Geist Gott sey, wie Vater und Sohn, nicht anders einsehen als eine Lehre von vielen Göttern: er denckt wie seine Vorfahren, das sey eine Gotteslästerung, daß sich Jesus selbst zum Gott gemacht. Er erwartet zwar einen Messias, aber einen, der Israel erlösen und nicht noch 1700 Jahr nachher in der Gefangenschaft und im Elende lassen sollte, einen der König seyn und ein herlich Reich anfangen, nicht aber am Holtze als ein Missethäter gehenkket werden sollte, einen, der nicht das ewige Gesetze Mosis, abschaffen, sondern völlig im Schwange bringen sollte. < > er die von den Evangelisten angeführte Beweißthümer aus dem Alten Testamente, daß Jesus der Messias sey, *er soll Nazarenus heißen, aus Egypten hab ich meinen Sohn gerufen, ich will sein Vater seyn und er soll mein Sohn seyn* etc.: so findet er entweder gar nichts davon im Alten Testament daß auch die Worte von gantz was andern handeln. Er findet also seiner Einsicht nach nichts als Blendwerck und Betrügerey in diesem vorgegebenen Beweise. Diese und hundert dergleichen scheinbare Einwürffe, die er begreiffen kann, sind ihm von seinem Rabbiner dem er wie < > von Jugend auf, mit dem größten Haß wird < > beygebracht werden: er hat gelernt täglich seinem Gott im Gebete zu dancken, daß er ein Jude gebohren sey, er höret von zarter Kindheit an, daß die sich ins Verderben stürzen, die den Gott ihrer Vater verlassen. So bekommt er nohtwendig einen solchen Abscheu wieder das Christenthum, den er, wenn wir wollen menschlich urtheilen, unmöglich überwinden kann. Sind ihm andere Dinge unbegreiflich, so daß sie ihn wollen irre machen: so denckt er, wie auch ein Christe bey solcher Gelegenheit dencket, das gehe über seine Einsicht, das können dennoch seine Lehrer beantworten; er wolle sich an das halten was er verstehe. Wir müssen nicht von Menschen fordern, was die Natur den Menschen, nemlich die Kraffte desselben übersteiget, und was denen angebohrene Regeln, wonach ein Mensch dencket und will entgegen ist. So wird man wohl begreiffen, daß es einem Juden der nach seiner Art recht unterrichtet ist nicht möglich sey ein Christe zu werden. Paulus hat schon die Hoffnung der Bekehrung mehrer Juden fast gantz aufgegeben und wendet sich dafur zu den Heyden und wir lesen nicht, daß nachher bis auf jetzige Zeiten aus diesem Volcke ein besonderer Zuwachs zum Christentum kommen sey. Vielmehr haben sie für und wieder um ihres Glaubens willen die graulichste Verfolgung und Marter hertzhafft ausgestanden. Und man mag insgemein mit bestand der Wahrheit sagen, daß die Juden so heutiges Tages Christen werden, fast alle Betrüger sind die Liederlichkeit und gehoffter Vortheil dazu bewogen hat.

Translation

Moreover, with the Jews I could deal especially with the topic, why have not more of them converted to Christianity, since they live amongst Christians, can read their books, which are quite often printed by them, are quite often enticed towards Christianity and have principles in common with Christians. The mob only looks askance at the Jews' cruel impenitence and wickedness. But, dear people, no one likes to go to Hell. If those people could realize that salvation is open to them in Christ, they would surely take it. But it is still not so easy for them to realize it as you might think. The witness and information the Jew has received from his ancestors is totally different from what the Evangelists and Apostles have said about it. And since these witnesses come from the highest council in Jerusalem, from seventy distinguished authorised persons, and the New Testament itself acknowledges that the ancestors of the Jews today had a totally different opinion of Christ's intention and deeds, so the Jew trusts in his own ancestors and the whole high council more than in any of Jesus' followers' witness. There is a clear admonition in the Law of Moses that he must not accept many Gods and that there is only one God: but he cannot comprehend the teaching of Jesus' being God as well as the Father in any other way than as a doctrine of many Gods: like his ancestors he thinks it was a blasphemy that Jesus made himself a God. Certainly he expects a Messiah, but one who will redeem Israel and not one who will keep it still in imprisonment and misery 1700 years later, one who will be King and start a glorious Kingdom but not one who will be hanged like a criminal, one who will not repeal the eternal Law of Moses but one who will bring it fully up to date. And when he [reads] the Old Testament proofs quoted by the Evangelists, that Jesus was the Messiah, *Nazarenus he shall be named, from Egypt I have called my son, I shall be his father and he my son* etc. not only will he not find anything about it in the Old Testament, he will find that even the words deal with something totally different. So he finds according to his inspection nothing in these faked proofs but deception and fraud. These, and a hundred such feigned objections as he can comprehend, the Jew has learned from his Rabbi, by whom he has been taught with the greatest hatred since he was young. He has learned to thank his God daily in his prayers that he was born a Jew. From his earliest childhood he hears that those bring disaster on themselves who leave their father's God. So he necessarily gets a disgust of Christianity such as he – if we want to judge from a human point of view – cannot possibly overcome. If other topics that make him confused seem incomprehensible to him, he thinks, just as a Christian thinks in such a case, that these things are beyond his reasoning but that his teachers might be able to give an answer while he himself should stick to what he is able to comprehend. We should not demand of humans what goes beyond human nature, which means what goes beyond his abilities and what contradicts the innate rules according to which a human being thinks. So it may be understood, that for a Jew who has been properly taught in this way, it is impossible to become a Christian. Paul eventually gave up hope of a broader conversion of the Jews and instead turned to the Gentiles, and we do not read that thereafter and until now a particular increase has come to Christianity from this people. Moreover, on behalf of and for the sake of their belief they have sincerely suffered the cruellest persecution and torture. And one may generally say truly, that almost every Jew nowadays who becomes a Christian is motivated by indiscipline and hope of advantage.

THE PHILOSOPHICAL CONTEXT OF HERMANN SAMUEL REIMARUS'
RADICAL BIBLE CRITICISM

Jonathan Israel

Hermann Samuel Reimarus (1694–1768), philologist, Bible critic, and philosopher, was in no doubt himself as to the severity of his philologico-philosophical assault on the Christian religion. At one point he suggests that Celsus and Porphyry themselves could scarcely have sharpened it any further;[1] and even more acerbic was his attack on the Jewish legacy to humanity. While it is true that in the early sections of his *Apologie* Reimarus recounts his estrangement from Christianity, and Christianity's inheritance from the Jews, as a gradual process of doubt and questioning, driven principally by textual and philological concerns, it is equally true that in the later stages of his intellectual evolution he built his general outlook around what he saw as an all-encompassing and surpassing principle of 'reason'. 'Reason' he holds aloft and extols, but also very closely entwines with what he sees as the general progress of philosophy in the history of the world.

In a remarkable passage in which he asserts that philosophy bequeathed more to the development of the Christian religion than the latter ever gave to philosophy, he contends that the history of religion proves beyond all doubt the indispensability of philosophy to the progress of morality and indeed religion itself. 'Die Lehre von der Einheit Gottes', he points out, by way of example, 'und dessen Anbetung ohne Bilder, welche Moses aus der geheimen Weissheit der Egyptischen Priester mitgebracht hatte, aber ohne vernünftige Gründe bloss als ein Gebot vortrug, hatte bey den Israeliten nicht eher Eingang, als bis sie in der Gefangenschaft mit vernünftigen Heyden umgegangen waren.'[2]

But what kind of philosophy did Reimarus embrace? Philosophically, he was undoubtedly something of a hybrid figure, with one foot, or part of a foot, in the Radical Enlightenment, and the other, or one and a half feet, in the moderate Enlightenment. In this present paper I shall focus

---

[1] Hermann Samuel Reimarus, *Apologie oder Schutzschrift für die vernünftigen Verehrer Gottes* (ed.) G. Alexander (2 vols. Frankfurt, 1972), i, p. 61.
[2] Ibid., i, 112–13.

on three main dimensions of Reimarus' philosophical activity and conclusions. Firstly, I argue that despite some obvious differences between his
public position and his clandestine outlook, the general standpoint to be
found in both the published works and the secret *Apologie* of this unusually widely read and erudite professor, forms a philosophically coherent
whole, which in the main can be deemed a single and in some ways rather
original system. Secondly, I argue that the oft-repeated claim that Reimarus' critique of revealed religion, as it is put in Alan Kors' Oxford *Encyclopedia of the Enlightenment*, arose chiefly 'under the influence of English
deism', or as a recent Dutch scholar expresses it 'following the English
deists, among them John Toland, Anthony Collins, Thomas Chubb and
Thomas Woolston',[3] is not at all a satisfactory designation of his orientation; indeed I think this thesis, frequently repeated though it is, is basically
untrue and seriously misleading.

Thirdly, while agreeing that Reimarus is a key *exemplum* of the phenomenon, highlighted in particular by Martin Mulsow, of a split intellectual personality who can be said to be radical in some respects but
moderate in others, and moreover that it was precisely his being moderate
in some ways which enabled him to be subversive in others, I nevertheless contend that Reimarus' intellectual radicalism was not very extensive
in scope, indeed was almost entirely confined to his attack on revealed
religion and ecclesiastical authority (both of which he kept strictly private) plus his likewise largely silent plea for a broader toleration. Beyond
these three points, there is very little that is even mildly radical in Reimarus' thought. On the contrary, his core ideas would seem to share many
characteristics with the kind of conservative providential Deism represented also by Challe, Wollaston and Voltaire. Finally, I shall claim that his
underlying aversion to Spinozism and disinclination to invoke Spinoza's
(or Bayle's) name,[4] despite the fact that he was clearly thoroughly famil-

---

[3] John Stroup, 'Hermann Samuel Reimarus' in Alan Kors (ed.) *Encyclopedia of the
Enlightenment* (4 vols. Oxford, 2003), iii, p. 417; M. H. De Lang, "Literary and historical Criticism
as Apologetics", *Nederlands Archief voor Kerkgeschiedenis* lxxii (1992), pp. 149–65, here,
p. 151; the source of this misleading *idée fixe* seems to be especially the writings of Henning
Graf Reventlow, see, for instance, Henning Graf Reventlow, 'Das Arsenal der Bibelkritik
des Reimarus' in *Hermann Samuel Reimarus (1694–1768) ein "bekannter Unbekannter" der
Aufklärung in Hamburg* (Göttingen, 1973), pp. 44–65, particularly pp. 44, 57–8; see also
Günter Gawlick, 'Der Deismus als Grundzug der Religionsphilosophie der Aufklärung',
Hermann Samuel Reimarus (1694–1768) ein "bekannter Unbekannter", pp. 18–19.

[4] Jürgen von Kempski, 'Spinoza, Reimarus, Bruno Bauer – drei Paradigmen radikaler
Bibelkritik', in *Hermann Samuel Reimarus (1694–1768) ein "bekannter Unbekannter"*,
pp. 96–112, here, p. 97.

iar with the *Tractatus Theologico-Politicus* and the *Ethics*, as well as with Bayle's works I would argue, should be bracketed together with a wider, underlying antagonism in his writings, and inherent in his general system, regarding all materialist, one-substance and pantheistic positions.

Numerous modern commentators on the *Fragmentenstreit*, the Reimarus controversy of the 1770s in Germany, have insisted, often with some emphasis, that Reimarus in his clandestine *oeuvre* and secret religious philosophy was 'strongly influenced by English Deism' as well as by Leibniz and Wolff.[5] One commentator even claims that 'Wolff's influence on Reimarus served as a medium through which the thought of John Locke impinged on him' – despite the fact that the widely-read Reimarus in reality shows practically no interest in Locke at all. Indeed, this commentator devotes several pages, in a short general introduction to an English translation of 'fragments' from Reimarus' *Apologie* to exploring the different ways 'English influence was exerted upon Reimarus' while saying nothing about the other sources of inspiration of this pivotal German Enlightenment figure.[6] Were it really true that the 'influences that shaped [Reimarus'] private thought came primarily from two sources, Christian Wolff and English Deism', this would certainly be a striking and rather curious combination; however there seems to be no factual basis for this particular *idée fixe* in the literature about Reimarus. It is true, of course, that Reimarus went on a study trip for five months or so to England, in the summer and autumn of 1721;[7] but his stay in England was much shorter than his stay in Holland, and if one looks at the footnotes and references in the *Apologie*, and counts them, it is obvious by any reasonably impartial standard that the references to Jean Le Clerc, Bayle, Bekker, Van Dale,[8] and Spinoza are more numerous and important than those to the English deists and that, in any case, while he acknowledges that he found Toland's essay *Hodegus*, or the Pillar of Cloud, useful, remarking 'ich habe derselben mit Nutzen bedient',[9] Reimarus is generally very critical of Toland

---

[5] M. H. De Lange, 'John Toland en Hermann Samuel Reimarus over de wonderen in het Oude Testament', *Nederlands Theologisch Tijdschrift*, xlvi (1992), pp. 1–9 here, p. 6; besides Reventlow, Gawlick and Stroup, cited above, see Peter Stemmer, *Weissagung und Kritik. Eine Studie zur Hermeneutik bei Hermann Samuel Reimarus* (Hamburg, 1983), p. 8.

[6] Charles H. Talbert, 'Introduction' to Reimarus, *Fragments* (London, 1979), pp. 11, 14–18.

[7] Wilhelm Schmidt-Biggemann, 'Einleitung' to Hermann Samuel Reimarus, *Kleine gelehrten Schriften* (Göttingen, 1994), pp. 9–65, here, pp. 17–20.

[8] Reimarus, *Apologie*, i, p. 480 n. d, 908, 914–15 and vol. ii, p. 388.

[9] Reimarus, *Apologie*, i, p. 434; De Lang, 'John Toland', p. 7; Henning Graf Reventlow, 'Arsenal der Bibelkritik', p. 55.

and like most German commentators at the time, regards him anyway as essentially a Spinozist. Reimarus rebukes Toland especially for representing such ancient philosophers as Pythagoras, Anaxagoras, Socrates, Plato and Aristotle as 'pantheists' whereas to Reimarus' way of thinking it seemed clear that they were 'gewiss keine Pantheisten gewesen, sondern haben Gott, als ein immateriellen Geist, von der körperlichen Welt, die er geschaffen hat, genugsam unterschieden'; and even if some of them did envisage God as a life-giving force permeating Nature, held Reimarus, nevertheless 'so sind sie doch noch himmelweit von dem *Spinozismo* entfernt gewesen'.[10]

Of course, one might argue that there is no particular reason to single out either English Deism or Dutch freethinking as having been especially predominant as 'influences' in Reimarus' religious critical thinking or rather what became his religious critical thinking after he began to work on the first draft of his *Apologie*, probably shortly after 1735, the date of the publication of the Wertheim Bible and the start of one of the greatest intellectual controversies of eighteenth century German culture.[11] While Reimarus specifies his undoubtedly very numerous sources in his *Apologie* only rather rarely and sporadically,[12] much of his approach to linguistic research and philology, as well as New Testament criticism, and his attitude to wider philosophical questions, plainly actually derives, as Wilhelm Schmidt-Biggemann has stressed, from his teacher and father-in-law, Johan Albert Fabricius (1668–1736).[13] Crucial also, if in a more negative way, were the exegetical principles expounded by Johann Lorenz Schmidt in the preface (and subsequent explanatory essays), to his 'Wertheim Bible' of 1735, a text concerning which Reimarus in 1736 published a curiously cryptic review, seemingly adopting an unambiguously negative attitude towards Schmidt's hermeneutics, accusing him of basing his translation on his own philosophical principles rather than the intended sense of the original wording.[14] Similarly, Jewish and partly Jewish sources like Van

---

[10] Reimarus, *Apologie*, ii, p. 658.

[11] Wilhelm Schmidt-Biggemann, *Theodizee und Tatsachen. Das philosophische Profil der deutchen Aufklärung* (Frankfurt, 1988), pp. 76–8; Stemmer, *Weissagung und Kritik*, pp. 91–2, 97–8, 144–5.

[12] Ibid., p. 145.

[13] Reimarus, *Apologie*, ii, pp. 529, 578.

[14] Reimarus, *Kleine gelehrte Schriften*, pp. 306–7; Stemmer, *Weissagung und Kritik*, pp. 128–9, 131–2, 144; Almut and Paul Spalding, 'Die rätselhafte Tutor bei Hermann Samuel Reimarus: Begegnung zweier radikaler Aufklärer in Hamburg', *Zeitschrift für Hamburgische Geschichte* lxxxvii (2001), pp. 49–64, here, p. 50.

Limborch's colloquium with Isaac Orobio de Castro, Manesseh ben Israel, and the *Hizzuk Emunah* of Rabbi Isaac of Troki supplied additional components of his critical armoury. In the course of highlighting what he sees as misreadings and distortions in New Testament claims of continuity with the Old Testament, for example, Reimarus styles Isaac of Troki 'der gründlichste und stärkste Wiedersacher des Christenthums'.[15] Besides all this, one must bear in mind that Reimarus was also entirely familiar with the arguments of Socinus, Crell and other Socinians.[16]

Yet all these streams converged with particular force in the late seventeenth and early eighteenth century in the Dutch context. Nor must one forget that Grotius, whom Reimarus frequently cites in the *Apologie*, was for him a key guide, as indeed he had been earlier for Anthony Collins,[17] Reimarus remarking at one point that 'Grotius hat in seinem bundigen Commentari den buchstäblichen und historischen Sinn der meisten Schrifftörter glücklich aufgedeckt...'[18] Johann Niklaus Sinnhold, who wrote the most detailed account of the great Wertheim controversy of the later 1730s, at one point remarks of its freethinking compiler, Johann Lorenz Schmidt, that he followed a pernicious line of naturalists, deists, Socinians and Arminians who all misinterpreted Scripture and were all *Glaubens-genossen* [fellow-believers] of Spinoza, Grotius and Le Clerc.[19] Yes, indeed, and there would appear to be excellent reasons for saying much the same of Reimarus too.

It is clear enough that Reimarus was influenced by Bayle's comments on the Old Testament, which together with his sensational discussion

---

[15] Reimarus, *Apologie*, ii, p. 268.
[16] Ibid., ii, pp. 269–70.
[17] Stemmer, *Weissagung und Kritik*, pp. 31–2.
[18] Reimarus, *Apologie*, i, p. 728 and ii, p. 270; 'die Engländer', remarks Reimarus, at one point, 'haben sich durch den Collins genöthiget, die buchstäbliche Weissagungen von Christo beynahe aufzugeben, und bloss eine accommodationem darin zu erkennen. Der gantze Brief an die Hebräer ist voll von solchen Beweisen, die den Schreibern A. T. Meynungen antichten, davon ihre Worte nichts enthalten. Es würde aber ein gantzes Buch erfordern, wenn ich alle und jede Stellen so umständlich durchgehen wollte. Collins hat mehrer widerlegt, so weit seine Einsicht reichte; und Grotius ist ihm vorgegangen, nur dass dieser hie und da eine doppelte Erfüllung des Alten Testaments im Neuen einiger Maassen zu harmonieren. Wer sieht aber nicht, dass Grotii Erklärungsart eine gantze fremde und wieder all Deutung anderer Schriftsteller lauffende, und daher nur eigentlich zur Rettung des N. T., erfundene Regel voraussetzt; in dem Homero, und Mose selbst, alchymistische Geheimnisse suchen, und auch in den Profan-Scribenten Weissagungen von Christo finden könnte? In der That ist diese Methode nichts besser als die Allegorie und accommodatio.'
[19] Johann Niklaus Sinnhold, *Historische Nachricht von der bekanten und verrissenen sogenannte Wertheimischen Bibel* (Erfurt, 1737), p. 8; Stemmer, *Weissagung und Kritik*, p. 107.

of Manichaeism were certainly one of the most important spurs to his vehement anti-Scripturalism.[20] Yet possibly even more significant for his discussion of wonders and miracles, and the general development of his conception of *critique*, was Jean Le Clerc, whom he met personally during his stay in Holland between the spring of 1720 and early 1722, and by whom he was clearly impressed and who, he noted, 'judicirt und critisirt sehr frey über alle Leute'.[21] Our conclusion about the Dutch context, then, should probably be to say not that it was more important than other strands of his intellectual background, such as Fabricius and the 'left Wolffianism' of Schmidt, but merely that it was certainly more important than the British context. The fact that this directly clashes with the marked tendency in the work of German scholars such as Günter Gawlick, and particularly Henning Graf Reventlow, insistently to affirm that German Deism in general, and Reimarus' attack on revealed religion, in particular, emanated essentially from the seed-bed of British ideas should be attributed simply to the lack of any real empirical grounds for this remarkably strongly rooted bias in the older German historiography, which often evinced a strong preference, and also in other areas of culture, for finding British rather than French, Dutch or Jewish influences.

The frequent stress on English influence in the older historiography about Reimarus, then, is both groundless and highly misleading. In the key philosophical – as distinct from some of the Biblical critical – sections of his works, Reimarus makes no appeal whatsoever to Toland, Collins, or Tindal, mentions Hobbes only in passing, (in connection with his discussion of Rousseau's idea of the 'state of nature') and, as far as I can determine, reveals absolutely no interest in Locke whatsoever. Nor is this really very surprising, since Locke's influence on the German Enlightenment was by and large not very great. In fact, Reimarus makes it perfectly clear in the body of his two major texts, that his chief aim philosophically, and this is what any careful, close reader of German philosophy in the third quarter of the eighteenth century would, after all, surely expect, is to render as effective as possible his general critique of materialism, purely mechanistic systems, and Spinozism. In the published works, Spinoza is

---

[20] Reimarus, *Apologie*, i, pp. 233–6; Henning Graf Reventlow, 'Arsenal der Bibelkritik', p. 53.
[21] Reimarus, *Apologie*, i, pp. 314, 323, 325, 480, 509, 777, 857 and ii, pp. 270–1, 387; William Boehart, 'Hermann Samuel Reimarus in der "Gelehrten Republik" des 18. Jahrhunderts. Fragen nach den Grenzen einer "bürgerlichen" Aufklärung', in D. Fratzke and W. Albrecht (eds.) *Lessing zur Jahrtausendwende. Rückblicke und Ausblicke. '40. Kamenzer Lessing-Tage'* (Kamenz, 2001), pp. 127–40.

cited primarily as the chief example and general *princeps* or exponent of all would-be systematic atheistic and materialist thinking.[22]

Spinoza's *Tractatus Theologico-Politicus* is also, of course, one of the multiple sources of Reimarus' corrosive Bible criticism. He cites Spinoza in particular with respect to the late composition of the *Pentateuch* and Ibn Ezra's apparent realization of this.[23] However, just as Reimarus is strongly antagonistic towards Spinoza's philosophy so he clearly distances himself from his particular style of anti-Scripturalism. For if both thinkers see Scripture as a purely human document devoid of divine inspiration, they sharply diverge over the intrinsic value and status of the Bible. Where Spinoza designates Christ the direct 'mouthpiece' of God, a man whose grasp of morality was perfect, Reimarus represented Jesus as a failed Jewish reformer whose ignominious death led his disciples to mislead everyone by falsely reinterpreting him as a spiritual Messiah.[24] Where Spinoza attributes important moral value to the prophecies of the Old Testament, Reimarus held that the contents of all the books which the Jews gave out as a supernatural Revelation of God actually contain only very inferior 'Begriffe von Gott, seinen Eigenschaften, seine Erscheinungen, seine Wundern, seinen Geboten und Satzungen, und von seiner gantzen Haushaltung in dem Geschlechte Israels [...]. Furthermore, in the Old Testament, contends Reimarus, one finds 'keinen Spuhr von der Seelen Unsterblichkeit, oder von einem künftigen Leben, vorhanden sey [...],'[25] scarcely a complaint likely to have occurred to Spinoza.

Yet Spinoza is only very rarely the explicit target of Reimarus' sallies. Mostly, in both *Die vornehmsten Wahrheiten der natürlichen Religion* (1754), a work admired by Kant for at least a decade after its publication,[26] and in his somewhat original treatise on animal life, Reimarus targets La Mettrie or Buffon, whom he also accuses of expounding a simplistic *Mechanismus* of animal bodies, as representing the view that nature blindly forms life and creates species without the intervention of any divine Creator.[27] At the same time, though, La Mettrie is also deployed, as Reimarus himself

---

[22] Hermann Samuel Reimarus, *Die vornehmsten Wahrheiten der natürlichen Religion* (2 vols. Göttingen, 1985), i, pp. 6–7, 113, 188–91 and, ii, pp. 722, 734.

[23] Ibid., i, p. 857.

[24] Schmidt-Biggemann, *Theodizee und Tatsachen*, p. 82; Arno Schilson, 'Lessing and Theology' in B. Fischer and Th. C. Fox (eds.) *A Companion to the Works of Gotthold Ephraim Lessing* (Rochester, N.Y., 2005), pp. 163, 165.

[25] Reimarus, *Apologie*, i, p. 721.

[26] Manfred Kuehn, *Kant. A Biography* (Cambridge, 2001), p. 141.

[27] Reimarus, *Vornehmsten Wahrheiten*, i, pp. 273–6, 314–18, 346, 353, 360, 598–9.

explains at one point, as a way of reinforcing and redoubling his attack
on Spinozism by demonstrating, or so he thought, that Spinozism, like all
atheism, undermines the morality society always requires for men to live
by.[28] Once again, it is worth pointing out that neither La Mettrie, whose
intellectual context was rooted in Holland, and especially in Boerhaave
and Spinoza, nor Buffon were in any way representatives or offshoots of
the English context or British Enlightenment thought.

What is correct, on the other hand, is that Reimarus' own physico-
theology shows many parallels and resemblances with the Newtonian
philosophy. Even so, here too, though, there is no particular reason to link
this aspect of his thought closely with England. Reimarus rarely mentions
Newton or the British Newtonians, and physico-theology as a general
phenomenon in the early and mid-eighteenth century saturated not only
British but also a great part of western European thought, not least the
thought-world of his own cherished teacher Fabricius, who had translated
Fénelon's *Démonstration de l'existence de Dieu* (1713) into German and was
one of the earliest important advocates of physico-theology in Germany.[29]
It is clear, moreover, that Reimarus' own favourite physico-theologians
are Swammerdam, Derham, Nieuwentyt, Fabricius and Réaumur, so that
here, once again, we see how cosmopolitan and rich his erudition and
thought-worlds were and how very little reason there is, no matter how
many times the opposite has been claimed, to attribute his philosophical endeavours chiefly to English stimuli. At the core of his enterprise,
rather, was his uninterrupted striving to combat Dutch and French one-
substance doctrine and materialism, French materialism that is historically situated, as commentators in the 1750s generally tended to perceive
it, as the outgrowth of Spinozism.

Reimarus' *Vornehmsten Wahrheiten der natürlichen Religion*, though
aimed at the Deists and materialists, and warmly praising the physico-
theologists, was at the same time, a work inspired by a truly rigorous naturalism of a special kind, being in essence – in this respect reminiscent of
Nieuwentyt – an ostensible essay in defeating the materialists at their own
game. Consequently, his style of argument in some ways resembles that
style characteristic of the Spinozists and materialists themselves.[30] Thus,
he uses exclusively naturalistic arguments. Eager to prove, for instance,

---

[28] Ibid., ii, pp. 734–43.
[29] Gerhard Alexander, 'Die Sprache des Reimarus', in *Hermann Samuel Reimarus (1694–1768) ein "bekannter Unbekannter"*, pp. 128–47, here, p. 130.
[30] Reimarus, *Vornehmsten Wahrheiten*, i, p. 82.

that men have not existed on earth eternally but arose at a certain point, and then developed through stages from primitive beginnings and from very small numbers, Reimarus offers the linguistic evidence, that almost all European languages are related and may be conjectured to have developed from only a few primal languages and, ultimately perhaps, a single root.[31] The arts, crafts and sciences, he adds, had to be learnt only very slowly and painfully over long periods of time.[32]

But the divergences between him and the materialists are always more striking than the similarities. Reimarus' brand of naturalism leads him to assert that the origin of men and animals cannot lie in the world 'or in nature'. The crux of his argument here is that there is no 'natural' and convincing way of explaining how the advent of the first men, and the first animals, could have emanated directly from nature or the world. His materialist 'opponents' imagine, he says, that the warmth of the sun may have somehow animated inanimate matter and from this brought forth creatures, and eventually men. But such evolutionary notions, he holds, are inherently unconvincing when considered as naturalistic arguments. This claim does perhaps display a feature which Reimarus might be said to share with the Radical Enlightenment broadly conceived – namely the thesis that everything that is true is either according to reason or contrary to reason and that nothing is admissible in philosophy which is 'above reason' as this concept was understood and endorsed by Locke, Le Clerc, Leibniz, Wolff and the Newtonians.[33]

But if he is close to Spinoza and Bayle in claiming that there is no such thing in philosophy as 'above reason', his 'naturalism' at the same time drives a powerful wedge between him and the Spinozists. For at the heart of his counter-argument lies his contention that the materialist philosophers do not understand the laws of nature, as recent science has demonstrated them: they would not have 'made Nature their god,' he says, had they grasped its laws.[34] It contradicts all our experience and reason itself, he argues, to hold that raw matter itself, warmed by the sun, can create living species. The physical world of matter and pure body, he insists,

---

[31] Ibid., i, pp. 58–63, 65–7.

[32] Von Kempski, 'Spinoza, Reimarus', pp. 106–7.

[33] Reimarus, *Die vornehmsten Wahrheiten*, i, pp. 127–48; Jürgen von Kempski, 'Hermann Samuel Reimarus als Ethologe' in Hermann Samuel Reimarus, *Allgemeine Betrachtungen über die Triebe der Thiere* (Göttingen, 1982), i, pp. 21–56, here, pp. 24–5.

[34] Reimarus, *Die vornehmsten Wahrheiten*, i, pp. 127–48; Jürgen von Kempski, 'Hermann Samuel Reimarus als Ethologe' in Hermann Samuel Reimarus, *Allgemeine Betrachtungen über die Triebe der Thiere* (Göttingen, 1982), i, pp. 21–56, here, pp. 24–5.

lacks movement and is wholly lifeless and therefore is in no way an active agent.[35] Hence, the world is created and shaped, given its reality and forms, by a self-sufficient active cause which is external to it,[36] a truth which directly contradicts, he says, Spinoza's definition of substance in his *Ethics* and his doctrine that the physical universe is the only substance, which can, alternatively, be called 'God'. Hence, Spinoza's system, he claims, 'der Erfahrung und der wirklichen Welt widerstreitet' [contradicts experience and the real world], being based on false premises.[37] And with this, he argues, collapses Spinoza's conception of the necessity and determined character of all that exists, even if we must accept, as he willingly agrees, that everything that happens in nature of a physical character, and in our world, functions exclusively naturally and mechanistically.[38]

One must, holds Reimarus, always adduce something extra, beyond the laws of natural forces, and external to the principle of matter itself, from which one understands why the general laws of the universe are as they are and not otherwise. Here Reimarus reveals that strand of Leibnizian-Wolffian influence that undoubtedly plays an integral part in his system. He invokes Leibniz's *Theodicy* and cites a key passage where Leibniz holds that the mechanical laws governing nature are not altogether the outcome of necessity, maintaining rather that 'elles naissent du principe de la perfection et de l'ordre; elles sont un effet du choix et de la sagesse de Dieu.'[39] This confirms as indeed Reimarus himself expressly admits that he was profoundly influenced in philosophical matters by Leibniz as also by Pufendorf,[40] even though, as we shall see, it would be quite wrong to suggest that Reimarus can be satisfactorily or accurately described as any kind of Leibnizian or Wolffian.

Equally, he held, one must look beyond mere physical nature to grasp the essence of human life, even though the human body, with all its parts and organs, functions, he grants, just like a machine. For while the human body is in this sense a machine, a person is far more than a 'machine', our soul being constituted of quite a different substance from our bodies.[41] Here, once again, Reimarus selects La Mettrie and his *l'Homme machine*

[35] Reimarus, *Vornehmsten Wahrheiten*, i, pp. 83–4, 127.

[36] Ibid., i, pp. 158, 167.

[37] Ibid., i, 188; Rüdiger Otto, *Studien zur Spinozarezeption in Deutschland im 18. Jahrhundert* (Frankfurt, 1994), pp. 35, 172.

[38] Reimarus, *Vornehmsten Wahrheiten*, i, pp. 196–7.

[39] Ibid., i, pp. 202–17; Schmidt-Biggemann, 'Einleitung', pp. 50–1.

[40] Ibid., p. 45.

[41] Reimarus, *Vornehmsten Wahrheiten*, ii, pp. 475–7, 489–91.

as the prime target of his attack. If men and animals are constructed in essentially the same way, according to La Mettrie, for Reimarus mankind is something qualitatively quite different from the animal realm, and Man's nature is especially created to enable him to people the whole of the earth, dominate all the animals and direct everything to his own uses and satisfaction, all points directly contradicting Spinoza's stance.[42] While all animal life is orientated towards the here and now, Reimarus seeks to show that men are designed by nature, by their very constitution, and hence by the Creator, to aspire to what he calls a higher, purer and more lasting perfection and beatitude than can be attained in this life.[43] This, he held, together with what seemed to him the unanswerable claims of physico-theology more broadly, amounts to a valid proof of the immortality of the soul.

In his *Allgemeine Betrachtungen über die Triebe der Thiere, hauptsächlich über ihre Kunsttriebe* (1760), published when he had reached the age of sixty-six, Reimarus, who all his life remained deeply fascinated by animal behaviour, carries further his physico-theological differentiation between men and animals. This work was partly a reply, as has often been remarked, to Condillac's recently published *Traité des animaux* of 1755.[44] Reimarus' book also deals extensively with the ideas about animals of Descartes, Leibniz, Malebranche, Buffon and La Mettrie, a list chiefly striking perhaps for its omission of Locke. For where Condillac was undoubtedly an ardent admirer and defender of Locke and while Locke had introduced a philosophically novel way of distinguishing between animals and humans, Reimarus, once again, shows no interest whatsoever in Locke's approach.[45]

Except for Locke, Reimarus has an interesting critique to offer of all the earlier theorists on the subject of animals. While Condillac receives more attention than anyone else, getting sixteen pages, the sections assigned to Buffon and La Mettrie are also substantial and of crucial significance for grasping Reimarus' in some ways rather novel philosophical position. Basically, his treatise on animals is a continuation of *Die vornehmsten Wahrheiten der natürlichen Religion* especially in that Reimarus is here again chiefly attempting to combat French materialism (minus Diderot who, as usual, scarcely figures), and hence ultimately to combat

---

[42] Ibid., ii, p. 676.
[43] Ibid., ii, pp. 704–9; Schmidt-Biggemann, 'Einleitung', pp. 41, 46–7.
[44] Ernst Mayr, 'Geleitwort' to Reimarus, *Allgemeine Betrachtungen über die Triebe der Thiere*, i, pp. 9–18, here, pp. 13–14.
[45] Reimarus, *Allgemeine Betrachtungen über die Triebe der Thiere*, i, pp. 67, 319–20, 324–6.

Spinozism, whose modern representatives Buffon and La Mettrie, in particular, in Reimarus' eyes were. What is striking here, once again, is not English influence but, on the contrary, precisely the lack of any British dimension to his discussion.

Enlightenment philosophical interpretation of the animal world, it has been aptly said, can usefully be divided into three main traditions.[46] Firstly, there is the doctrine of the soulless animal-machine developed by Descartes and Buffon and taken to an extreme point by La Mettrie, the conception which is Reimarus' primary target.[47] Secondly, there was Locke's thesis that animals have souls akin to, but different in their intellectual capacity from, the souls of men, souls which are *tabula rasa* at birth and become orientated towards particular patterns of behaviour through their needs, experience, and acquisition of knowledge, a doctrine developed and defended by Condillac who also thought that an animal's earliest moments and early development are essentially a learning experience.[48] This too, in the form it is given by Condillac, is rejected by Reimarus who, in one of his most acute philosophical passages, points out that there is no discernible process of learning or improvement in the behaviour of animals and insects, since these practice unchanging, systematic skills; insects, birds and mammals, in other words, know how to do what they do, without any learning, hesitation or inaptitude from the outset.[49] Thus, spiders spin their cobwebs, ant-eaters dig their holes even before they know how flies and the other insects which they eat taste, indeed before they even know that such little creatures exist.[50] Experience and reason hence play no part, holds Reimarus, in the acquisition of animal skills. Animals, held Reimarus, have souls, certainly but not reason, not the power to compare ideas or images and draw conclusions, or the capacity to change their ideas or improve their knowledge and hence their behaviour.[51] Between the ape and the dumbest human, he asserts (perhaps rather dubiously), there is a much greater gulf than between the dumbest human and a Leibniz or Newton.

---

[46] Ibid., pp. 14–15.

[47] Ibid., i, p. 227.

[48] Étienne Bonnot de Condillac, *Traité des animaux* (ed.) M. Malherbe (Paris, 2004), pp. 149–54.

[49] Reimarus, *Allgemeine Betrachtungen*, i, p. 325.

[50] Ibid., i, p. 326.

[51] Ibid., i, pp. 327–30, 333–4, 444; Reimarus *Apologie oder Schutzshcrift*, ii, p. 501.

The third line of traditional argument regarding animals, and the one characteristic of physico-theology, was the idea developed by Swammerdam, Réaumur and the abbé de la Pluche, namely that the key to understanding animals is the concept of innate God-given instinct or drives, the ingrained nature which all classes of animals have, and which, while quite different in their determined nature from the mechanism of mere machines, is nevertheless externally determined or rather implanted by the divine Creator: 'die Kunsttriebe der Thiere sind demnach keine Vollkommenheiten, welche sie selbst durch andere Kräfte erworben hätten, sonder angeborenen und völlig determinirte Grundkräfte jeder Arten der Thiere, welche, so wie die Thierarten selbst, ihren ersten Ursprung ausser der Natur in einem Wesen haben müssen, das die Einpflanzung dieser Triebe in die Natur durch eine Einsicht aller möglichen Vollkommenheiten, nach den Bedürfnissen jeder Arten des Lebens zu ihrer Wohlfahrt abgemessen hat.'[52]

Hence, for Reimarus, animals neither learn from experience, nor draw inferences, nor in any way participate in the progress and work of reason together with humans; and this is clear proof, he thinks, of the fact that the divine *Werkmeister* infused life and motion into the world, not only imparting to Nature all mechanical laws, rules and order but also imparting to souls all regular skills and abilities.[53] Although he lends an apparently Leibnizian twist to his argumentation by claiming that all God-given drives imparted to animals tend to the well-being and propagation of each species of creature,[54] he is nevertheless here rather critical of Leibniz, holding that when one looks at his model more closely, animal bodies remain in a definite sense pure machines, receiving no influence from the soul.[55] In fact, he mounts a general rejection of Leibniz's pre-established harmony as being excessively mechanistic in character.

A striking difference between Reimarus and the Radical Enlightenment as I have tried to define it is that even while he manages to separate morality from faith and does so no less emphatically or effectively than Spinoza or Bayle, tying morality to reason rather than religion, nevertheless, unlike them, Reimarus endeavours to anchor ethics in a surrogate

---

[52] Reimarus, *Vornehmsten Wahrheiten*, i, p. 448.

[53] J. Jaynes and W. Woodward, 'In the Shadow of the Enlightenment: Reimarus and his Theory of Drives', *Journal of the History of the Behavioural Sciences* x (1974), pp. 144–59, here, p. 147.

[54] Reimarus, *Allgemeine Betrachtungen*, i, pp. 66, 68, 448.

[55] Ibid., i, pp. 292–6.

form of theology, turning ethics into a system broadly opposed to sensualism, worldly pleasure and the body. Reimarus contends that the divine Creator in His wisdom would not have bestowed such a noble capacity as our spirit, a spirit-based reason, the tool which enables men to unearth the deepest truths, and leads them on to morality and religion merely so that our spirit and reason should assuage such base sensual desires as hunger and lust.[56]

One of the many points on which Reimarus emphatically diverges from Spinoza is in his account of Solomon, a figure lionized by Spinoza as a model for mankind and the ultimate philosopher, but roundly disparaged by Reimarus. 'Es ist nämlich bald zu sehen, dass seine meisten und vornehmsten Beschäftigungen dahin gingen, bey Pracht und Überfluss herrlich und in Freuden zu leben, und sich mit der Wollust nach aller Herzens Neigung zu ersättigen. Der Grundsatz seines Predigersbuchs besteht darin: es sey dem Menschen nichts besser, als Essen und Trinken und frohlig seyn bey seiner Arbeit; alles andere sey eitel. Gantz Juda und Israel folgte darin seiner Lehre und Exempel: sie assen und trunken und waren fröhlig.'[57] Above all Reimarus objects to his sexual preoccupations and practices. 'Nichts aber konnte weiter getrieben seyn als sein Serrail, darin er 700 Weiber und 300 Kebsweiber, also Tausend in allen, ein gantzes Regiment von Schönen, zu seiner Wollust gehalten haben soll.'[58]

Reimarus' unwavering insistence on the immateriality and immortality of the soul is indeed more stridently and insistently expressed than by other providential Deists such as Wollaston or Voltaire.[59] In his eyes, the Old Testament's manifest inadequacy on these points was clear evidence of its inferiority as a religious text. 'Wenn die Menschen nicht aus dem NT, oder vielmehr aus ihrer Catechismus-Lehre, gewohnt wären, mit gewissern Wörtern and Redensarten christliche Begriffe zu verknüpffe, und mit dem Vorurteil zur Lesung des AT's kämen, dass darin eben dasselbe unter gleichen Ausdrücken verstanden werde; so müsste es allen einleuchten, dass das gantze AT von keiner Unsterblichkeit der Seele und ewigen Seligkeit oder Verdamniss wisse, sondern dieselbe vielmehr ausdrücklich leugne; und dass sie auf keine andere Erlösung, als von ihrer Gefangenschaft, durch einen weltlichen König gehoffet haben.' When we

---

[56] Ibid., i, p. 334.

[57] Reimarus, *Apologie*, i, p. 624; F. Lötsch, 'Was is "Ökologie"?' *Hermann Samuel Reimarus. Ein Beitrag zur Geistesgeschichte des 18. Jahrhunderts* (Koln, 1987), pp. 82–5.

[58] Reimarus, *Apologie*, i, p. 625.

[59] Ibid., i, pp. 769–819.

come across the terms 'Seele' und 'Geist' in the Old Testament, Reimarus points out, 'und sie gantz christlich verstehen; so betriegen wir uns'.[60]

Philosophically and morally, the primary point for Reimarus was that while God can reveal no more than what is universal and material, philosophy cannot, on that ground, reduce everything to one substance. Here is a conception which Reimarus turns equally against the Spinozists and naturalists on one side, and, in his secret *Apologie*, against mysteries, miracles and the principle of Christian Revelation on the other.[61] Here too we clearly perceive not only the radical component in Reimarus' thought but also the immense gulf separating him from philosophical Spinozism in its broadest sense and from the Radical Enlightenment conceived as a wider movement of thought and social reform. It is also here, I would argue, that we find the philosophical grounding of Reimarus' social and political conservatism. For the work of the providential Creator, according to Reimarus, is perfect and geared to securing the happiness of all his creatures, so that the essential framework of social, economic and political life is, for him, as for the Newtonians, something which must be judged to be broadly as it should be.[62]

This is not to deny that, like any *Aufklärer* worthy of the name, Reimarus aspires to improve the world and engineer major changes in society: but a widening of religious toleration and weakening of ecclesiastical authority are the only substantive changes that are of real importance to him, and even then his hoping for these things was not sufficiently urgent to motivate him to agitate for them publicly. In practical terms Reimarus' Enlightenment is a silent protest against the intolerance shown to those who, like the Socinians and deists, seek to base their religion on reason alone. Protestant societies, like Lutheran Germany, complains Reimarus, claim to be tolerant; but the truth is that, Protestant, Catholic or Jew, one must have faith in something supernatural and hence irrational, no matter what, in order to be tolerated. How ironic it was, notes Reimarus, that in the Netherlands, England and Germany all organized religions are allowed except for those, like Socinianism, Arianism and Deism which on principle reject everything irrational.[63] 'Eine reine vernünftige Religion zu

---

[60] Ibid., i, p. 787.

[61] L. P. Wessell, *G. E. Lessing's Theology. A Reinterpretation* (The Hague, 1977), pp. 76–7.

[62] Jean-Marie Paul, "Reimarus et le Curé Meslier: Évolution et Révolution", in J. Moes and J.-M. Valentin (eds.) *De Lessing à Heine. Une siècle de relations littéraires et intellectuelles entre la France et l'Allemagne* (Paris, 1985) pp. 73–91, here, p. 85.

[63] Reimarus, *Apologie*, i, pp. 133–5.

haben und zu üben, is wenigstens in der Christenheit nirgend erlaubt'. Here, interestingly, he cites the indeed very pertinent example of Uriel da Costa, and Van Limborch's dialogue with Isaac Orobio de Castro.[64]

The conviction that men are in need of emancipation from a vast tangle of error pervading all institutions and aspects of society, fundamental to the thought-world of more obviously radical figures such as Knutzen, Gabriel Wagner, Lau, Schmidt, Lessing or Struensee, no less than Du Marsais, Toland, Collins, Meslier, Diderot Helvétius or d'Holbach, is largely missing from the physico-theological *Weltanschauung* of Reimarus. This is not to say, assuredly, that a providential Deist absolutely could not be broadly radical with respect to social questions or to deny that weakening ecclesiastical authority would itself have vast social consequences. Reimarus wanted to live in a different sort of world from that in which he did live. One element he shares with both the Radical Enlightenment and Voltaire is his denunciation of 'priestcraft', in which context he cites David Hume's *Essays* as a text which effectively shows that it was with their construction of 'another world' that priests manage to 'move this world at their pleasure'.[65] His vehement denunciation of the behaviour of not just the Spaniards but of all the Europeans in the New World and the radical consequence he seems on the point of drawing that the structures of empire in the New World lack all legitimacy likewise need to be born in mind. What must the Amerindians think of the Europeans, he asks, 'Leute, welche durch Menschen-Dieberey und List andere zu Sklaven machen und ihres Eigenthums berauben; Leute, die der Völlerey und Geilheit ergeben sind, und auch die Einfalt der wilden Lebensart durch starkes Getränke und Schwelgerey zu verderben suchen.'[66]

This is undoubtedly part of a larger indictment of Christian society intended to show that the very belief-structure of Christianity leads to ruinous social and political consequences. Yet in general the Newtons, Wollastons and Voltaires tended to be socially conservative rather than radical and this, arguably, is true of Reimarus too. It was precisely their common and pervasive stress on a providential Creator and physico-theology which provided the basic sanction for existing political, family, racial and other social hierarchies and institutions as well as for man's dominion over the world and over animals.

---

[64] Ibid., i, p. 134.
[65] Ibid., ii, p. 281.
[66] Ibid., i, p. 154.

Reimarus, then, proves to have been coherent in his philosophy, but at the same time, a strange mix of radical and conservative impulses regarding politics, society and public debate. Here the contrast with Johann Lorenz Schmidt, whom Lessing mentions in his foreword to the *Fragmente eines Ungenannten* as a possible author of the *Apologie* (as part of his strategy of diverting attention from Reimarus),[67] whom Reimarus knew (and apparently helped in the early 1740s),[68] and who was no less an enemy of mysteries and miracles but less inclined toward physico-theology, seems instructive. Schmidt is less inclined to stress the immateriality and immortality of the soul than Reimarus and generally harder to separate from the materialists, even though in his Wertheim preface and other writings he claimed (unlike Reimarus, in his *Apologie*) not to be attacking the Christian religion. As Reimarus himself points out, in his published critique of the Wertheim Bible, it is often difficult to tell Schmidt's 'left -Wolffian' Deism apart from the anti-Scripturalism of a Collins or Tindal.[69] Reimarus aptly refers to Schmidt's 'collusion' with the enemies of religion. Furthermore, where Schmidt hurled himself into the great public controversy precipitated by his *Wertheim Bible* (1735), full-frontally engaging his many critics, and later also publicized and translated Tindal, Du Marsais, Boulainvilliers and Spinoza into German, plainly seeking to extend awareness of a broad range of radical thought into that language, Reimarus remained distinctly reticent by comparison. In the *Vorbericht* of his *Apologie*, he affirms that his vast text 'mag in Verborgenen, zum Gebrauch verständiger Freunde liegen bleiben; mit meinem Willen soll sie nicht durch den Druck gemein gemacht werden, bevor sich die Zeiten mehr aufklären. Lieber mag der gemeine Hauffe noch eine Weile irren, als dass ich ihn, (obwohl es ohne meine Schuld geschehen würde), mit Wahrheiten ärgern, und in einen wütenden Religions-Eiffer setzen sollte. Lieber mag der Weise sich, des Friedens halber, unter den herrschenden Meynungen und Gebräuchen schmiegen, dulden und schweigen, als dass er sich und andere, durch gar zu frühzeitige Äusserung, unglücklich machen sollte.'[70]

This timidity or quietism is another factor which sets Reimarus apart from Spinoza and, I would argue, the Radical Enlightenment as a whole. Indeed, one might well wonder how the times could become more

---

[67] Gawlick, "Der Deismus", p. 16.
[68] Spalding, 'Rätsselhafte Tutor', pp. 61–4.
[69] Reimarus, *Kleine gelehrte Schriften*, p. 302; Stemmer, *Weissagung und Kritik*, p. 128.
[70] Reimarus, *Apologie*, i, p. 41.

'enlightened' if those who were most 'enlightened' preferred not to cir-
culate or publish their works. In any case, it would seem that Reimarus
refrained from doing so out of fear of the prevailing intolerance and the
probability of harsh consequences which would destroy both his peace
of mind, and that of others, along with his comfortable position in Hamburg society.[71] The discreditable and thoroughly wretched fate of Schmidt
indeed makes it only too understandable that Reimarus should have conducted himself in this fashion. But by the same token Schmidt's insistence
on proclaiming the truth as he saw it and refusal to surrender to conventional views display a much more broadly and openly reformist and
oppositional orientation.

---

[71] Boehart, 'Hermann Samuel Reimarus', pp. 134–5.

LIVING IN THE ENLIGHTENMENT:
THE REIMARUS HOUSEHOLD ACCOUNTS OF 1728–1780

Almut and Paul Spalding

From the moment when he moved back to his native Hamburg from Wismar early in 1728 to take up a teaching post at the college-preparatory *Akademisches Gymnasium*, Hermann Samuel Reimarus kept meticulous household financial records. At his death forty years later, his daughter Elise seamlessly continued them. Originally intended merely as a record of financial transactions, these documents now provide a rich source of information on the Reimarus family, bearing witness to over five decades of material, social, economic, political, religious, and intellectual life. Based primarily on these records, this chapter will present Hermann Samuel Reimarus as citizen of Hamburg, rooted in Lutheran tradition and social networks even while he actively contributed radical ideas to the Enlightenment movement.

Four vellum bound volumes of Reimarus' financial accounts from 1728 to 1780 survive, covering Hermann Samuel Reimarus' entire marriage. During several years, an unusually high number of births and deaths in the family and the disposal of his father-in-law's and brother-in-law's remaining papers apparently sapped Hermann Samuel Reimarus' energy too much to worry about book-keeping. As a result, gaps of a few years exist in the financial records, mostly in the 1730s. From 1742 on, the records are unbroken and complete. On their right-hand pages, these volumes list expenses, on left-hand pages, income. In the very back of three of the octave-size books, Hermann Samuel Reimarus had entered the dates and salaries of household employees. Carefully guarded by the descendant family into the twentieth century, three of the four volumes are now deposited in the Staatsarchiv Hamburg, while one – chronologically the third – remains in private hands.[1] This third volume, which documents

---

[1] Bestand 622–1/86, Signatur A-18, vols. 1 (1728–1749) and 2 (1750–1758); and Signatur F- (1773–1780), Staatsarchiv Hamburg (in the following abbreviated as StA HH). Now in private hands in Australia, the third volume (1759–1772) was still in Hamburg when Almut Spalding examined it for the first time. For the sake of readability, subsequent references to these *Haushaltsbücher* will be given as "HB" with volume number and date.

the transition from father to daughter, includes a separate, loose sheet where Hermann Samuel Reimarus had tallied assets and liabilities shortly before the end of his life.

Spanning over fifty years and two generations, these records have no equivalent among published, contemporary household records in Germany. Of comparable significance internationally are the account books of Voltaire or Jefferson.[2] By their nature, these records indicate only activities that cost or earned money. But when supplemented by other sources, they offer abundant information on housing and hygiene, food and drink, clothing and fashion, religious and intellectual life, music and entertainment, professional activities and travel. They also reveal extensive relations of the Reimarus family across all social ranks, both with well-known contemporaries and with people otherwise very poorly documented.

EIGHTEENTH-CENTURY HAMBURG AND THE REIMARUS FAMILY

The free imperial city of Hamburg, along with its royal Danish suburbs of Altona and Wandsbek, formed the largest and most cosmopolitan German-speaking urban centre in the eighteenth century. It was a hub of international commerce, sugar refining, music and theatre, journalism and the book trade. Though officially Lutheran, the area hosted a great diversity of religious groups in conditions of striking tolerance for the time, including Roman Catholics, Calvinists, Mennonites, and Germany's largest Jewish community. Key Enlightenment circles also emerged here and came into conflict with traditional thought and power. The Reimarus family lived at the very centre of this early modern urban culture. It consumed products from around the world, cultivated relations with persons at a wide remove, enjoyed the benefits of high culture in the form of theatrical and musical performances, and interacted with a wide social spectrum of city dwellers.

The present authors, who have prepared a critical edition of these household records, wish to express their gratitude to members of the extended Sieveking family, including the late Hildegard Sieveking of Hamburg, Dr. Hinrich Sieveking of Munich, and the late Ulrich Sieveking of Sydney, for making these materials available.

[2] The most similar contemporary, published account book for Germany is *Lübeck 1787–1808: Die Haushaltungsbücher des Kaufmanns Jacob Behrens des Älteren*, ed. Björn Kommer (Lübeck: Graphische Werkstätten, 1989). For Voltaire's and Jefferson's account books, see *Voltaire's Household Accounts, 1760–1778*, ed. Theodore Besterman (NY: Pierpont Morgan Library, 1968) and *Jefferson's Memorandum Books... 1767–1826*, eds. James Bear and Lucia Stanton (Princeton, NJ: Princeton UP, 1997).

For the first fourteen years of their marriage, Hermann Samuel Reimarus (1694–1768) and his wife, Johanna Friederica née Fabricius (1707–1783), rented living quarters, initially near the *Johanneum* and St. John's Church, in a narrow street called *Stavenporte*, then for several years on fashionable *Neuenwall*, and finally for a decade on *Grosse Beckerstrasse*. With the death of Johanna Friederica Reimarus' brother-in-law, Dr. Joachim Diederich Evers (1695–1741), who was also Hermann Samuel Reimarus' colleague at the *Akademisches Gymnasium*, the Reimaruses inherited the former Fabricius property *auf dem Plan*, a corner house across the street from the school and St. John's Church complex. After remodelling that "corner house" to accommodate a large family, the Reimaruses lived there from 1742 until 1753, when Hermann Samuel Reimarus acquired a larger property next door. This house would remain the Reimarus family home for three decades, well past Hermann Samuel's own lifetime.[3]

Even by the standards of the eighteenth century, the Reimarus household was relatively large. Of the couple's seven children, whose date and hour of birth – and death – Hermann Samuel carefully recorded in a family genealogy, at most four were alive at the same time. Only three reached adulthood: Johann Albert Hinrich (1729–1814), Margaretha Elisabeth ("Elise," 1735–1805), and Hanna Maria (1740–1819). But in 1742, the family took in as their own the four orphaned children of Friederica Reimarus' deceased sister, Catharina Dorothea Evers née Fabricius (1705–1737), following the death of their father.[4] This increased the Reimarus-Evers household to the size of fifteen persons, including in addition to the parents eight living children, a governess formerly in Evers' employ, and four domestic servants: a manservant, a female cook, a maidservant, and a wet nurse. At various times, the household also included a dog and occasionally additional animals, observations about which Hermann Samuel included in his book on animal behaviour.[5]

---

[3] References to the "corner house" (*Eckhaus*) are frequent in the household records, e.g., HB 1, 30 Apr. 1742; HB 2, Nov. (2x) and Dec. 1758, as are references to the "large house" (*grosses Haus*), e.g., July (3x), Oct., Dec. 1753. For details on the Reimaruses' homes, including maps and illustrations, see Almut Spalding, *Elise Reimarus (1735–1805): A Woman of the German Enlightenment* (Würzburg: Königshausen & Neumann, 2005) 50–51, 57, 67, ill. 10–11.

[4] For relevant genealogical tables, see A. Spalding, 518–522.

[5] *Allgemeine Betrachtungen über die Triebe der Thiere...*, vol. 1, 2nd ed. (Hamburg: Bohn, 1762) 27–28; see also 32–33, 55–57, 85. Purchase of dogs: HB 2, 9 Oct. 1752; HB 3, 27 May 1768; other domestic animals: "Henne mit 11 Kücken," HB 1, March–May 1732; "Pfingstlamm" (2x, for school age children Albert Hinrich and Elise, respectively), HB 1, 4 May 1742.

The relatively prosperous Reimarus family benefited from the access Hamburg offered to the world's goods. When Hermann Samuel was furnishing his home for his new bride in the autumn of 1728, for instance, he bought an English watch and furniture, Spanish champagne (*Palma*) und French wine (*Pontac*), East Indian tea table-cloths, and American beaver pelts to line a nightgown.[6] Thereafter, his growing family consumed goods in the opulent variety possible for the privileged of this major urban area. The family sweetened their Indian tea with Caribbean sugar in Dresden porcelain, played with cards from Brussels, enjoyed Virginia tobacco out of English snuff-boxes, and read books imported from Holland and Italy by the light of Russian candles.[7] The Reimarus parents and growing children, women and men, cultivated the fashionable public wardrobe that spread primarily from the French court to people of station throughout urban, western Europe and the American colonies.[8] Rich in imported fabrics and accessories, this fashion included Silesian linen, Danish gloves, Bohemian jewellery, and Scottish pearls and earrings.[9]

Thanks to Hamburg's location at the intersection of postal routes and the family's solid economic footing, the Reimaruses could maintain a regional and international network of acquaintances with relative ease. As their household records attest, they travelled to and corresponded

---

[6] HB 1, 7 and 20 Sep.; 11 and 28 Oct. 1728.

[7] Tea and sugar, e.g., HB 1, Easter 1728 and numerous other instances. Dresden porcelain, HB 2, 20 Aug. 1750. Playing cards from Brussels, HB 3, 24 June 1763. Tobacco, e.g., HB 1, Jan.–Feb. 1732 and numerous other instances. English snuff-box, HB 3, 17 Aug 1763. Books from Holland, HB 1, June–Aug. 1730, 4 March 1748; HB 2, March 1755; from Italy, HB 2, Dec. 1755, 11 Nov. 1756, 22 May 1757. Russian candles, e.g. HB 2, 19 Aug. 1754 and numerous other instances.

[8] The great wave of modern international fashion flowed from the French royal court at Versailles during the reign of Louis XIV (1643–1715). During the eighteenth century, the costume of aristocratic Paris, focused on ostentation, became the ideal for what people wore everywhere. See Max von Boehn, *Modes and Manners, vol. 4: The Eighteenth Century*, trs. from the German by Joan Joshua (London: Harrap, 1935) 32, 149; Millia Davenport, *The Book of Costume*, vol. 2 (NY: Crown, 1948) 652; Daniel Roche, *The culture of clothing: Dress and fashion in the 'ancien régime'*, trs. from the French by Jean Birrell (Cambridge: Cambridge UP, 1994) 13–14, 29, 48.

In Hamburg, the adoption of French aristocratic fashion by the merchant and educated classes began appearing clearly in the 1660s, and soon spread even among servants and pedlars, gaining vigour from the settlement of French Huguenot refugees in the city after the revocation of the Edict of Nantes in 1685. See Ernst Finder, *Hamburgisches Bürgertum in der Vergangenheit* (Hamburg: Friederichsen, de Gruyter & Co., 1930) 75–76. The Reimarus family patronized business people of French descent in Hamburg, including clothiers and wigmakers such as d'Arien, de Fontaine, Dumars, Miton, and Royé.

[9] Silesian linens, HB 2, 10 March 1751; Danish gloves, HB 1, 24 Dec. 1745; Bohemian jewellery, HB 2, 17 May 1755; Scottish pearls and earrings, HB 3, Dec. 1768.

with friends and relatives in Schleswig-Holstein, Copenhagen, Swedish Pomerania, Lübeck and Bremen, Greifswald, Göttingen and Jena. Evidence also appears of Hermann Samuel Reimarus' correspondence with scholars in wider Germany and beyond: Leipzig, Tübingen, Oxford and Rome. When Johann Albert Hinrich was studying medicine abroad at Leiden, London, and Edinburgh, his father and sister were able to keep postal contact during the entire three and a half years' duration of the programme (1754–57).

The Reimaruses were able to enjoy the diverse stage and musical offerings of a great city. While Hermann Samuel does not appear to have frequented the theatre much himself, he regularly paid for his teenage daughters' attendance at pantomimes, French comedies, at least one recorded tragedy, and an opera, presumably an Italian performance by the popular Mingotti troupe, in the former riding house at the city wall, the *Dragonerstall*.[10] Occasionally Hermann Samuel Reimarus himself visited the Hamburg opera house and musical performances in the *Drillhaus*, the favorite secular location of concerts before a municipal concert hall was completed in 1761. Church music, an important Hamburg tradition, surrounded the family, directed by the city music director (*Kantor*), Georg Philipp Telemann (1681–1767), who was also Reimarus' colleague at the *Johanneum* for forty years and an immediate neighbour. Telemann's successor, Carl Philipp Emanuel Bach (1714–1788), would become a close friend of the younger Reimaruses, Johann Albert Hinrich and Elise.

As the financial records attest, the family came into contact with people of all civic estates. They dealt not only with the educated and powerful, including civic senators and syndics, merchants, jurists, pastors, professors, physicians, journalists, and musicians, but also with shopkeepers, tradespeople, moneylenders, private tutors, professional women and widows, servants, day labourers, and welfare recipients. They encountered not only the orthodox Lutherans who predominated in their city, but also Mennonites, e.g., merchants Gerhard Beetz and Ernst Gevers in Altona;[11] French Reformed, e.g., Hamburg merchant de la Fontaine, and the pastor of the French Reformed congregation, Pierre Jean Géraud (1703–1785);[12]

---

[10] During Hermann Samuel Reimarus' lifetime, HB 1, Nov.–Dec. 1730; 17 Jan., Feb. 1749; HB 2, Apr. 1751; 21 Nov. 1752; 14 and 21 Nov., 6 Dec. 1753; 15 and 21 Feb., 10 March, 27 Sep., 7 Nov., and Dec. 1754; 28 May and 20 Aug. 1755; 18 Feb. 1756; Oct. 1758; HB 3, 14 Oct. 1765; Sept. 1766; Oct. 1767.

[11] For Beetz: HB 2, 24 Jan. 1757, 24 July 1763, 1 Feb. 1766; for Gevers: HB 1, 9 July 1747.

[12] For de la Fontaine: HB 3, Jan. 1764; for Géraud: HB 3, 25 June 1766.

Anglicans, e.g., merchant Gregory Evatt and tutor George Gregory;[13] Jews, e.g., rabbi Jacob Bassan (1704–1769) and a scribe Ruben;[14] and persons considered "freethinkers," such as Johann Lorenz Schmidt (1702–1749, with the Hamburg alias of "Schroeder").[15]

One particular example of modern urban multi-culturalism that the family embodied was its adherence to both Lutheranism and Enlightenment. The former had been the established civic religion since the time of the Reformation, whereas the latter emerged only in the eighteenth century as an international intellectual movement that sought to evaluate tradition by a bold use of reason, and to propose reforms accordingly. Hermann Samuel Reimarus, his son Johann Albert Hinrich, and daughter Elise are rightfully considered as belonging firmly to the Enlightenment movement. Less known are the family's deep, strong, and extensive roots in Lutheran tradition, and the cordial and even intimate relations that these Enlightenment figures also maintained with traditionally religious individuals. The household records contribute much detail on the participation of their authors, Hermann Samuel and Elise Reimarus, in both Lutheranism and Enlightenment.

LUTHERAN HERITAGE

Lutheran contemporaries sometimes referred to Hamburg as the "Zion of the North," because of the fame of its preachers and the firmness of its magistrates' commitment to maintaining the privileged local status of orthodox Lutheranism. The city had early joined the Protestant Reformation of Christian faith and life in the 1500s, making the Lutheran church the official religion in the municipal territories. Lutheranism enjoyed this privileged status in Hamburg until the end of the German empire (the "Holy Roman Empire of the German Nation") in 1806.[16] Five "main churches," whose pastors belonged to the clerical elite of the Lutheran world, dominated the city's skyline. Innumerable smaller churches and chapels stood within the city walls and outside, in the surrounding vil-

---

[13] For Evatt: HB 3, 10 Sep. 1762, 24 June 1763; for Gregory: HB 1, Nov. 1764 and numerous additional entries in 1748–49; in HB 2, 1752–53 and 1758; and in HB 3, 1759.

[14] For Bassan: HB 3, Juni–Sep. 1760; for Ruben: HB 3, 7 July 1768.

[15] HB 1, 4 June, 1 Nov., Dec. 1742; Sep. 1743; Sep. 1744.

[16] For a survey of what Joachim Whaley calls Hamburg's "struggle for political stability and purity of belief" during this period, see his *Religious Toleration and Social Change in Hamburg 1529–1819* (Cambridge: Cambridge UP, 1985) 8–44.

lages and farmland that Hamburg controlled. Intimately related to the churches were civic institutions such as an orphanage, hospital, reformatory, almshouses, and many schools, administered by clergy and lay civic leaders – among them the prestigious Latin school, the *Johanneum*, and the *Akademisches Gymnasium*.

Hermann Samuel Reimarus came from a family that boasted many clerics. Some of them attained high social and ecclesiastical rank, while others remained impoverished country pastors. Two great-great-grandfathers, a great-grandfather, and a grandfather had been Lutheran pastors in Mecklenburg and Pomerania. On his father's side, an uncle became a superintendent of pastors, or church provost (*Probst*). An uncle and two cousins in Holstein all rose to the position of "ducal court preacher." One of them, cousin Georg Heinrich Reimarus (1688–1735), became general superintendent of the church in ducal Holstein and vice president of the supreme church consistory. A maternal cousin of Herman Samuel Reimarus became pastor of Hamburg's Church of the Holy Spirit and a related almshouse known as the *Gasthaus*.[17] Female relatives also played key roles in these clerical networks. Four sisters of Hermann Samuel's paternal grandfather married pastors. In Hermann Samuel Reimarus' own generation, female cousins on both his paternal and maternal side married clergymen. Among the latter was Anna Cäcilie Wetken, who married Johann Georg Bötticher (b. 1695), church provost in Neumünster. Hermann Samuel Reimarus' sole sister Agatha Johanna (1692–1720) married Ernst Heinrich Schultz, a pastor in Danish Altona just outside Hamburg's western city gates.[18] The Reimaruses maintained regular ties with all these clerical relatives, as indicated through correspondence and material or monetary gifts recorded in the financial accounts.

Non-clerical relatives of Hermann Samuel Reimarus made important contributions to church-related institutions of care and education. An uncle of his mother, Hermann Wetken (d. 1712), had founded Hamburg's *Wetkensche Armenschule*.[19] Hermann Samuel's maternal grandfather,

---

[17] "Johann Jacob Wetken (1691–1741)": *Lexikon der hamburgischen Schriftsteller bis zur Gegenwart*, ed. Hans Schröder (1851–53), *Deutsches Biographisches Archiv*, ed. Bernhard Fabian, with Willy Gorzny et al. (München: Saur, 1986) fiche 1359, 338.

[18] Particularly valuable for Reimarus' family connections is Hermann Samuel Reimarus' personal copy of his father's genealogical publication, *Das Geschlecht-Register Der Vier Reimarorum... colligiret von Nicolao Reimaro* (Lauenburg: Pfeiffer, 1720), with manuscript additions by Hermann Samuel Reimarus, StA HH, Bestand 622–1/86, G 1.

[19] Friedrich Georg Buek, *Genealogische und Biographische Notizen über die seit der Reformation verstorbenen hamburgischen Bürgermeister* (Hamburg: Meißner, 1840) 15.

Johann Schultze (1647–1709) had been rector of the *Johanneum*, where Hermann Samuel's paternal uncle Christian (1664–1716) and his father Nicolaus Reimarus (1663–1724) taught – the latter for four decades.

Relatives of Hermann's wife Johanna Friederica also saw service to the Lutheran church and its institutions. Her great-grandfather and great-uncle were pastors in Bergedorf, south of Hamburg, while her paternal grandfather served as choir director and organist, first in Itzehoe northwest of Hamburg, then in Leipzig. Her father Johann Albert Fabricius (1668–1736), after studying theology in Leipzig, began his Hamburg career as secretary to one of the "main pastors," Johann Friedrich Mayer (1650–1712), and in 1699 became professor of ethics and eloquence at the *Akademisches Gymnasium*.[20] A classical scholar of world repute, he also became known as a major Christian apologist by translating and writing works on "physico-theology," the attempt to draw conclusions about God from the physical world while remaining true to traditional Christian belief.[21]

Hermann Samuel Reimarus himself led a life that contemporaries took to be religiously exemplary. After studying at the Lutheran universities of Jena and Wittenberg and serving as rector of the Latin school in Wismar (1723–1727), during the decades of teaching Hebrew to many aspiring theology students at the *Akademisches Gymnasium* he developed a reputation as a Christian apologist. He edited a commentary on the biblical book of Job, criticised a notoriously rationalist translation of the Pentateuch or first five books of the Bible, known as the "Wertheim Bible," and delivered funeral sermons on such orthodox worthies as his father-in-law Fabricius and the senior pastor in Hamburg, Friedrich Wagner.[22] He also

---

[20] Erik Petersen, *Johann Albert Fabricius en Humanist i Europa*, 2 vols. (København: Museum Tusculanum, 1998) 1: 38, 49, 175–87.

[21] Petersen 2: 691–748, 837–38. Among Fabricius' friends were the pastors of St. John's and the orphanage chapel, Nicolaus Staphorst (1679–1731) and Joachim Morgenweg (1666–1730), respectively: 2: 480.

[22] The commentary on Job is *Johann Adolph Hoffmanns Neue Erklärung des Buchs Hiobs* (Hamburg: Felginers Wittwe, 1734). The critiques of the Wertheim Bible appeared without title or author in the literary journal *Hamburgische Berichte von Gelehrten Sachen*, 1736 (6 and 10 Jan.), 9–18; new ed. by Wilhelm Schmidt-Biggemann in Hermann Samuel Reimarus, *Kleine gelehre Schriften* (Göttingen: Vandenhoeck & Ruprecht, 1994) 299–309; see the article by Ursula Goldenbaum in this volume. The funeral sermons, delivered on behalf of the *Akademisches Gymnasium*, were published as *Monumentum Doloris Communis de Obitu Viri Summe Reverendi, Amplissimi, et Longe Doctissimi, Johannis Alberti Fabricii…* (Hamburg: Conrad König, 1736), new ed. in *Kleine gelehre Schriften*, 333–50; and as *Civitatis et Ecclesiae Purioris Sensum Acerbum ex Insperato Obitu Viri Summe Reverendi, Excellentissimi, Amplissimi Friederici Wagneri…* (Hamburg: Jeremias Conrad Piscator, 1760), new ed. in *Kleine gelehrte Schriften*, 397–410.

published his own theological reflections based on reason.[23] Contemporaries not only understood these works to be compatible with traditional doctrine, but celebrated them as a defence of Christianity against Deism and atheism.

As the financial records clearly reflect, Hermann Samuel and his family lived their year according to the city's traditional Christian chronology, marking off seasonal quarters for business and social purposes by the religious celebrations of Easter in the springtime, St. John's Day at midsummer (June 24), Michaelmas in the autumn, and Christmas in winter (December 25).[24] Other important church commemorations by which they dated their lives included Three Kings or Epiphany (6 January), St. Antony's Day (17 January), Shrove Tuesday (Fastnacht, the day before Ash Wednesday), Quasimodo (first Sunday after Easter), Ascension (40 days after Easter), Pentecost (seventh Sunday after Easter), St. Martin's Day (11 November), and Advent Sunday (the first of four Sundays before Christmas). At the end of some years in his financial records, Hermann Samuel expressed thanks for God's blessings.[25]

The family actively engaged in church life. At St. Peter's, the main church of the parish to which they belonged, they recorded the baptisms of their infants, posted the banns before their children's weddings, and buried and memorialized their dead. Hermann Samuel Reimarus presumably occupied a pew in St. John's, the chapel of the *Akademisches Gymnasium*, as a perquisite of his job, perhaps the pew that his widow Johanna Friederica rented there following his death.[26] He acquired several Bibles, hymnbooks, and communion books, some for the use of specific family members.[27] Like all members of his family, Hermann Samuel Reimarus served as godfather at the baptism of numerous children of relatives, friends, colleagues, and servants.[28] He also contributed regularly to city

---

[23] *Die vornehmsten Wahrheiten der natürlichen Religion* (1754), repr. with introduction, ed. Gerhard Gawlick (Göttingen: Vandenhoeck & Ruprecht, 1985); and *Die Vernunftlehre* (1760), repr. in 2 vols., ed. F. Lötzsch (München: Hanser, 1979).

[24] For instance, rent for housing in Hamburg was charged at six-monthly intervals, payable either at Easter or Michaelmas, as the financial records regularly indicate.

[25] Examples are at the end of the following years: 1733, 1743, 1745, 1751, 1752, 1753.

[26] HB 4, July 1776.

[27] For example, HB 1, 8 April 1729; HB 2, 20 June and 20 Dec. 1755.

[28] Entries for monetary gifts on the occasion of "Gevatterstand" are too numerous to list in their entirety. Examples of Hermann Samuel Reimarus' baptismal sponsorship among relatives, friends, and servants or long-time business relations include infants of the following: his father's sister in Pomerania, Hedwig Kanzau née Reimarus (d. 1766), HB 1, Jan.–Feb. 1731; his son Johann Albert Heinrich's lifetime friend and founder of the

institutions of social welfare such as the orphanage, hospital, and alms-houses, to the rebuilding of St. Michael's Church after its destruction by lightning in 1750,[29] and to such emergency causes as relief for flooding victims and ransom for sailors enslaved by North African Moors.[30] The Reimaruses also gave annual and occasional monetary gifts to needy rela-tives and acquaintances, particularly widows and orphans.

The family cultivated friendly relations with local pastors. The "arch-deacon" of St. Peter's, Johann Brameyer (1685–1741), baptized all three Rei-marus children who were to reach adulthood.[31] A particularly close friend of Hermann Samuel Reimarus was Johann Andreas Geismer (1695–1759), whom he had known since they were fellow students at the *Akademis-ches Gymnasium*.[32] Following his theological studies, Geismer returned to Hamburg only shortly before Reimarus himself to become became a seamen's chaplain (1727–1733), and then adjunct pastor and pastor in the village of Billwerder, slightly upriver from Hamburg along the Elbe River.[33] Hermann Samuel Reimarus often visited Geismer in Billwerder, and for more than a decade used this quiet place as a retreat for himself and his family. In a couple of letters home from Geismer's parsonage one summer, Hermann Samuel described accompanying his friend into the countryside to baptize a child and finally gaining the sleep he had sought.[34]

Another pastor to whom the Reimaruses were quite close was Georg Hei-nrich Schultze (1718–80), a former student of Hermann Samuel Reimarus

---

Handlungs Akademie, Johann Georg Büsch (1728–1800), HB 3, Aug. 1768; printer Carl Ernst Bohn (1749–1827), HB 2, Sep. 1754; former maidservant Antje Liebers née Stapelfeld, HB 1, Feb. 1749; and tailor Johann Nicolaus Mester (d. 1774), whose mother-in-law Elisabeth Anna Ernsting née Ahrens had been a servant in the Fabricius household and also served the Reimaruses as nurse and washerwoman, HB 3, 5 Feb. 1765.

[29] Hermann Samuel Reimarus paid a contribution towards the rebuilding of St. Michael's church generally once a year, in Feb. or March, such as in HB 1, 1750, 1751, 1752, 1753, 1754.

[30] "Sclaven-Becken," HB 1, 9 July 1749; HB 2, 9 Jan. 1750, 10 Jan. 1751.

[31] Basic data on the life and career of Brameyer appear in Herwarth von Schade, *Hamburger Pastorinnen und Pastoren seit der Reformation: Ein Verzeichnis,* Im Auftrag des Kirchenkreisvorstandes des Kirchenkreises Alt-Hamburg in der Nordelbischen Ev.-Luth. Kirche, ed. Gerhard Paasch (Bremen: Temmen, 2009) 44. The baptismal records of the Reimarus children appear in Taufbuch St. Petri 1720–40, StA HH, Bestand 512–2 St. Petri, A VIII b 1 g, pp. 282, 412, and 533.

[32] C[arl] H[ieronymous] W[ilhelm] Sillem, ed., *Die Matrikel des Akademischen Gymnasiums in Hamburg 1613–1883* (Hamburg: Gräfke & Sillem, 1891) p. 83, matriculation no. 1873.

[33] Schade, 84.

[34] Hermann Samuel Reimarus to Johanna Friederica Reimarus, Billwerder, 28 June and 1 July 1746, StA HH, Bestand 622–1/86, B 1. References to visiting Geismer and Billwerder include financial record entries: HB 1, June and October 1743, April 1745, 18 May and July 1746; and HB 2, 21 Aug. 1751, May, 26 June and 23 Aug. 1752, 14 and 22 June and 15 Aug. 1753, 23 May and 5 Aug. 1754, 20 May, 1 July, and 28 Sep. 1755, 15 July and 2 Aug. 1756.

who began his pastoral career in Cuxhaven. The Reimaruses offered him gifts for his wedding and at the birth of children for whom they served as godparents. Hermann Samuel Reimarus almost surely played a key role in Schultze's appointment in 1758 as pastor of St. John's Church, directly across the street from the Reimarus home. The Schultzes' quarters in the St. John's complex also housed one of the two pumps where the Reimaruses fetched their water, which added to the families' frequent interactions, as decades of customary payments of Christmas gifts to the Schultzes' servants attest.[35] Finally, Hermann Samuel Reimarus was close friends with the prefect, schoolmaster, and senior canon of the Hamburg cathedral chapter, Christian Franciscus Schwäneschuh/Schwaeneschuch (1697–1774). The men became such close acquaintances as to loan one another large amounts of money over many years.[36]

The tutors whom the Reimarus family hired for their children included theology graduates on their way into the pastorate, as well as a musician soon to occupy a prominent organist's position. Johann Gerhard Sucksdorf (1716–1783) taught the children German, history, and religion for twelve years (1743–1756), during the last two of which he also served as catechist at the Hamburg reformatory (*Werk- und Zuchthaus*). The entire Reimarus family shared his painfully long wait for a pastoral post. When he was finally appointed pastor in the village of Döse, downriver from Hamburg at the mouth of the Elbe, Hermann Samuel Reimarus presented him with a monetary gift in celebration.[37] Barthold Nicolaus Krohn (1722–1795) also taught the youngest surviving Reimarus daughter, Hanna, for two years before finding an appointment as pastor of St. Mary Magdalene Church

---

[35] On Schultze, see Schade, 238. References to Schultze in the financial records: HB 2, 11 Aug. 1750 (wedding gift); 28 Aug. 1758 (Friederica R. godmother's gift); 3 June 1769 (Elise R. godmother's gift); and yearly tips to Schultze's maids "for the water," every December from 1759 until Schultze's death.

[36] Schwaeneschuch is listed under "III. Ein Hochwürdiges Dom-Capitul" in the annual *Hamburgischer Staats-Calender*, for example, in the 1765 edition, ed. Matthias Rohlfs (Hamburg: Conrad König), unpaginated. Hermann Samuel Reimarus' loans to Schwaeneschuch appear under the following household record entries: HB 1, April 1745; HB 2, 5 July 1758; HB 3, 12 July 1759. In turn, the following entries attest Schwaeneschuch's loans to Reimarus: HB 2, 15 Jan. 1753 and Nov. 1758; HB 3, 1 May and Nov. 1759; 13 and 31 May, and 6 Sept. 1760; 5 Jan. and 19 Nov. 1761; 11 and 19 Nov. 1763; Nov. 1764; 16 Nov. 1765; Oct. 1766; Nov. 1767.

[37] Schade, 258. Sucksdorf's tutoring salaries are attested from 1743 to 1756 on a quarterly basis: HB 1, from 24 June 1743; to HB 2, 21 August 1756. Conversations about Sucksdorf appear in numerous letters by Johann Albert Hinrich Reimarus to his sister Elise in the 1750s, see Almut Spalding, *Elise Reimarus* (note 3) 86.

in Hamburg.[38] Among church musicians, Knut Lambo (1714–1783) tutored Elise Reimarus and perhaps also her younger sister on the harpsichord before gaining appointment as organist at St. Nicolas' Church.[39]

There were also two former Roman Catholic clergymen whom Reimarus hired as tutors for his children. Roche Bagard, an immigrant from France and Lutheran convert from a monastic order, for eight years (1742–1749) taught the Reimarus and Evers children French.[40] For instruction in English, the older Reimarus children had had another teacher, but the youngest, Hanna, learned English with a former Scottish priest (1758–1759). In Hamburg he was known by the last name of Coleman. Actually, he had been born Peter Alexander MacGregor, from a clan that staunchly supported the Stuarts. Following the Battle of Culloden (1746), where one of his brothers was killed, he had fled to Hamburg, converted to Anglicanism, and sought further protection from persecution by the English by assuming a new last name.[41] Reimarus probably knew about this background and meant to assist the refugee Coleman and his young family by initially doubling his salary.[42]

---

[38] Schade, 148. HB 2, Jan., 30 March, 28 June 1758; 6 Feb., 13 April, 25 June, October 1759; April, June, and 10 June 1760. On the last date, Hermann Samuel Reimarus presented Krohn with a monetary gift to celebrate his new pastorate. In 1779, on Elise Reimarus' initiative, Krohn would become one of the subscribers to Mendelssohn's Hebrew Bible in German, see Almut Spalding, *Elise Reimarus* (note 3) 270.

[39] HB 1, 7 July and 6 Oct. 1748. Johann Albert Hinrich Reimarus referred to Elise's earlier musical training in a letter to her from Leiden, 27 April 1754, Ley XIIr, StA HH, uncatalogued to date.

[40] Entries of payments to Bagard are numerous in HB 1 between June 1742 and June 1749. Bagard was probably still unmarried when he was tutor to the Reimaruses. Living in the same house as the organist at the Church of the Holy Spirit and the *Gasthaus*, and widowed probably with very young children, he married his second wife, Elisabeth Behrens née Reinshagen (1711–1789), in 1753 very shortly after the death of his first wife, Marie Du Moulin. Following his employment in the Reimarus household, Bagard held a similar position as French tutor to the future enlightened merchant and Hamburg senator, Johann Michael Hudtwalcker (1747–1818).

[41] Printed family tree, StA HH, Bestand 741–2 Genealogische Sammlungen, Coleman-MacGregor N. Coleman had been ordained priest in Germany in 1730 and spent some time in Vienna and Silesia before leaving Scotland for good. He married a native of Silesia, Johanna von Schalscha (1727–1788). Their son John Francis Charles Coleman (1751–1826), already born in Hamburg, was the future private secretary of the English Merchant Venturers.

[42] HB 2, 21 June and Aug. 1758; HB 3, 13 Apr., 22 June, Dec. 1759. The 1758 entries explicitly list the English tutor's (*Sprachmeister*) salary as 12 marks per month, even though by then, only Hanna Reimarus was still receiving language instruction. In 1759, Coleman's monthly salary was reduced to 6 marks. This was exactly what the previous English tutor, George Gregory, employed until 1753, had received even teaching several students at once.

Reimarus also maintained contact with clergy from other traditions in other ways. He used his friendship with William Murray, Anglican chaplain of the English Merchant Venturers in Hamburg, to obtain books and a table service from England, and to send his own work to scholars in that country.[43] He carried on a correspondence with the Vatican librarian Cardinal Angelo Maria Querini (1680–1755), as discussed in another chapter in this volume.[44] Finally, he served in a court case as an expert witness on the side of the local Portuguese Jewish rabbi Jacob Basan (1704–1769).[45]

ENLIGHTENMENT

As is well known today, despite all appearances to contemporaries, Hermann Samuel Reimarus was anything but an orthodox Lutheran. His account books shed light on his evolution as an enlightened man who wrote, surreptitiously over three decades, a radical critique of the Bible that would reach full publication only in 1972.[46] Financial transactions show Reimarus' personal relations with other leaders of the Enlightenment. They show how the objects of his book-buying shifted from the traditional religious works typical of his first years at the *Gymnasium* (1728–34) to writings that would address a modern, enlightened Western European intellectual. They suggest an important origin of his scientific interests and an arena for his observations of animal behaviour: his active involvement in gardening.

Housebook entries substantiate Hermann Samuel's relations with leaders of the early, literary and publicistic phase of the Enlightenment in Hamburg. This phase centered initially on members of the *Teutschübende Gesellschaft* (1715–1717) and the first *Patriotische Gesellschaft* (1723–1730s), and contributors to the first German moral weekly, *Der Patriot* (1724–1726). Close friends and acquaintances in these circles included Reimarus' father-in-law Johann Albert Fabricius (1668–1736), professor of Classics at the *Akademisches Gymnasium*; syndics Johann Julius Surland

---

[43] HB 2, 7 Sept. and 27 Oct. 1753; 2 Oct. 1755. Murray appears in various years of the *Hamburgischer Staats-Calendar*, as in that of 1755, under "VII. Die Hochpreißliche Societät der alhier residirenden Englischen Adventurier-Kauf-Leute."

[44] HB 1, 29 August 1743, Jan. 1744, 27 May and Nov. 1746, and 4 April 1748.

[45] HB 3, June–Sept. 1760.

[46] *Apologie oder Schutzschrift für die vernünftigen Verehrer Gottes*, 2 vols., ed. Gerhard Alexander (Frankfurt a.M.: Insel, 1972). For the importance of Reimarus in the religious world of his time, see *Hermann Samuel Reimarus (1694–1768): ein "bekannter Unbekannter" der Aufklärung in Hamburg* (Göttingen: Vandenhoeck & Ruprecht, 1973).

(1687–1748) and Johann Klefeker (1698–1775); and mayor Conrad Widow (1686–1754). Frequent contacts with these individuals are traceable in the financial records through the customary holiday tips that Reimarus gave to servants of houses that he frequented. His gifts to the servants of the Fabricius household reflect his courting and marrying Johanna Friederica and their close ties thereafter. After Fabricius' death in 1736, the financial accounts substantiate Hermann Samuel's care of his father-in-law's legacy: bringing his manuscripts to publication, acquiring copper etchings of him, and repairing his grave.[47] Hermann Samuel Reimarus was a close friend of syndic Surland – as were their families – and regularly borrowed large sums from him.[48] Records of Hermann Samuel coming to dinner at the home of "H. K." and boating on the Alster with "S. K." probably refer to syndic Klefeker.[49] Hermann Samuel borrowed substantial sums from mayor Conrad Widow (1786–1754) and received presents from his family for writing and publishing memorials of Widow in Latin and German.[50]

Hermann Samuel also acquired books associated with leaders of this early phase of the Hamburg Enlightenment. He bought works by Thomas Lediard (1681–1764), secretary of the British envoys in Hamburg and director of the Hamburg opera; by senator and poet Barthold Heinrich Brockes (1680–1747); and by mayor Johann Anderson (1674–1743).[51] He bought other books from the auctions of estates of men in these circles, including Surland; the rector of the *Johanneum*, Johann Hübner (1668–1731); poet Friedrich von Hagedorn (1708–54); and Michael Richey (1678–1761), professor of history and Greek at the *Akademisches Gymnasium*.[52]

The early phase of the Hamburg Enlightenment continued in less influential groups for some years, including the *Freitags-Collegium von Rechts-gelehrten* (founded in 1722), the *Dienstagsgesellschaft hamburgischer Juristen* (1730s–40s), and the *Orden des guten Geschmacks* in Hamburg.

---

[47] Repair of the Fabricius family burial place in St. Peter's: HB 3, 28 Aug. 1760. After Hermann Samuel Reimarus' own death in 1768, his daughter Elise disposed of a large collection of Fabricius manuscripts: HB 3, July 1770.

[48] Records on transactions with the Surlands are numerous, at least one per year beginning in Nov. 1728. The last entries date from the auction of Surland's remaining papers, following the death of his widow, Rebecca Catharina née Fürsen (d. 1767): HB 3, May and Sept. 1767.

[49] HB 1, Jan. 1749; HB 2, 4 Sep. 1751 and 3 June 1757.

[50] HB 1, 9 Feb. and 24 July 1744, 6 Feb. 1746; HB 2, April 1755.

[51] HB 1, Sep. and Nov.–Dec 1730 (Lediard); June–July 1734 (Brockes); Nov. 1746 (Anderson).

[52] HB 1, March–May 1732 (Hübner); HB 2, 3 July 1755 (Hagedorn); HB 3, 25 Sep. 1762 (Richey).

Hermann Samuel's closest friend in his early Hamburg years was a member of both the *Freitags-Collegium* and *Dienstagsgesellschaft*, a man whom he called "Mon Frère" ("my brother"), his brother-in-law and colleague Joachim Dietrich Evers, whose orphaned children the Reimaruses would later raise as their own. Two other members of the *Freitags-Collegium* whom Reimarus visited occasionally were Dr. Georg Seitz (d. 1760), who transferred money for the Evers orphans to Hermann Samuel Reimarus; and senator Joachim Rentzel (1694–1768), whose son studied under Reimarus.[53] Hermann Samuel joined the *Dienstagsgesellschaft* in 1740 as its only non-juridical member.[54] Fellow members who appear in the household records, beyond Evers, were senator Christian Dresky (1698–1762), from whom Hermann Samuel borrowed large sums; and Conrad Dieterich Volckmann (1702–1751), judge at the lower court and son-in-law of mayor Anderson, whom Reimarus saw regularly.[55] The membership of the *Orden des guten Geschmacks* consisted mostly of men in the diplomatic service, whose leader in the 1730s was the diplomat, composer, and writer Johann Mattheson (1681–1764). Reimarus would compose the inscription for Mattheson's grave marker in St. Michael's church.[56] Other members of the organization included two of Reimarus' students, the lawyer Johann Joachim Borgeest (d. 1759), and Johann Jakob Wolf (d. 1744), secretary of the Hanoverian envoy.

Especially important for the Enlightenment in Hamburg from the 1730s to the early 1750s were social groups centered on the writer Friedrich von Hagedorn (1708–54). Unlike other documentation, the financial accounts

---

[53] For Seitz, e.g., HB 1, 6 Aug. 1743, 29 July and 28 Aug. 1745, 13 Aug. 1746, 3 Aug. 1747. For Rentzel, e.g., HB 1, Juni–Juli 1734, 15 Jan. 1738, and private lessons for his son Garlieb Rentzel (1727–1796) 20 Feb 1742.

[54] The first reference in the financial records to the *Dienstagsgesellschaft* appears in HB 1, June 1743.

[55] For Dresky, e.g., HB 1, 10 May 1749; HB 2, 18 June 1758; HB 3, 60: 12 Apr. 1760; 61: 21 Jan. and 3 Oct. 1761; 2 Nov. 1762; and 3 Oct. 1763; and private lessons for his son Johann Heinrich Dresky (1740–1805) Oct. 1760, 17 Apr. an 29 Sep. 1764. Regarding Volckmann, Reimarus made regular December payments to Volckmann's servants from 1743 until Volckmann's death in 1751; and had the Volckmann sons as private students: Johann Jakob (1732–1803), HB 1, 2 Sep. 1747; 8 May 1748; Peter Dietrich (1735–1792), HB 2, 14 Apr. and 10 July 1756; 4 Apr. 1757.

[56] HB 3, June 1767. Mattheson's grave was under the pulpit at the recently rebuilt main church St. Michael's, where Mattheson had personally borne the full and immense costs of the new organ. On a visit in October 1772, the British musicologist Charles Burney noted the "fine old-fashioned Latin inscription [by Reimarus], giving an account of his [Mattheson's] benefaction": *An Eighteenth-Century Musical Tour in Central Europe and the Netherlands*, vol. 2 of *Dr. Burney's Musical Tours in Europe*, ed. by Percy A. Scholes (London: Oxford UP, 1959) 221.

indicate little about Hermann Samuel Reimarus' relation with Hagedorn directly, beyond buying books from his postmortem auction and briefly encountering his servant and widow.[57] However, the records do document substantial interactions with many members of the Hagedorn circle. Those members included Reimarus' close friend Surland (see above), and the printer Johann Carl Bohn (1712–1773). Bohn sold Reimarus many books, bought from him manuscripts by Fabricius, published some of Reimarus' books (*Natürliche Religion, Vernunftlehre,* and *Triebe der Tiere*), borrowed large sums from him, and served him as a mediator of interest payments from investments in the region of northern Dittmarschen, along the North Sea coast of Holstein.[58] Bohn and Hermann Samuel Reimarus also served as godparents of each other's children and even grandchildren.[59] The above-mentioned William Murray helped arrange book orders and a tea service from England, as well as payment for several copies of Hermann Samuel's edition of Dio Cassius. Barthold Joachim Zinck (1718–1775), journalist and legation secretary, served as writing tutor to the Reimarus children for at least five years (1743–1748).[60] Another member of the Hagedorn circle was the rector of the *Johanneum,* Johann Samuel Müller (1701–1773), in whose courtyard stood the other pump where the Reimarus family fetched their water.[61] Finally, the Hagedorn circle included Dr. Christoph Lipstorp (1694–1754), Hamburg's city physician, to whom the Reimaruses occasionally turned for their medical needs.[62]

After Hagedorn's death in 1754, Hermann Samuel Reimarus became the centre of Hamburg's Enlightenment circle. Several figures in this group appear in the Reimarus account books: his students and subsequent lawyers, Johann Ulrich Pauli (1727–94) and Peter Dietrich Volckmann (1735–92); the architect Ernst Georg Sonnin (1713–94), whose reconstruction of St. Michael's Church the Reimaruses supported; and Johann Georg Büsch (see above).[63]

---

[57] HB 2, 3 July 1755, 6 Feb. 1758; HB 3, 4 Feb. 1761.

[58] Financial transactions with Bohn are too numerous to list in their entirety. Examples of entries for the year of the first edition of the *Vernunftlehre* are HB 2, 2 Feb., 14 Feb. (3x) and 14 Feb. 1756.

[59] Bohn was godfather to Hanna Maria Reimarus: Baptismal record, Taufbuch St. Petri 1720–1740, StA HH, Bestand 512–2 St. Petri, Sign. A VIII b 1 g, p. 533.

[60] HB 1, generally quarterly payments to Zinck from 24 June 1743 to 27 Sep. 1748.

[61] References to Müller are too numerous to list in their entirety. Reimarus made regular payments for access to water until Müller's death in 1773.

[62] HB 1, March–May 1732; HB 2, 25 Jan. 1753 (2x); 26 Jan. 1754; 28 Jan. 1755.

[63] Pauli: HB 1, 9 Feb. 1748. References to Volckmann are yearly payments to servants from 1743 until Volckmann's death in 1751. Sonnin also oversaw one of the Reimaruses'

Hermann Samuel's close acquaintances also included less well-known members of the early Enlightenment in Hamburg. One was Gerloff Hiddinga (1683–1766), contributor to the *Hamburgische Beyträge* and painter, who served as mathematics and drawing instructor to the children of the Reimarus household for at least six years (1742–1748). Another was Dr. Johann Heinrich Stüve (d. 1751), a book-keeper and patron of the notorius author of the rationalist "Wertheim Bible" of 1735, Johann Lorenz Schmidt. According to the household books, apparently Stüve helped Reimarus move from Wismar to Hamburg in the spring of 1728. Reimarus also had occasion to tip Stüve's coachman, and after Stüve's death borrowed money from his widow.[64]

Most provocative of all is the likelihood, according to a close reading of the financial records, that Reimarus employed Schmidt himself as a family tutor during the 1740s. While Hermann Samuel was careful not to record his own Bible project explicitly, he let slip at least one reference to personal association with this notorious biblical critic who had inspired Reimarus. From 1738 to 1746, Johann Lorenz Schmidt was living in Hamburg as a refugee from imperial justice, under the pseudonym "Johann Ludwig Schroeder/Schröter." Entries in the Reimarus financial records concerning a mysterious tutor named "Mons Schroeder" (Sept. 1744), apparently identical with a "Schreib[-] und Rechenmeister" for Johann Albert Hinrich Reimarus and his cousin Hermann Daniel Evers (Nov. 1742 and Sept. 1743), may be the only written evidence in Reimarus' own hand of his encounter with and patronage of Schmidt. It indicates a personal relationship between the men whose writings provoked the two great public theological debates of eighteenth-century Germany.[65]

Out of the Reimarus circle emerged the so-called second *Patriotische Gesellschaft* of 1765, the key group leading the later phase of the Enlightenment in Hamburg. Focused on practical reform of civic life, this

---

own construction projects. In 1770–71, following her brother's remarriage, Elise Reimarus hired Sonnin to remodel the Reimarus home, which subsequently became the residence also of Johann Albert Hinrich's new family. HB 3, 3 Sep., 8 Oct., 18 and 22 Nov. 1770.

[64] HB 1, Easter (2x) and 22 Nov. 1728; 4 June 1729; March–May 1732; HB 2, 25 May and 27 June 1753.

[65] For details, see Almut and Paul Spalding, "Der rätselhafte Tutor bei Hermann Samuel Reimarus: Begegnung zweier radikaler Aufklärer in Hamburg," in *Zeitschrift des Vereins für Hamburgische Geschichte* 87 (2001): 49–64. See also Paul Spalding, *Seize the Book, Jail the Author: Johann Lorenz Schmidt and Censorship in Eighteenth-Century Germany* (West Lafayette, IN: Purdue UP, 1998).

association appears in the financial records by October, 1766.[66] Among its earliest members were persons appearing frequently in the Reimarus financial records: Büsch, Pauli, Sonnin, and Hermann Samuel Reimarus' son, the young physician Johann Albert Hinrich Reimarus, and the printer Jeremias Conrad Piscator (1712–1788).

The book purchases documented in the household books also substantiate Hermann Samuel Reimarus' growing involvement in the Enlightenment. They indicate that by the 1740s, his interests were moving away from traditional religious literature to recent secular and scientific works. His early book purchases focused heavily on biblical, rabbinical, and theological writings. Biblical works included Hebrew Bibles and the Septuagint, and a recent synopsis of the New Testament. Rabbinical works included early commentaries (*Meckilta, Tanchuma*), the Babylonian and Jerusalem Talmuds, medieval travel accounts (Benjamin de Tudela), philosophy and correspondence (Maimonides), halachic compendia (Jacob ben Asher, Caro), popularized legal summaries and story collections (*Kol Bo, Maasehs Buch*), and late medieval and recent commentaries (Horowitz, Isaac ben Samson, Hazzan, Mosche Frankfurter, Peiser). Reimarus also bought some Christian tracts, disputations, and books, such as two volumes of Martin Luther.[67]

Already early on, Reimarus cultivated interests in matters beyond traditional theology. During his first Hamburg years, he bought a modern scholarly treatment of the Bible in the form of a recent critical biblical edition by the French scholar Calmet, and "physico-theological" poetry by his friend Brockes.[68] He also bought some contemporary social commentary (Lamy), a local work on firework displays (Lediard), and a medical manual (Dover).[69] But the great weight of Reimarus' book purchases

---

[66] HB 3, Oct. 1766 and Sep. 1767.

[67] In chronological order, HB 1, 30 June and Aug. 1729; April and Oct. 1731; Jan.–Feb. 1732; Jan.–March, April, and May 1734. Many of these books appear in *Auktionskatalog der Bibliothek von Hermann Samuel Reimarus*, ed. Johann Andreas Gottfried Schetelig (1769, 1770), index by Gerhard Alexander (Hamburg: Reimarus-Kommission der Joachim-Jungius-Gesellschaft der Wissenschaften, 1978, 1980).

[68] Augustin Calmet (1672–1757), *Commentaire littéral sur tous les livres de l'ancien et du nouveau testament* (1707–16); HB 1, Jan.–Feb. 1731. Barthold Heinrich Brockes, *Irdisches Vergnügen in Gott*, 9 vols. (Hamburg, 1721–48); HB 1, Jan–March, June–July 1734.

[69] François Lamy (1636–1711), *Lettres philosophiques … sur divers sujets importants* (Trevoux: Geneaux, 1703); HB 1, 6 May 1729. Thomas Lediard, *Eine Collection curieuser Vorstellungen in Illuminationen und Feuer-Wercken* (Hamburg: Stromer, 1730); HB 1, Sept., Nov.–Dec. 1730. Thomas Dover (1660–1742), *The Ancient Physician's Legacy to His Country*, 2nd ed. (London: Bettlesworth & Hitch, 1732), which Reimarus acquired in French translation, *Legs d'un ancien Médecin à sa patrie* (La Haye, 1734); HB 1, Jan.–March 1734.

changed in the direction of Enlightenment after the mid-1730s. This evidence substantiates the thesis that Reimarus departed from traditional biblical studies at just this time, inspired by the modern critical "Wertheim Bible" of 1735 that he himself commented on anonymously in the *Hamburgische Berichte*.[70]

The striking shift in book purchases is most visible after the several years with few or no entries in the financial records. The last recorded purchases of disputations and rabbinical works came in 1743–1744. Besides a Hebrew Bible for his son in 1746, Hermann Samuel Reimarus made no further explicit purchases of biblical or theological works for scholarly purposes during the remainder of his career. Instead, he was buying books typical of the Enlightenment, including works authored by women. They included classical works (Lucretius, Ovid, Lucian, Livy, Virgil, Aristophanes),[71] social commentary (Du Noyer, Leprince de Beaumont),[72] geography (Anderson),[73] science (Rösel, Buffon),[74] modern language grammars and dictionaries (Girard, Veneroni),[75] history (Willebrand, Campbell),[76] moral journals (Addison's *Spectator*),[77] a directory of contemporary scholars (Adam),[78] a numismatic

---

[70] Peter Stemmer, *Weissagung und Kritik: Eine Studie zur Hermeneutik bei Hermann Samuel Reimarus* (Göttingen: Vandenhoeck & Ruprecht, 1981).

[71] In chronological order, HB 1, March and 14 Oct. 1743; HB 2, 19 Aug., July, and Dec. 1759.

[72] *Lettres de Madame du Montier*, ed. Jeanne Marie Leprince de Beaumont (Amsterdam: Brund, 1720); Anne Marguerite Petit, Mme. du Noyer (1663–1719), *Lettres historiques et galantes* (Cologne: Marteau, 1711); HB 3, 18 Jan. 1746.

[73] Johann Anderson, *Nachrichten von Island...Gröneland und der Strasse Davis* (Hamburg: Georg Christian Grund, 1746); HB 1, Nov. 1746.

[74] Reimarus subscribed to August Johann Rösel von Rosenhof (1705–1759), *Insektenbelustigungen*, 3 vols. (1746–1755); and *Historia naturalis ranarum nostratium, oder die natürliche Historie der Frösche hiesigen Landes* (1758); HB 1, Nov. 1746; 9 Jan. and 4 March 1748; HB 2, 22 Jan., 31 July, and 13 Dec. 1751; 13 Jan. 1753; 21 Feb., and 9 July 1754; 21 Jan. 1755; 27 Nov. 1756; and July 1758. Similarly, Reimarus subscribed to several volumes of Georges Louis Leclerc, Comte de Buffon (1707-1788), *Histoire naturelle, générale et particulière*; HB 2, 7 Feb. 1754; HB 3, 6 July 1765; Aug. 1766.

[75] Gabriel Girard (1677–1748), *Les vrais principes de la langue Françoise* (Paris: Lebreton; Amsterdam: J. Wetstein, 1747); HB 1, 1 Dec. 1747. Sieur de Veneroni (1642–1708), *Italiänisch-frantzösisch- und teutsche Grammatica* (Frankfurt/Leipzig: Johann Philipp Andrea, 1747); HB 2, Dec. 1755.

[76] *Hansische Chronik* by Johann Peter Willebrand (1719–86), ed. Anton Köhler (Lübeck: gedruckt auf Kosten des Autors, 1748); HB 1, 4 March 1748. George Campbell (1719–96), *An* [sic] *Universal History, from the earliest account of time to the present* (London: printed for J. Bailey and others, 1736); HB 2, 20 Oct. 1755.

[77] HB 1, June 1749.

[78] Melchior Adam (d. 1622), *Vitae theologorum, Jureconsultorum, Politicorum, medicorum atque philosophorum maximam partem Germanorum nonnullam quoque exterorum*, 3rd ed. (Frankfurt/M., 1705); HB 1, 22 Apr. 1748.

work (Langermann and Hartmann),[79] maps (Rome, Hamburg),[80] and polit-ical/social registers (Gothaer Kalender).[81] Throughout his professional life, Reimarus also subscribed to a variety of German journals that were vital to the spread of Enlightenment in the North: the *Hamburgische Berichte, Freye Urtheile und Nachrichten, Reichspostreuter, Commentarii Hambur-gensis, Hamburger Relations-Courier,* and *Hamburgischer Correspondent.*[82] The latter two were the premier German newspapers of the time. In his last years he was subscribing to three journals simultaneously.

The household records document additional consumers and producers of enlightened knowledge in Hamburg with whom the Reimaruses came into contact. In addition to colleagues at the *Akademisches Gymnasium* mentioned above, they include the mathematician Christoph Heinrich Dornemann (1682–1753), the physicist Johann Christian Wolf (1689–1770), the moral philosophers Lukas Heinrich Helmer (1726–60) and Johannes Wunderlich (1718–1778), and the rhetoricians Paul Schaffshausen (1712–61) and Johann Heinrich Vincent Nölting (1736–1806).[83]

The enlightened network also included publishers and book traders from Hamburg and Altona. References to prominent families in the pub-lishing trade include the Bene family: Ida Elisabeth Bene (d. 1747), her son Johann Conrad (1694–1757), and his wife Agatha née Gehrke; the Felg-iner-Bohn family: Theodor Christoph Felginer (1686–1726), his wife Sophia Catharina (d. 1747), their son-in-law and successor, the above mentioned Johann Carl Bohn, and his son and successor, Carl Ernst Bohn; the Grundt family: Georg Christian Grundt (1695–1758), his wife Sophia Wendelina née Holle (d. 1768), and their son Heinrich Christian Grundt; and the

---

[79] *Hamburgisches Münz- und Medaillen-Vergnügen*, eds. Johann Paul Langermann and Christian Hartmann (Hamburg: Piscator, 1753); HB 2, 2 Apr. 1753.

[80] Giambattista Nolli (before 1692–1756), *Nuova Pianta di Roma* (Rome, 1748); HB 2, 11 Nov. 1756. "Riss von Hamburg," HB 2, Sep. 1758. Perhaps this anticipated publication of a Hamburg map was based on Johann Klefeker's hand-coloured 1758 drawing, "Charte zur Vorstellung der Post-Wege aus Hamburg..." (photomechanical reproduction with comments by Erich Kuhlmann, Hamburg: Vermessungsamt Hamburg, 1983).

[81] HB 3, April and Dec. 1767. His Daughter Elise continued subscribing to additional volumes after Hermann Samuel Reimarus' death.

[82] Reimarus paid journal and newspaper subscriptions on a yearly basis, usually early in January. Every single year in the financial records for which January entries exist lists payments for journals.

[83] Dornemann, HB 2, 9 July 1754. Wolf, HB 1, Dec. 1749; HB 2, March 1754. Helmer, HB 1, 9 Feb. 1748. Schaffshausen, HB 1, 1 June 1754; HB 3, 12 Dec. 1761. Wunderlich and Nölting had been Reimarus' students and became his colleagues only during the last years of his life. They appear in the financial records while still students: Wunderlich, HB 1, undated entries (ca. 1736–37 and 1738); and Nölting, HB 2, 31 Oct. 1753.

family behind the famous *Heroldsche Buchhandlung*: Johann Christoph Kissner (d. 1735), his son-in-law and successor, Johann Christian Herold (1703–1761), Herold's widow, Anna Maria née Kissner (d. 1788), their sons, Johann Heinrich (1742–1810) and Christian (b. 1750), and Johann Christian Herold's brother; and the Piscator family: Johann Georg Piscator (d. 1759) and his above-mentioned son, Jeremias Conrad Piscator.[84] Other local individuals in the publishing trade included Christian Wilhelm Brandt (d. 1761), Johann Gottfried Dalençon (1718–1795), Johann Conrad König (1695–1757), Luder Mencke, Karl Peter Petit, and Johann Winkelmann.[85]

The financial records also refer to colleagues in the wider Republic of Letters: in Lübeck, the book trader Peter Heinrich Tesdorpf (1712–1778), owner of a scientific cabinet who was particularly knowledgeable on insects; in Leipzig, the Arabist Johann Jakob Reiske (1716–1774); in Göttingen, the linguist Johann Matthias Gesner (d. 1761); in Amsterdam, the above-mentioned publisher and book trader Mosche Frankfurter (1672–1762); in Oxford, Benjamin Kennicott (1718–1783), the editor of a critical compilation of biblical manuscripts; in Edinburgh, the book traders Alexander Donaldson (d. 1794) and Alexander Kincaid (1713–1777); and in Rome, Cardinal Angelo Maria Querini (1680–1755), prefect of the Vatican library.[86]

Enlightenment networks are closely linked with forms of sociability involving new consumer goods, such as coffee and tea. In Hamburg, tea became the drink of choice for the well-to-do and educated elite, though over the course of the eighteenth century, tea became affordable to ordinary people as well. Indicative of the importance of respectable sociability

---

[84] References to book traders and publishers are too numerous in the financial records to list here in their entirety. The name Bene appears yearly from 1743 until 1780, generally with January payments for journals. The Felginer business appears 1728–1732, and after a gap in the records, from 1743 on under the name Bohn, generally with payments at the beginning of the year. Grundt, HB 1 and 2, January payments 1749–1758. Kissner, HB 1, undated entry (ca. 1728). Entries to Herold during 1749–1756 refer to Johann Christian Herold only, with financial transactions mostly in the summers. Other documents attest to contacts between the Reimarus and Herold families well into the subsequent generation. Piscator, HB 2, 1 Feb. 1758: HB 2, March 1768, 14 Feb. 1770.

[85] Brandt, HB 1, yearly payments, generally Jan.–March, 1730–1746. Dalençon, HB 2 and 3, numerous entries per year, 1752–1762. König, HB 1, March 1732. Petit, HB 1, April 1731. Mencke, HB 2, 31 March 1750. Winkelmann, HB 3, 4 Aug. and Oct. 1769.

[86] For Tesdorpf, e.g., HB 1, Aug. 1743; 9 Jan. and 4 entries for March 1748. Reiske, HB 2, 15 Apr. 1757. Gesner, HB 2, 26 Dec. 1752. Mosche Frankfurter, HB 1, April, May, and Oct.–Dec. 1731; Jan.–Feb. And May 1732. Kennicott, HB 3, 10 Sep. 1762 and 24 June 1763. Donaldson and Kincaid, HB 2, 24 Oct. 55. Quirini, HB 1, 29 Aug. 1743; Jan. 1744; 27 May and Nov. 1746; 4 Apr. 1748; HB 2, 12 März 1751; 17 Jan. and 7 Sep. 1752.

to the young Hermann Samuel Reimarus, his second recorded purchase
while setting up his household in Hamburg at Eastertime 1728 included
tea. During his first year of marriage, when tea was still heavily taxed, Reimarus spent one fifth to one quarter of his annual base salary (96 of 450
marks) on tea and tea paraphernalia. Coffee and its implements never had
the same importance in the Reimarus home. Hermann Samuel Reimarus
also frequented public establishments that served tea and functioned as
centres for intellectual exchange, as attested by records of special meals
at the *Baumhaus*, located at the entry to the Hamburg port.[87] The financial
accounts contain no references to the *Patriotisches Kaffeehaus*, an estab-
lishment associated with the *Patriotische Gesellschaft*,[88] but Reimarus may
have subsumed the cost of an occasional cup of tea or coffee under his
"pocket money" expenses.

In contrast to public coffee-houses, semi-public gatherings around tea
in private homes enabled women not only to participate in, but to take
leadership roles in social-intellectual exchange. Hermann Samuel Reimarus supported and encouraged female intellectual engagement, as the
financial records document extensively in connection with reading material by and for women, his daughters' education, and references to tea
consumption. Not by accident, shortly after Hermman Samuel Reimarus'
death, one of the earliest German literary salons would become known
as the "Reimarus tea table." Led by his daughter Elise, daughter-in-law
Sophie née Hennings, and eventually granddaughter Johanna Sieveking,
the tea table came to represent the epitome of late eighteenth-century
Enlightenment sociability. Its roots, however, date to the early eighteenth
century, when young Hermann Samuel Reimarus treated tea consumption as a matter of course.

The house books also indicate an early passion for gardening and for
visiting gardens in the countryside nearby. Besides encouraging sociability
in yet another venue, these activities inspired Hermann Samuel's increas-
ing focus on scientific observation and interest in scientific publications.
Until at least 1748, Hermann Samuel Reimarus rented a garden with a
small "house of pleasure" outside the city, and made numerous acquisi-
tions of plants and gardening tools.[89] Two of the gardens' owners are doc-

---

[87] Reference to the *Baumhaus*, HB 3, 22 Aug. 1759; 29 Sep. 1764; and Sep. 1765.
[88] Count Ahasverus v. Lehndorf, diary entry, 2 Dec. 1765 (or 1767?), quoted in Wilhelm
Stieda, "Hamburg im Jahre 1767," *Mitteilungen des Vereins für Hamburgische Geschichte*,
Bd. 14, Heft 2 (1923–1925): 179.
[89] References to gardens, gardening, plants, and tools are too numerous to list in their
entirety. For example, HB 1, Easter 1728, May–June 1729.

umented, a Mr. Koster and the senior councillor (*Oberalter*) Heinrich Otto Seumenicht (1684–1760).⁹⁰ The gardens are likely to have been located either to the northeast of the city along the Alster, in the neighbourhood called St. Georg that was known for its gardens, or just to the northwest of the city, outside the Wall Gate, where the land was undeveloped and rents were still cheap.⁹¹

Later, Hermann Samuel Reimarus appears to have given up maintaining a garden of his own, perhaps because his children were by then grown up, but he continued to visit the gardens of friends. The household books record his visits, in general chronological order, to the gardens of the pastor of the orphanage, Joachim Morgenweg, located near Altona; the estates Seestermühe and Jersbek of the Danish noble family of Hans-Heinrich von Ahlefeldt (1657–1720) and his son, Bendix von Ahlefeldt (1679–1757); the gardens of attorney Peter Draing (1693–1766); of the Canon and property owner, Dr. Heinrich von Meurer (1678–1744); of the senator and future mayor Martin Lucas Schele (1683–1751); gardens of the above named Seitz (in Bilwerder), Surland, and Volckmann; of the physician Dr. Joachim Momma (d. 1757); of the attorney Hermann Burmester (d. 1765), probably in Bergedorf; and the Wellingsbüttel gardens of sugar merchant and member of the extended Reimarus family, Arnold Amsinck (1723–1792).⁹² The financial records document numerous other excursions into the countryside around Hamburg, such as boat rides on the Alster, visits to Altona, Bergedorf, Billwerder, Blankenese and other places. These excursions served the Reimaruses, and particularly Hermann Samuel Reimarus, to pursue their interest in nature.

In their love of gardens and gardening, Hermann Samuel Reimarus and his friends embodied a new appreciation of nature, as also expressed in Fabricius' physico-theology and Brockes' nature poetry. Inspired by this new outlook, Hermann Samuel Reimarus maintained a correspondence on scientific topics,⁹³ increasingly turned to scientific reading, and

---

⁹⁰ Koster, HB 1, 18 Sep. 1744. Seumenicht, HB 1, 10 Nov. 1747.

⁹¹ Oscar L. Tesdorpf, "Mittheilungen aus dem handschriftlichen Nachlaß des Senators Johann Michael Hudtwalcker...," *Zeitschrift des Vereins für Hamburgische Geschichte* 9 (1890): 163–64.

⁹² Amsinck married one of the orphaned Reimarus nieces, Catharina Johanna Evers (1730–1797). Example of references to garden visits are HB 1, Easter 1728 (Morgenweg), March–May 1732 (Meurer, Draing, Schele), 6 Aug. 1743 (Seitz), 10 Aug. 1745 (Ahlefeldt), 13 Aug. 1746 (Surland), 1 Aug. 1749 (Volckmann); HB 2, June 1752 (Momma), Aug. 1752 (Ahlefeldt), 5 June 1759 (Burmester), and 7 June 1762 (Amsinck).

⁹³ 29 letters from Tesdorpf to Hermann Samuel Reimarus, 1745–1763, survive in the Staatsarchiv Hamburg.

began to make his own, careful observations of nature. Thus, the financial records document how more than thirty years of systematic exposure to, and interaction with nature prepared Reimarus' ground-breaking work on the instincts of animals.

CONCLUSION

The Reimarus household records offer abundant detail about far more than Hermann Samuel Reimarus' daily life, and his social and intellectual networks. Perhaps more than any other surviving document, these records show how he embodied the civic confessional tradition of Lutheranism even as he embraced radical Enlightenment.

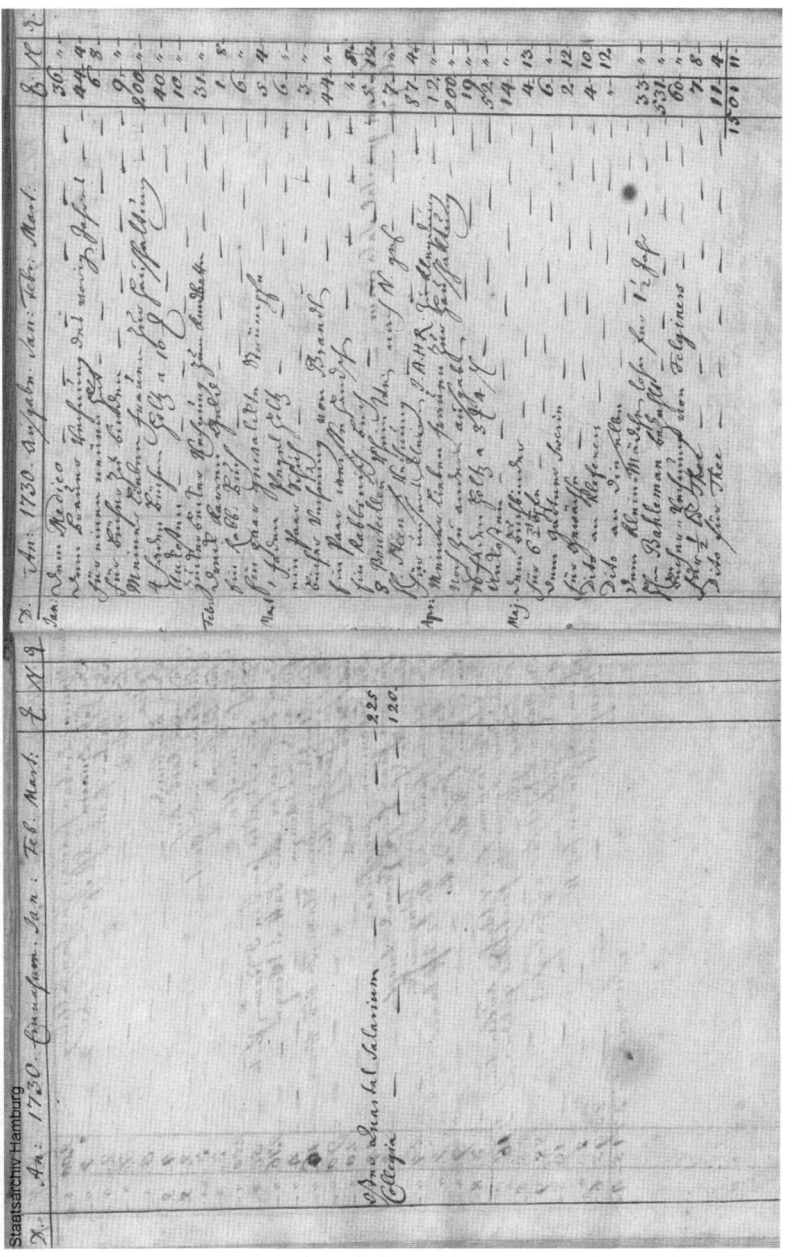

These pages of the first volume of the household account show conditions early in the Reimaruses' marriage. During the first months of the year 1730, expenses include six separate entries for book purchases, among them two rabbinical books; routine household items and special items like tea, wine, and beer; clothing; costs related to the birth of the couple's first child in November 1729; and charges for plants and gardeners' wages.

Courtesy of StA HH, 622-1-86 Familie Reimarus A 18 Band 1.

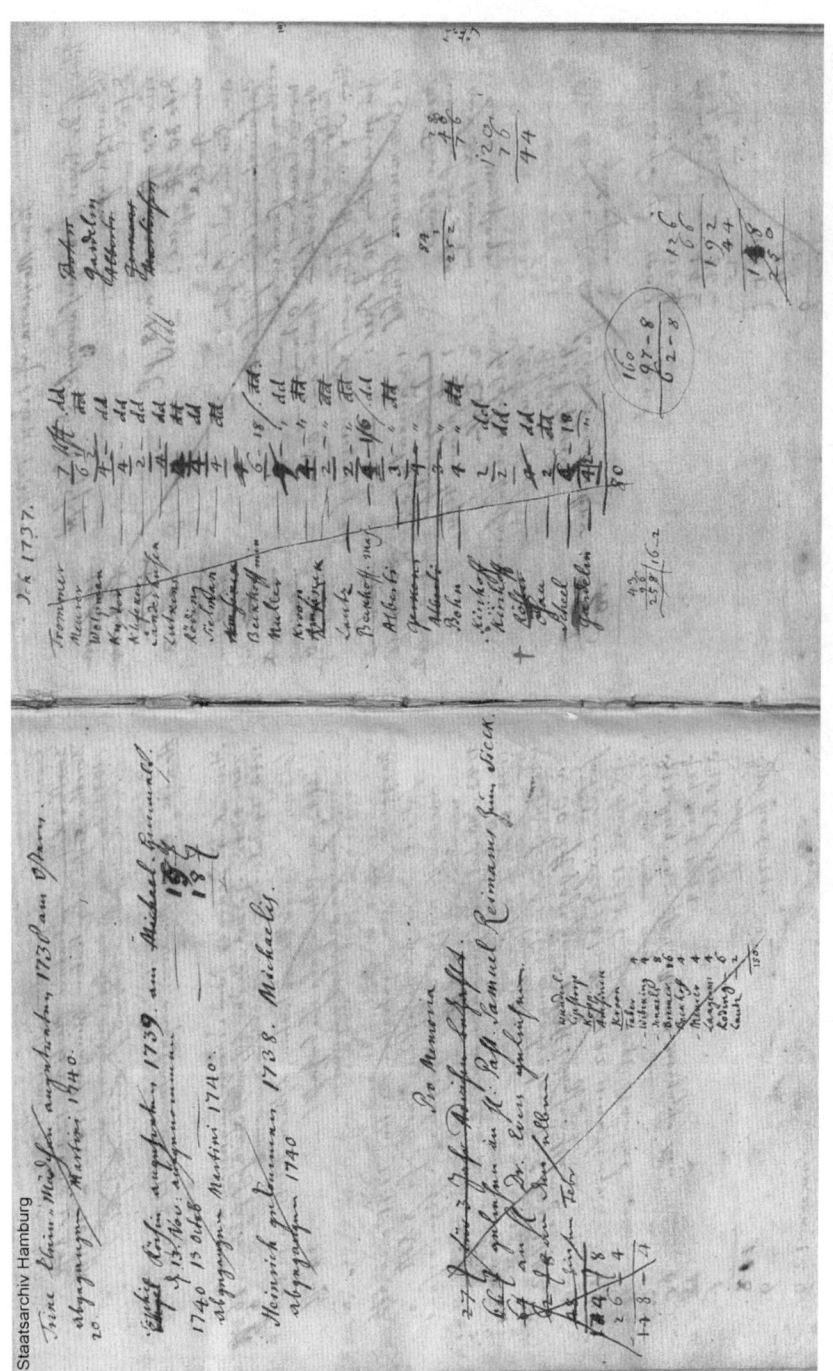

These end pages of the first volume of the account books list three domestic servants who were employed in the Reimarus household between 1738 and 1740; several loans that Hermann Samuel Reimarus had extended to relatives; and students who had taken private lessons from him in 1737.

Courtesy of StA HH, 622-1-86 Familie Reimarus A 18 Band 1.

Staatsarchiv Hamburg

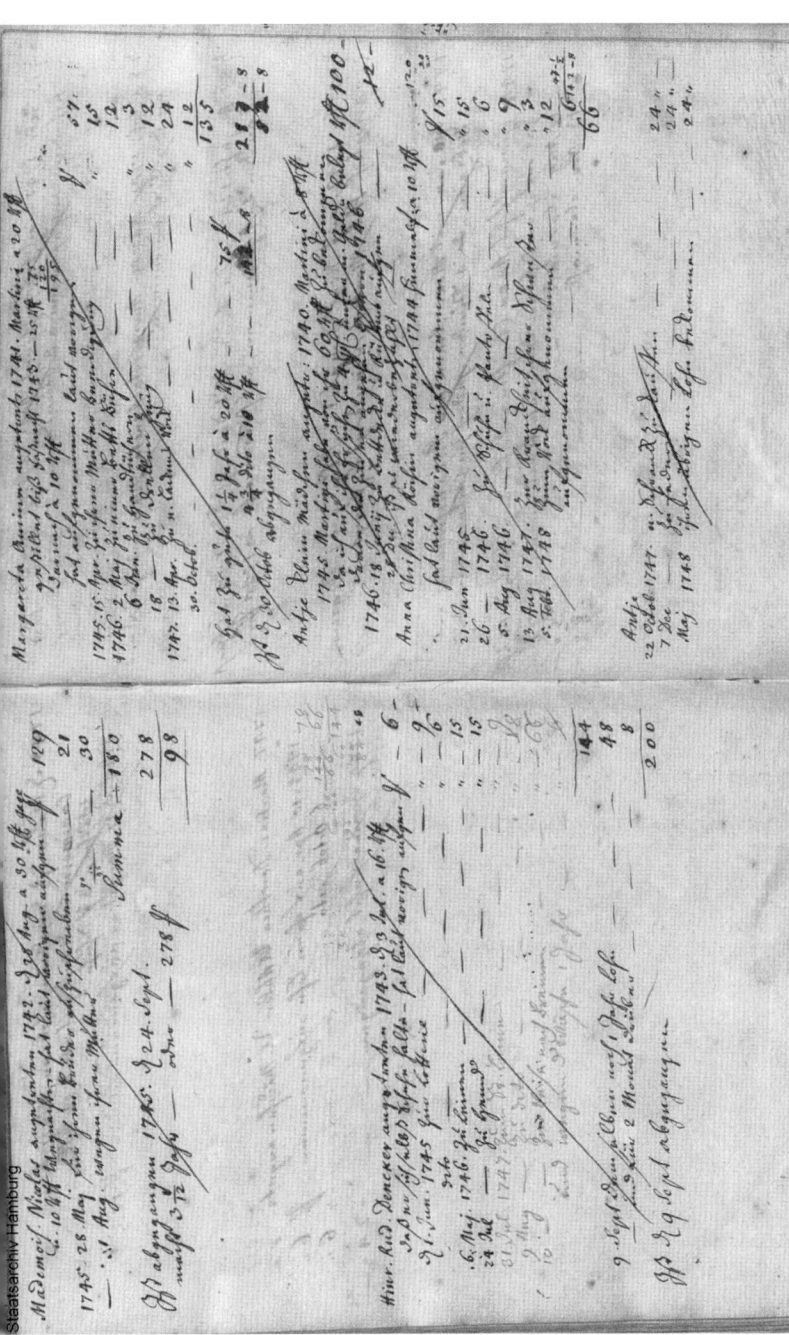

These end pages dating from the 1740s attest to the decade when the Reimarus household was largest, with eight living children and five domestic employees. Domestics included a live-in French teacher, Hermann Samuel Reimarus' personal male servant, a wetnurse for the youngest child, a maidservant, and a female cook. Hermann Samuel Reimarus carefully noted dates of their employment and salary, other benefits such as shoes, clothing, and bedding, and expenses paid for their relatives in cases of illness or death.

Courtesy of StA HH, 622-1-86 Familie Reimarus A 18 Band 1.

These pages from 1753 show that 25 years into his employment at the *Akademisches Gymnasium*, private lessons to students continued to provide a significant portion of Hermann Samuel Reimarus' income compared to his quarterly salary. Expenses in August and September of that year included moving costs for son Johann Albert Hinrich, who had spent a year studying medicine in Göttingen and was moving on to Leiden. Not only that year, but also the following year when the younger Reimarus would study in Edinburgh, copies of the Dio Cassius sent to book traders abroad would serve to finance Johann Albert Hinrich's studies.

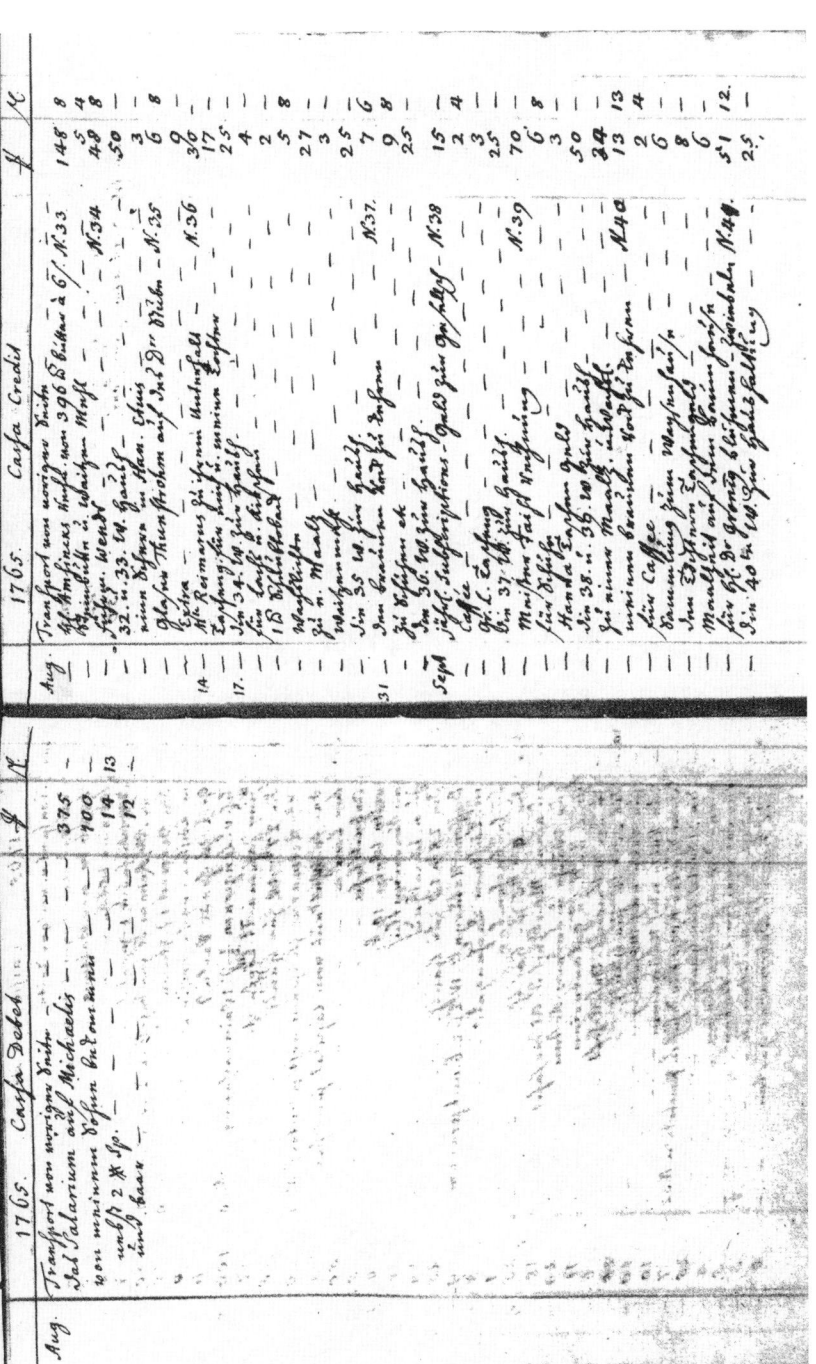

The first entry for September 1765 shows Hermann Samuel Reimarus' first annual dues payment for the newly founded Patriotic Society. On the income side, a payment from his son Johann Albert Hinrich covers both his rent and expenses to care for his two young children, who were being raised by Elise in the Reimarus home.
Courtesy of private collection.

INDEX OF NAMES